The Possible Dream

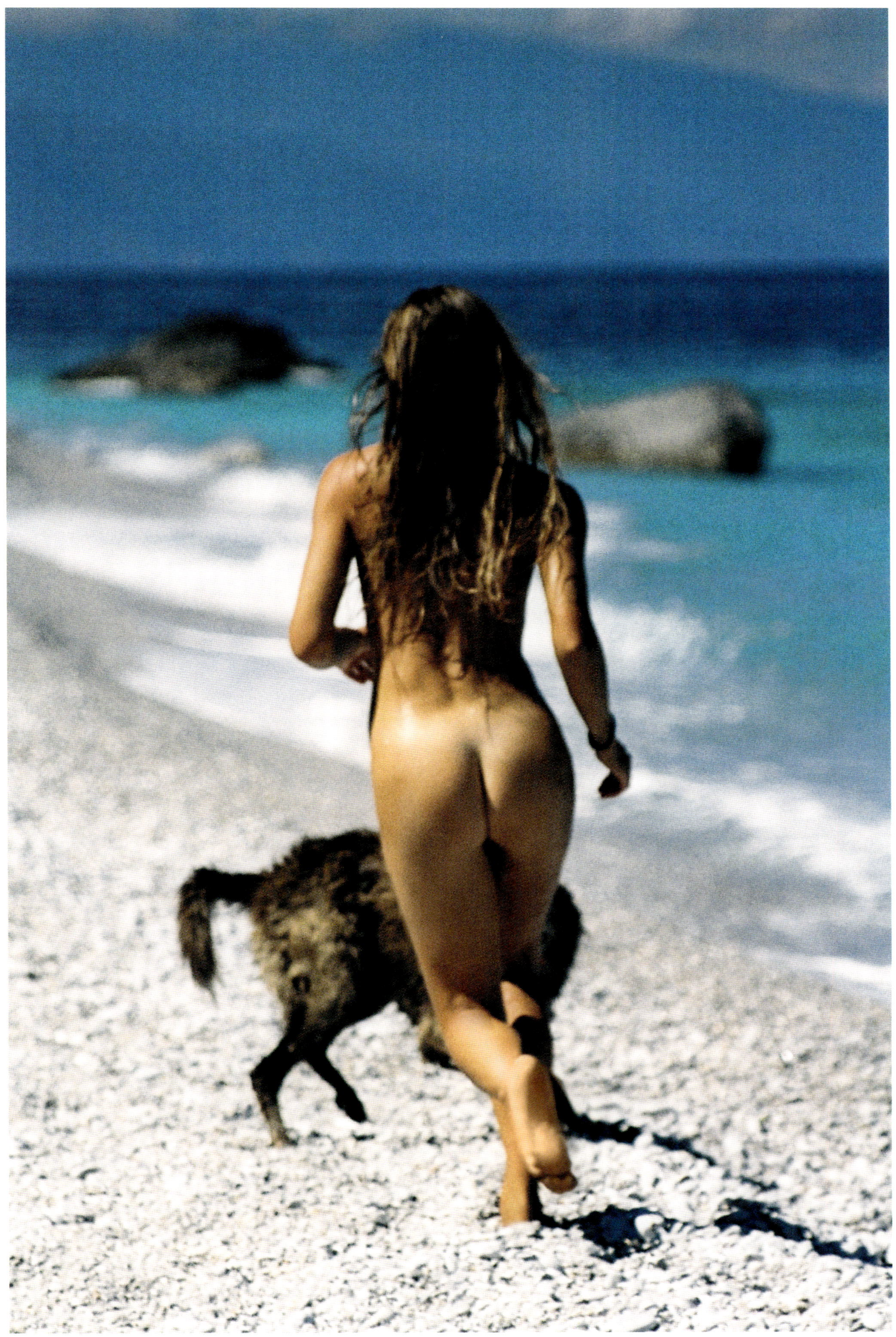

THE POSSIBLE DREAM

Akila Berjaoui

PRESTEL
Munich · London · New York

"When setting out on a journey, do not
seek advice from those who have
never left home."

Rumi

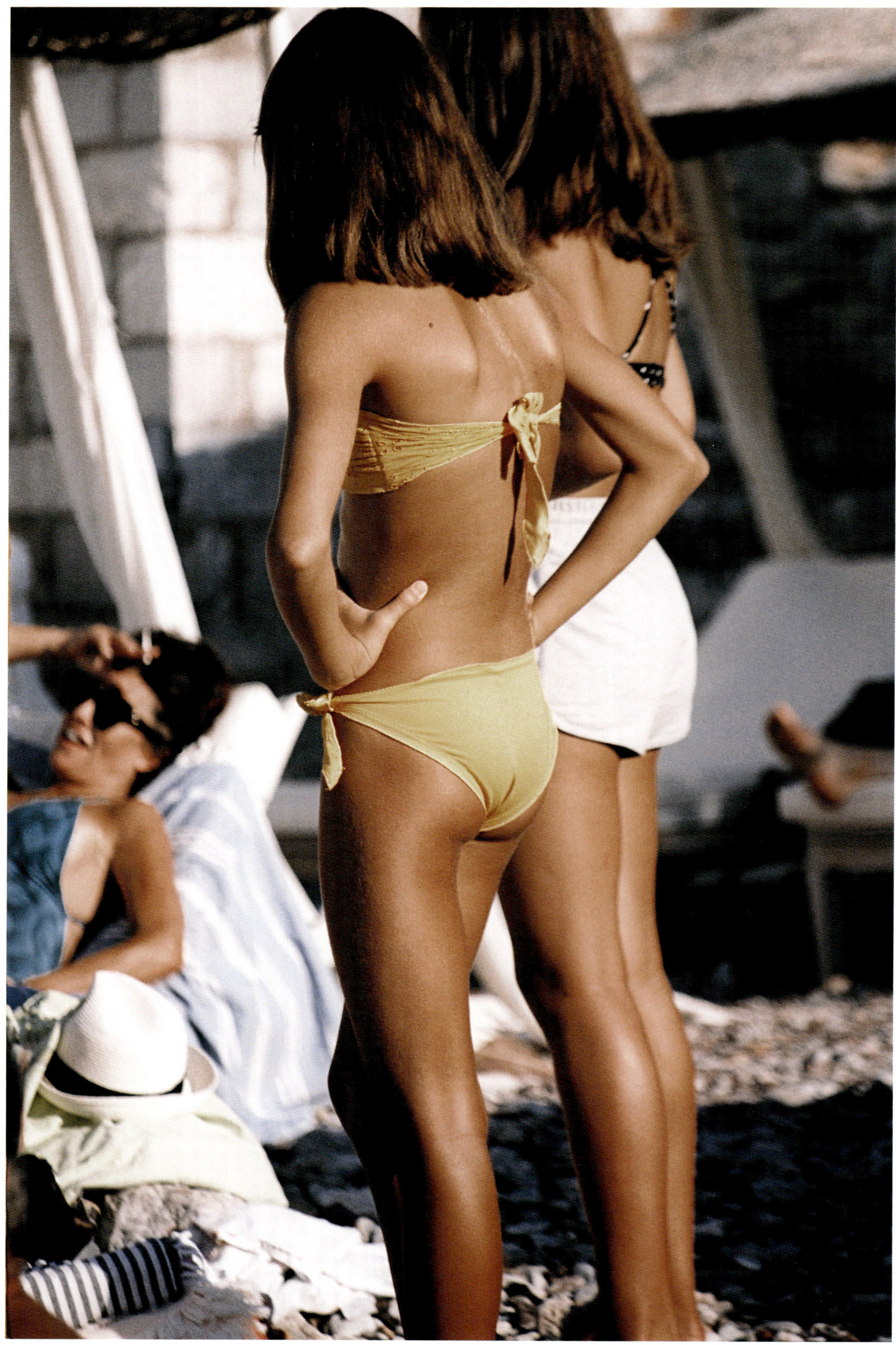

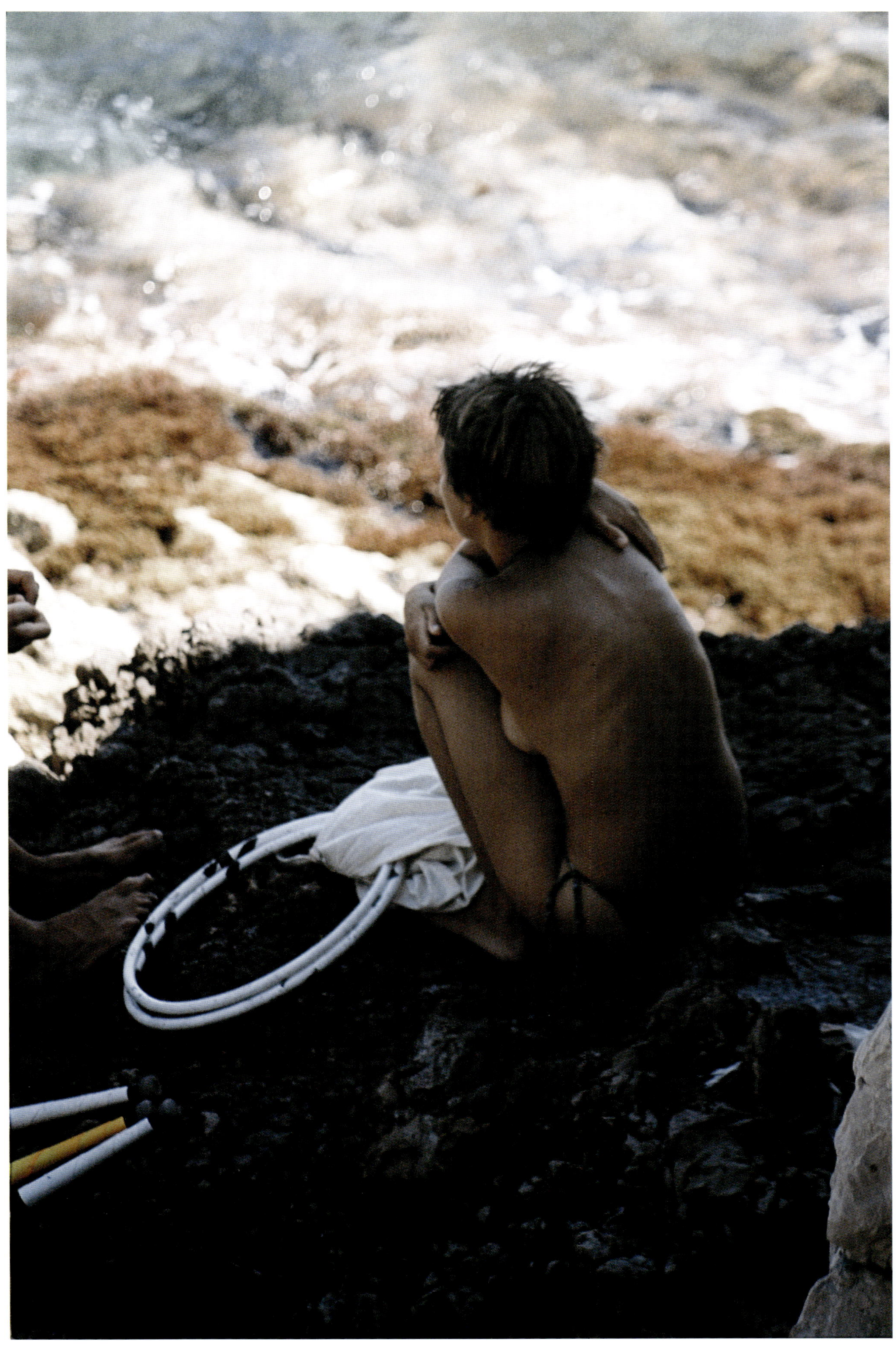

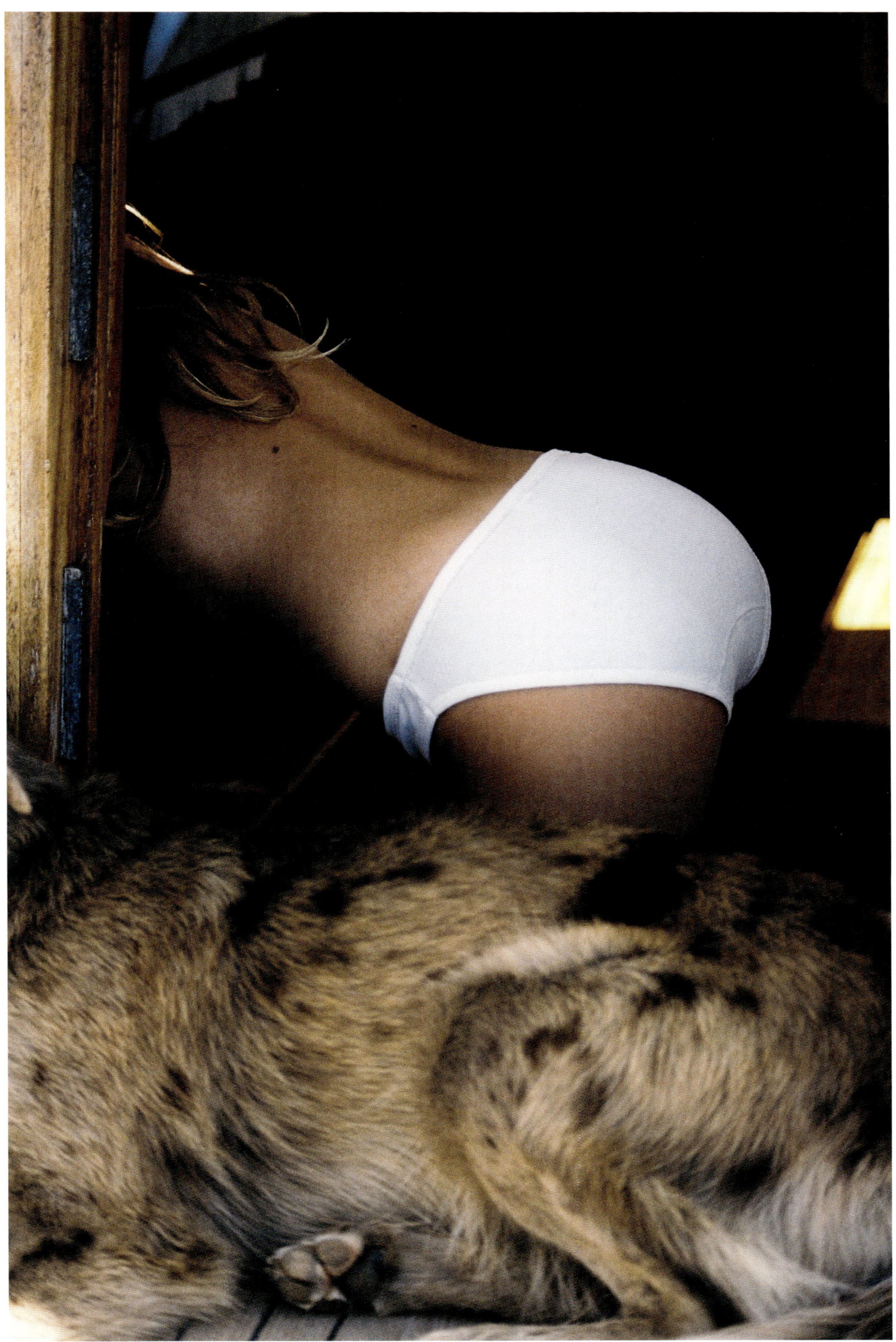

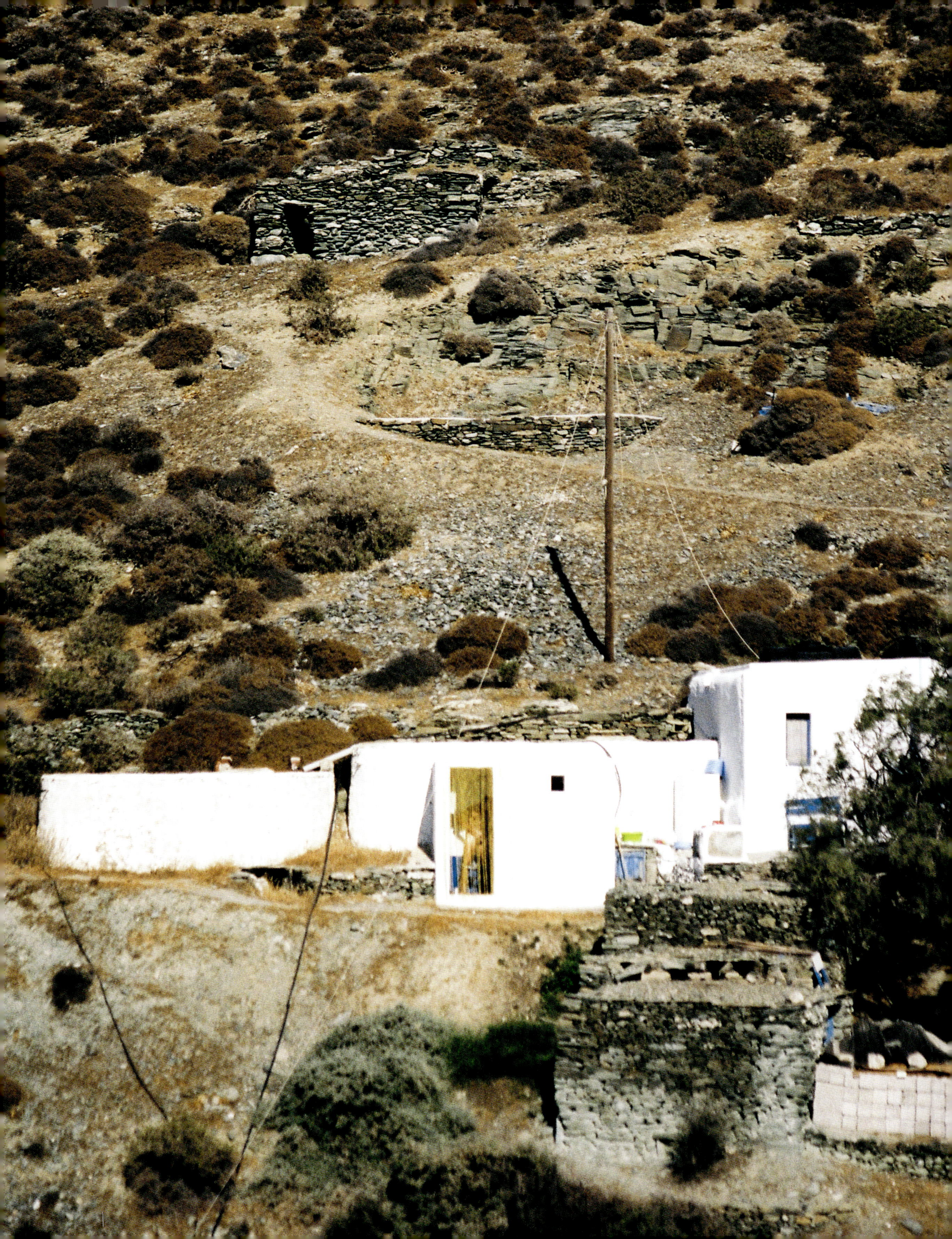

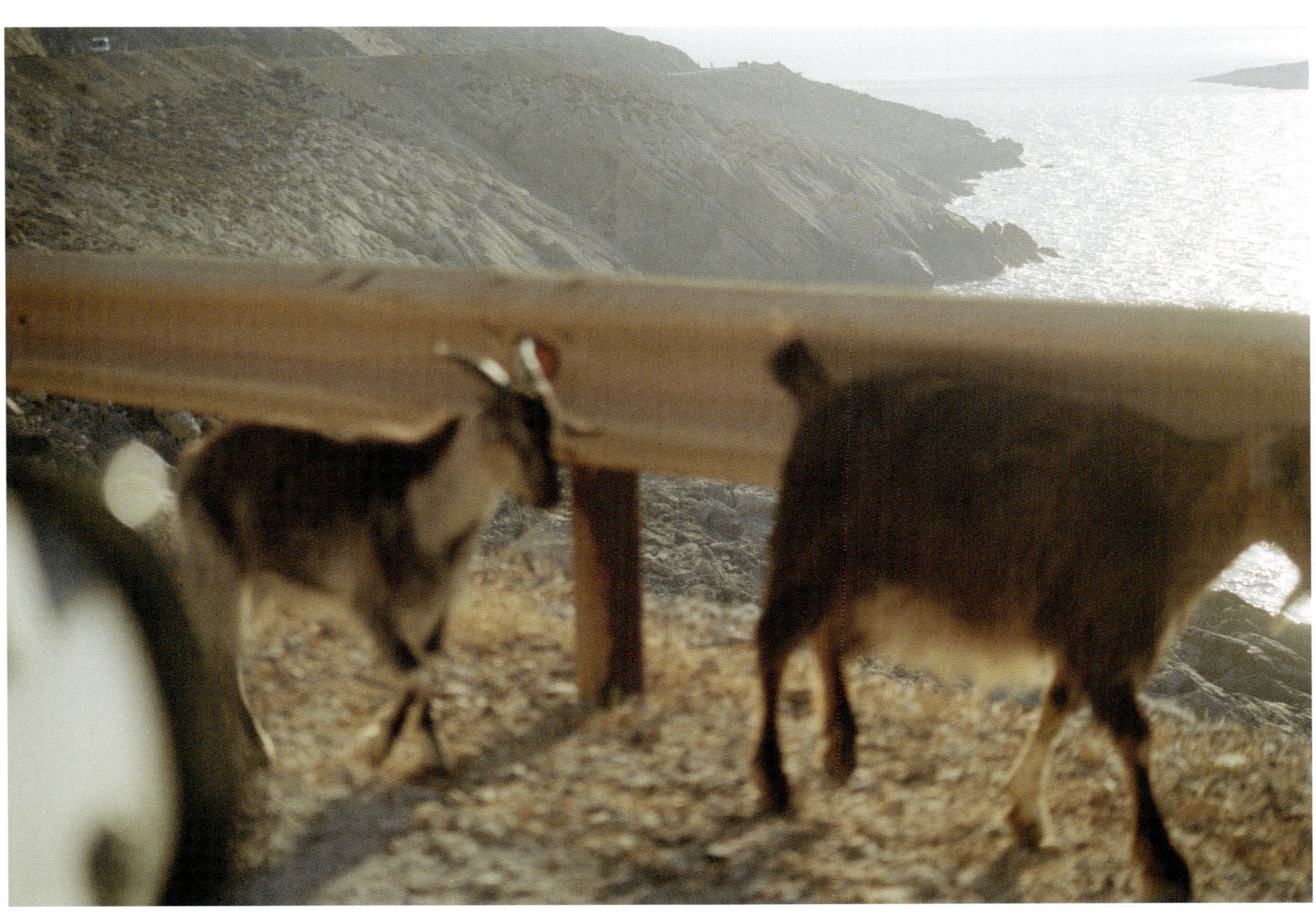

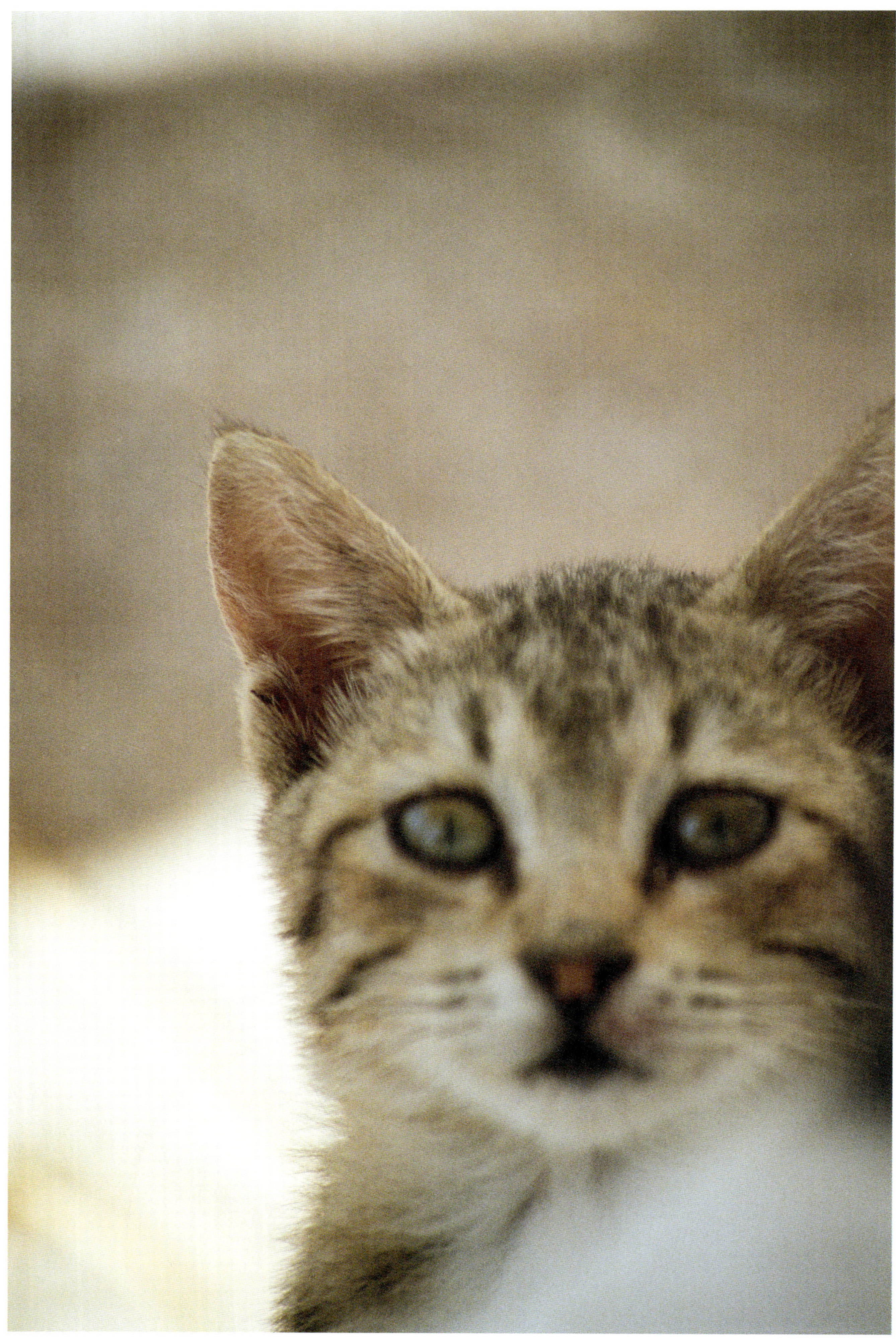

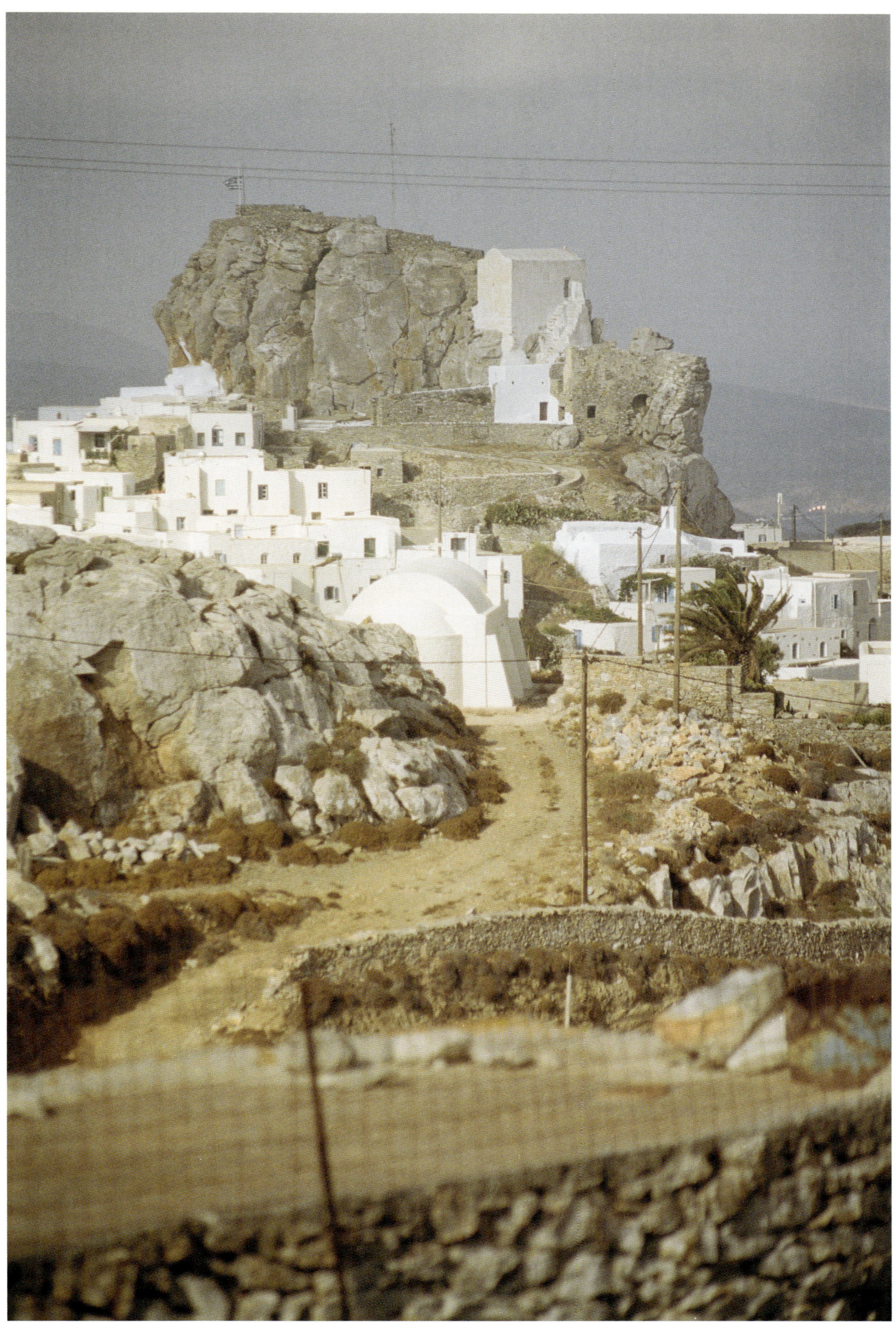

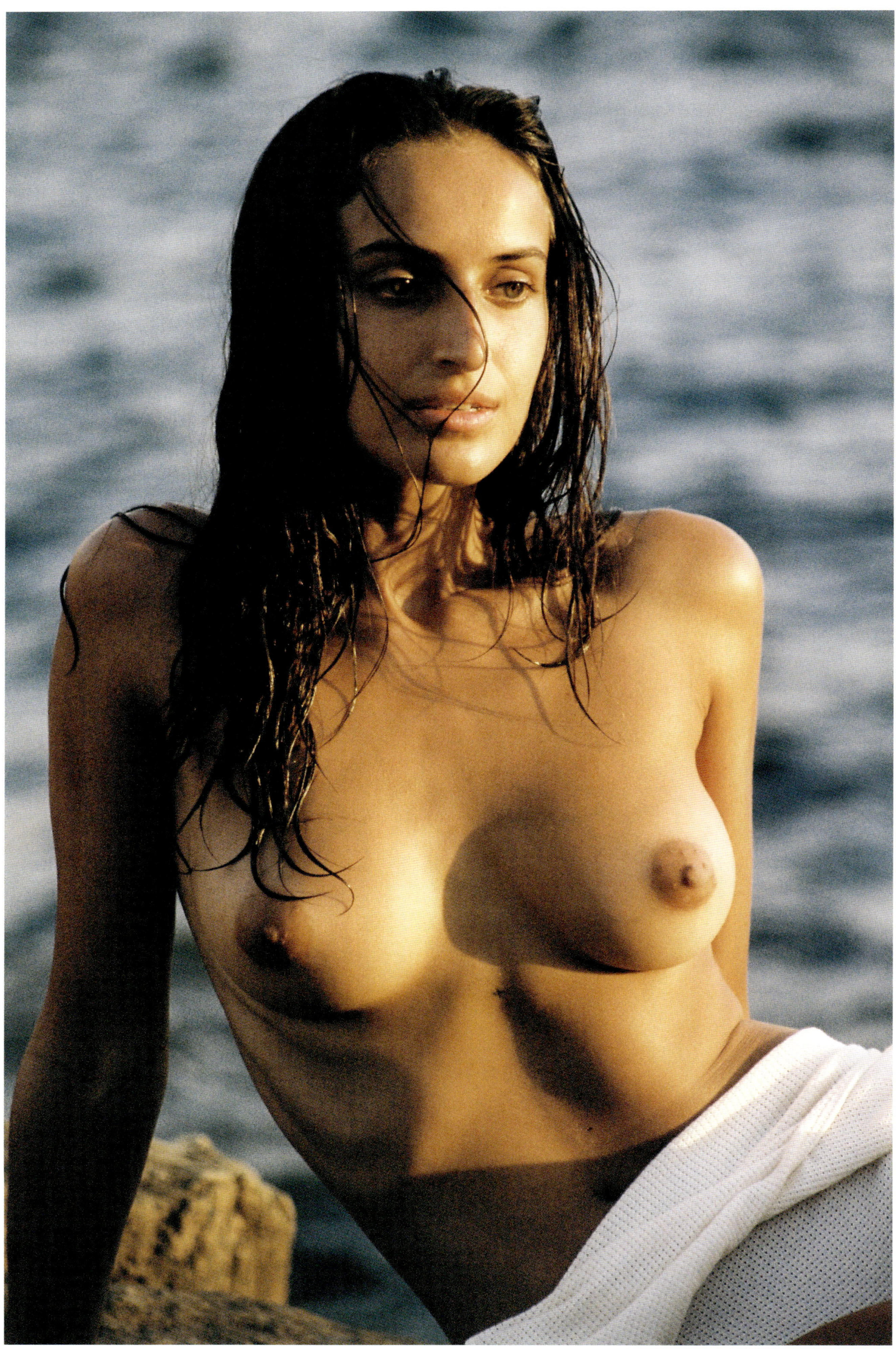

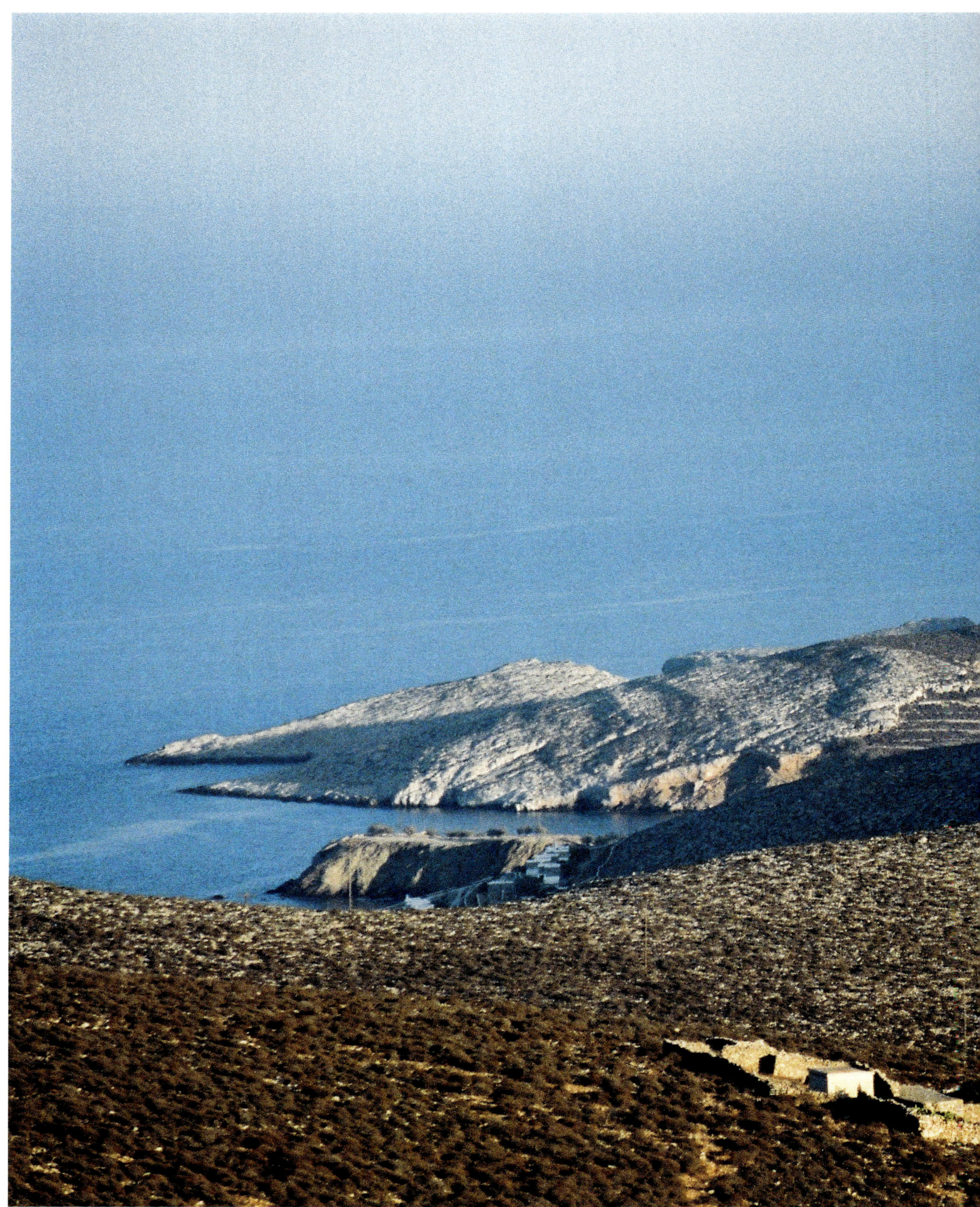

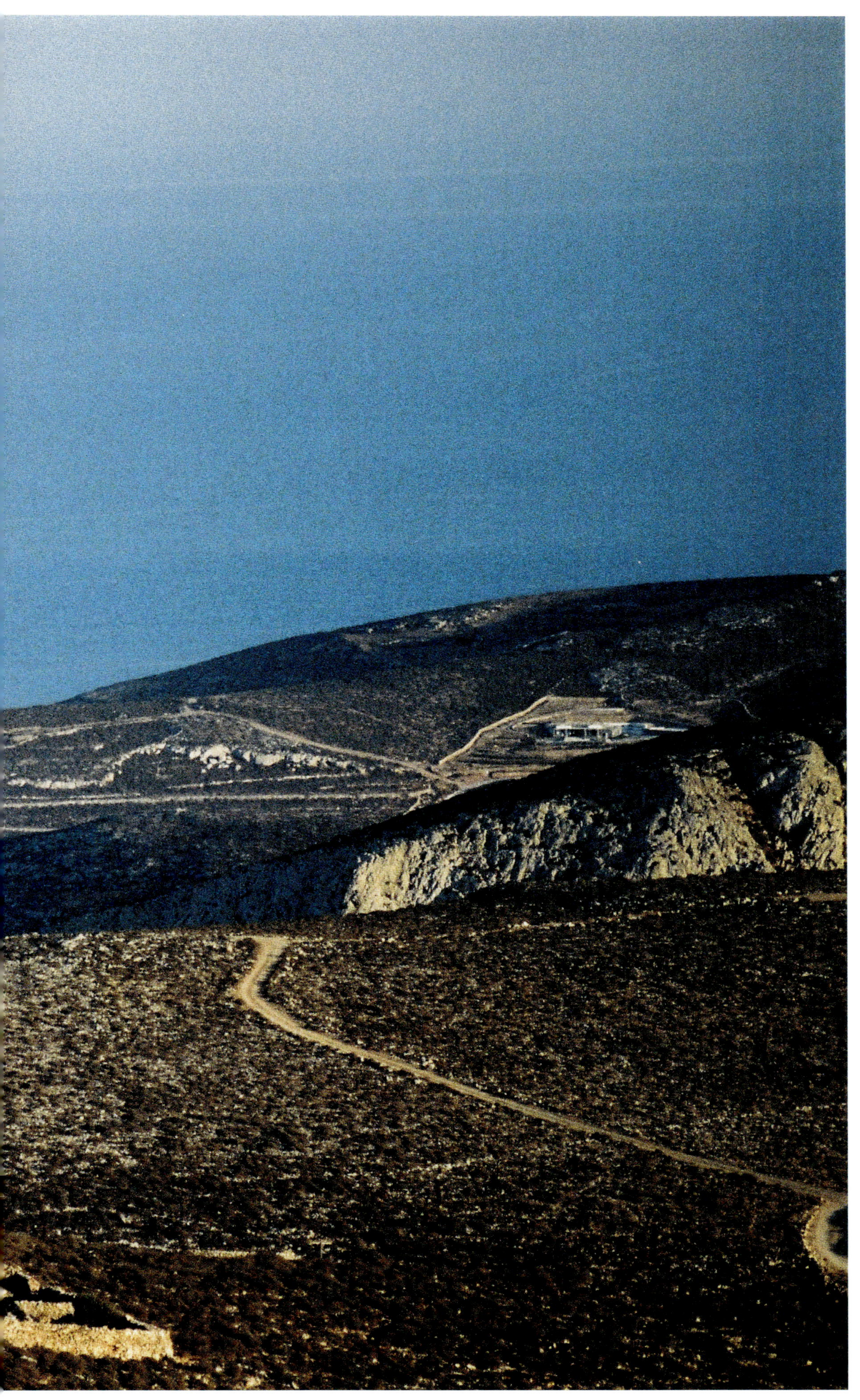

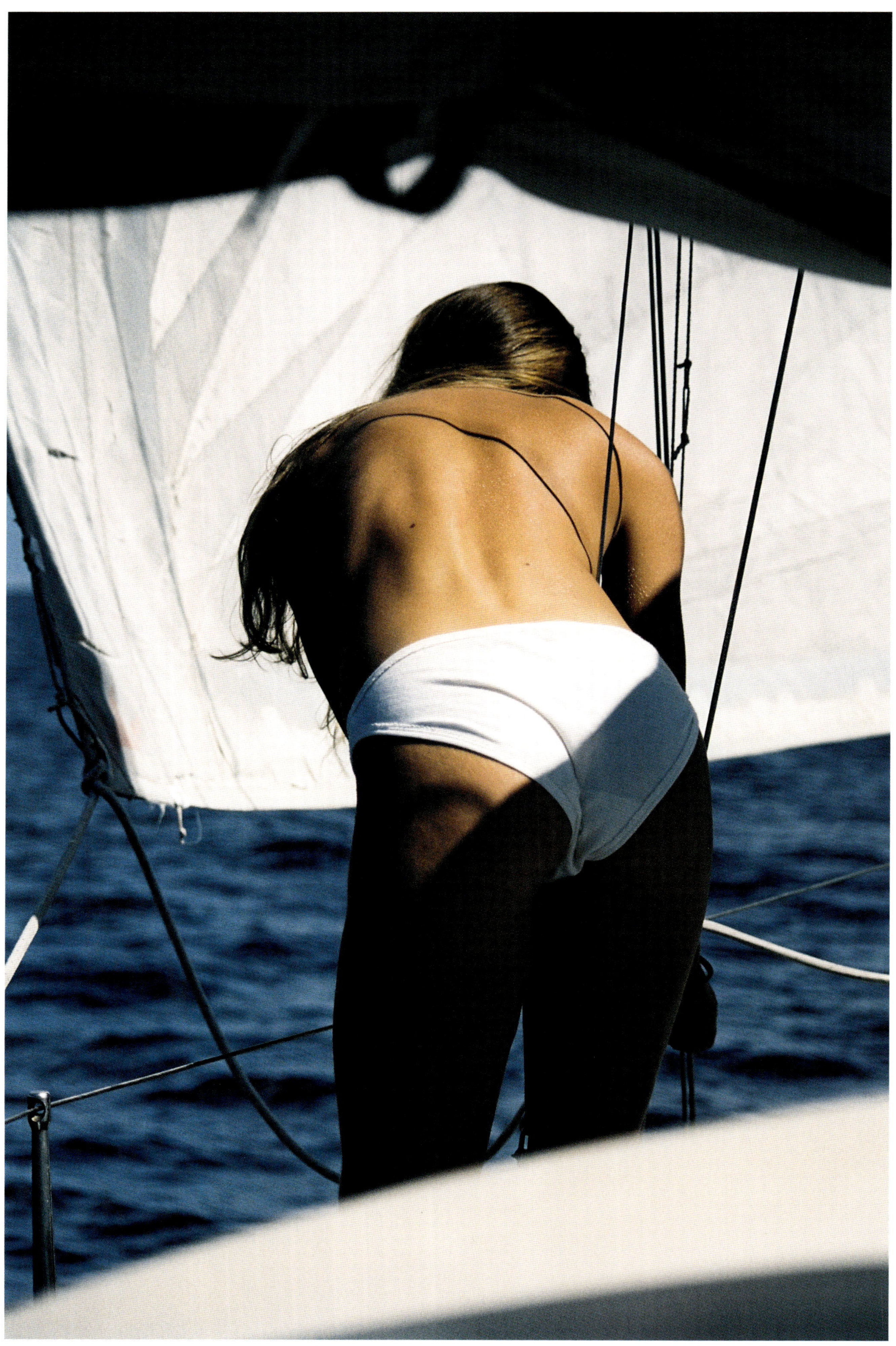

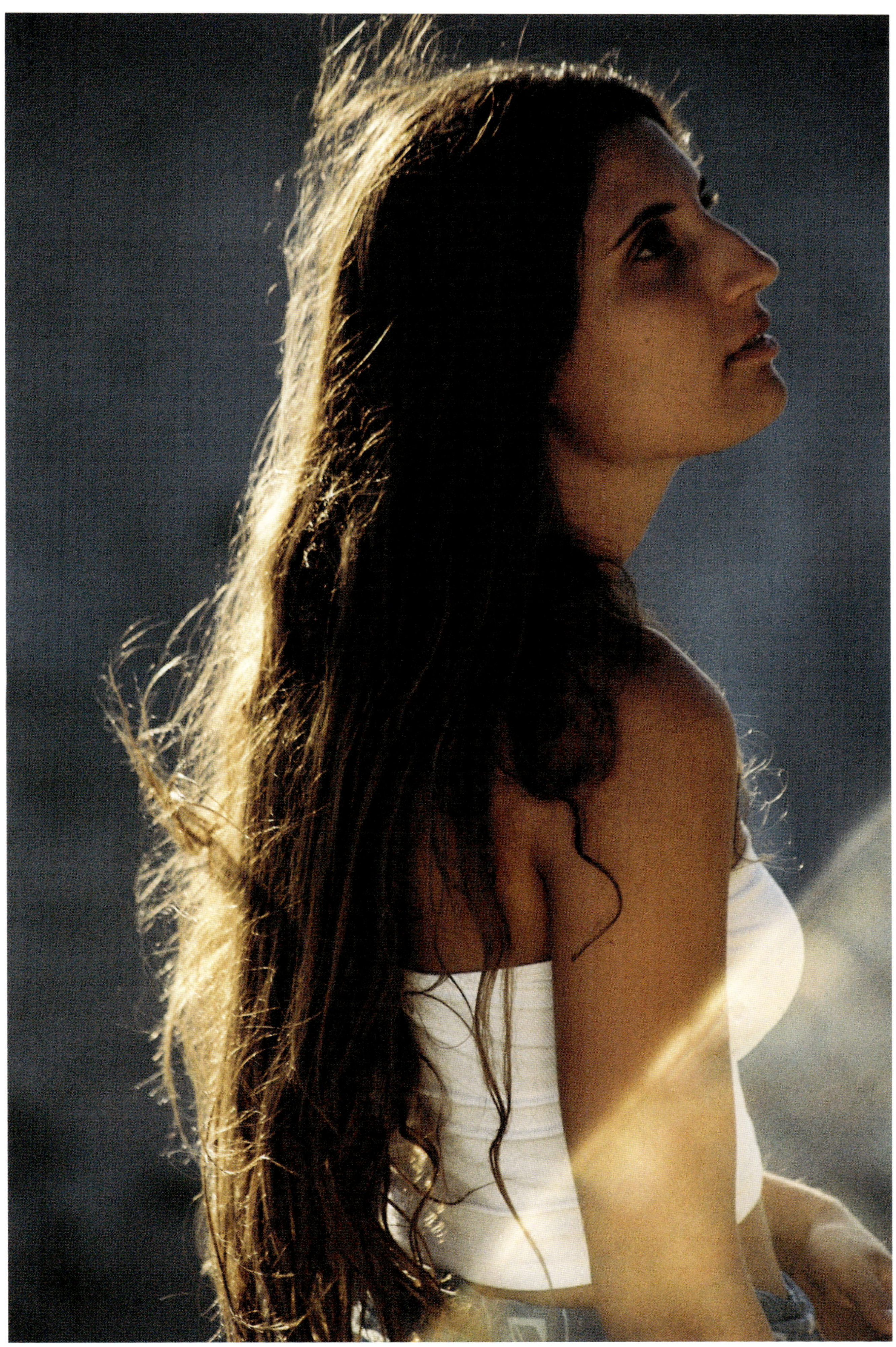

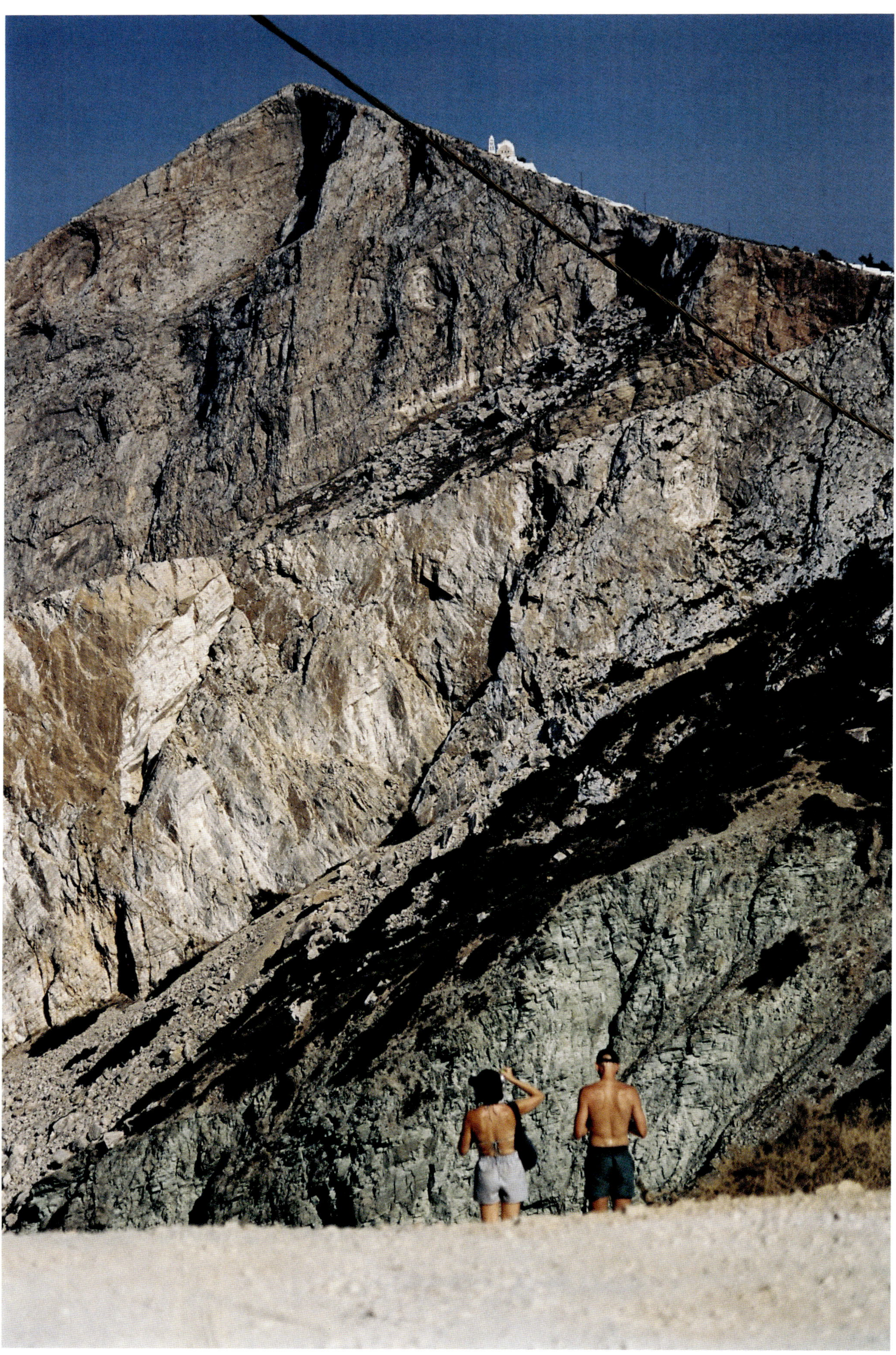

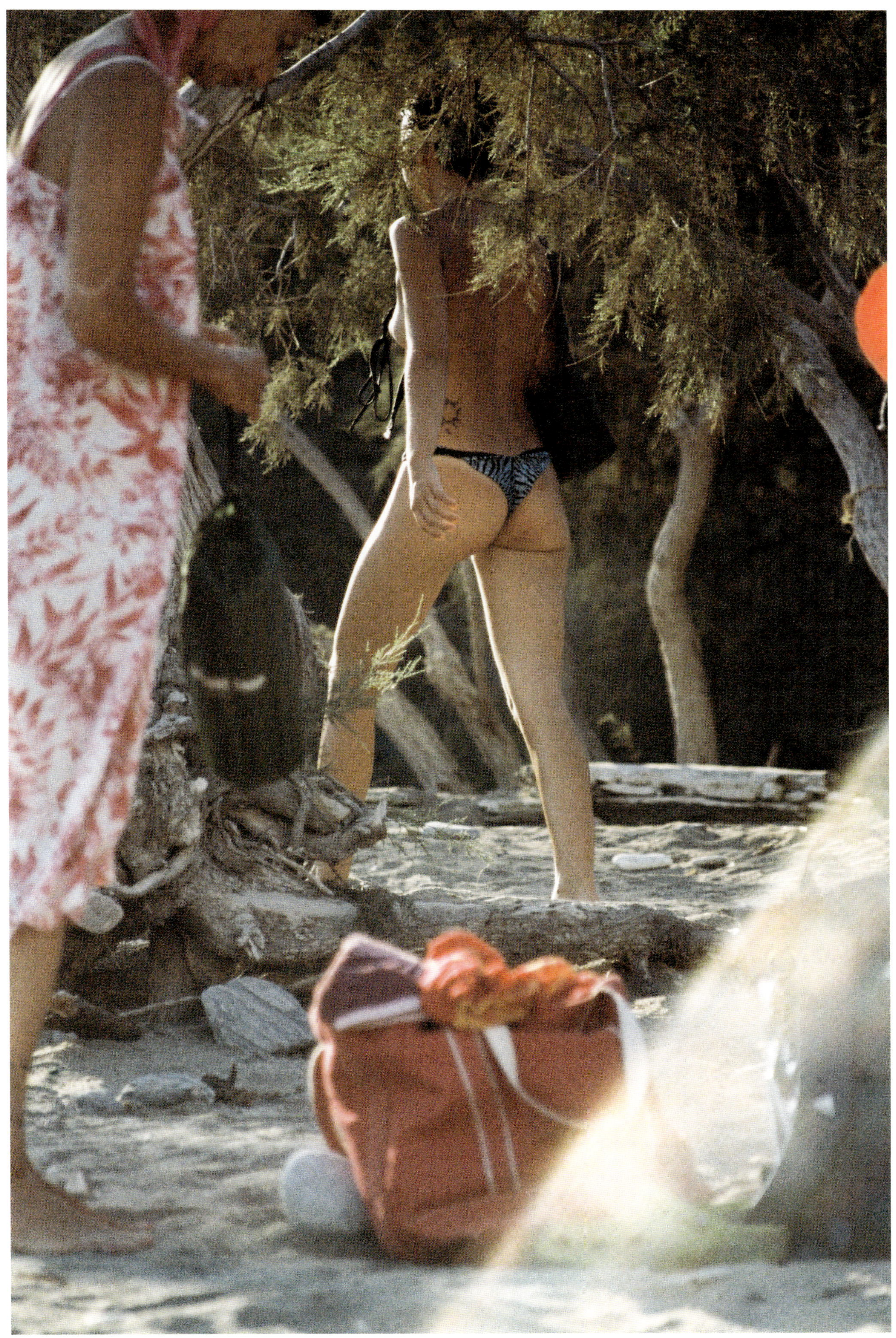

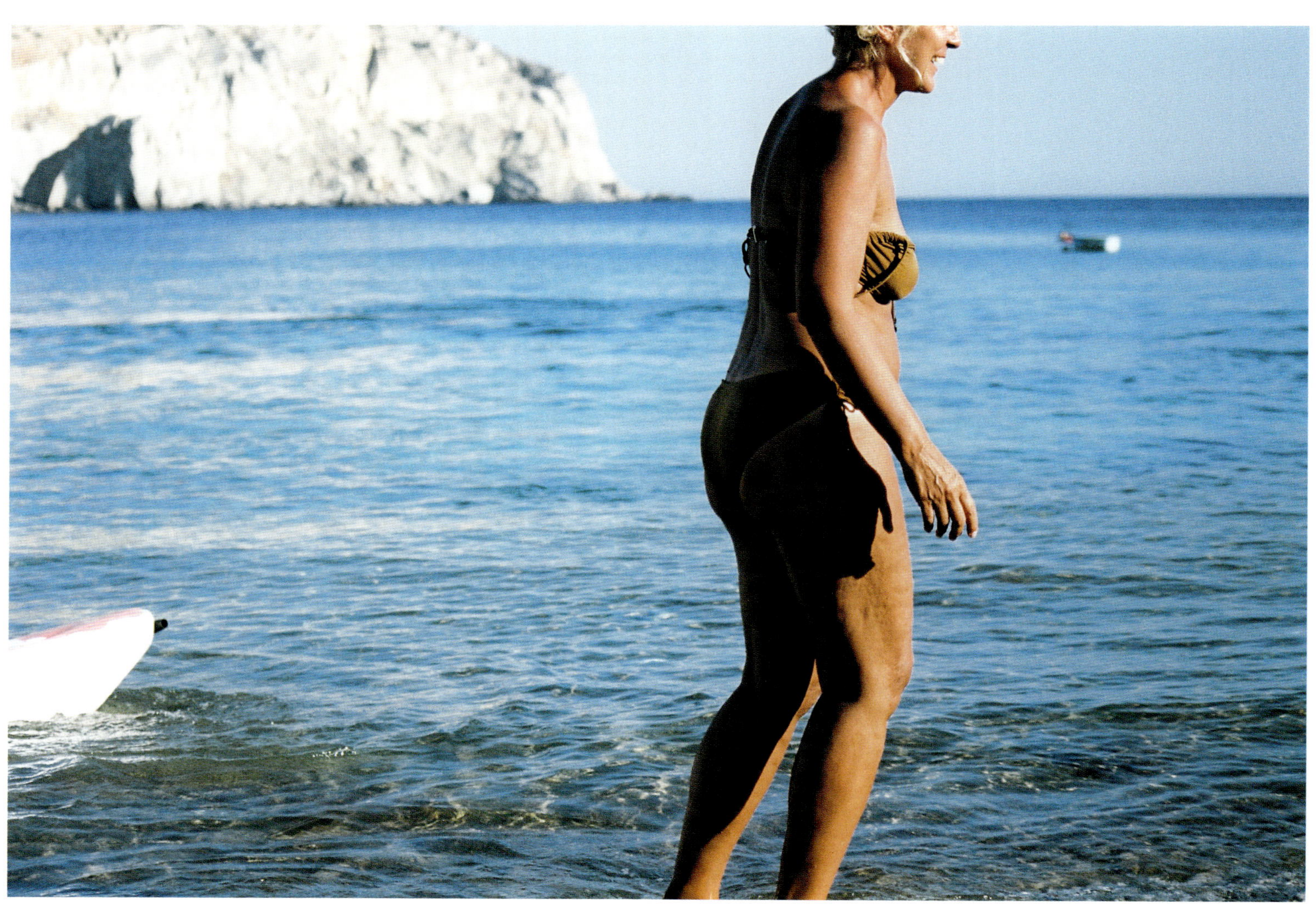

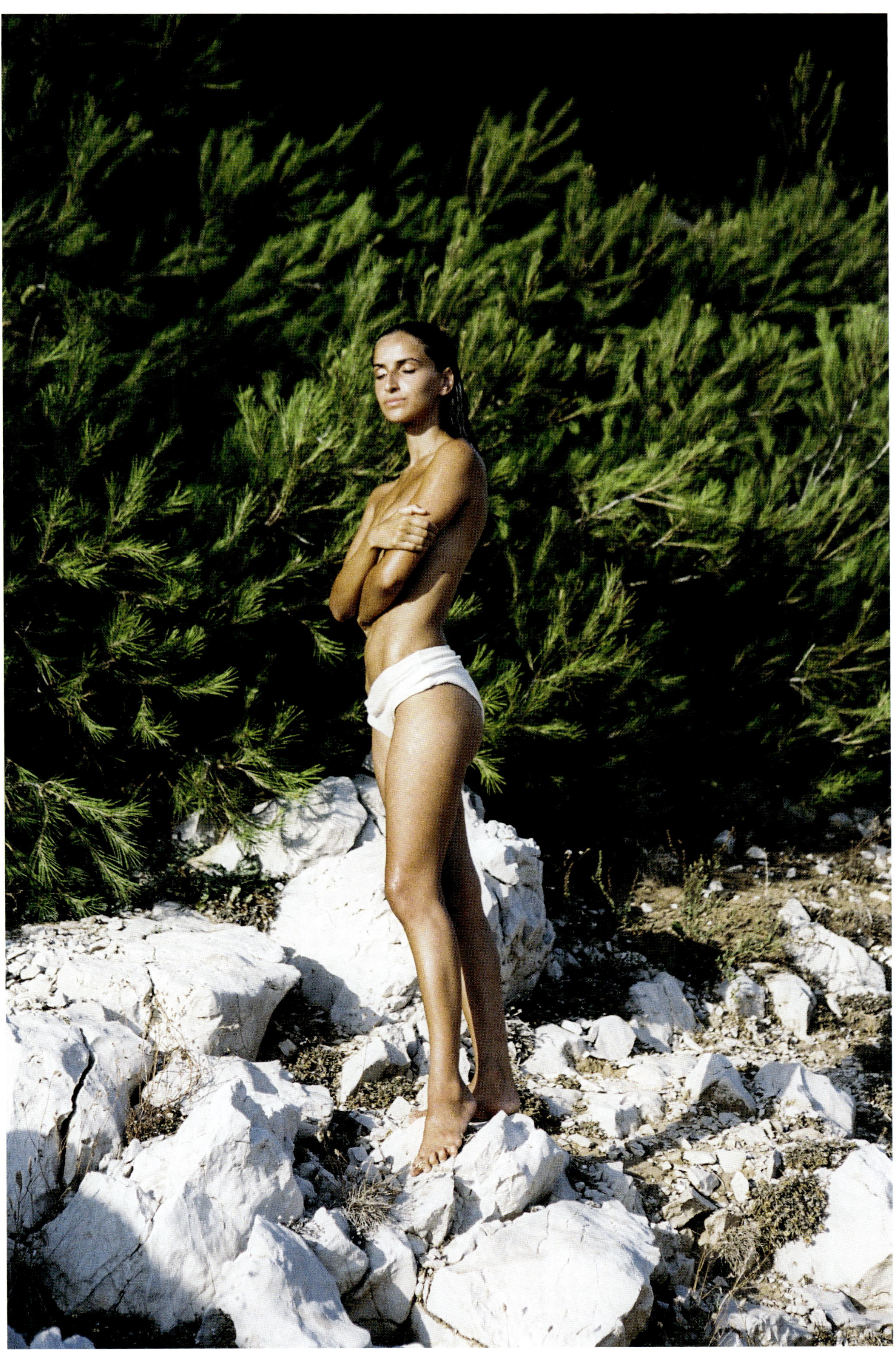

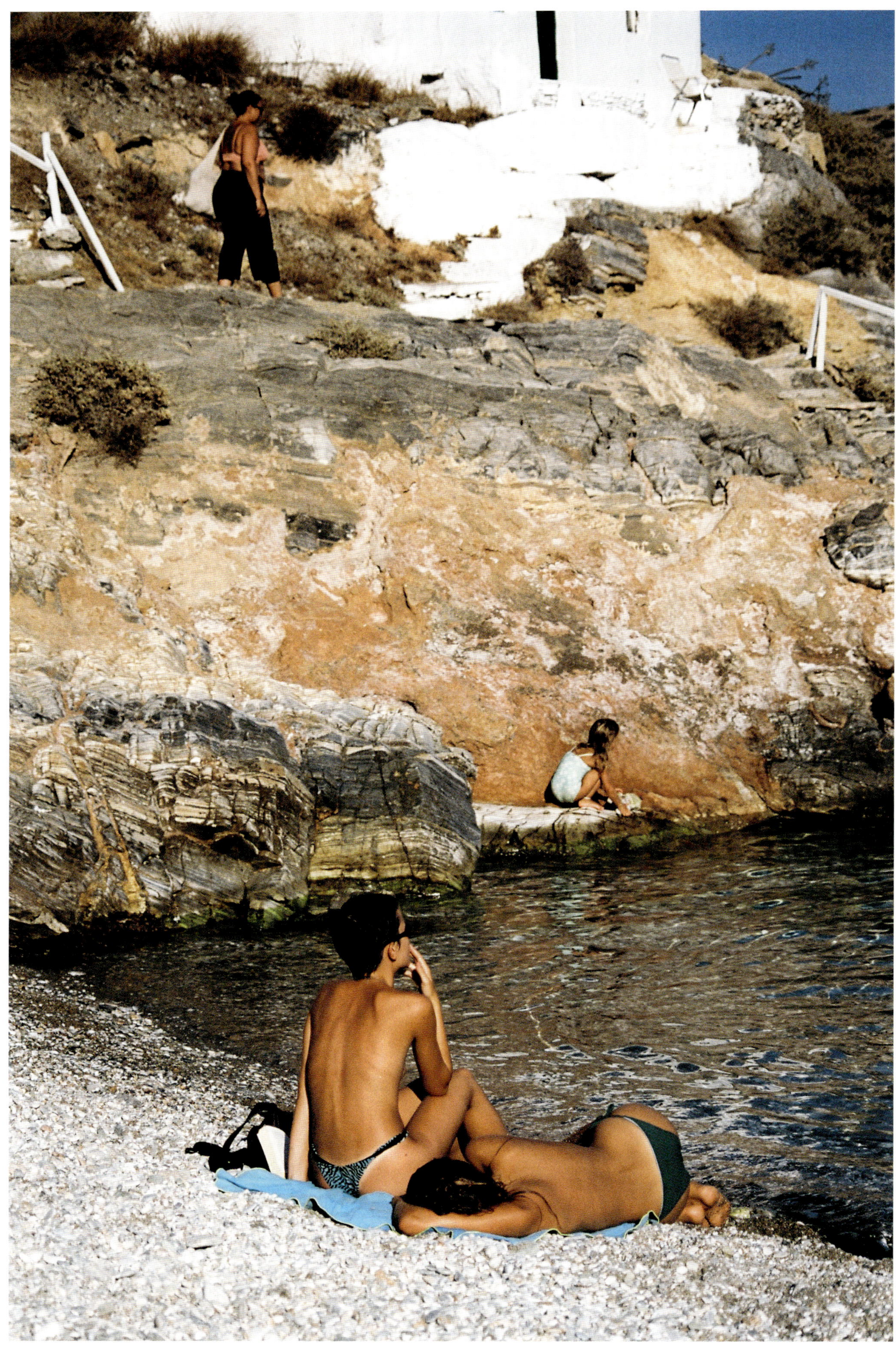

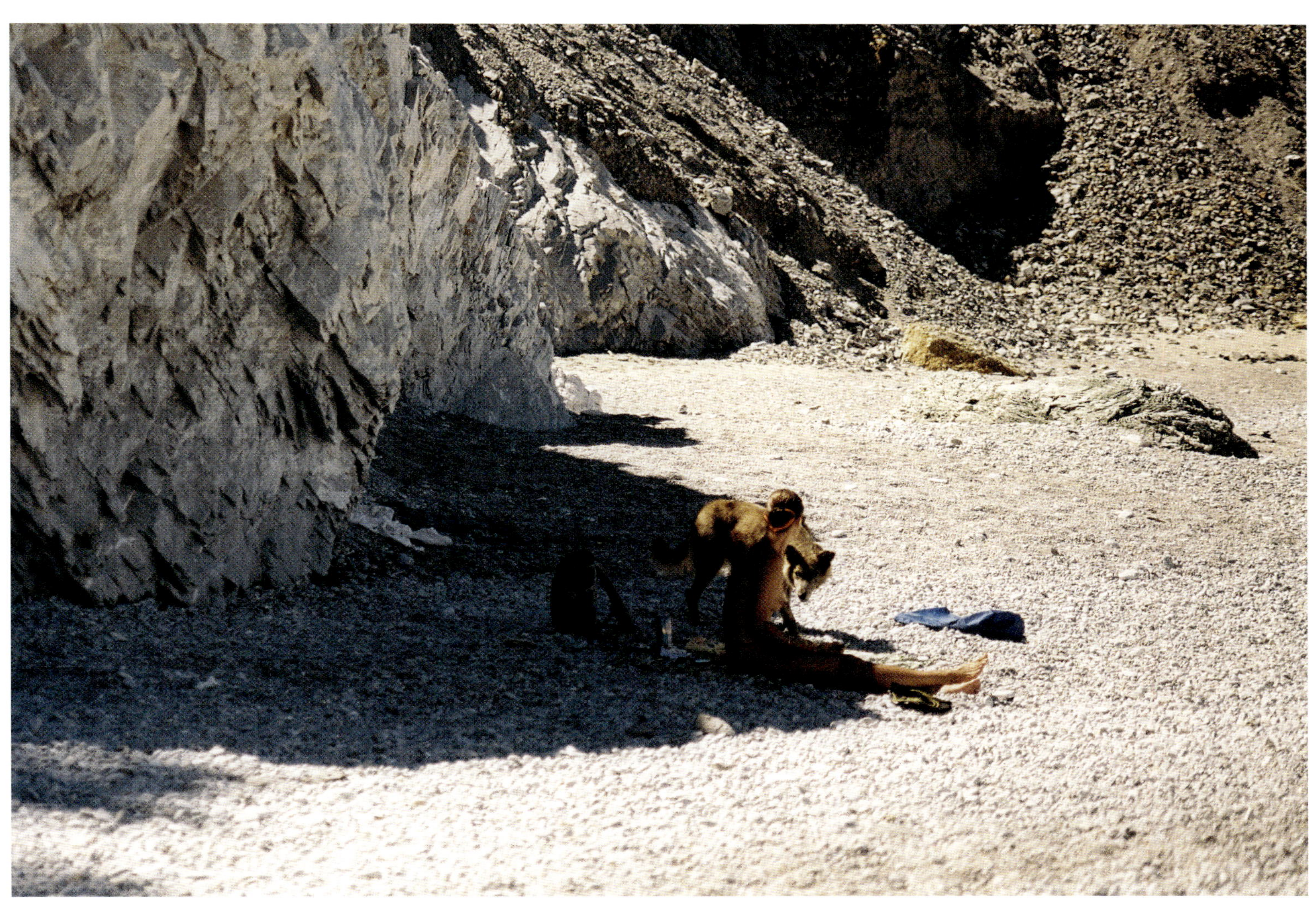

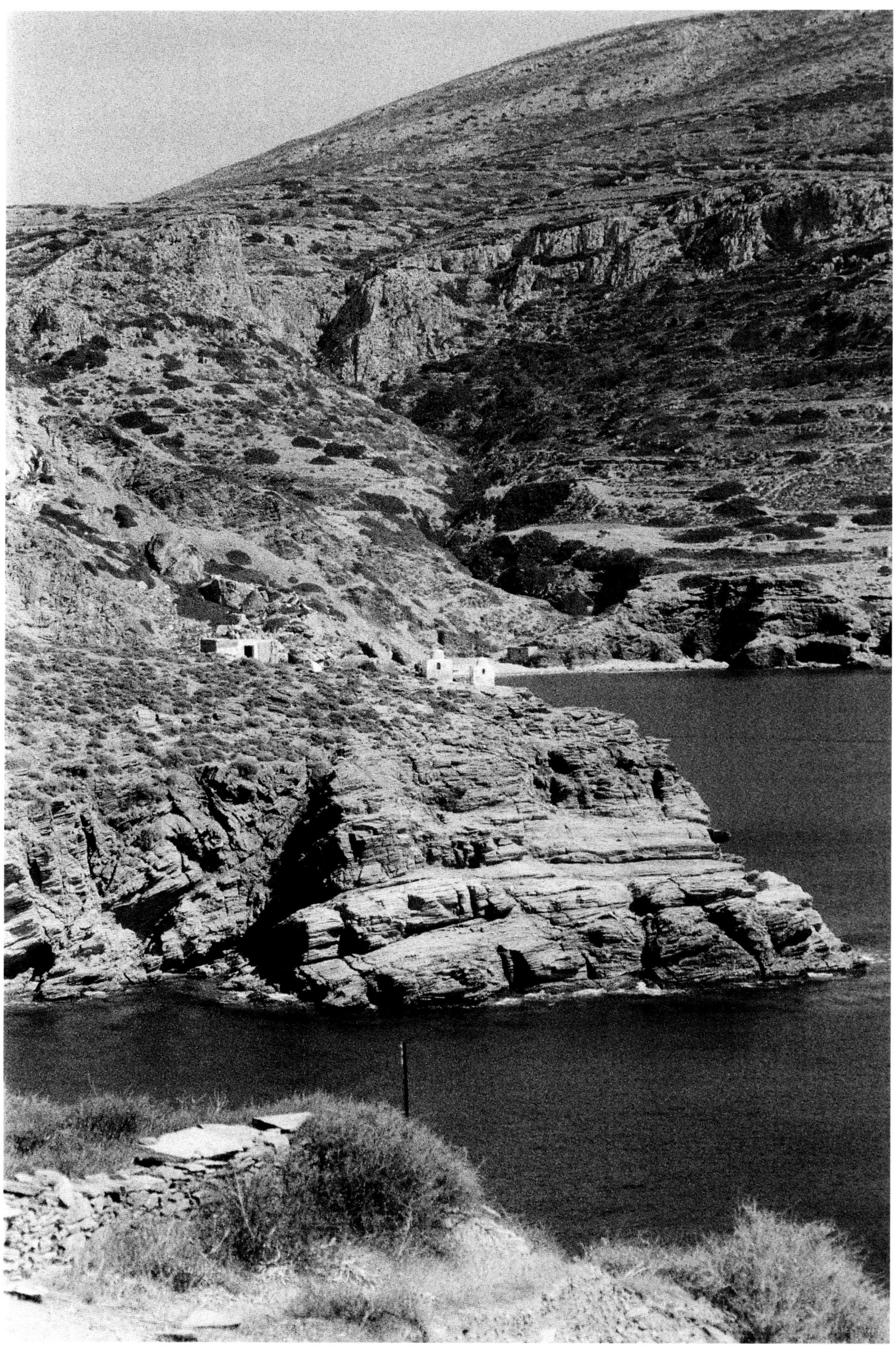

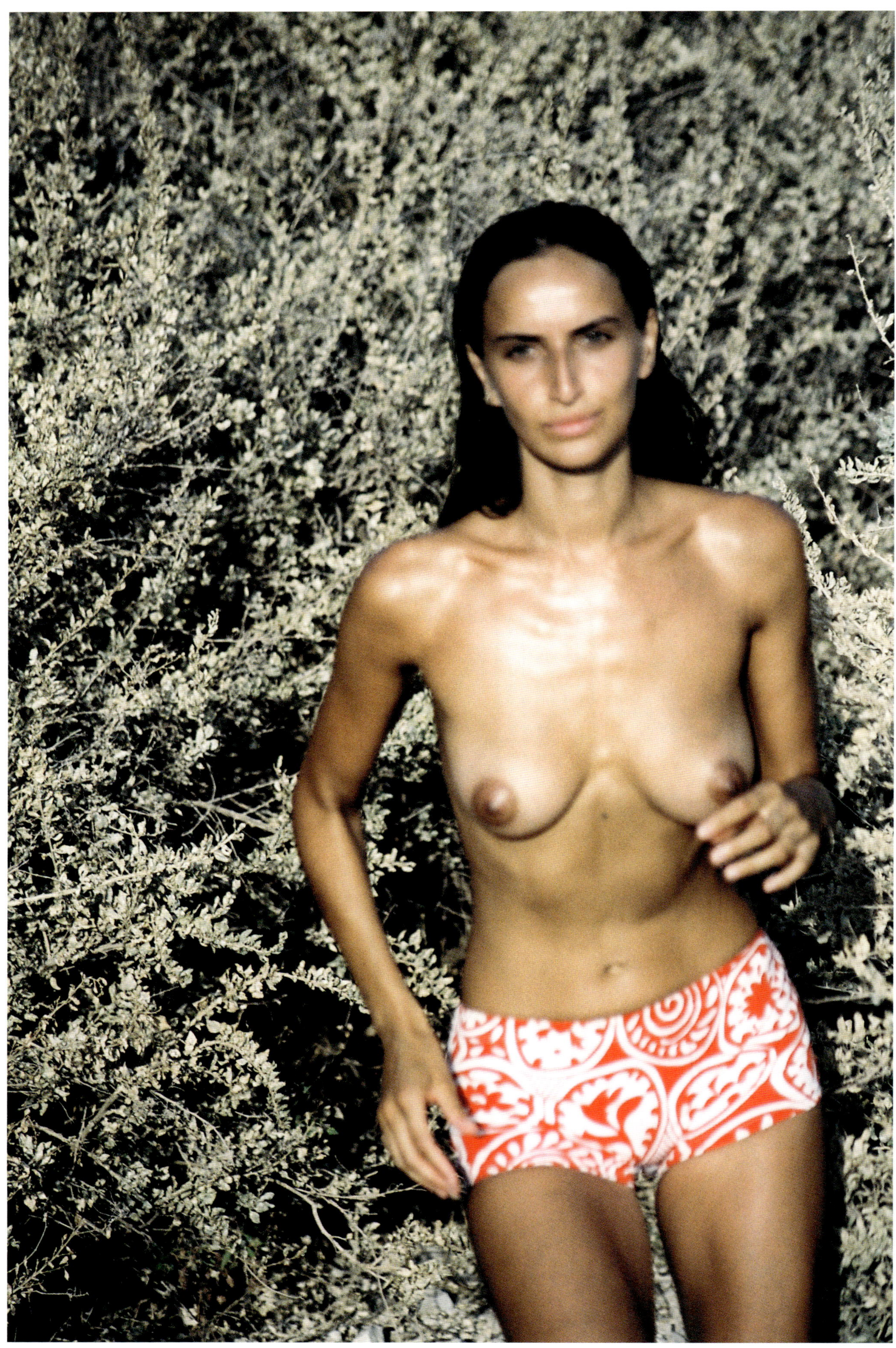

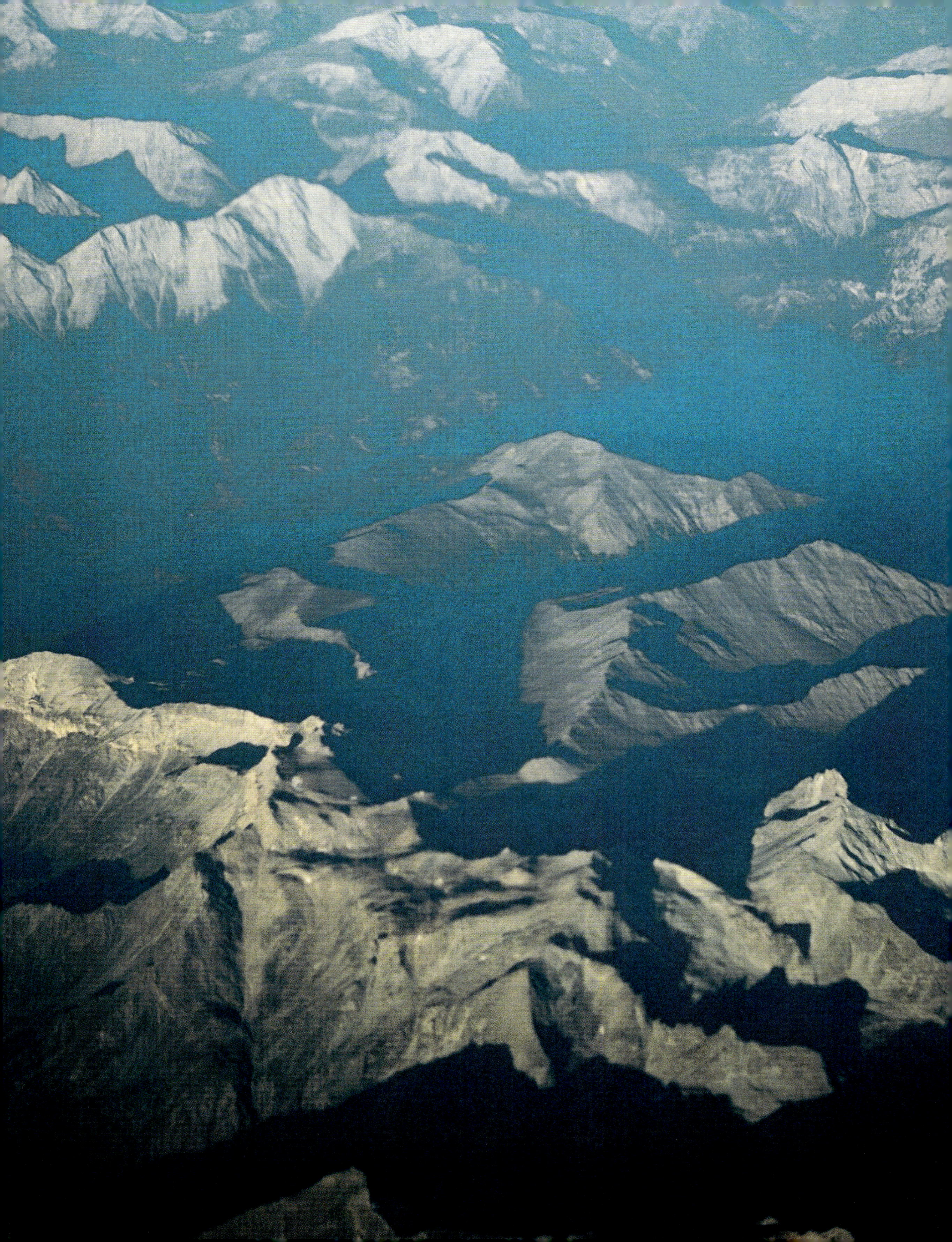

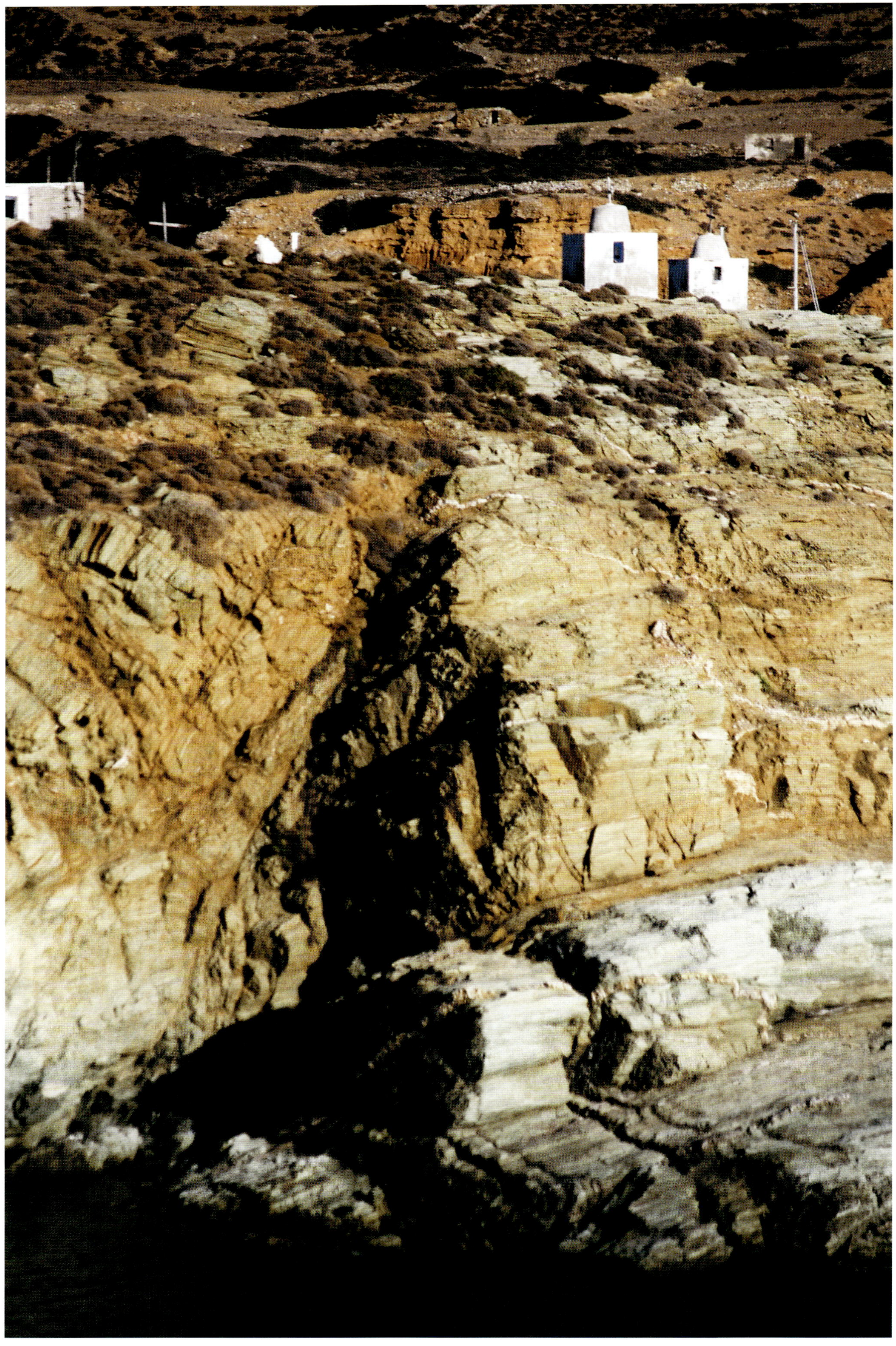

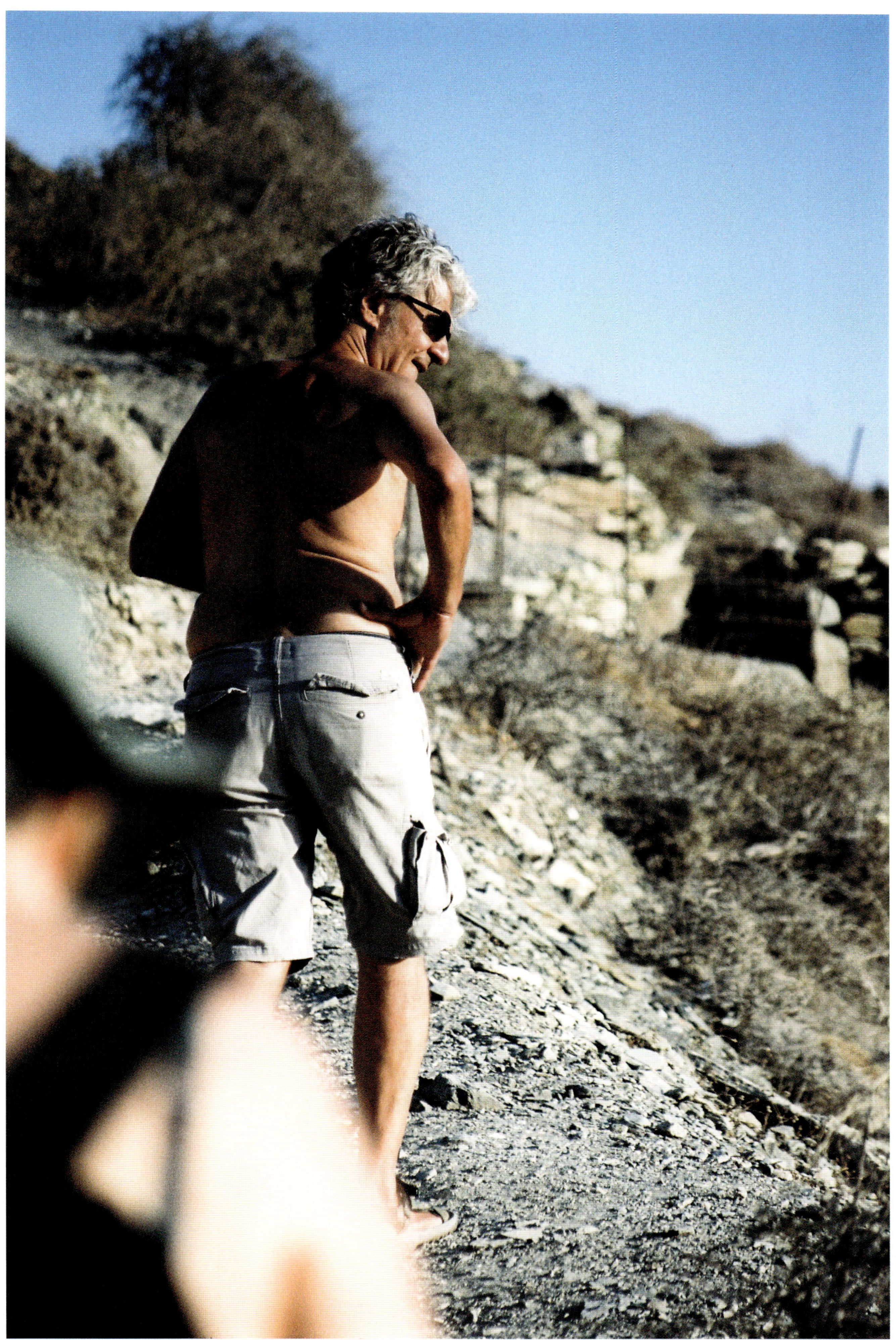

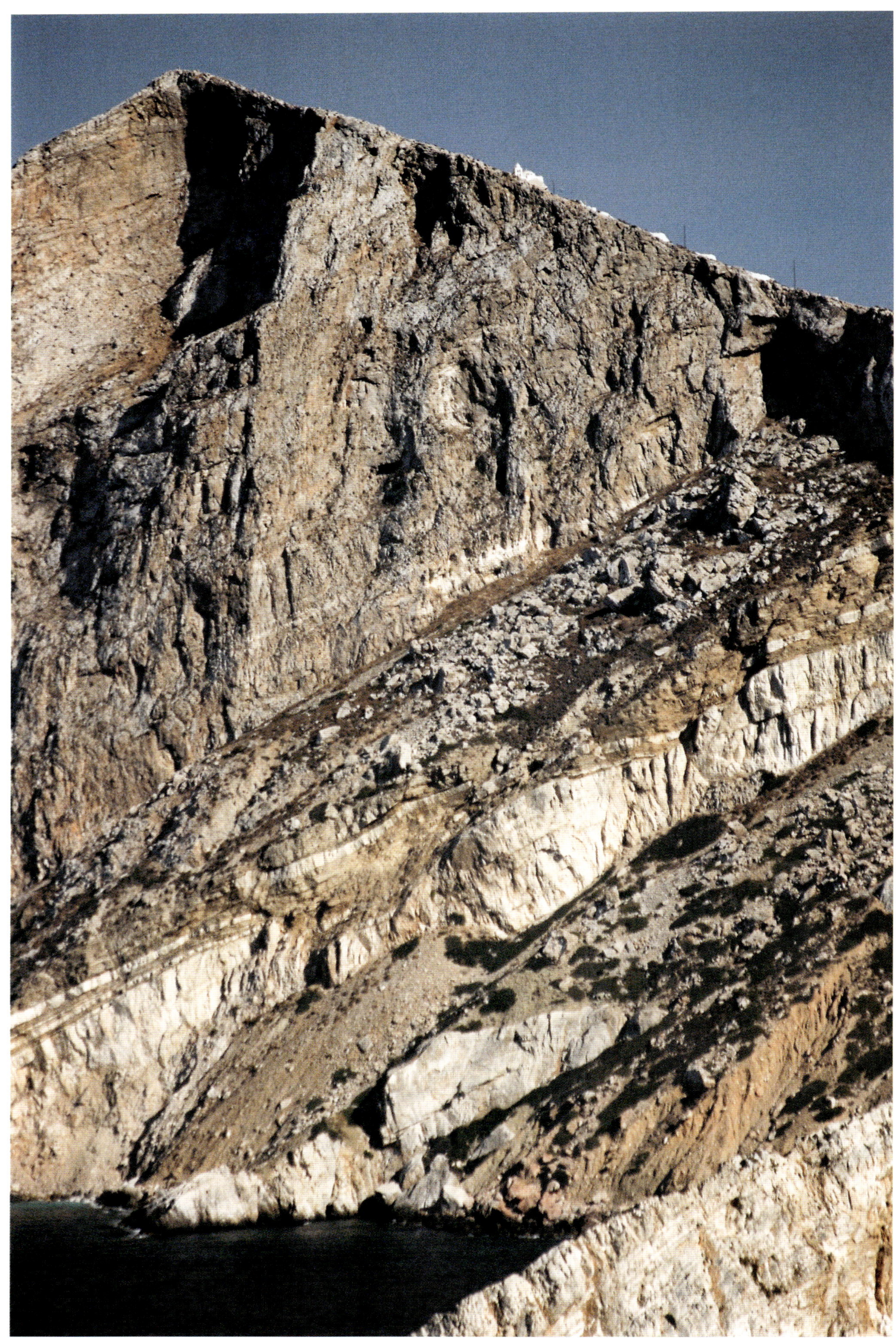

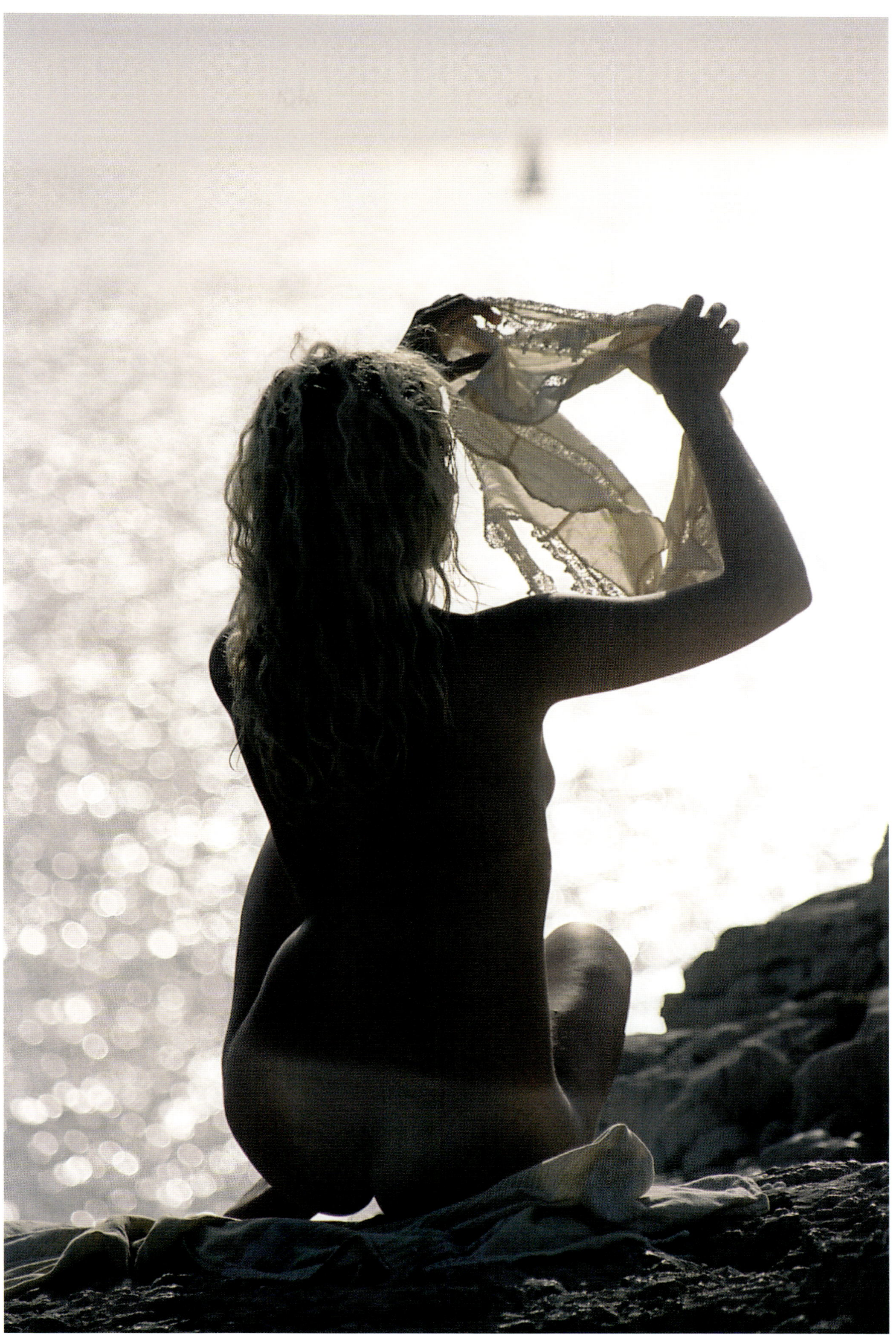

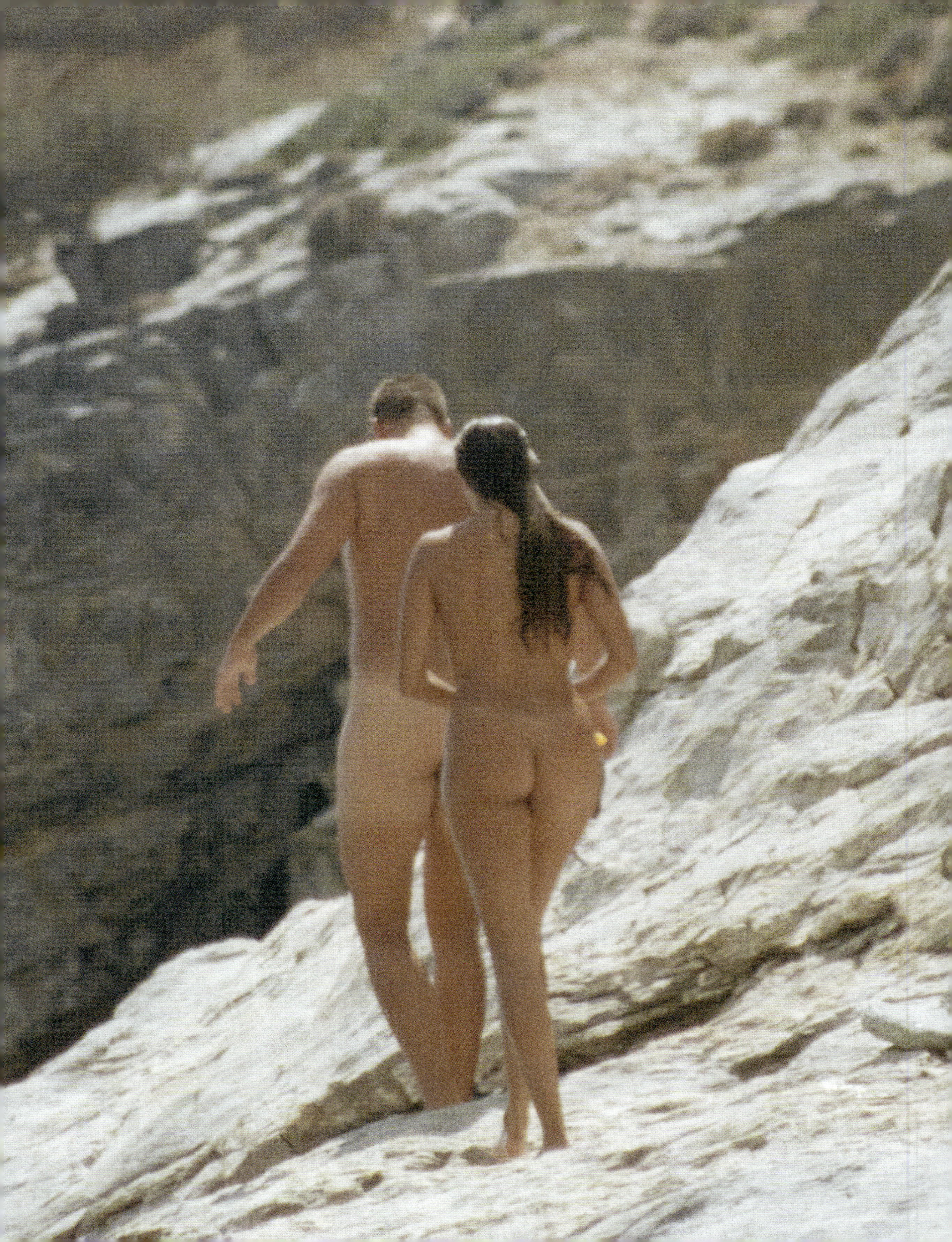

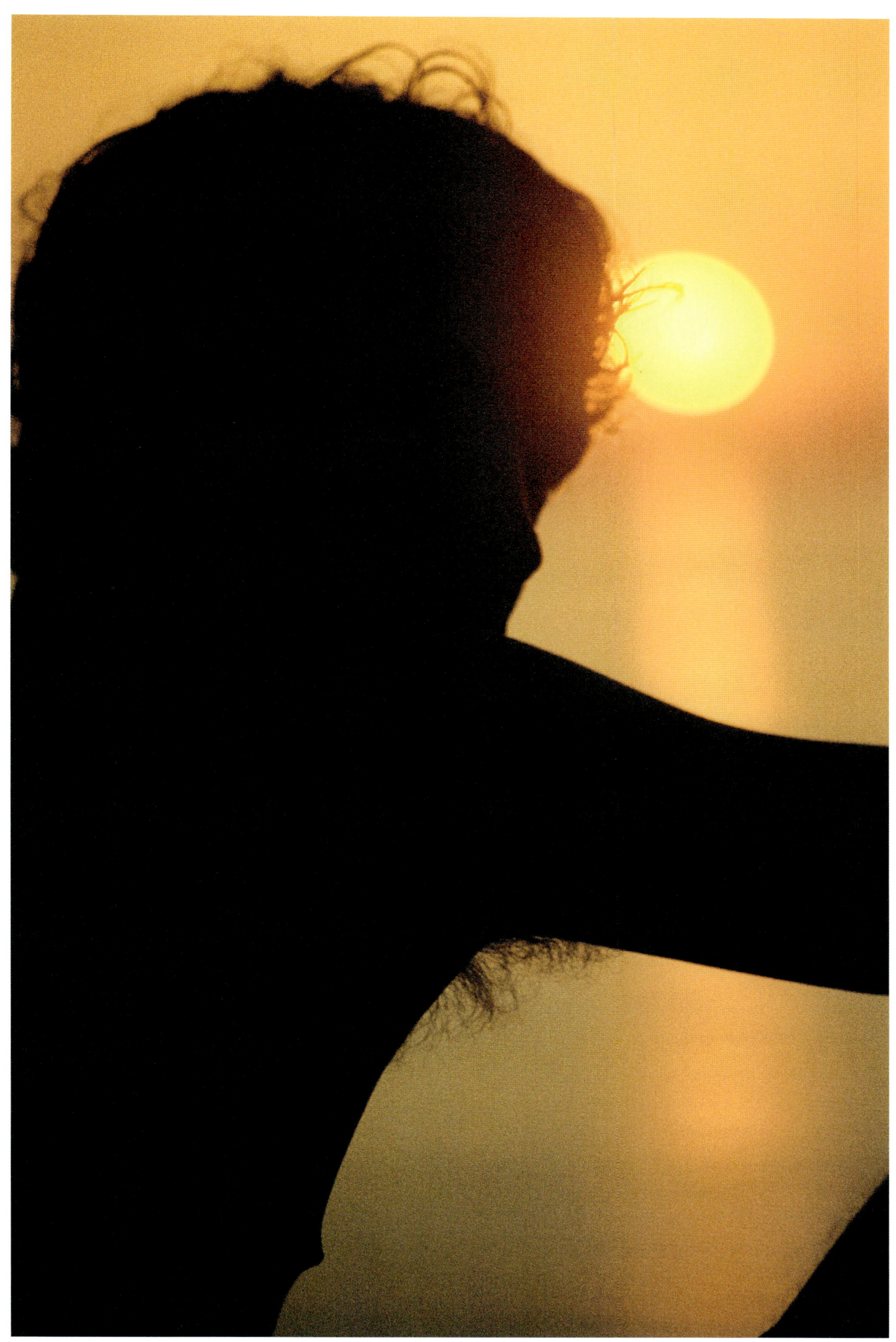

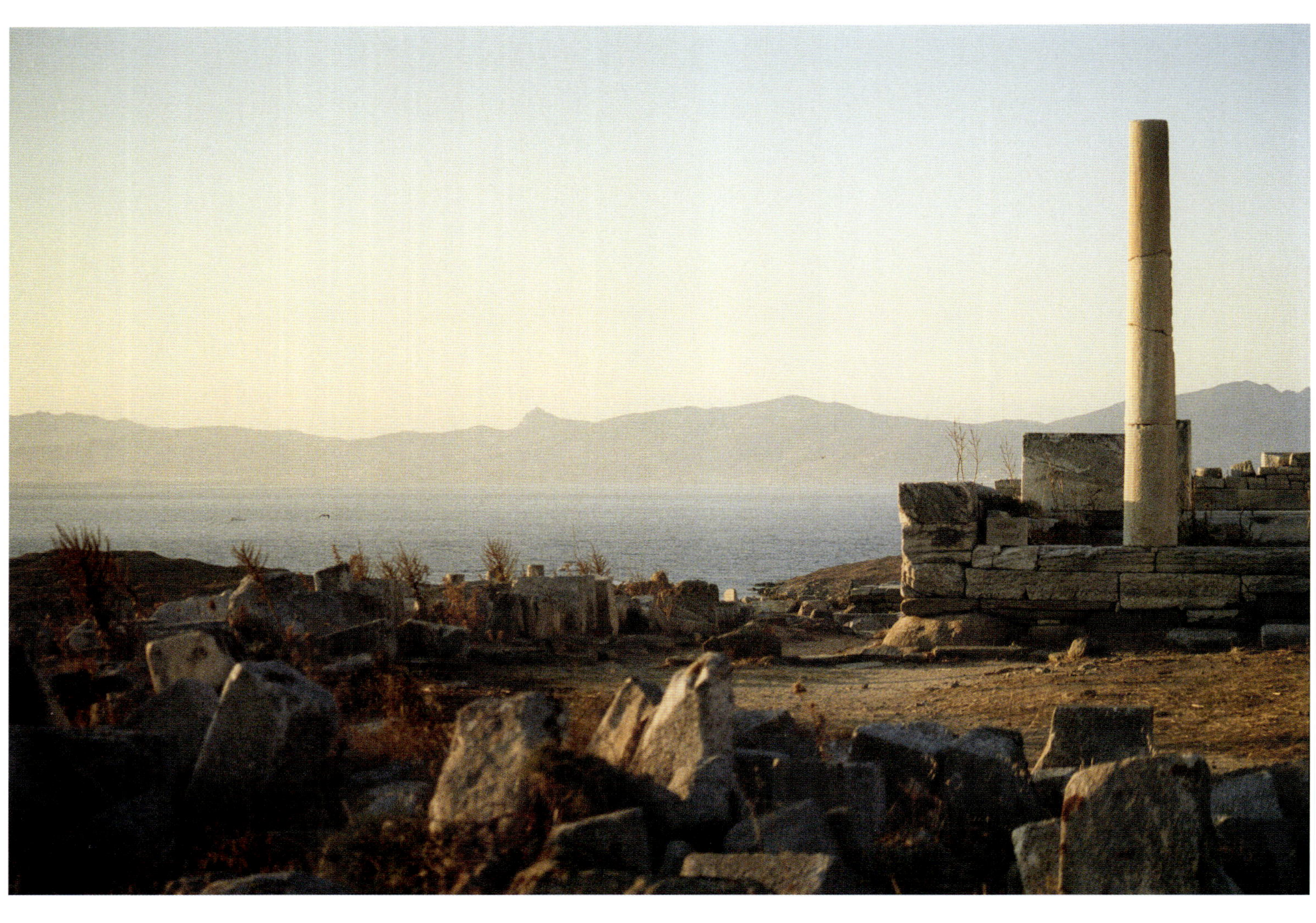

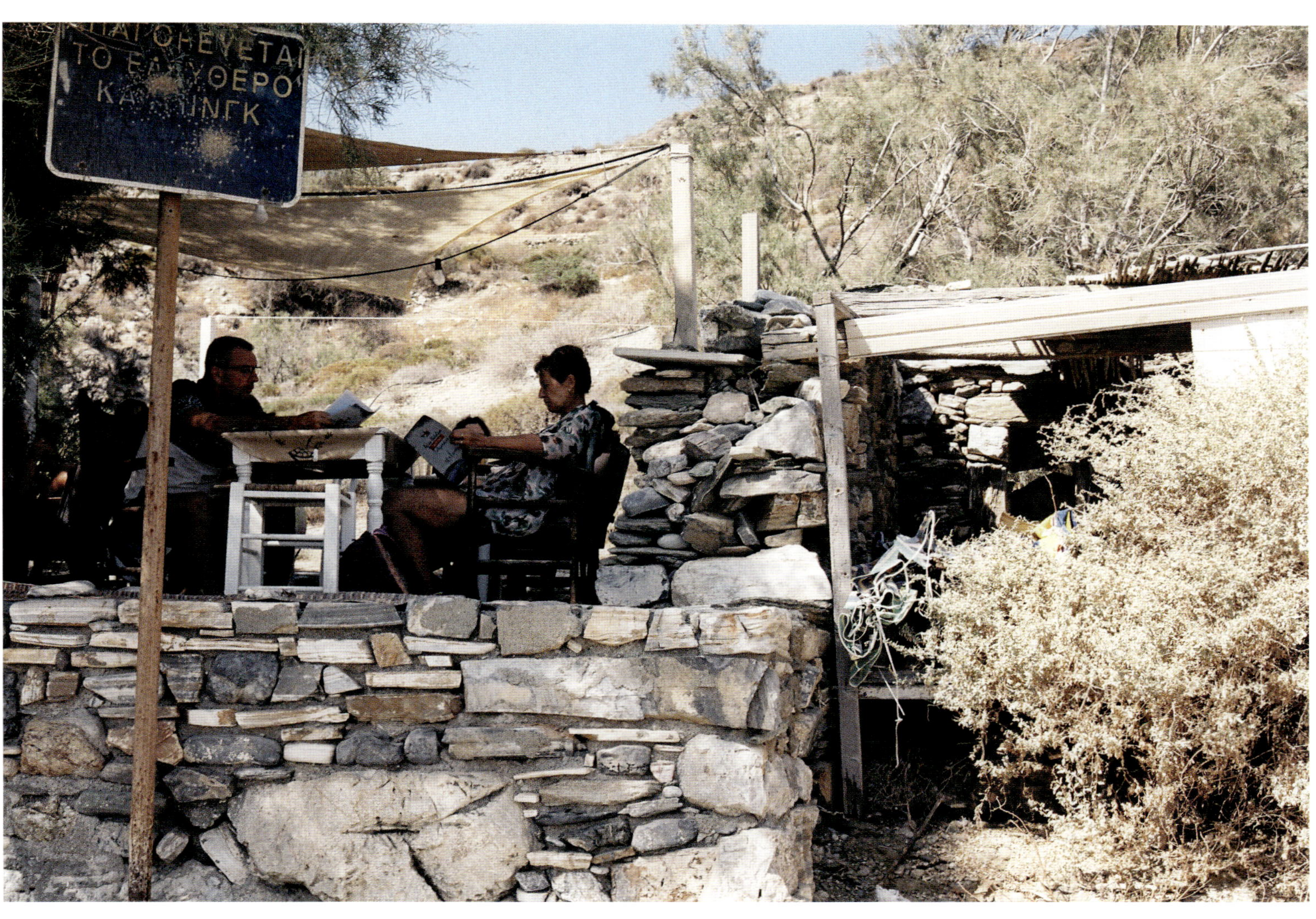

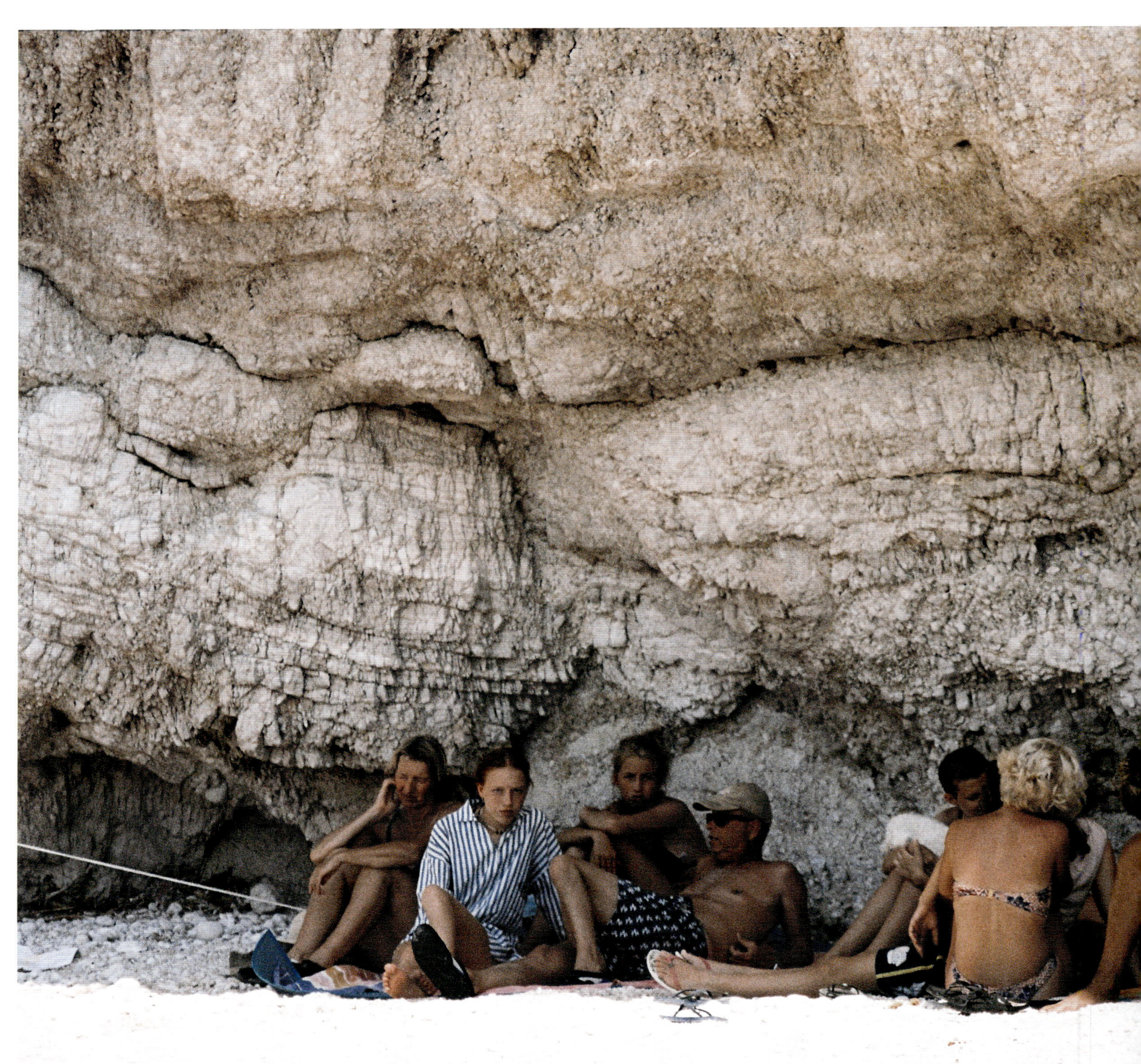

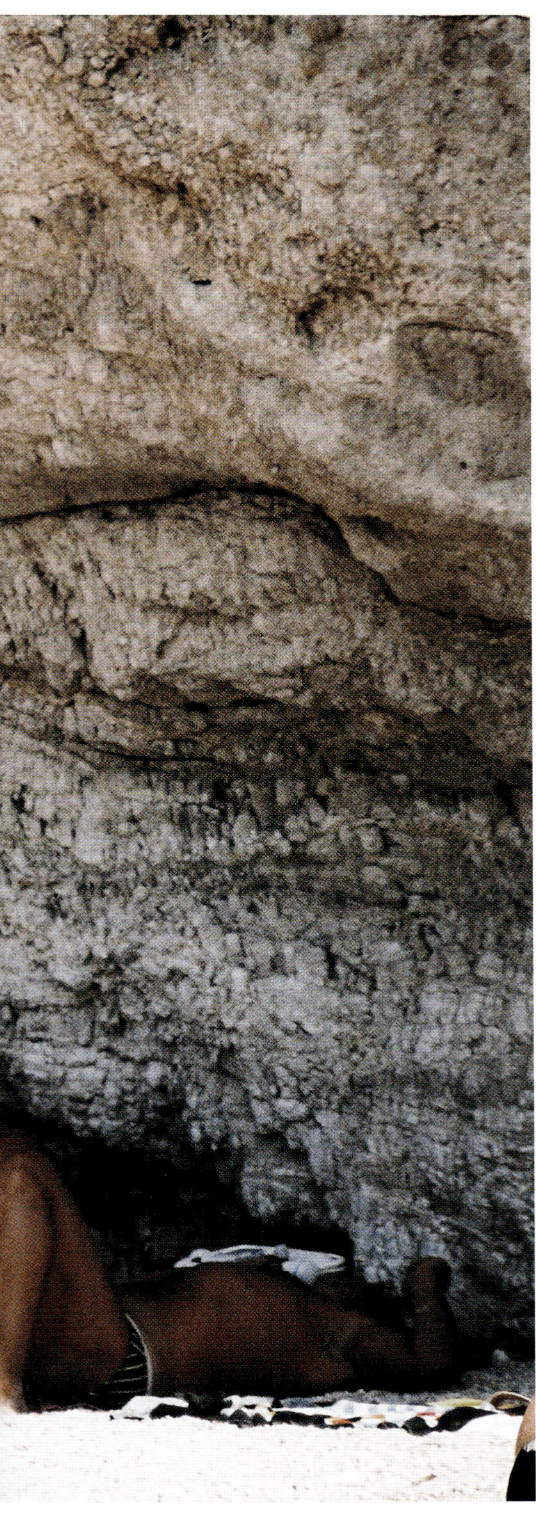

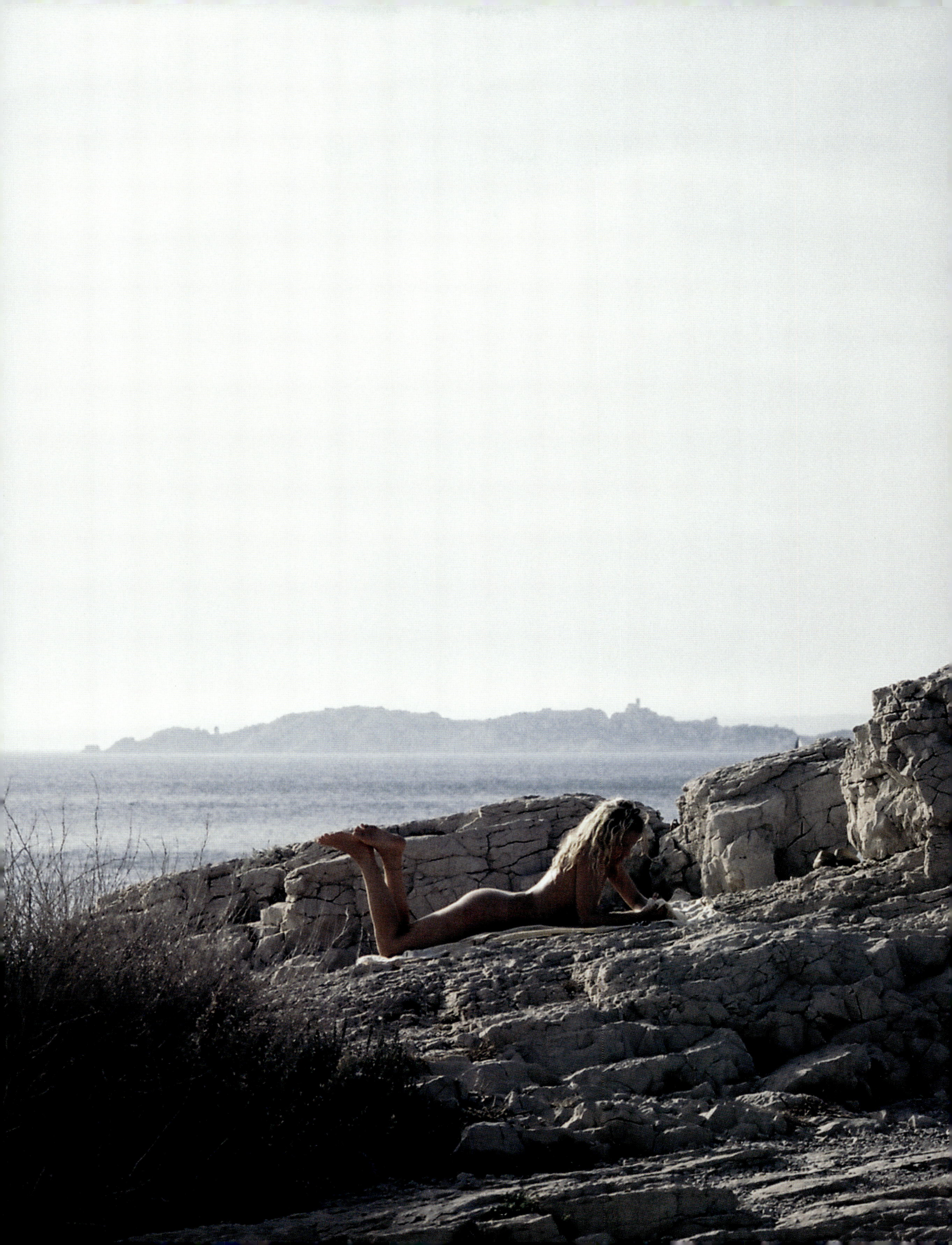

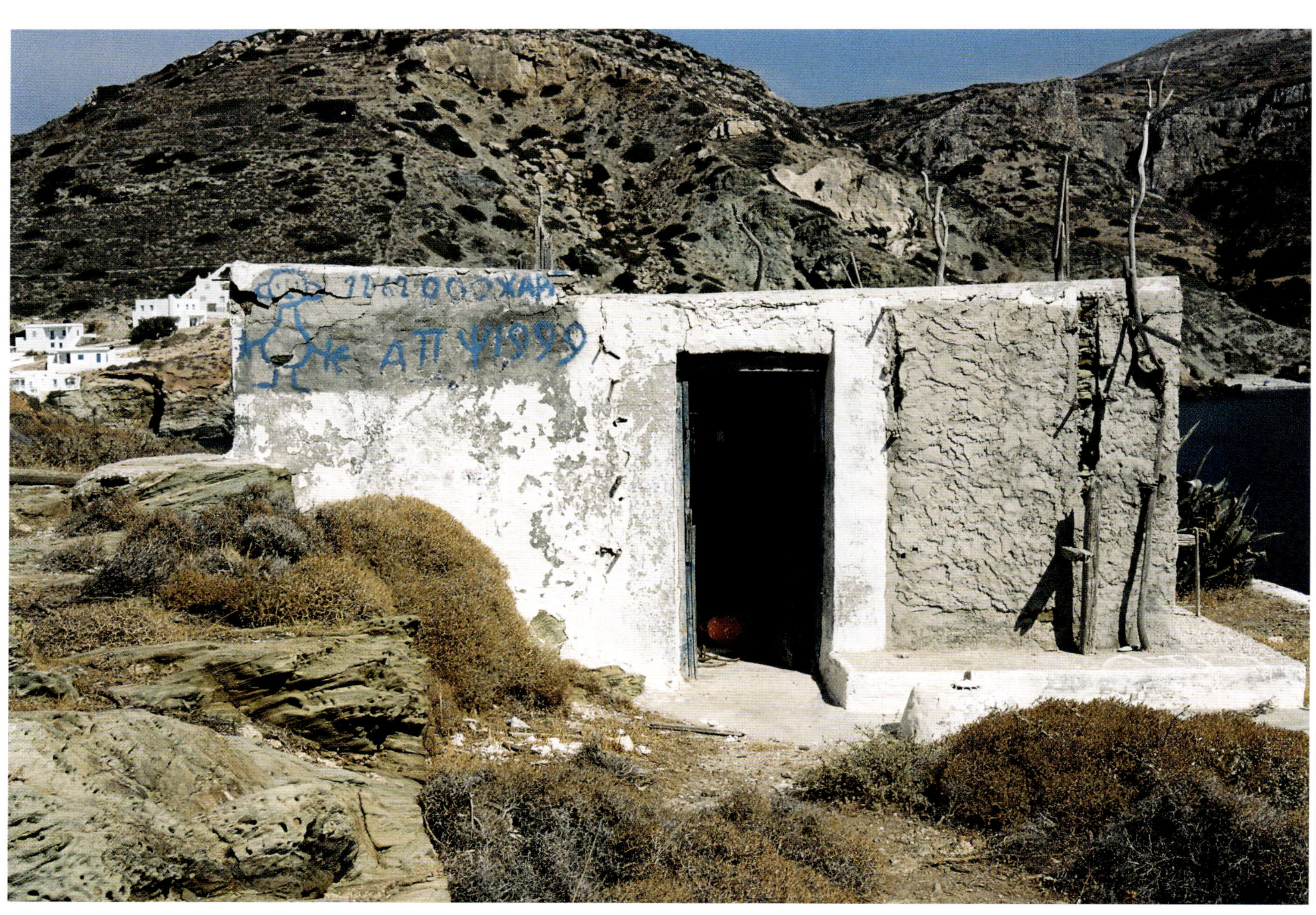

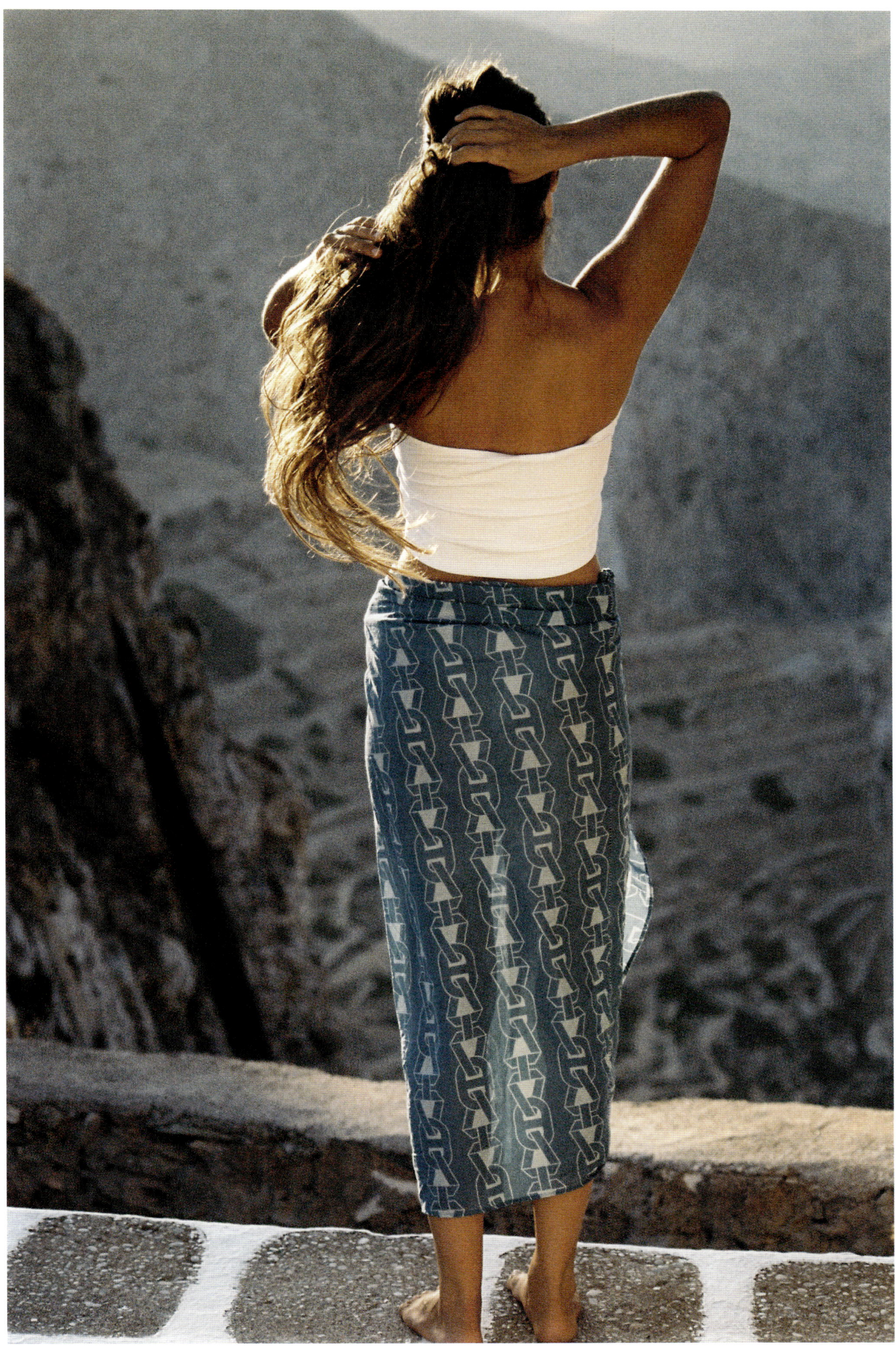

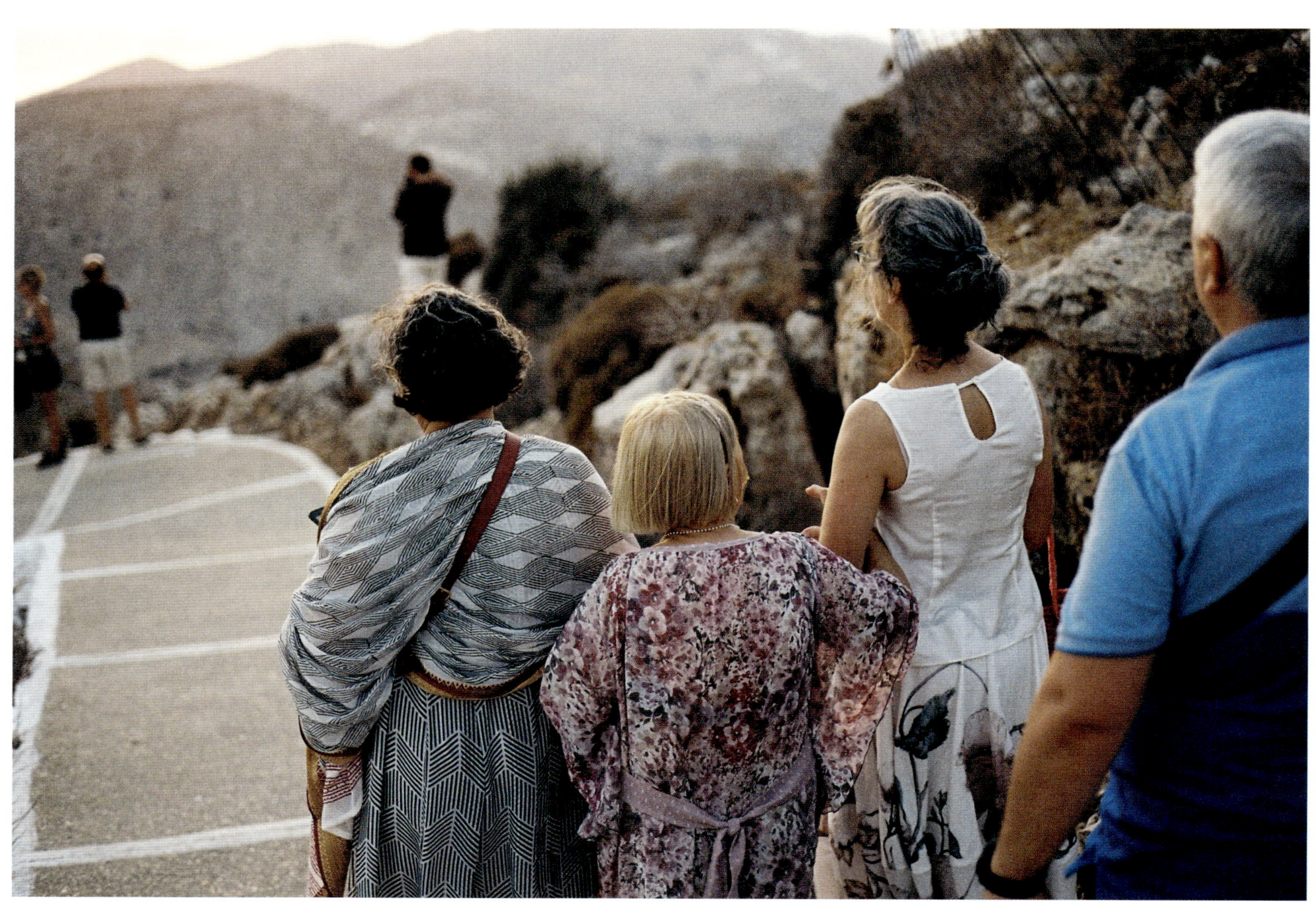

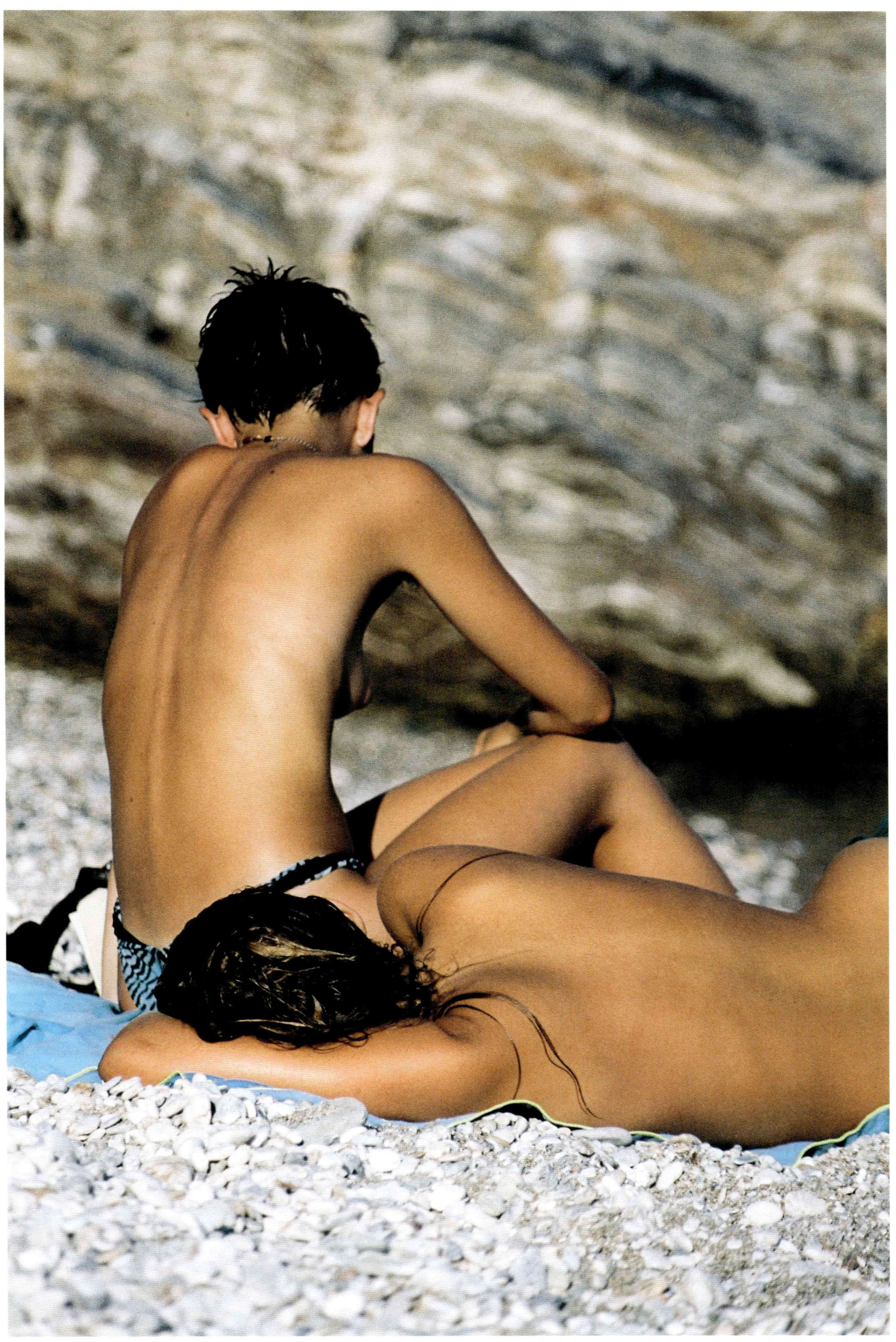

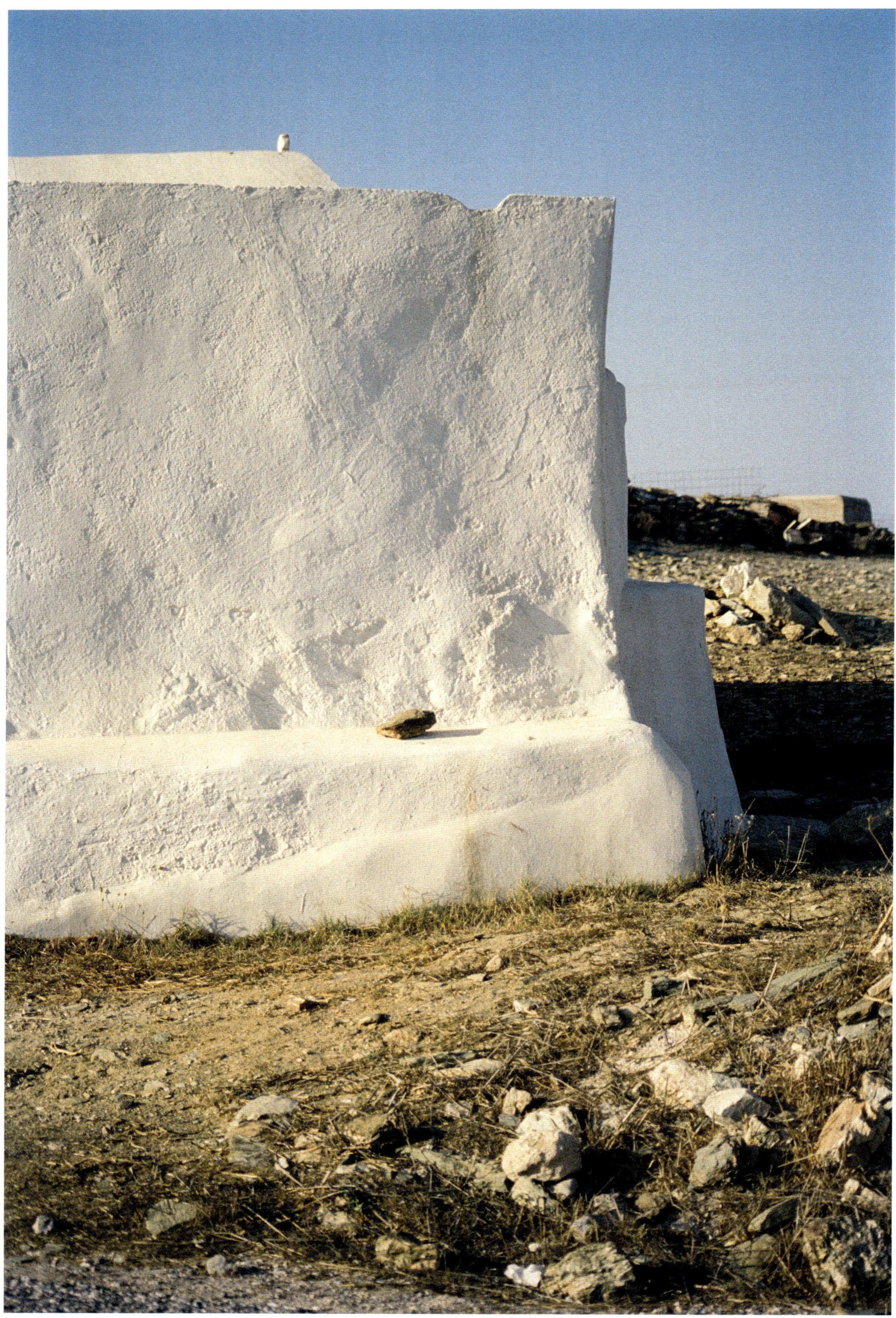

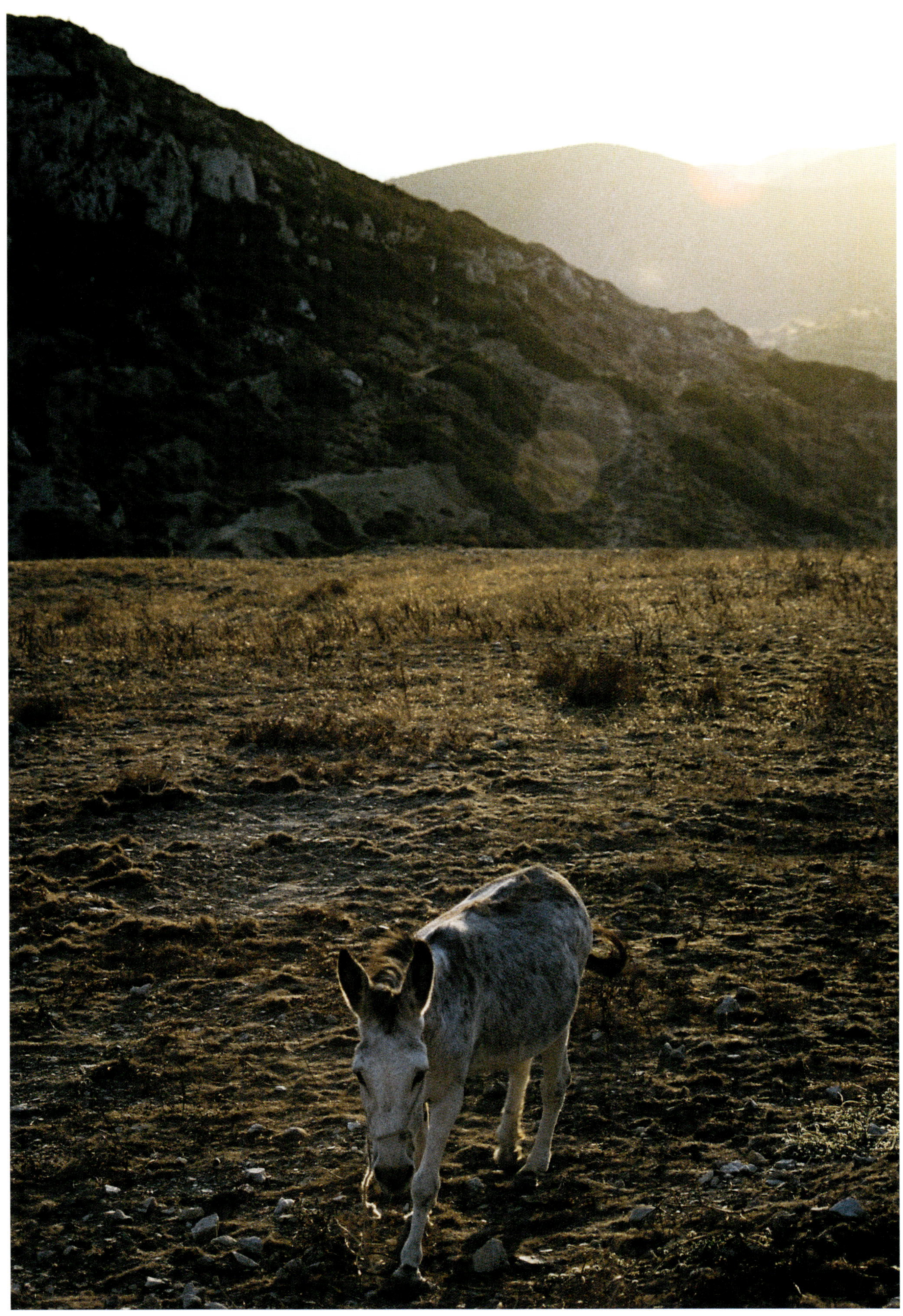

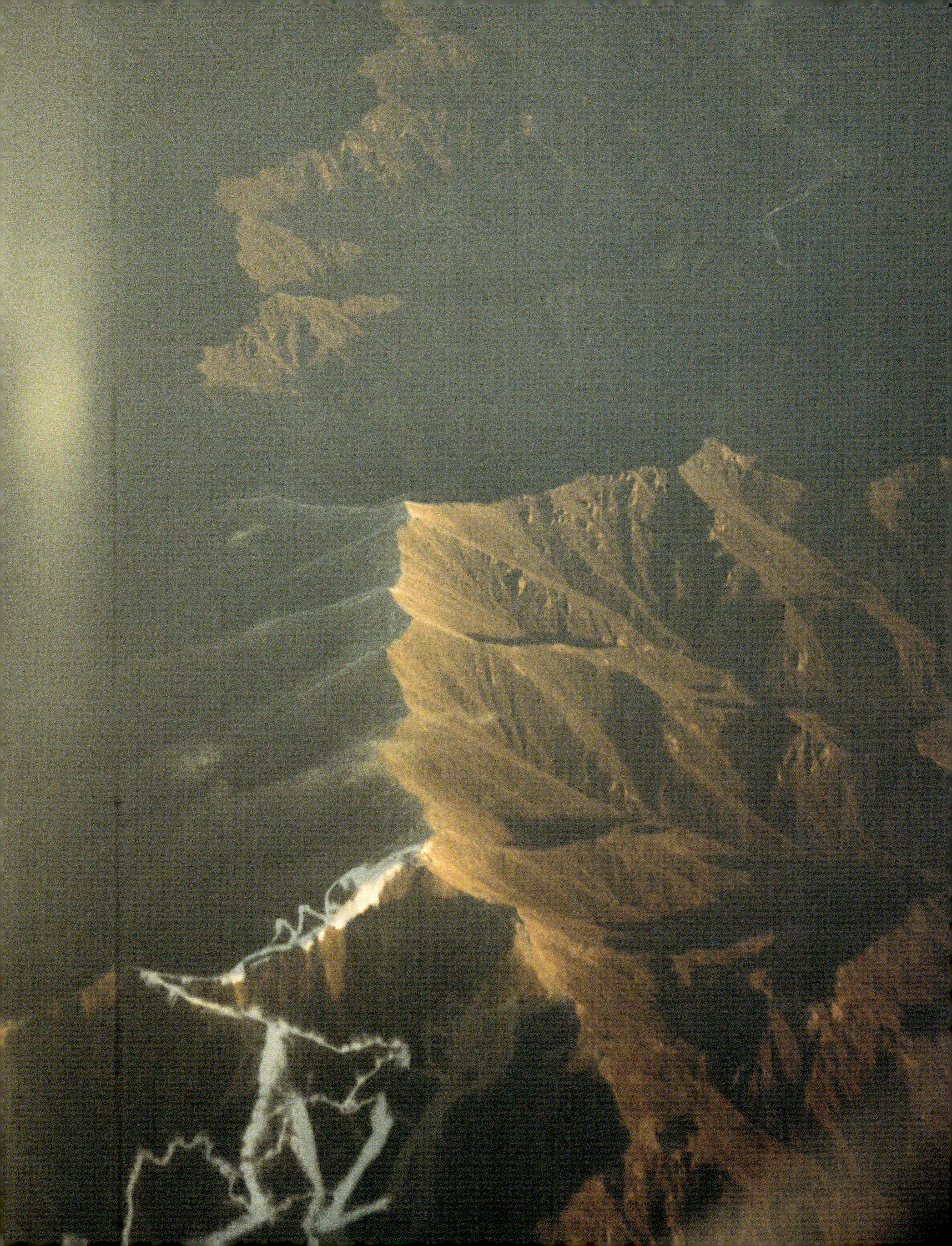

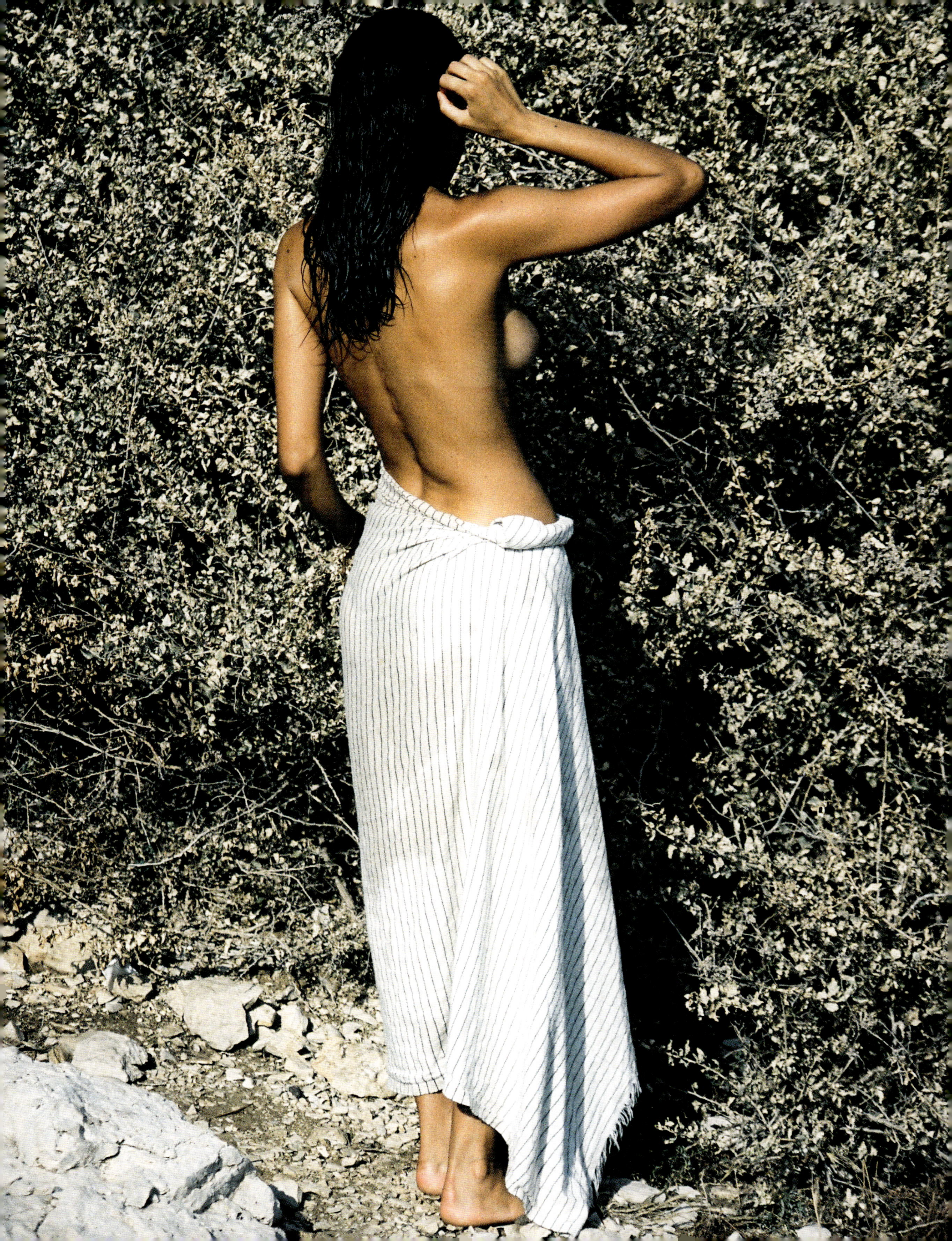

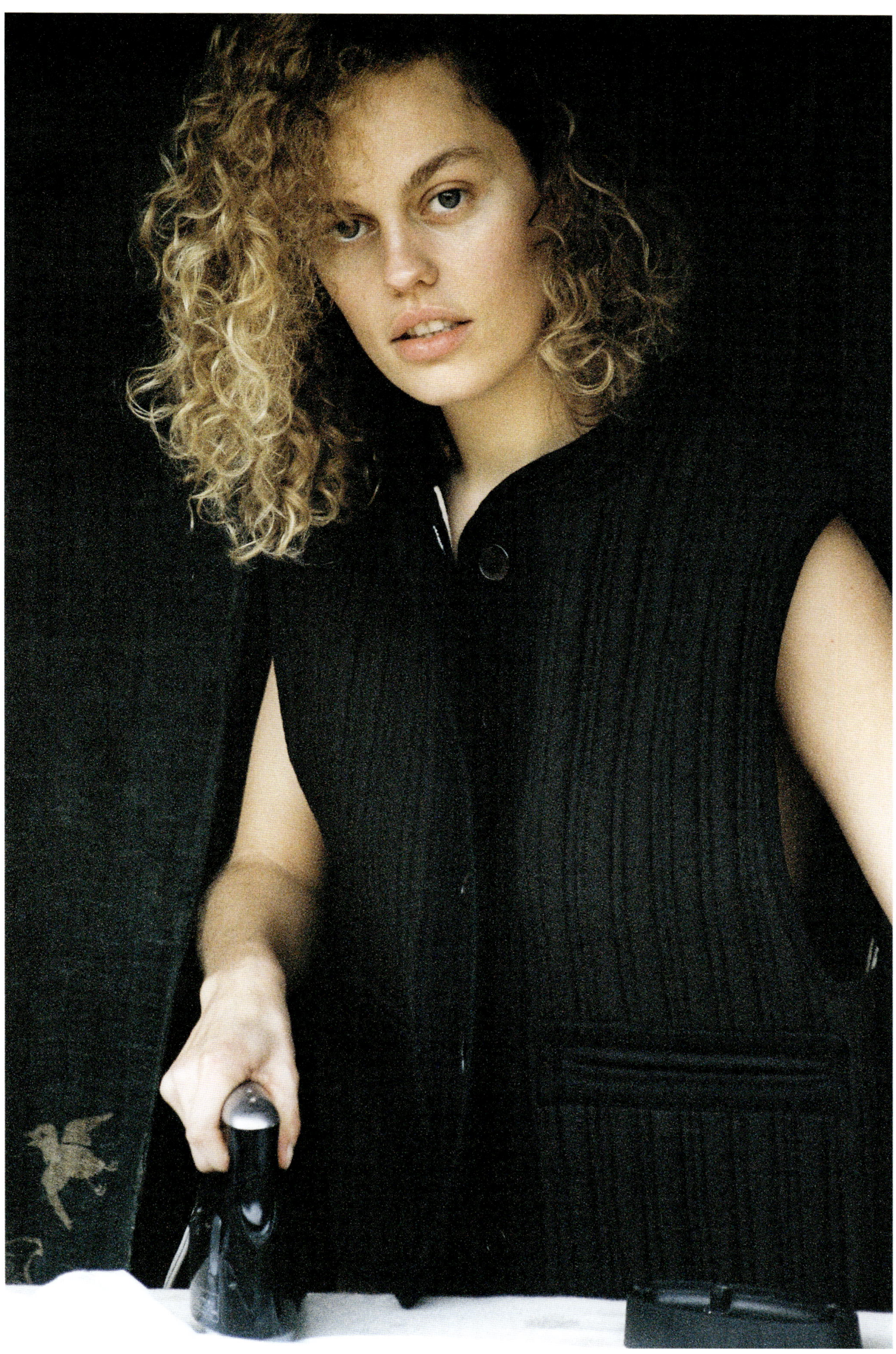

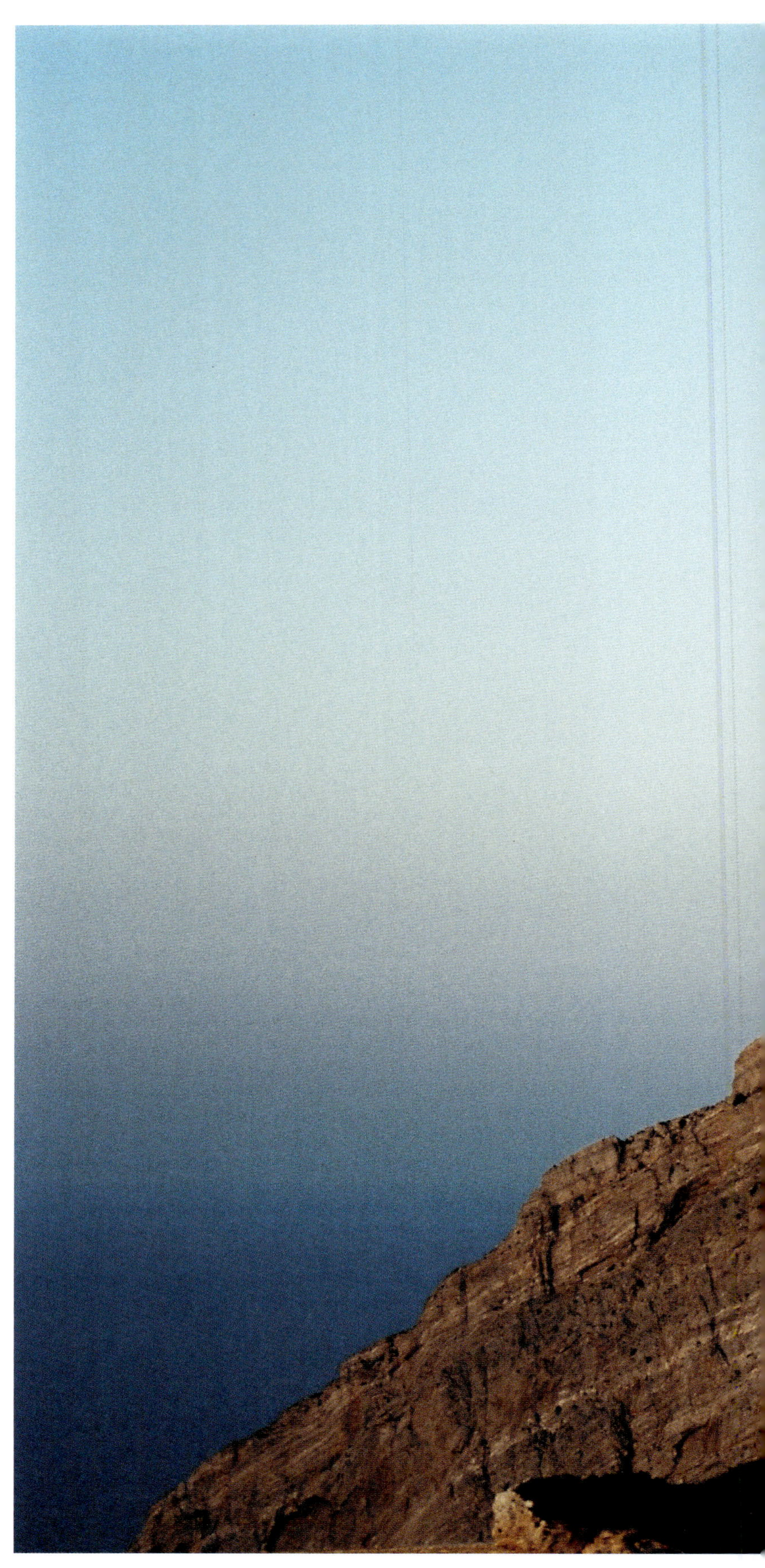

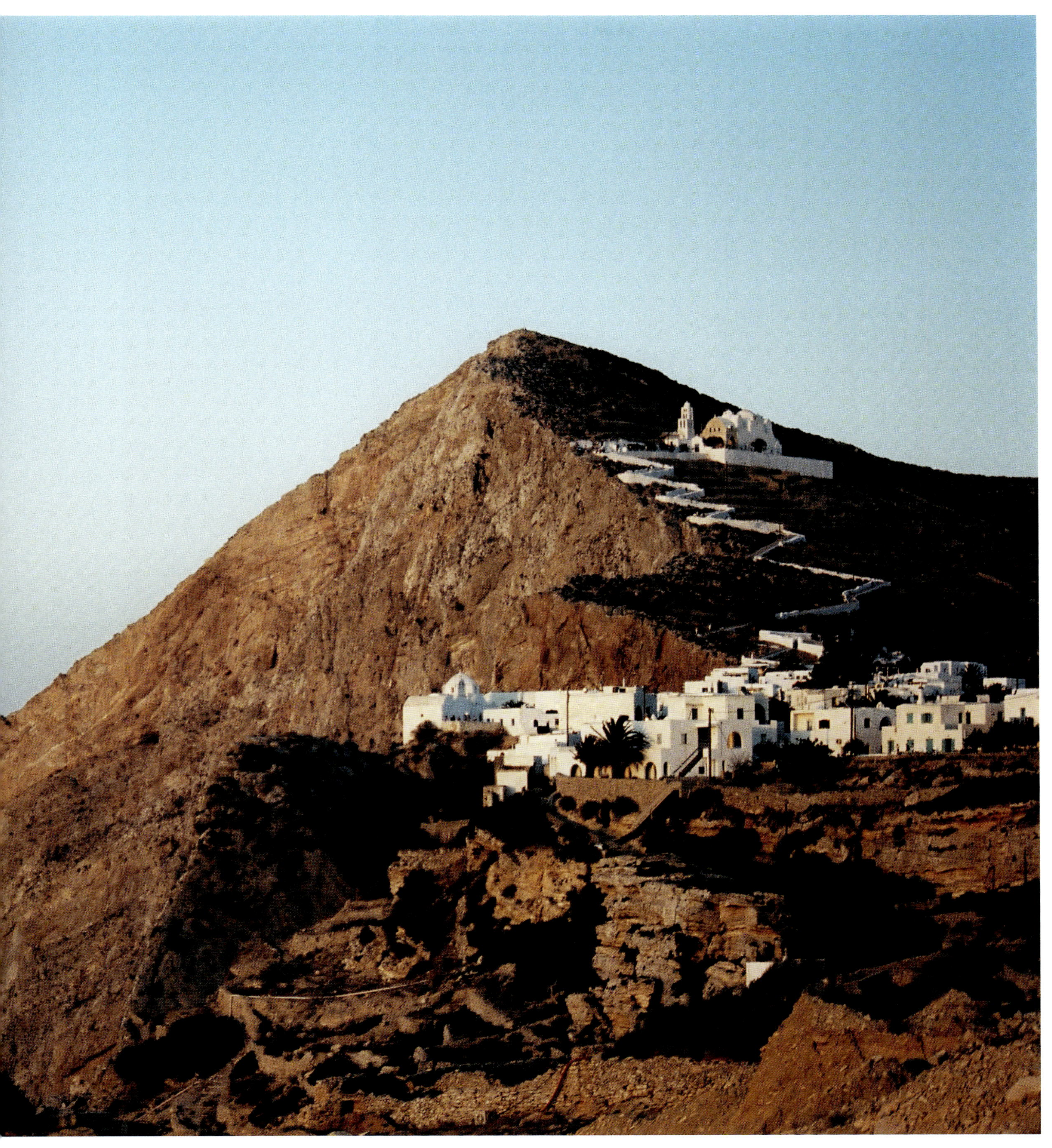

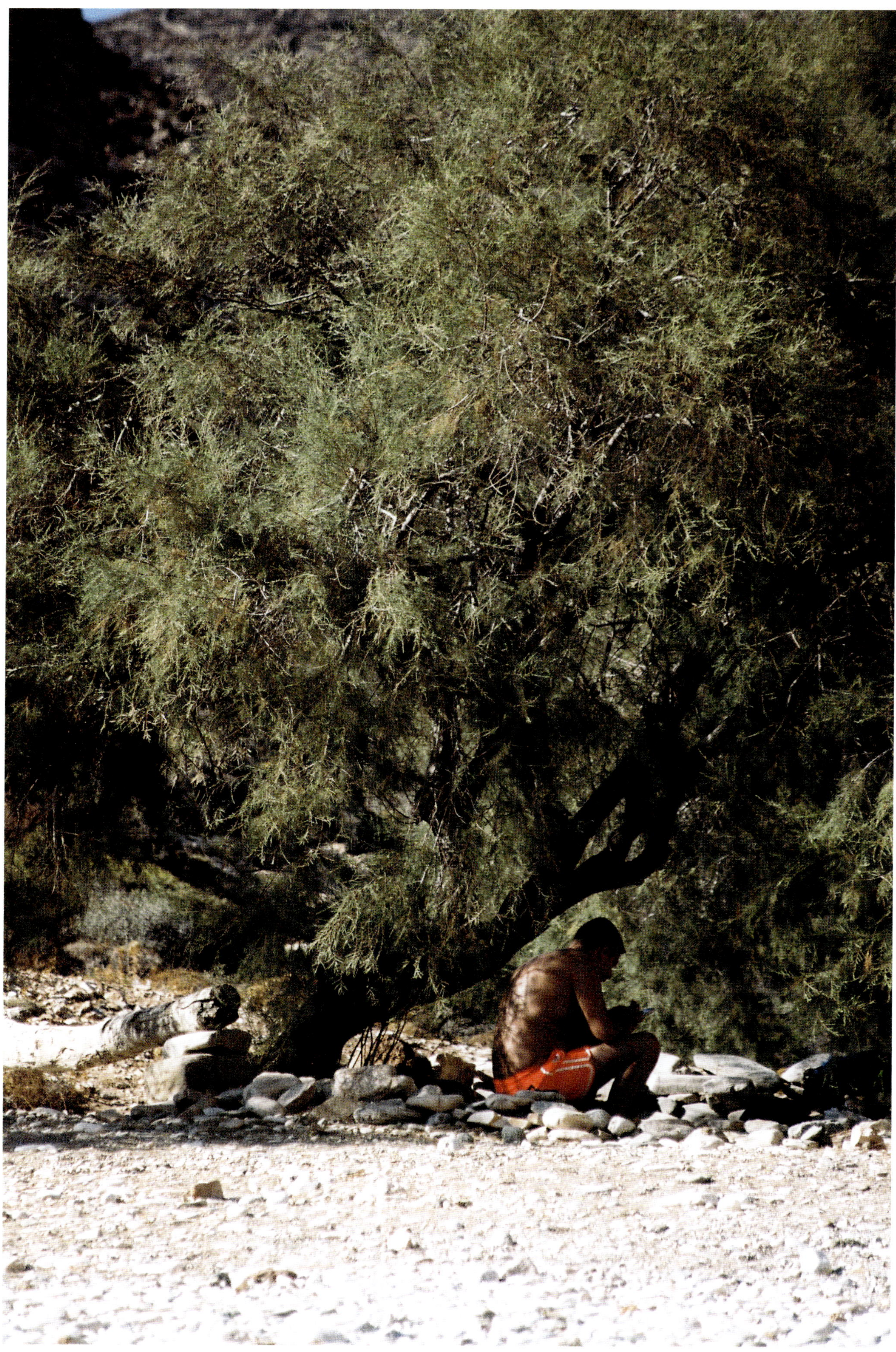

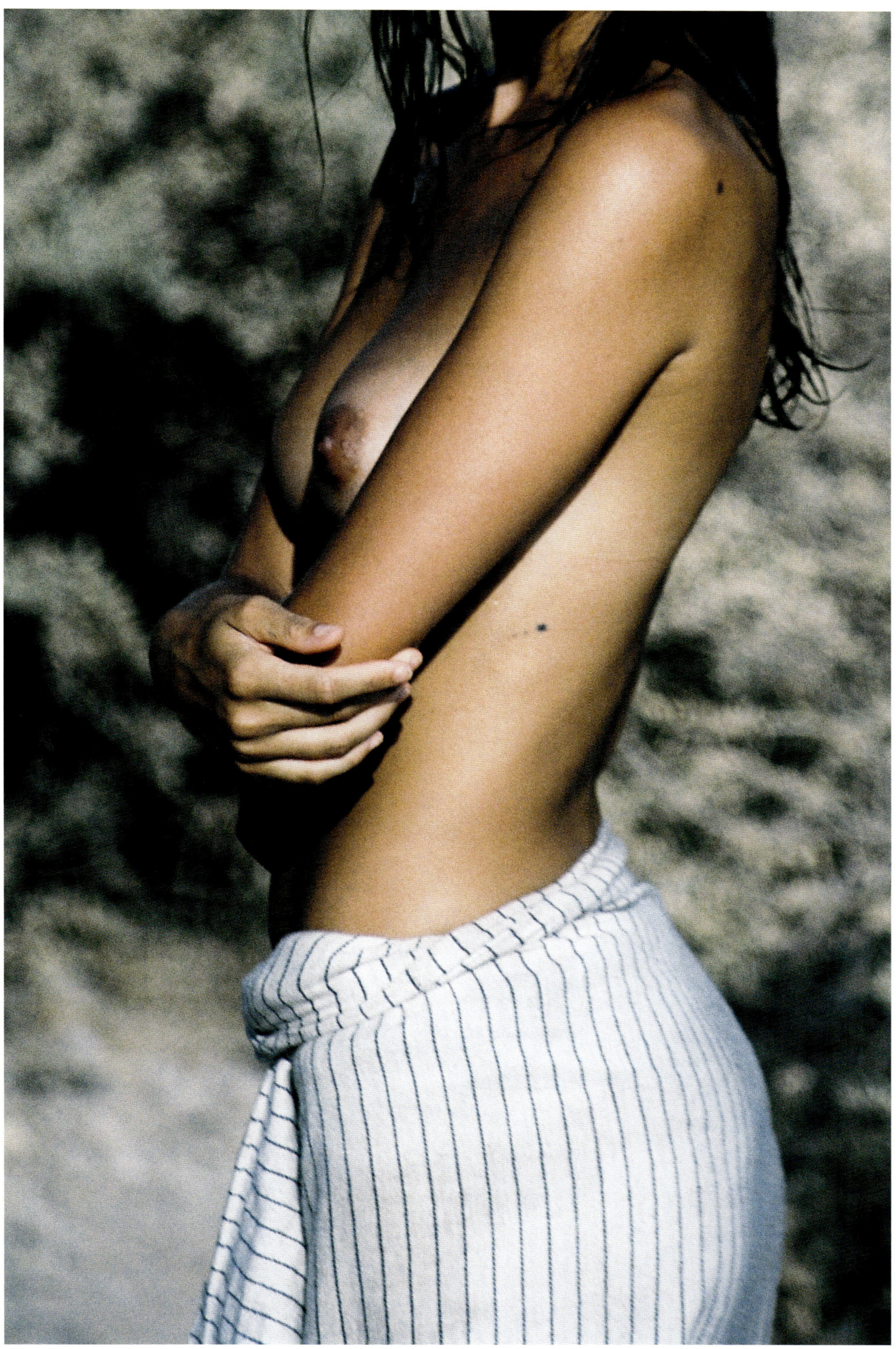

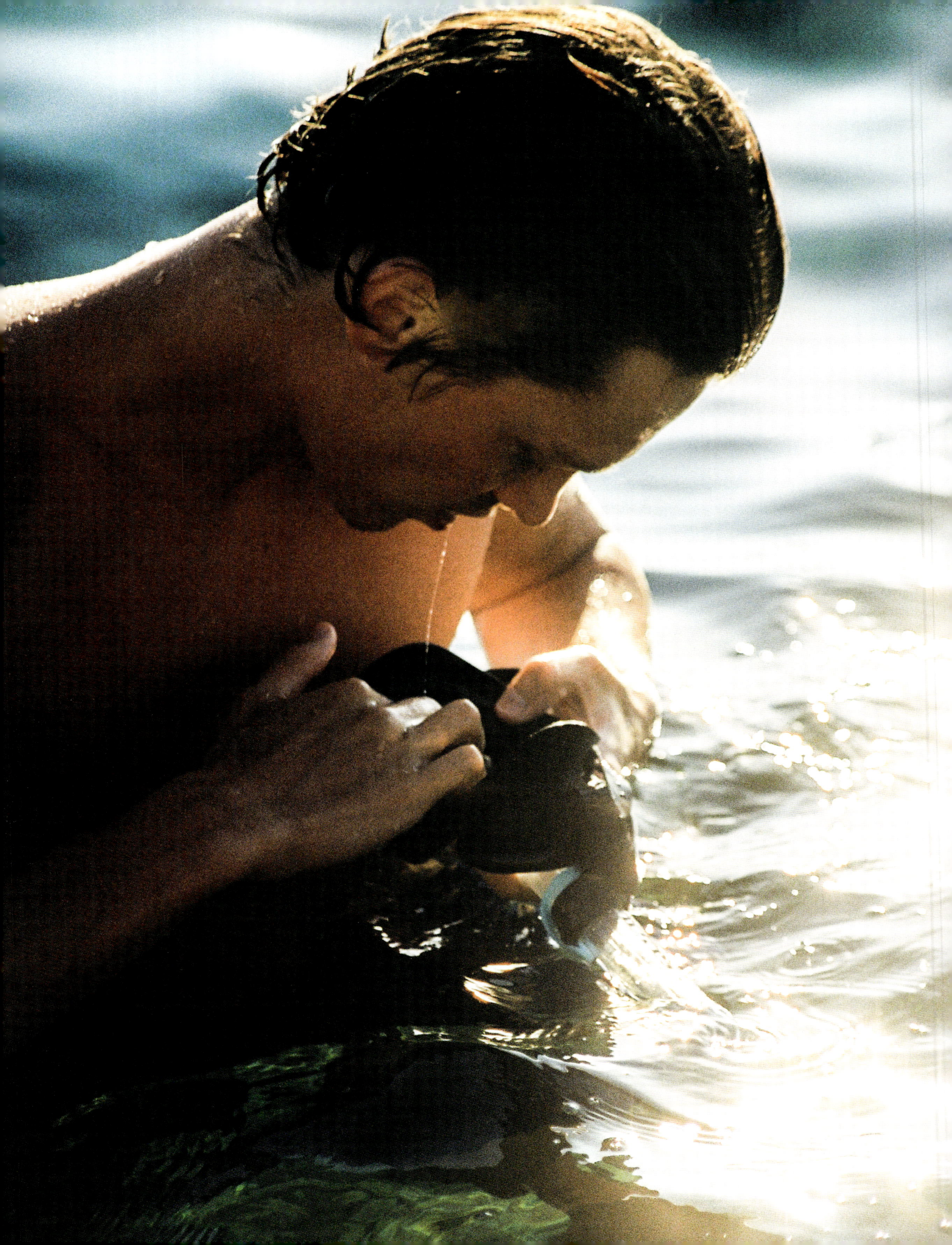

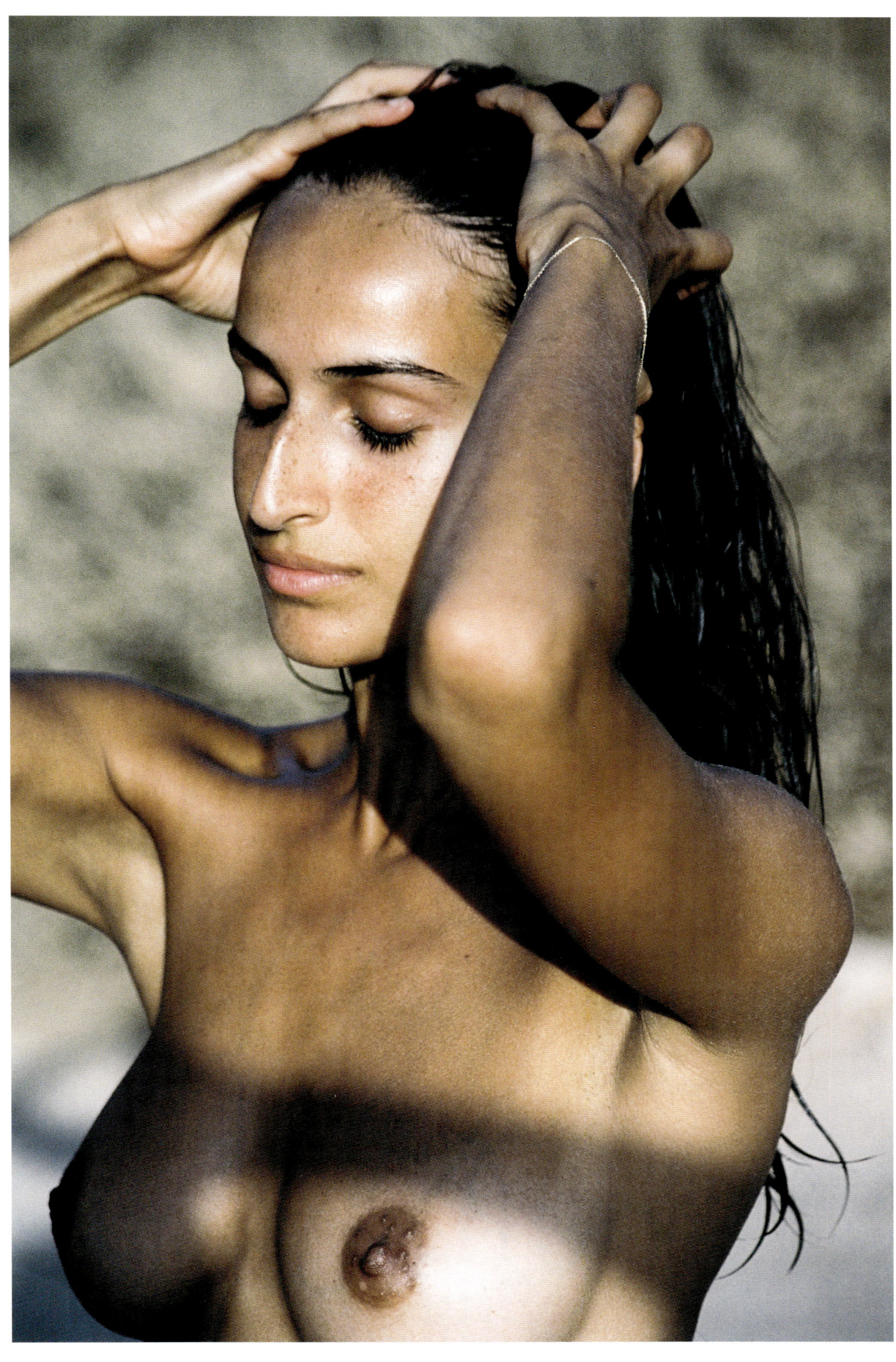

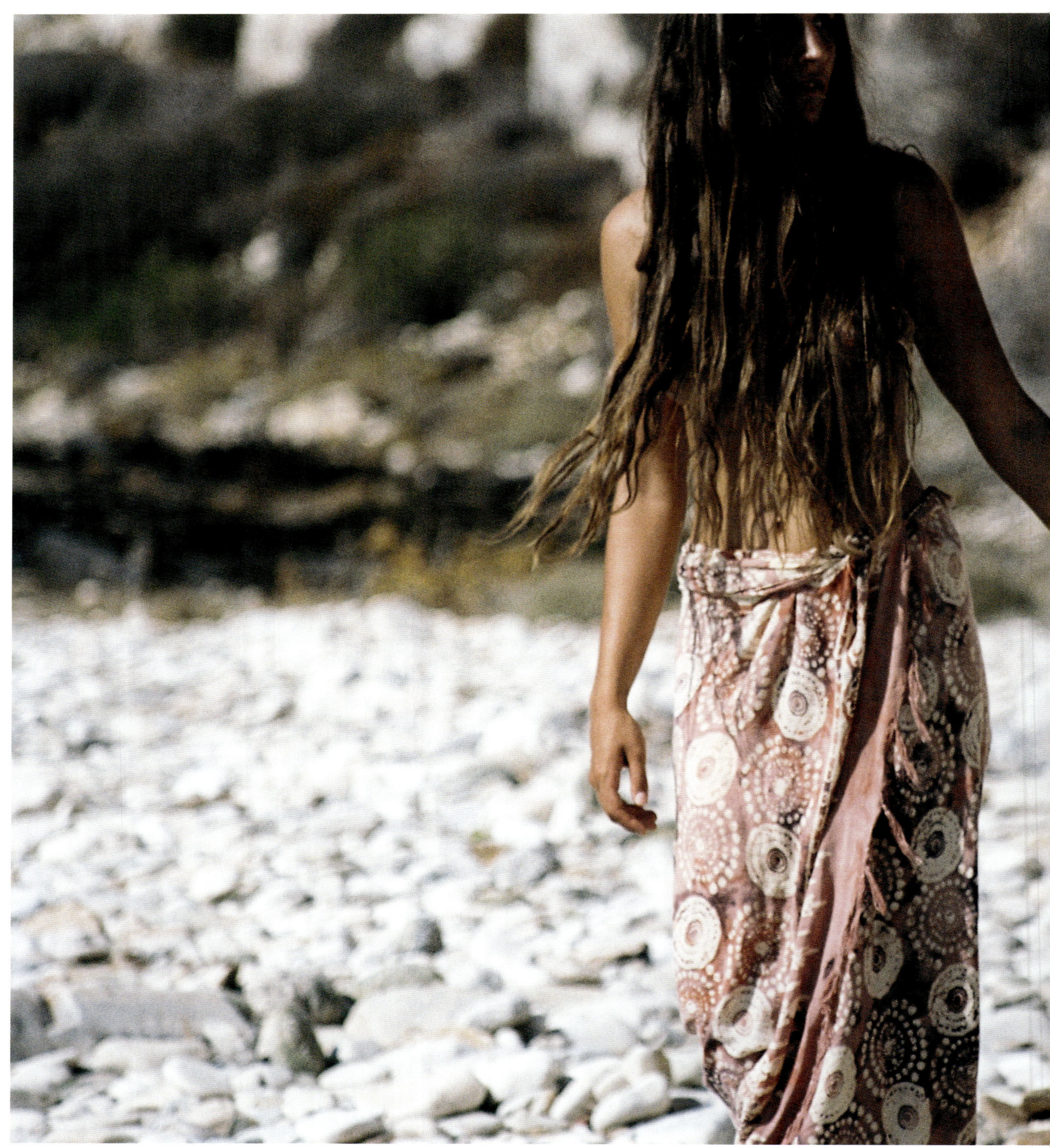

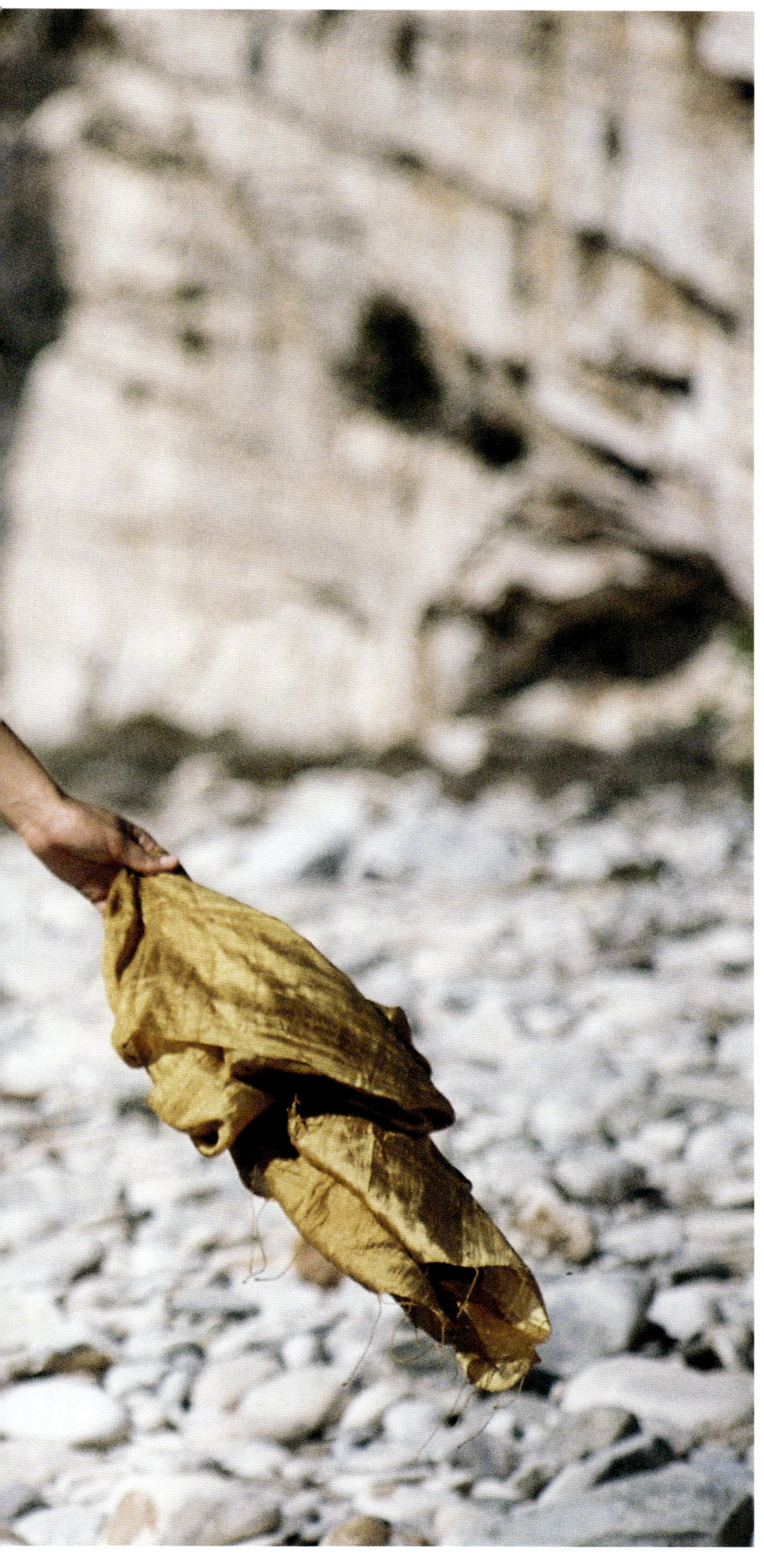

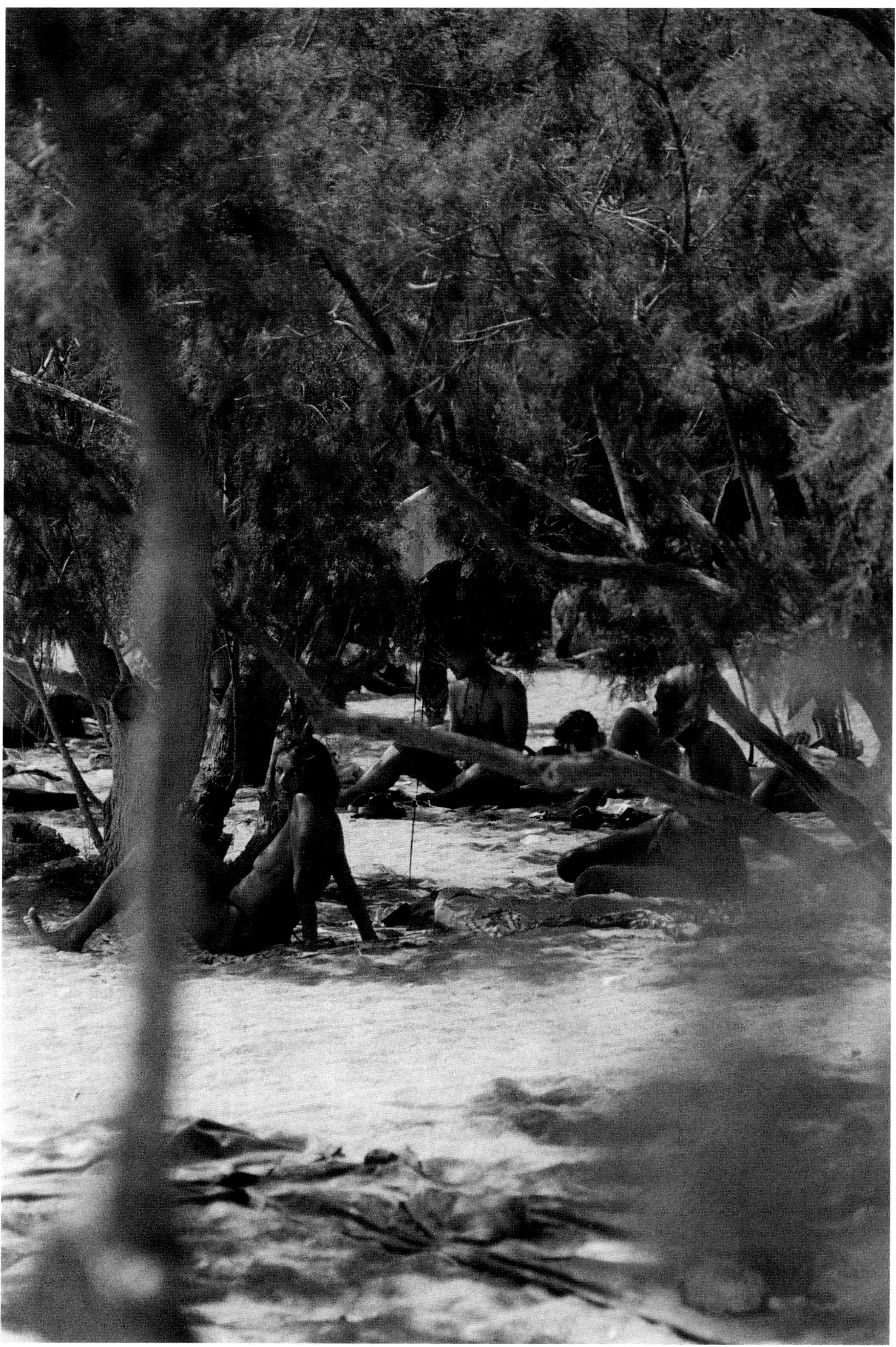

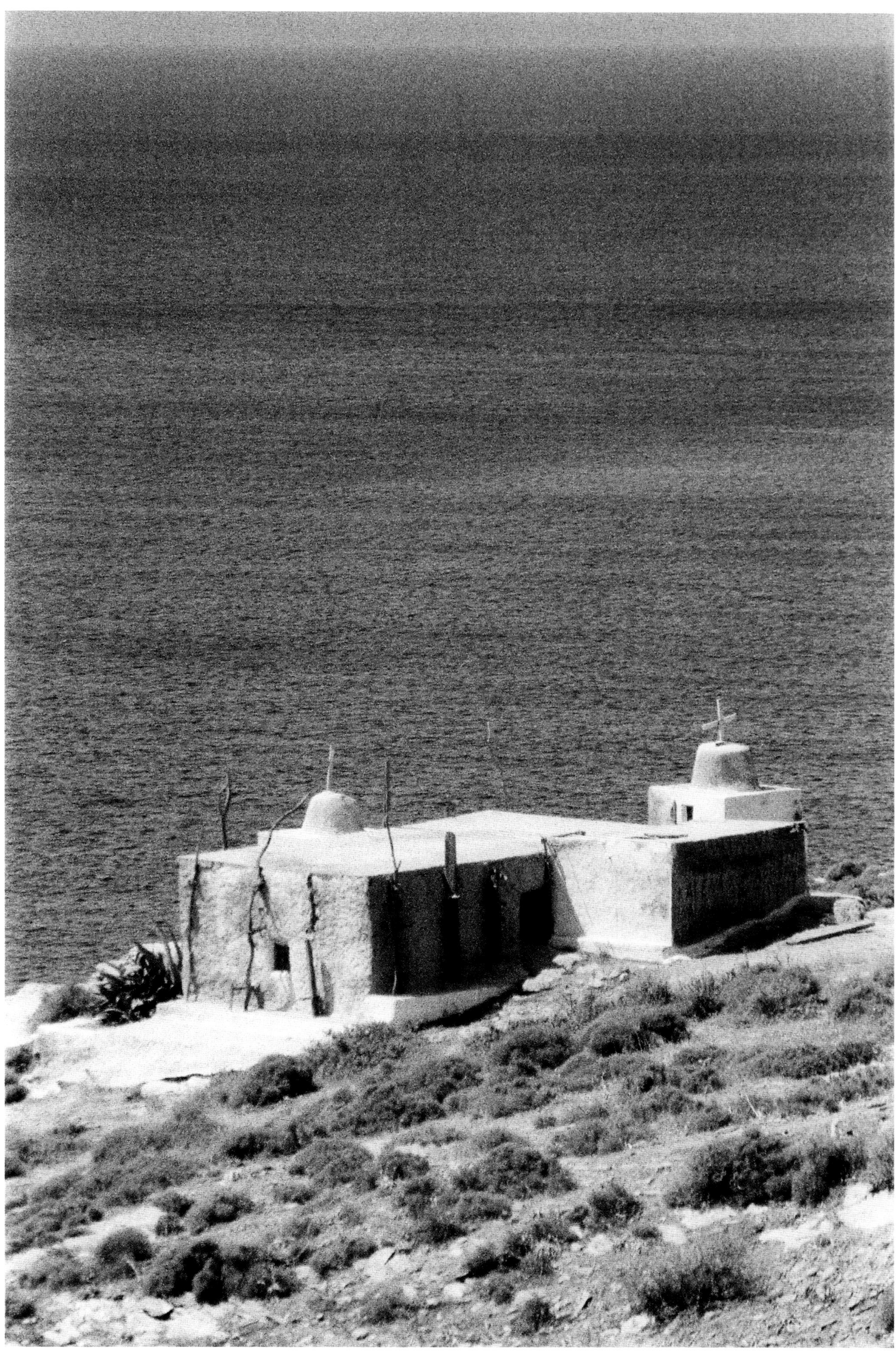

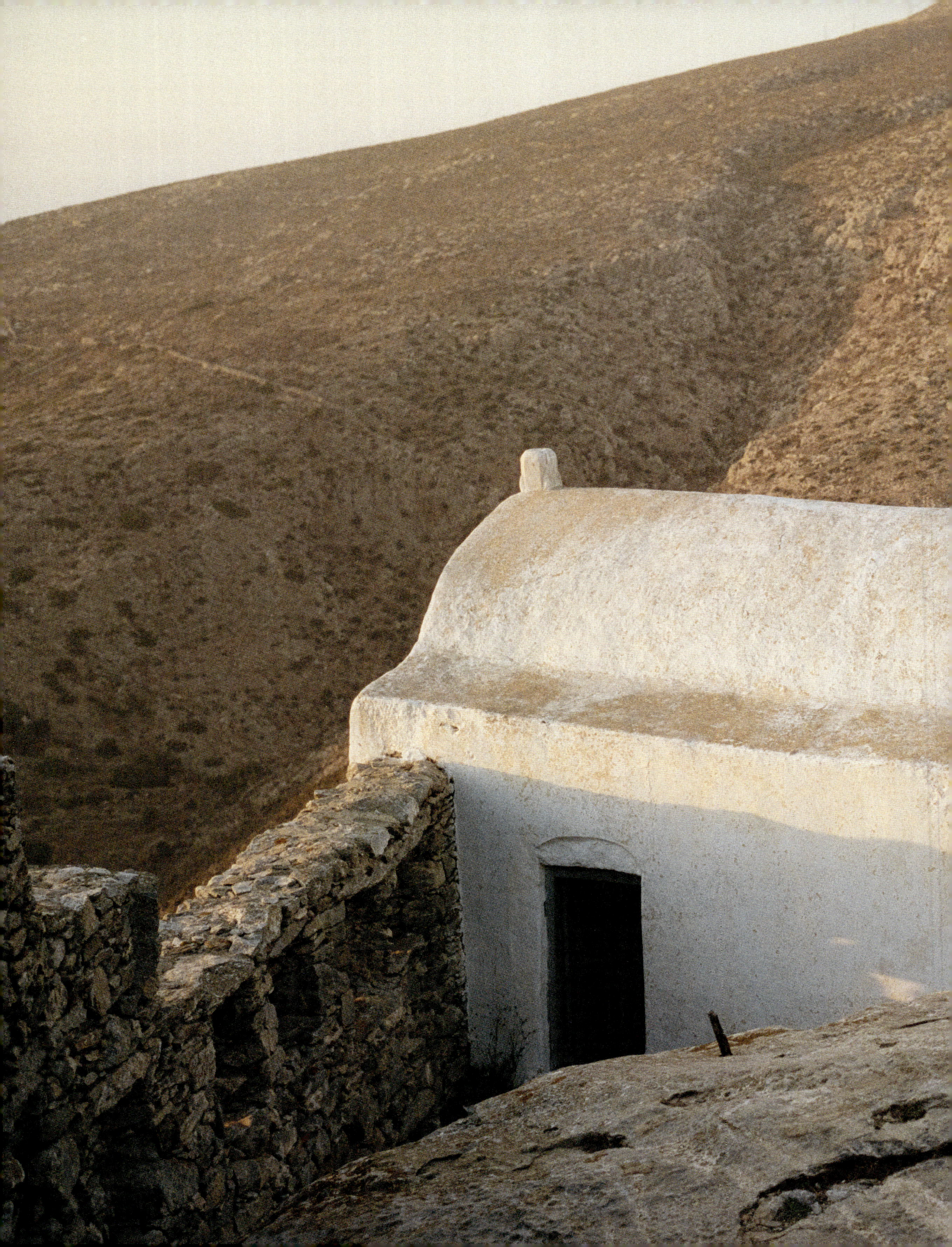

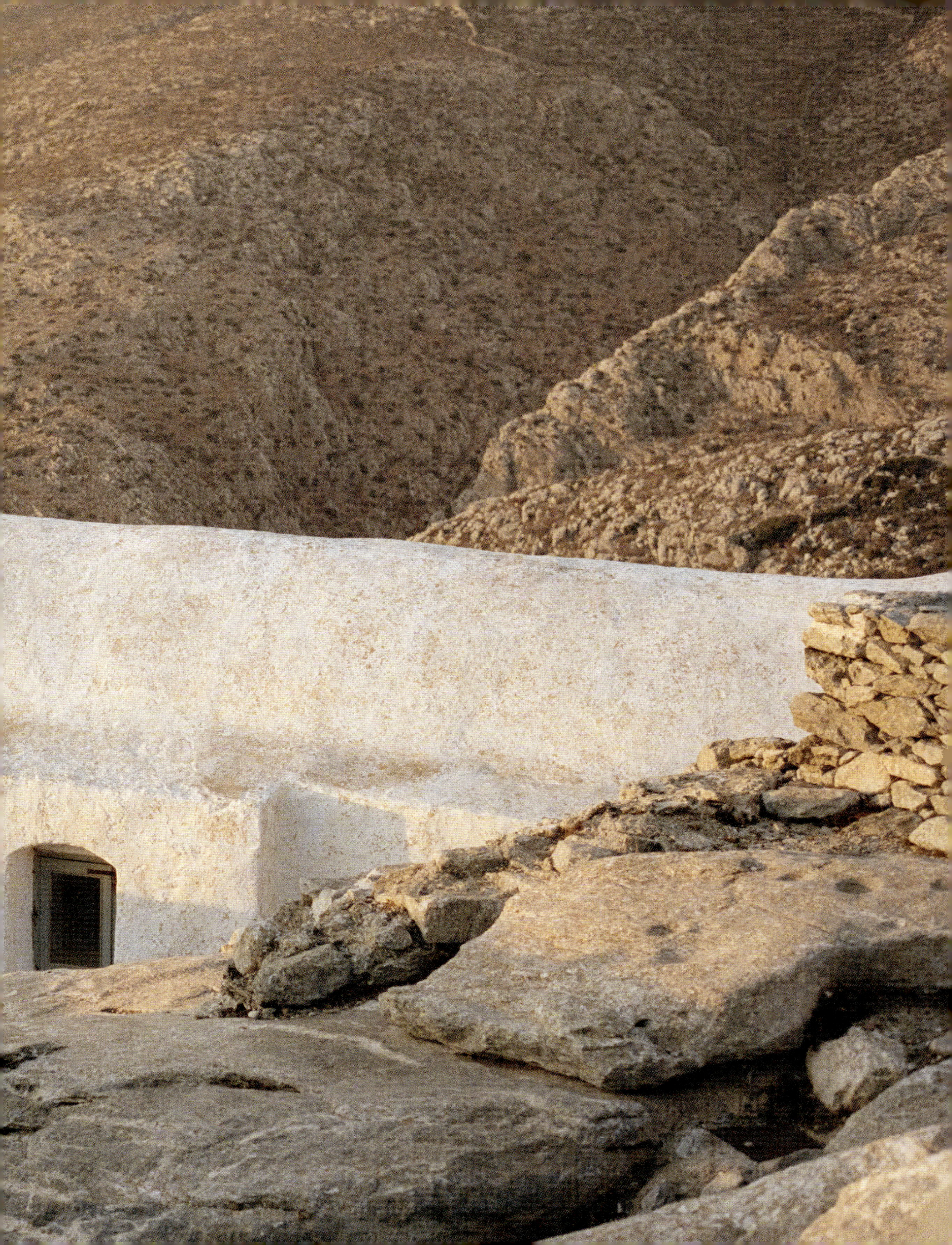

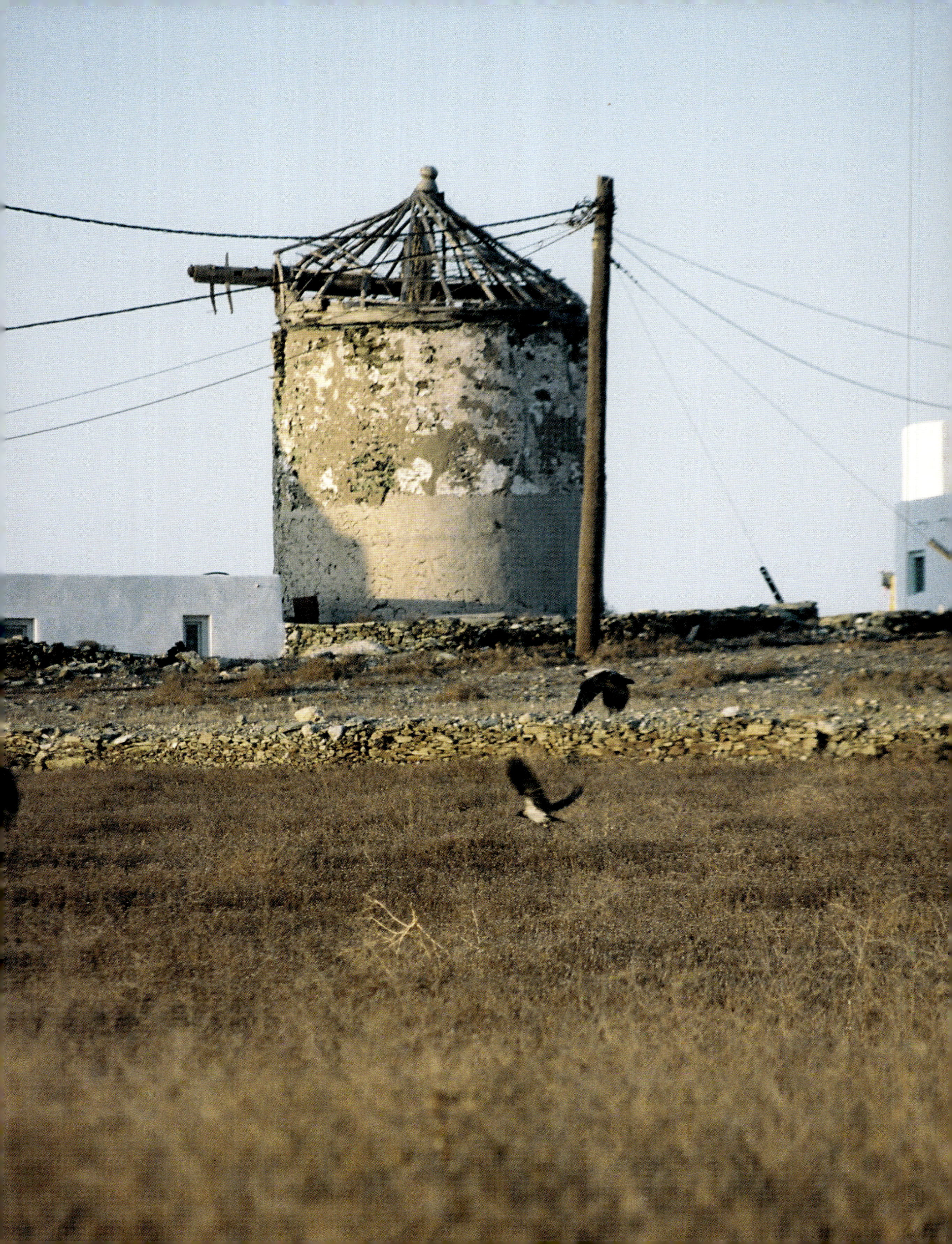

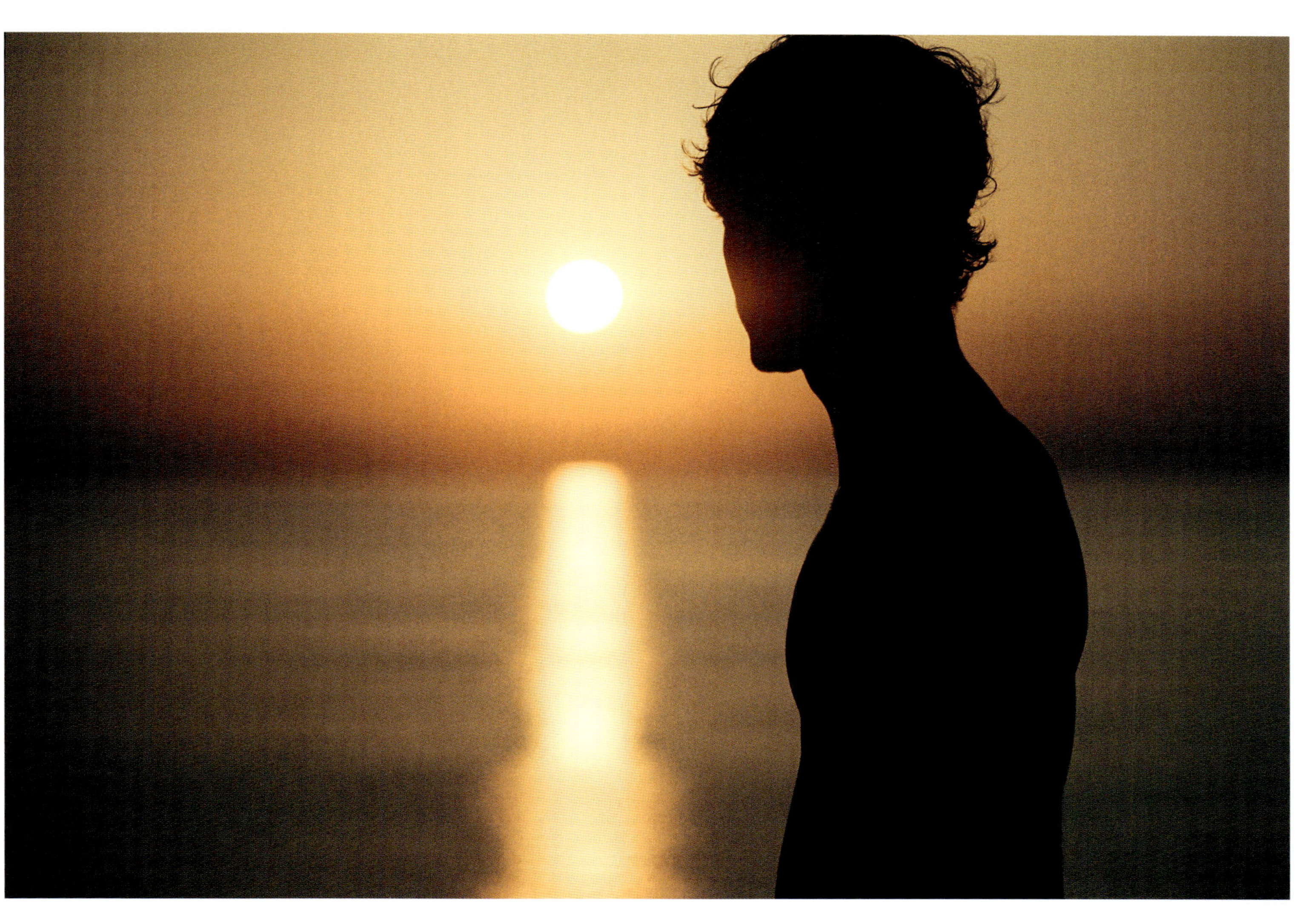

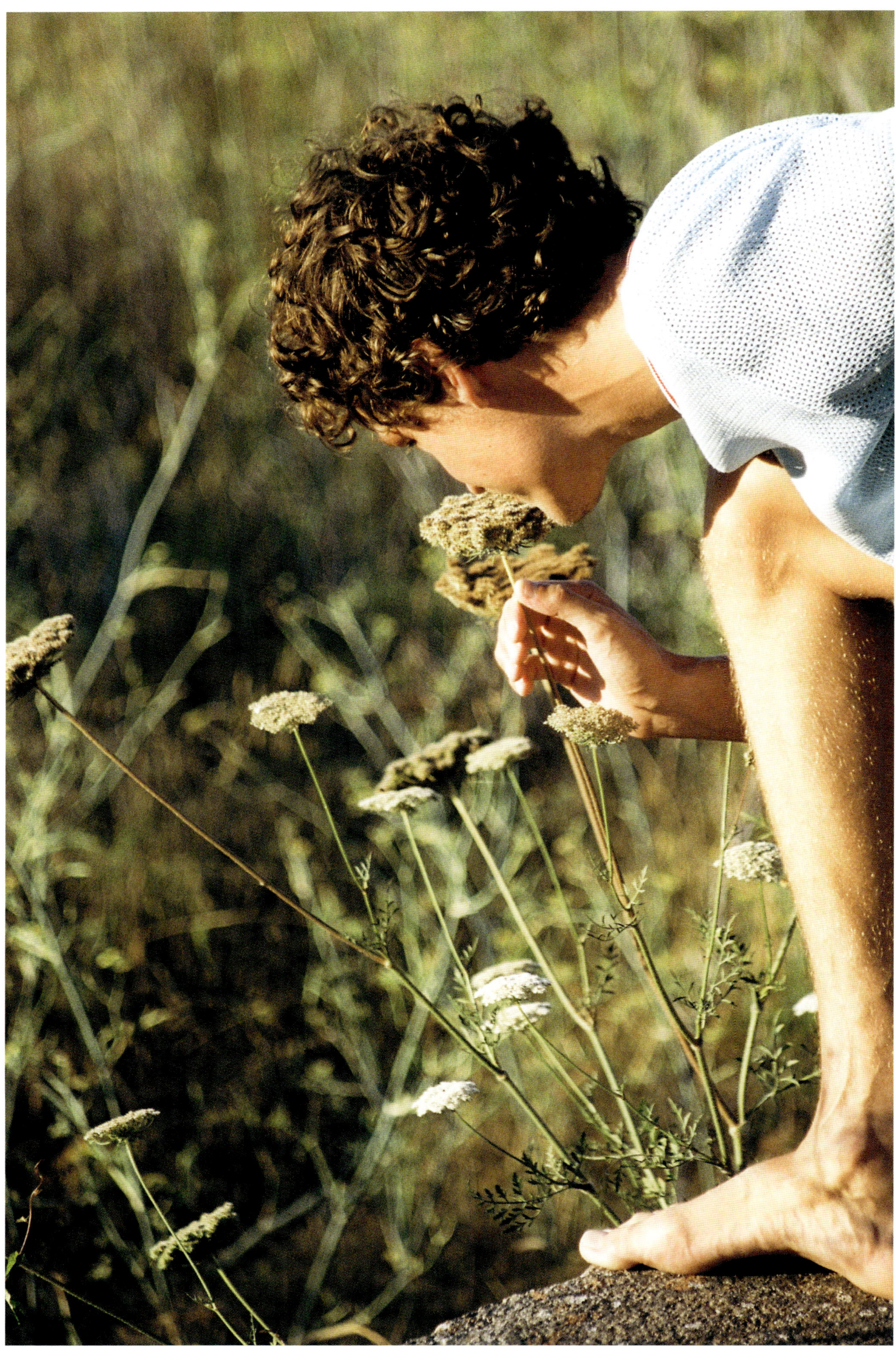

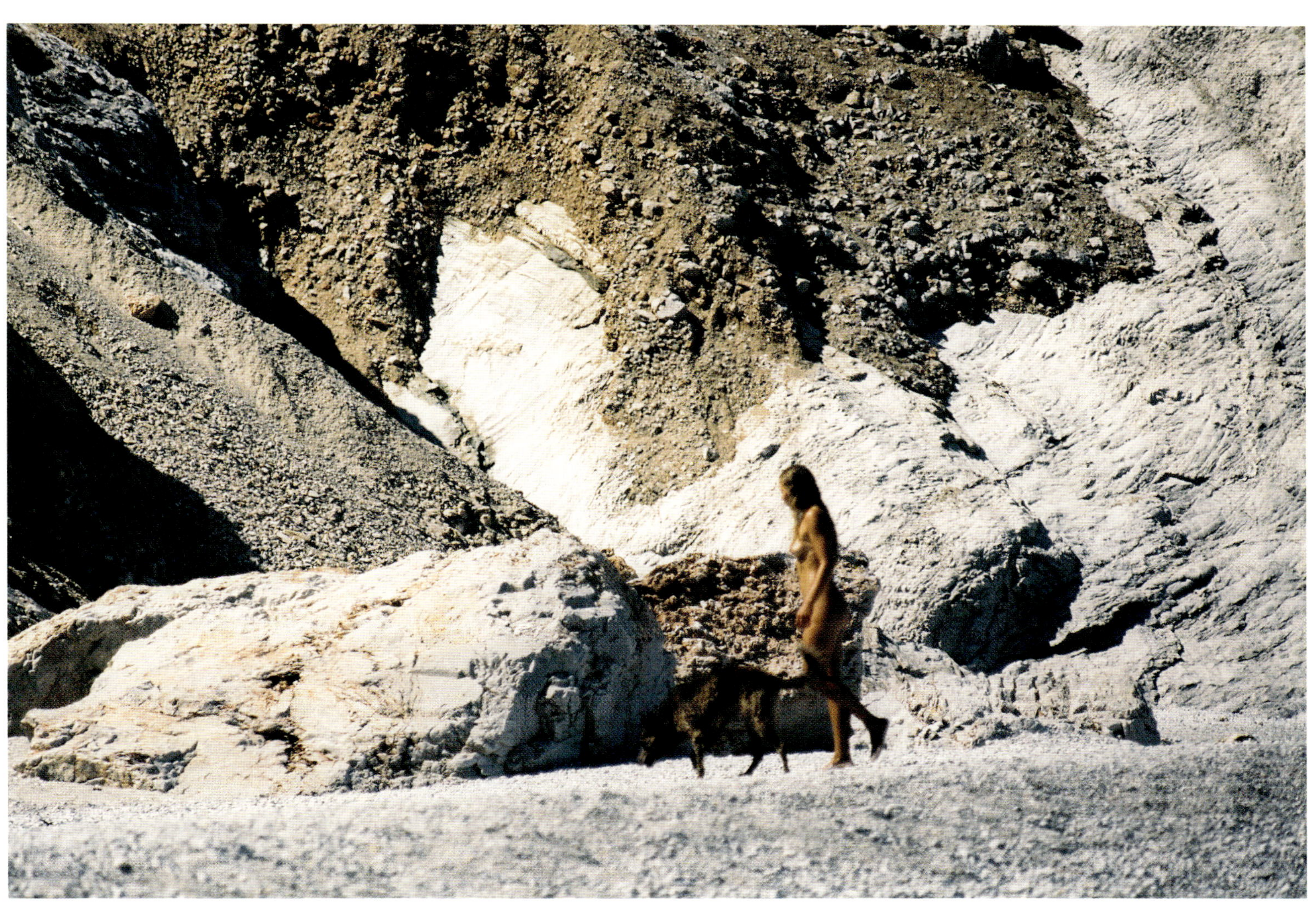

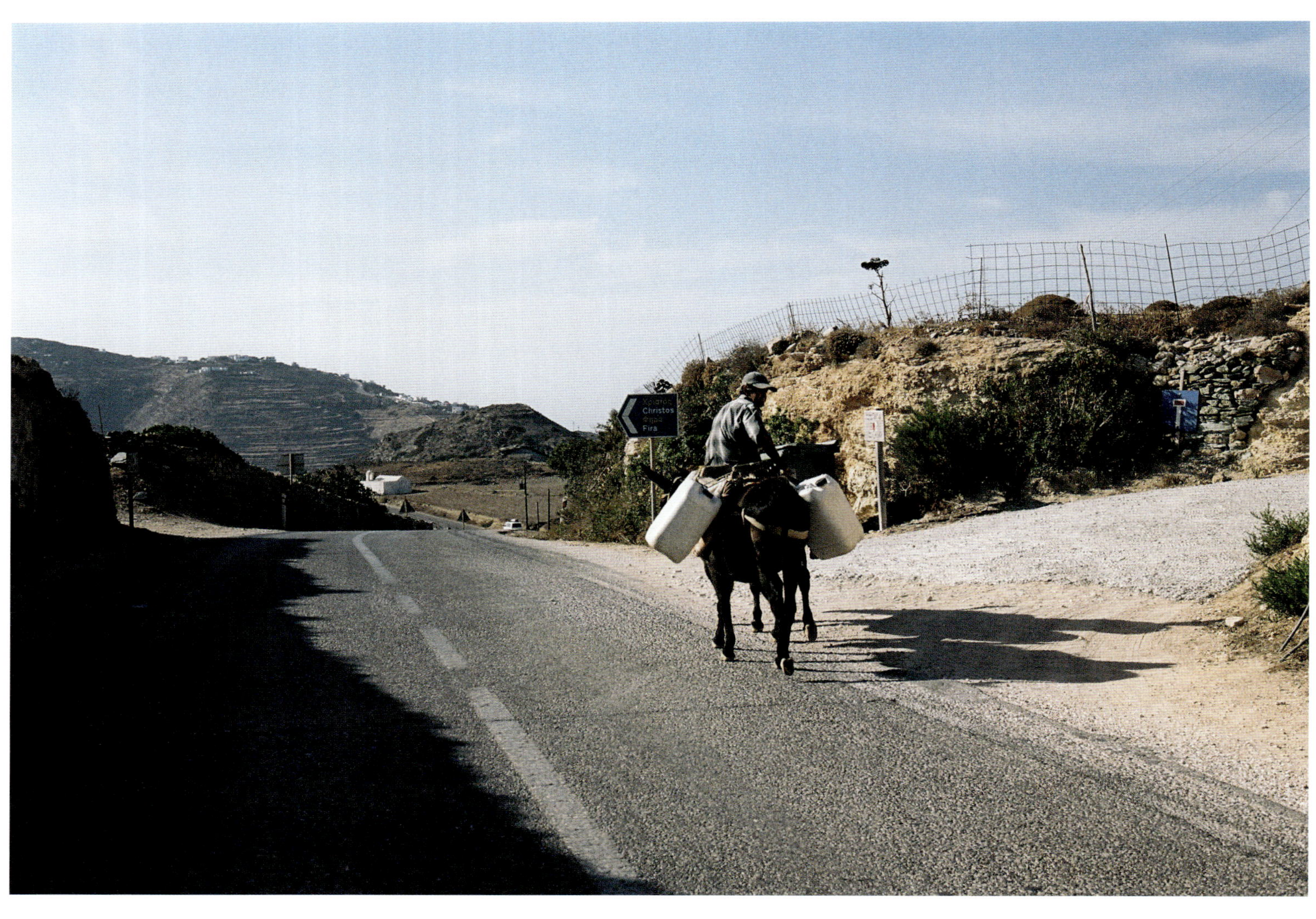
Christos
Fira

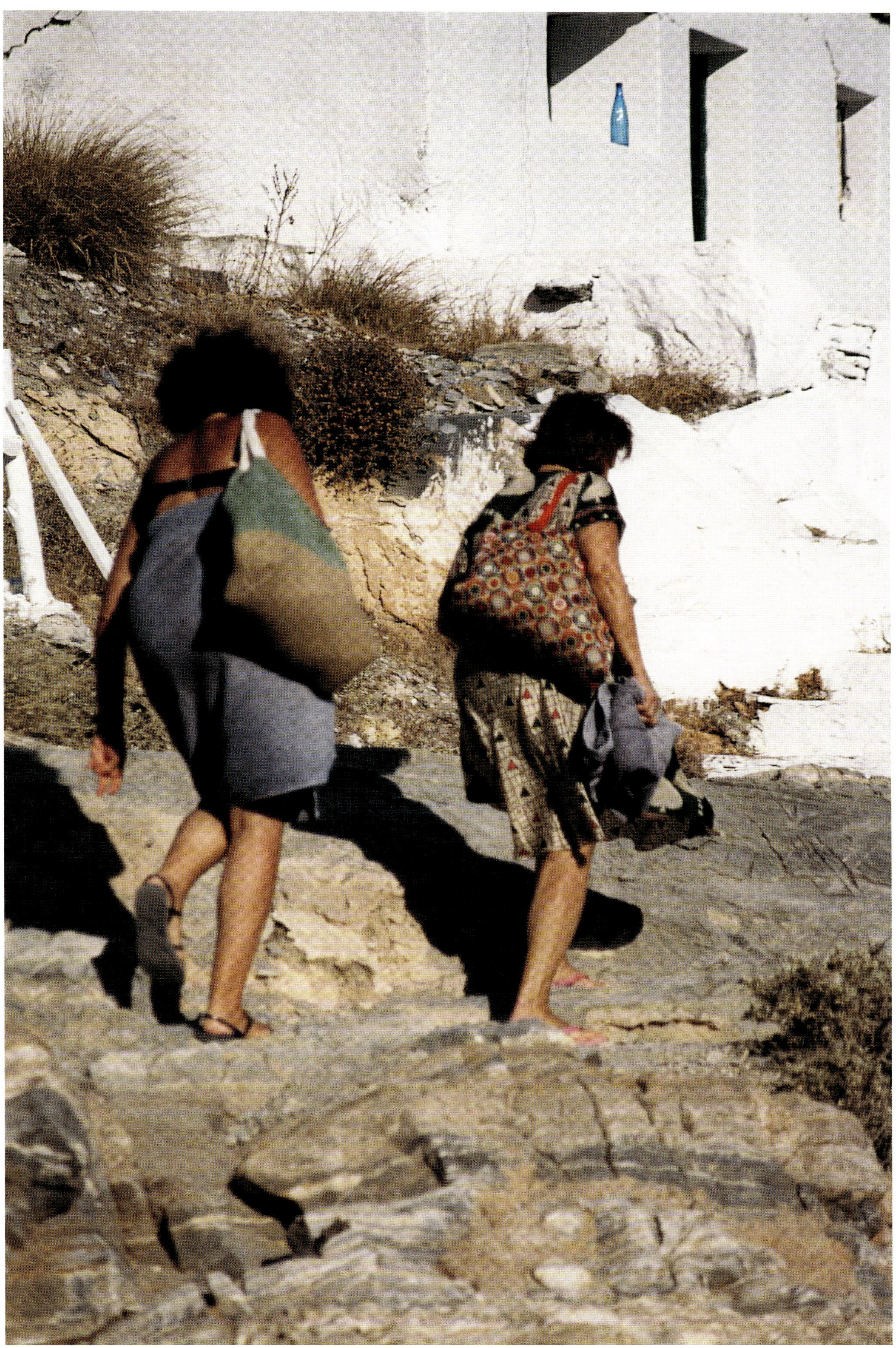

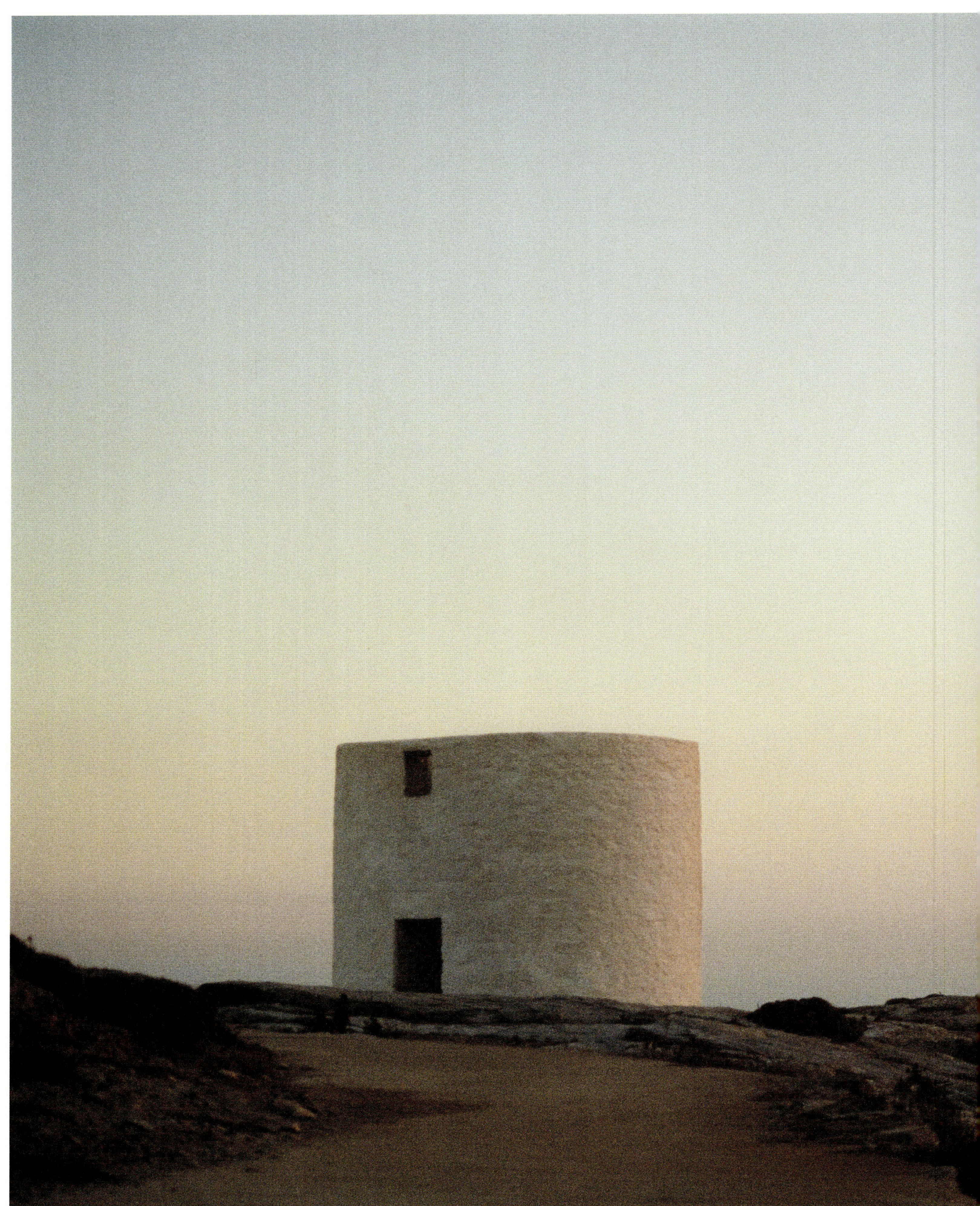

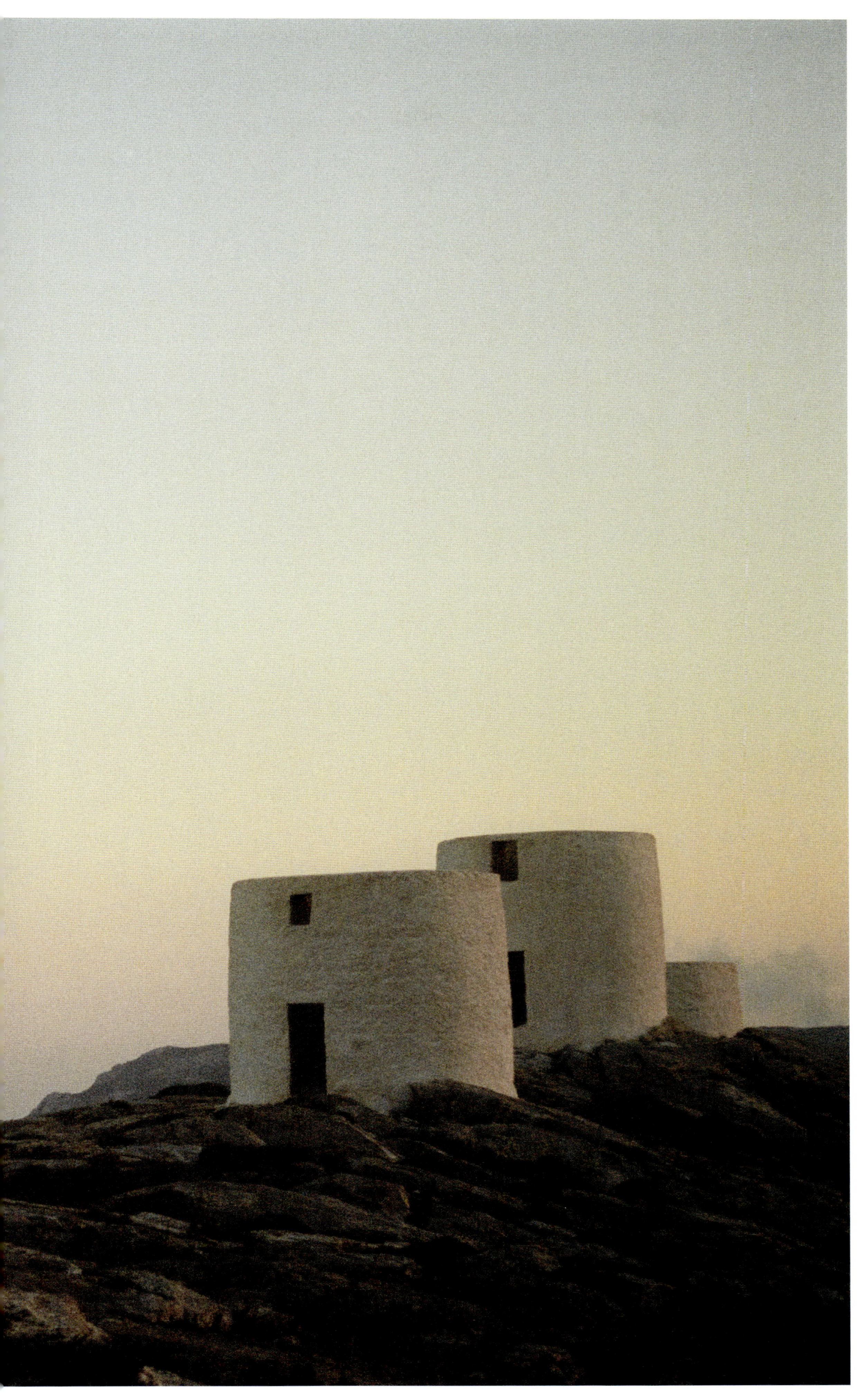

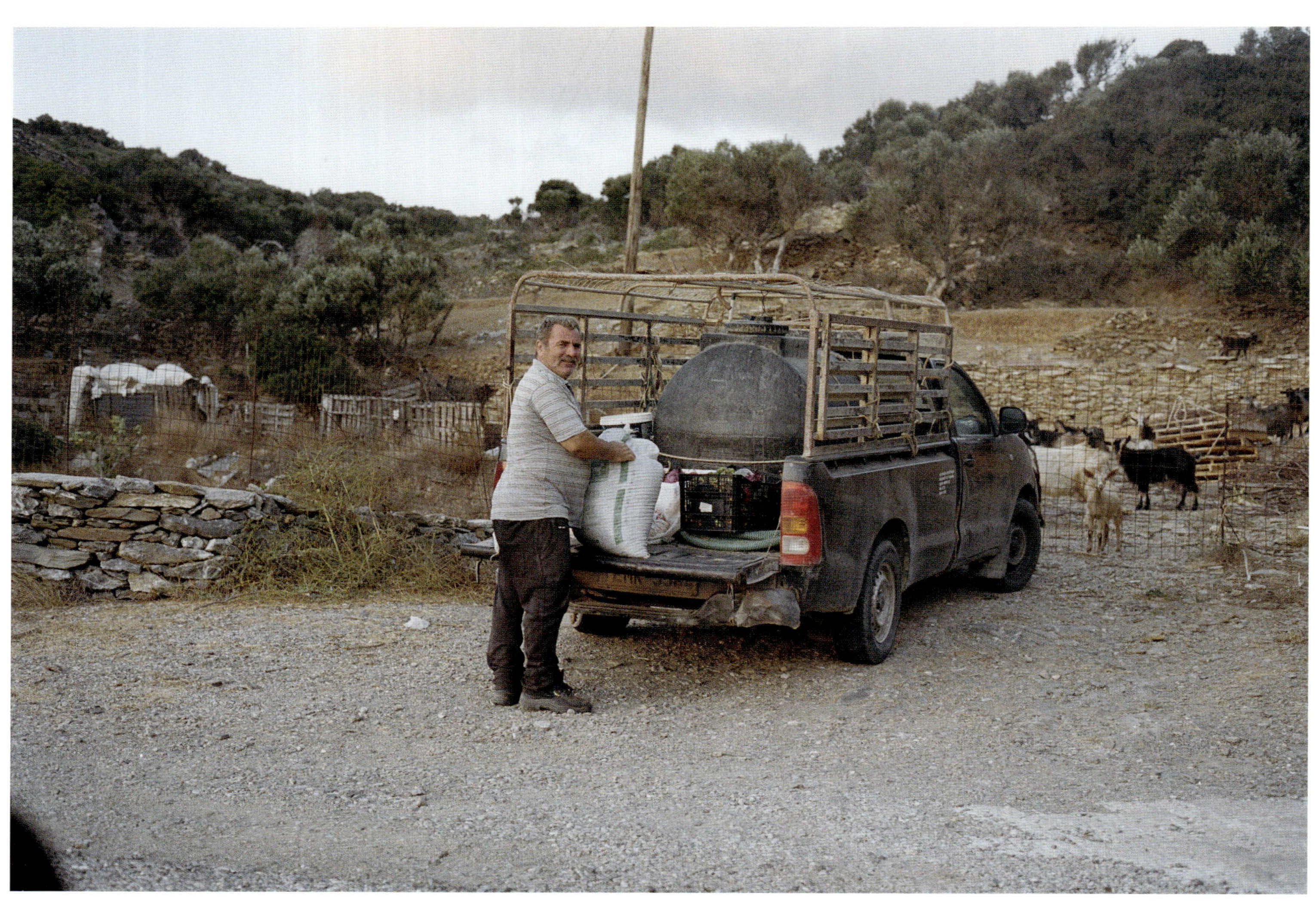

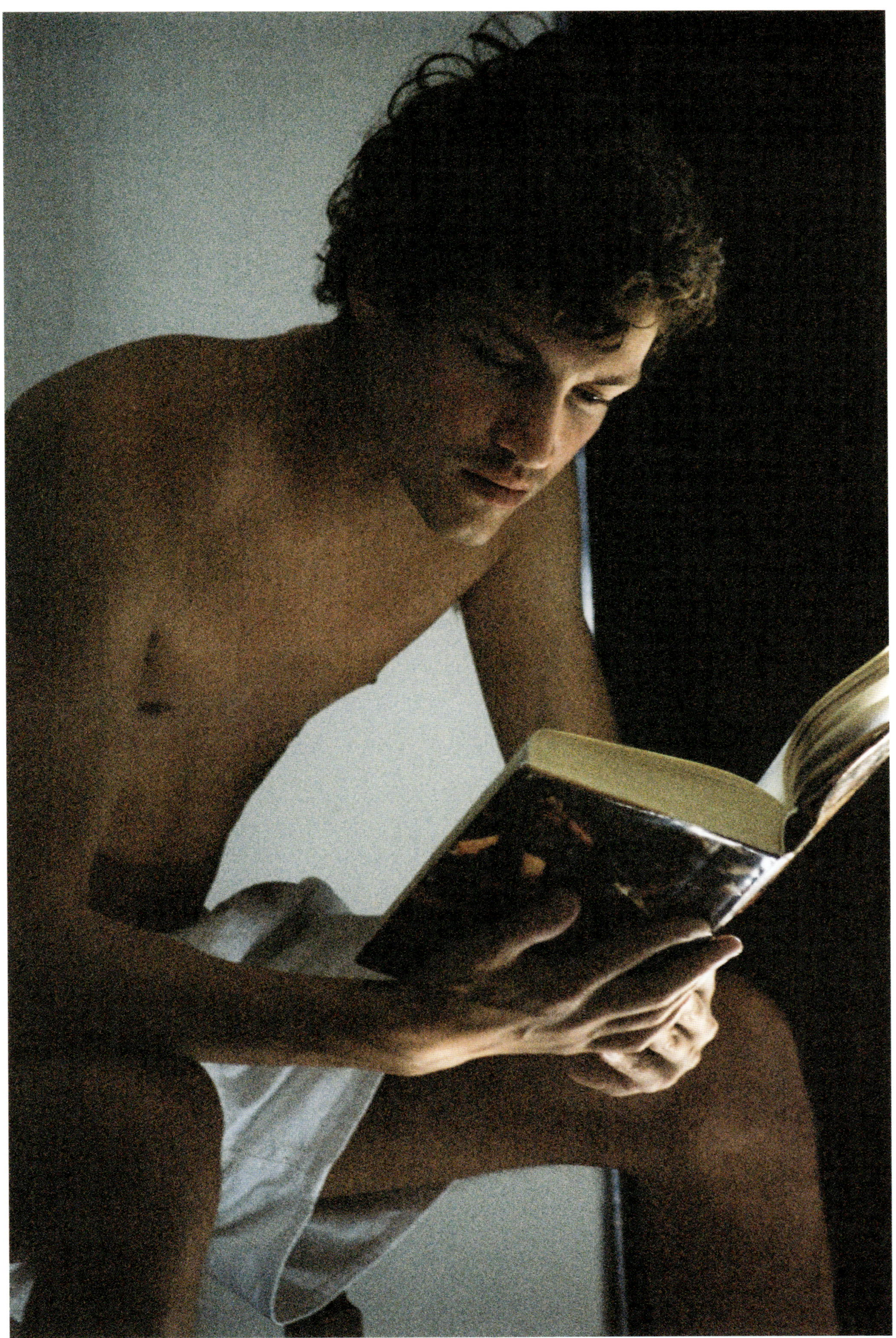

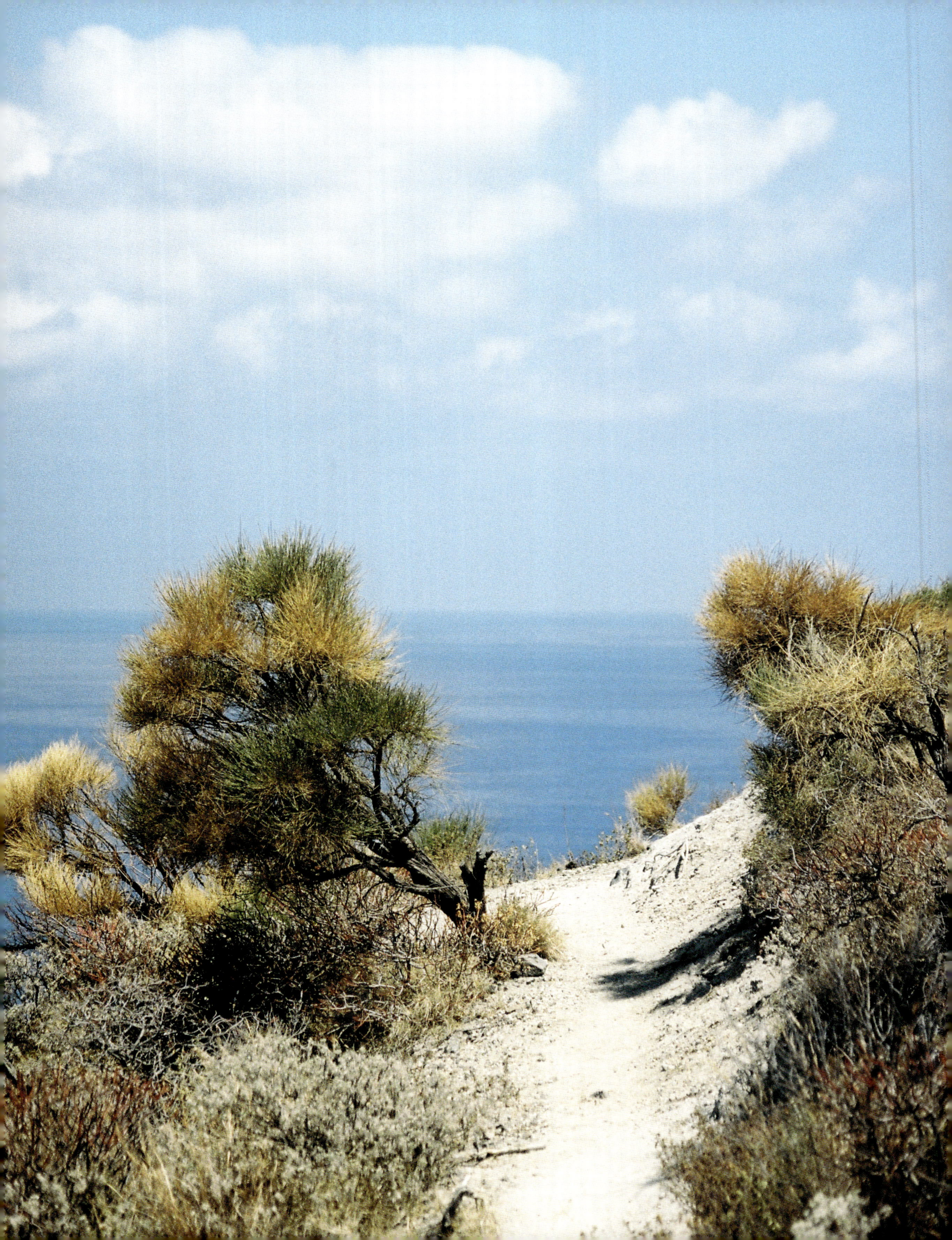

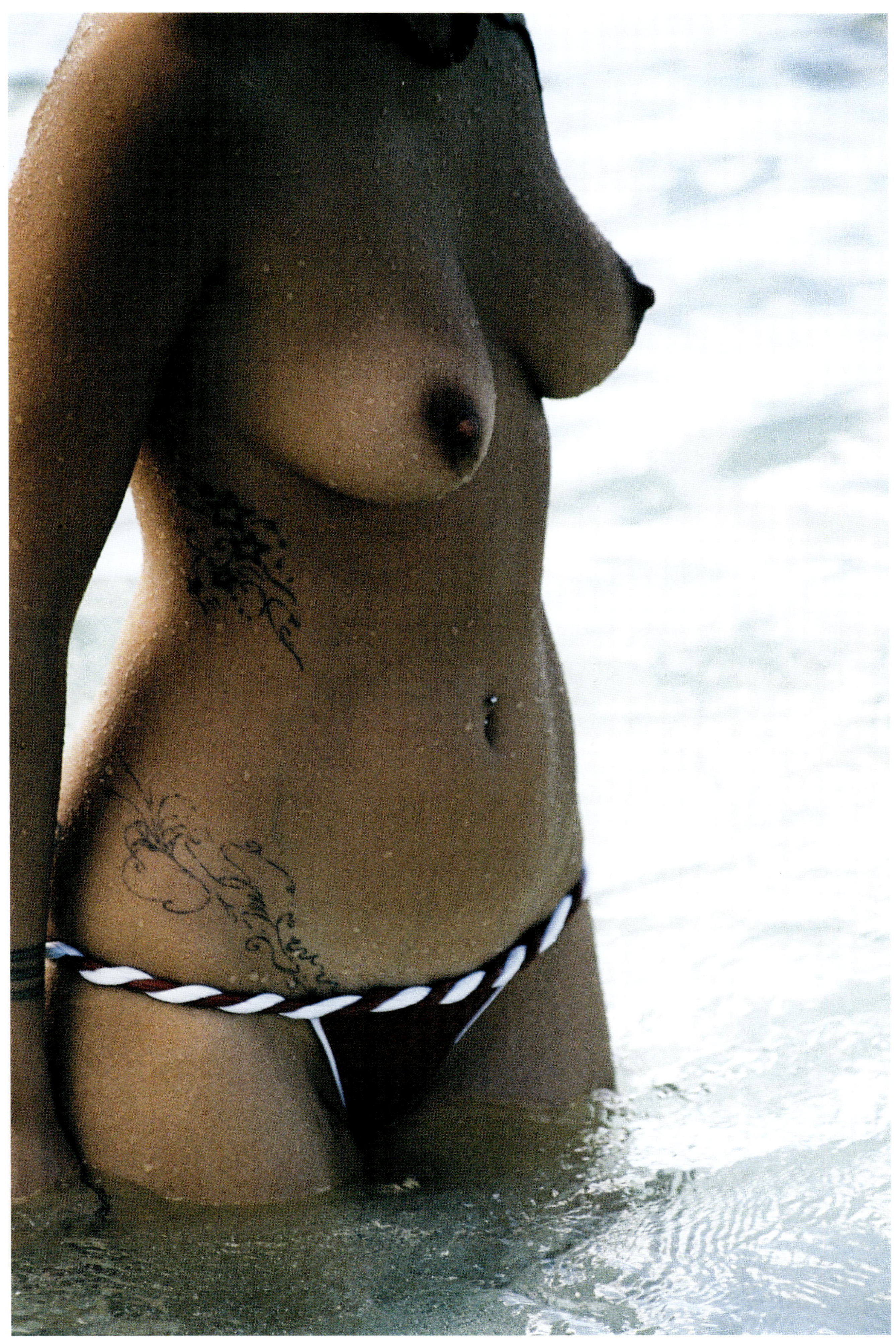

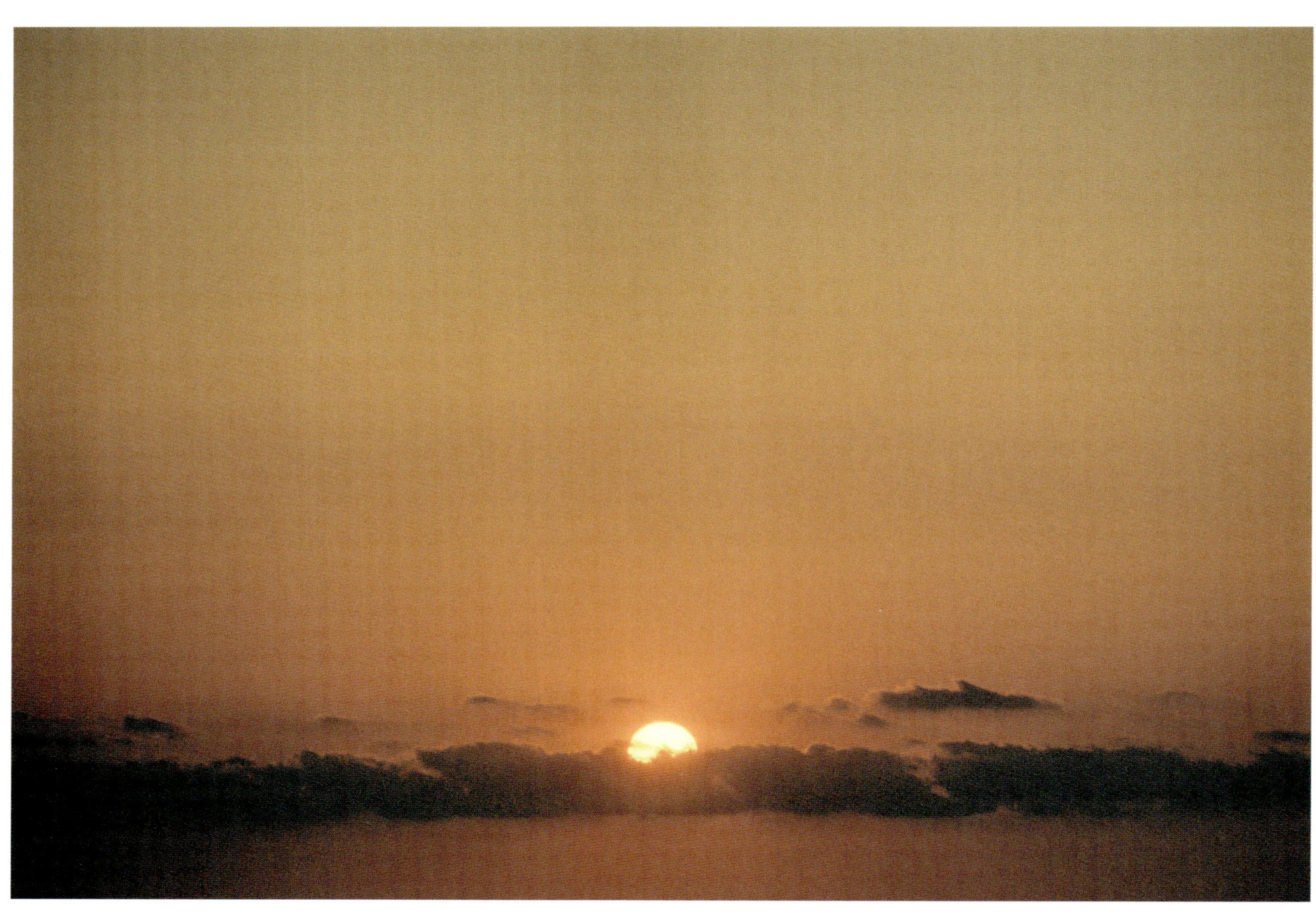

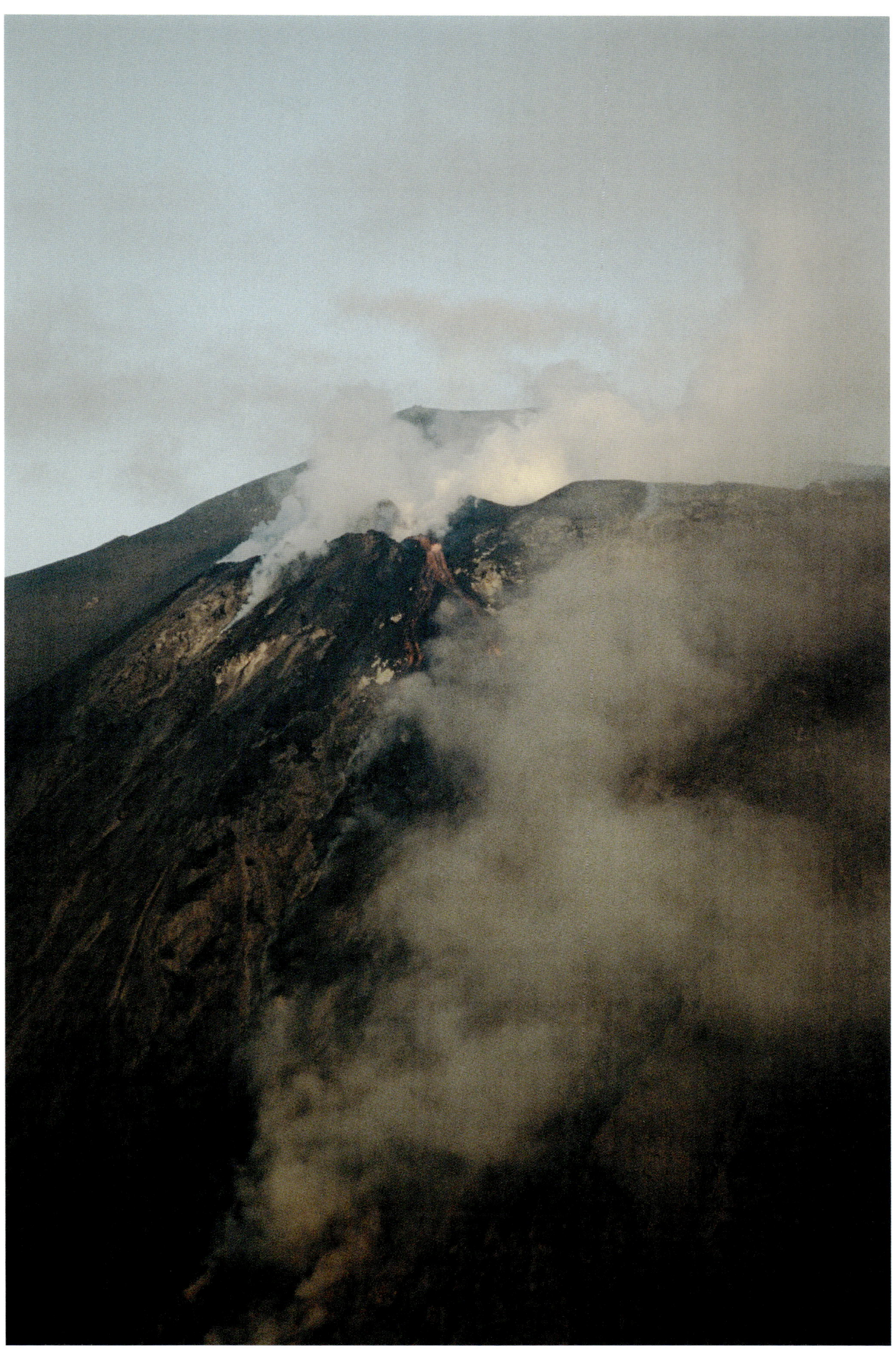

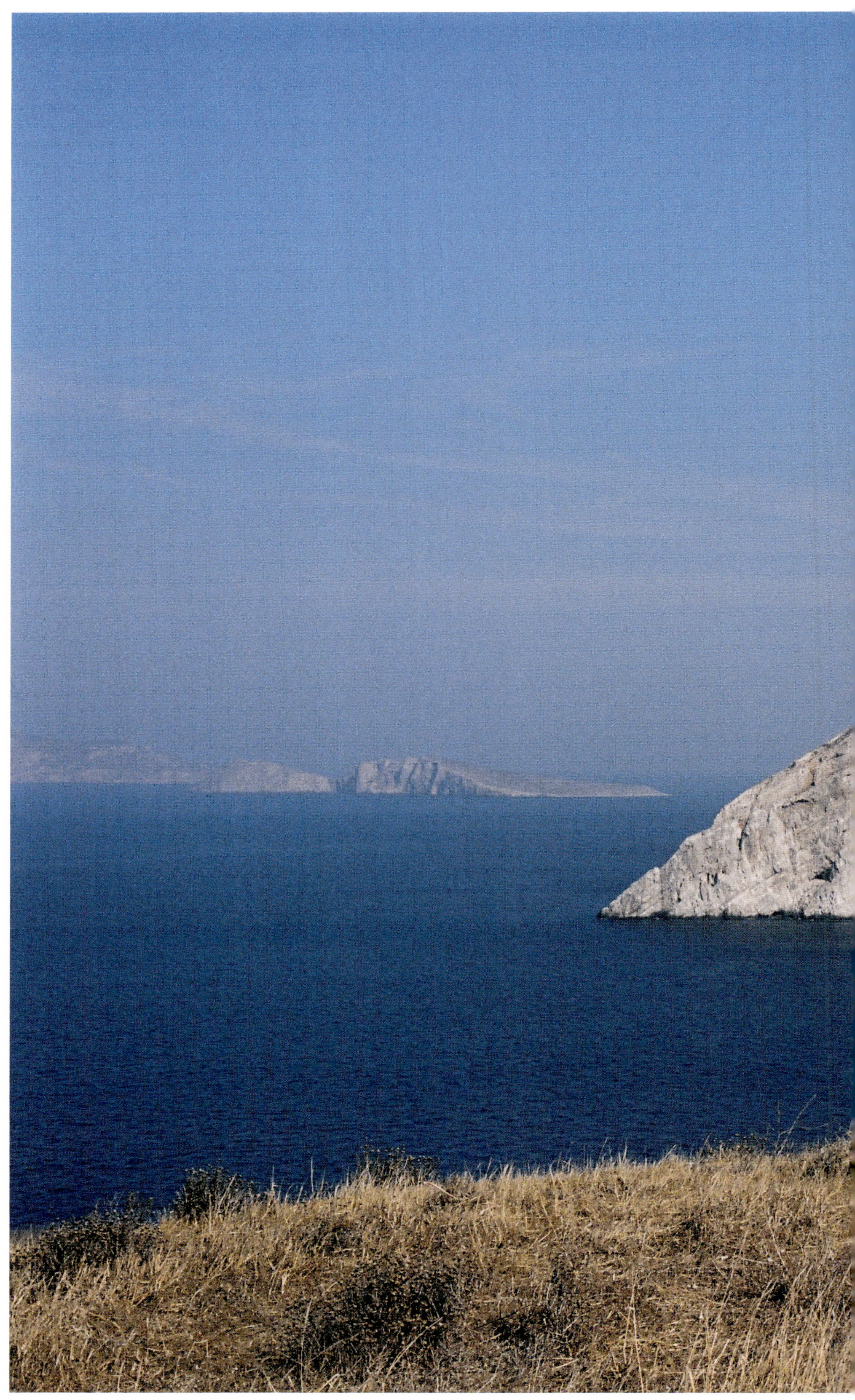

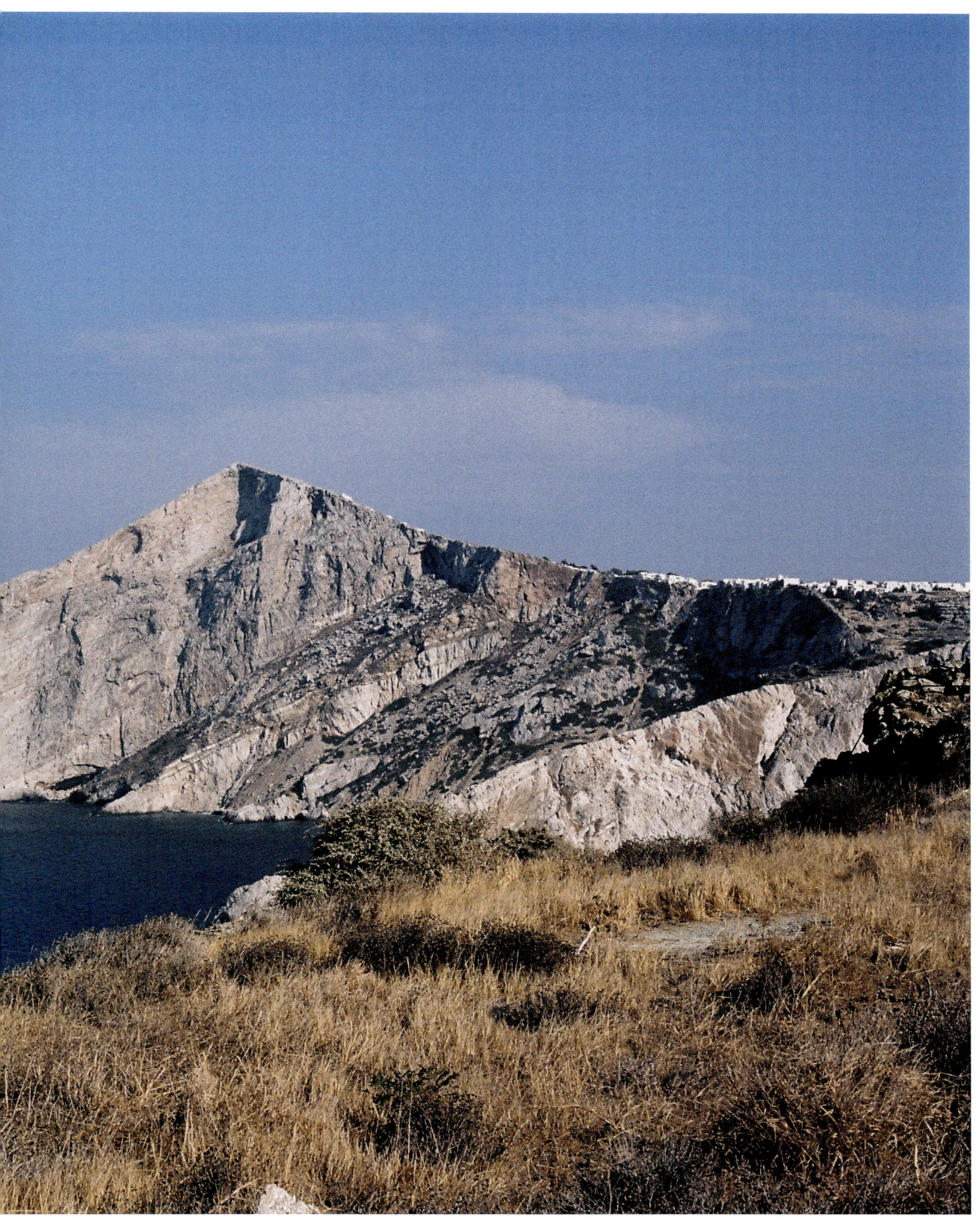

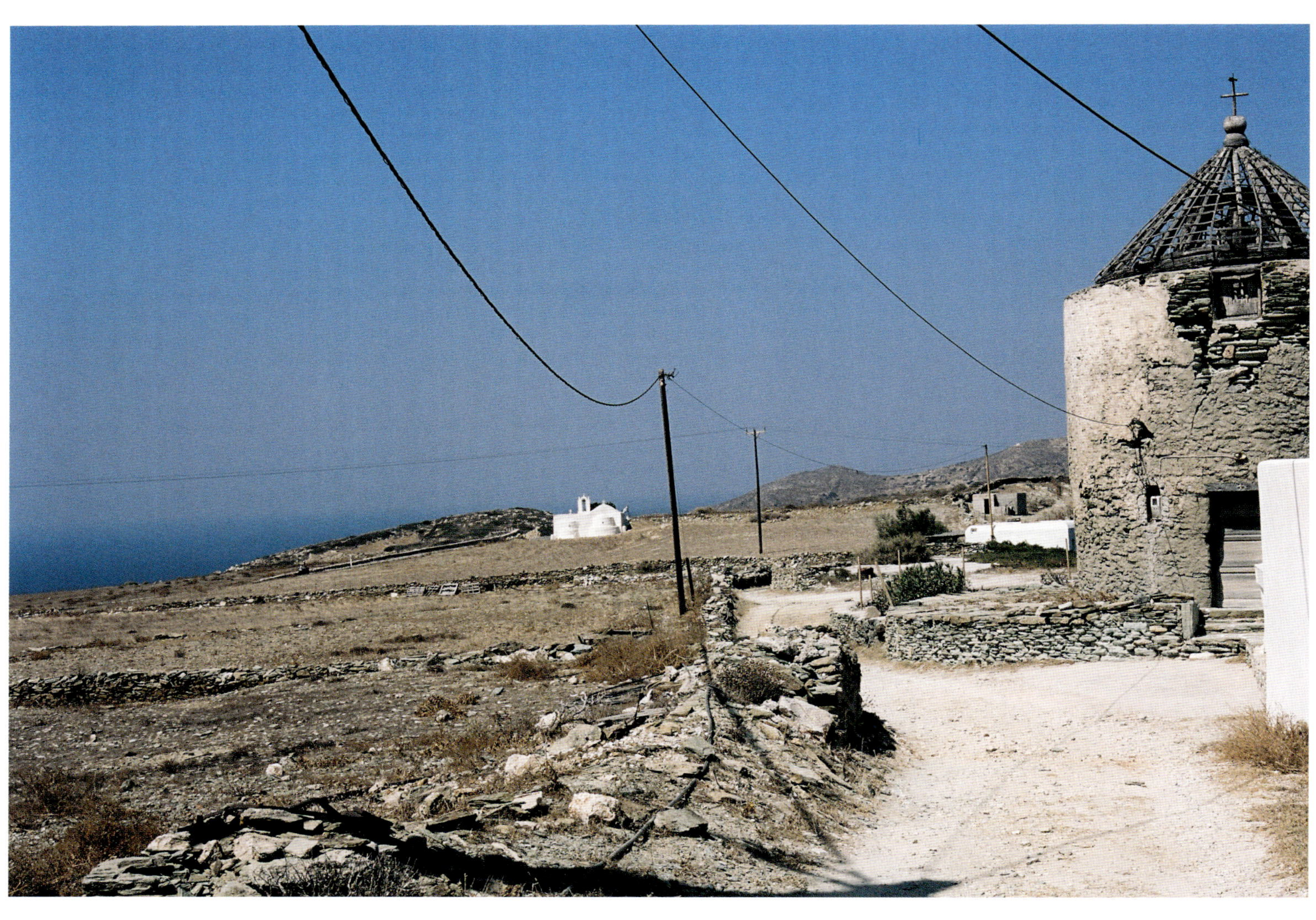

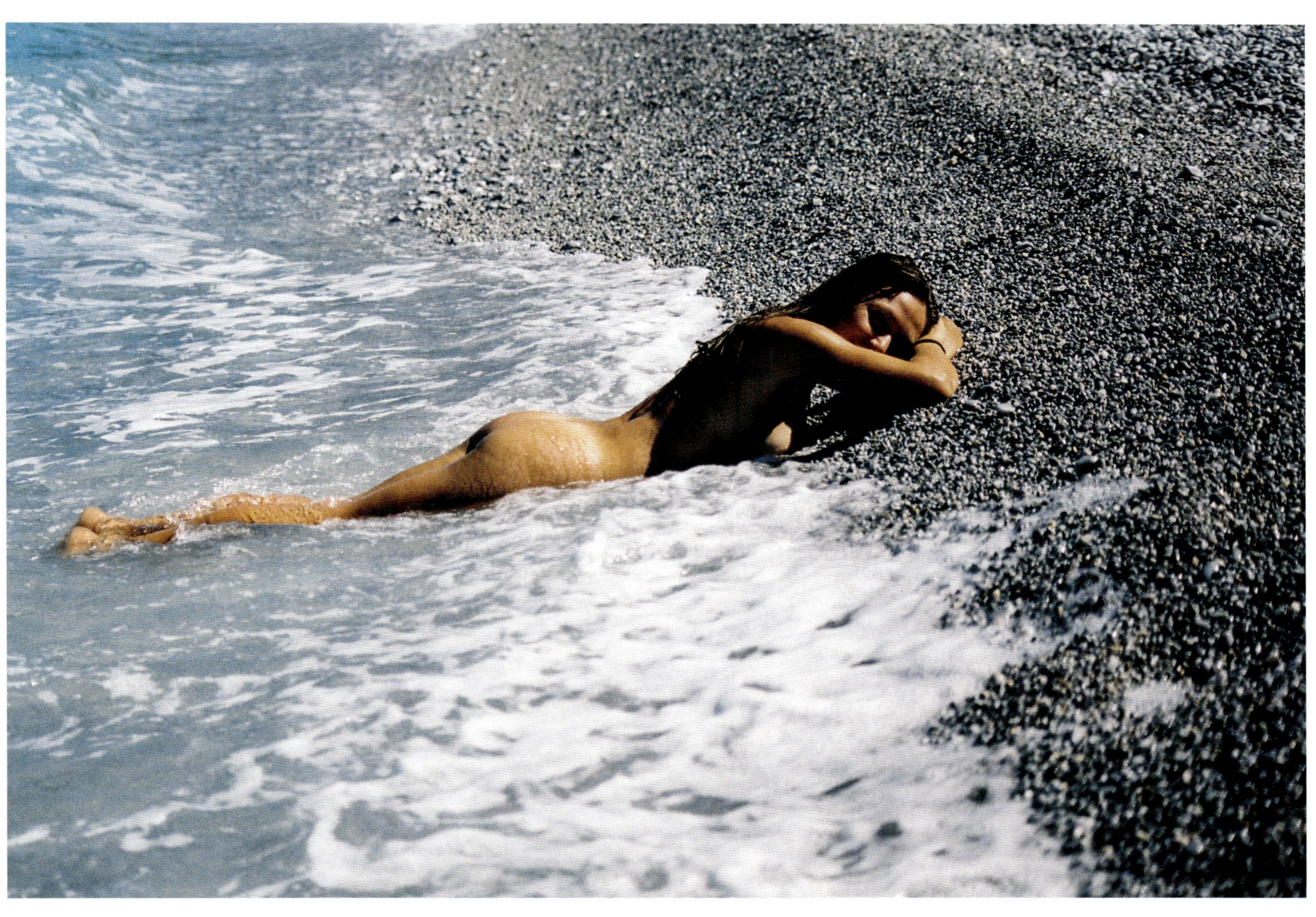

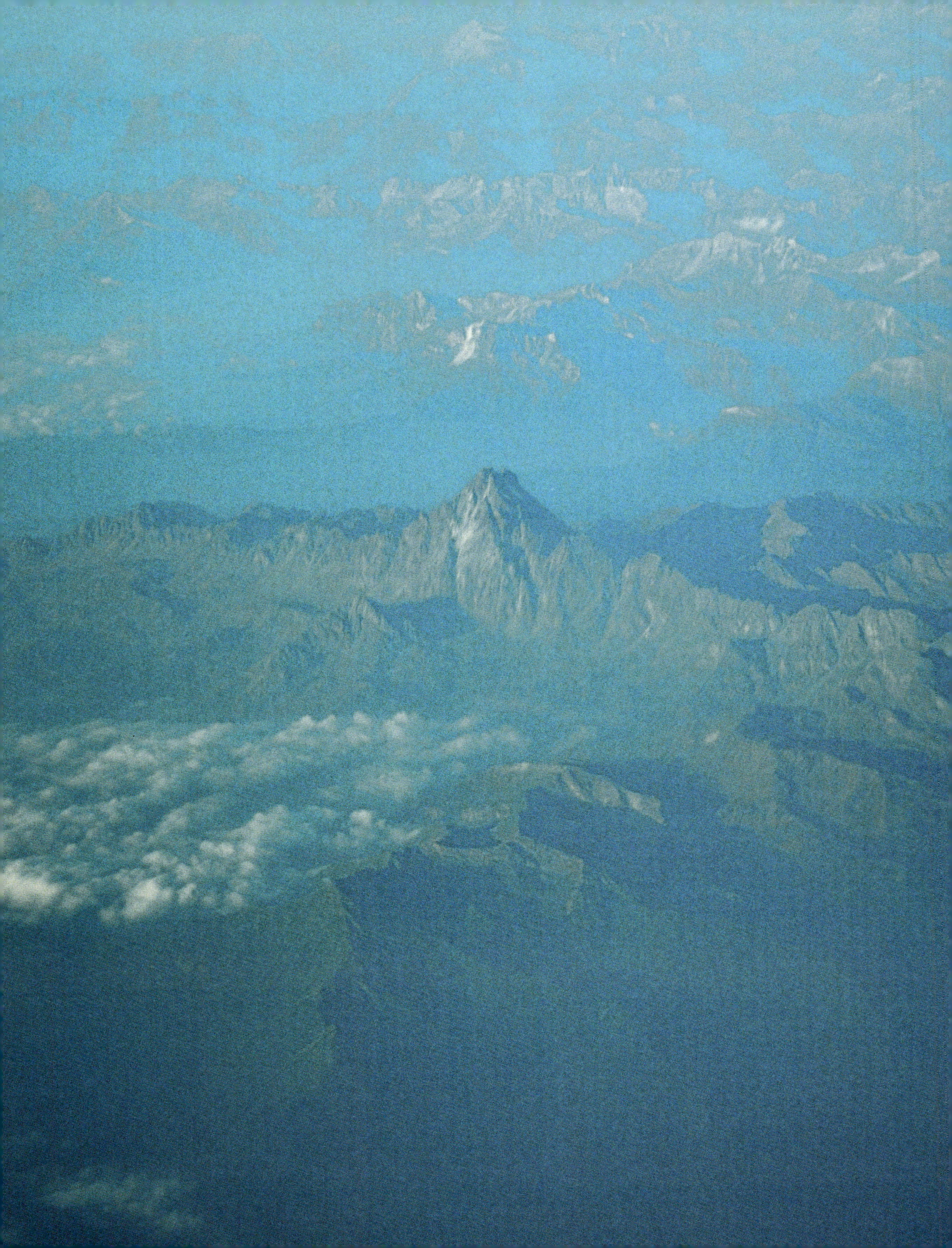

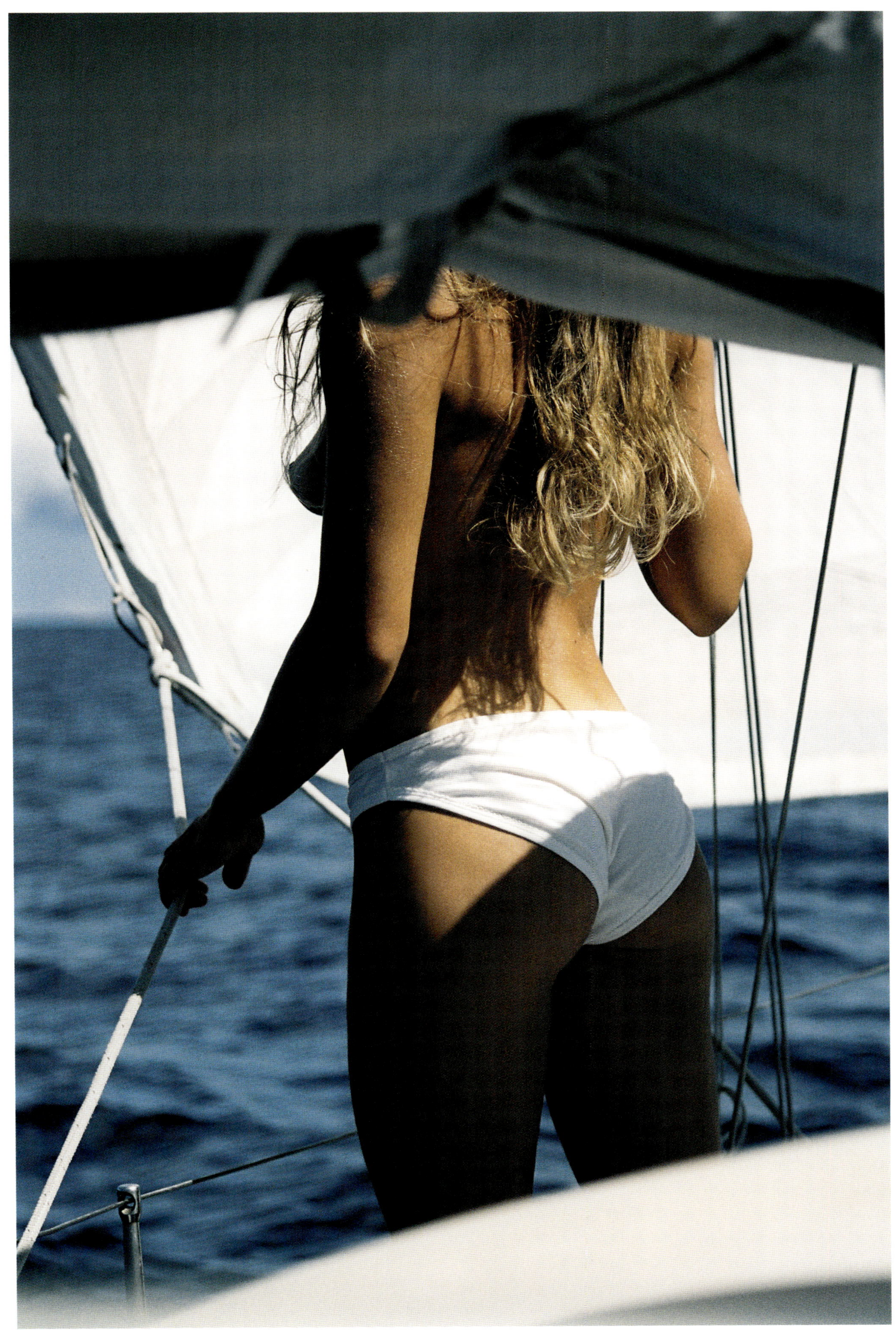

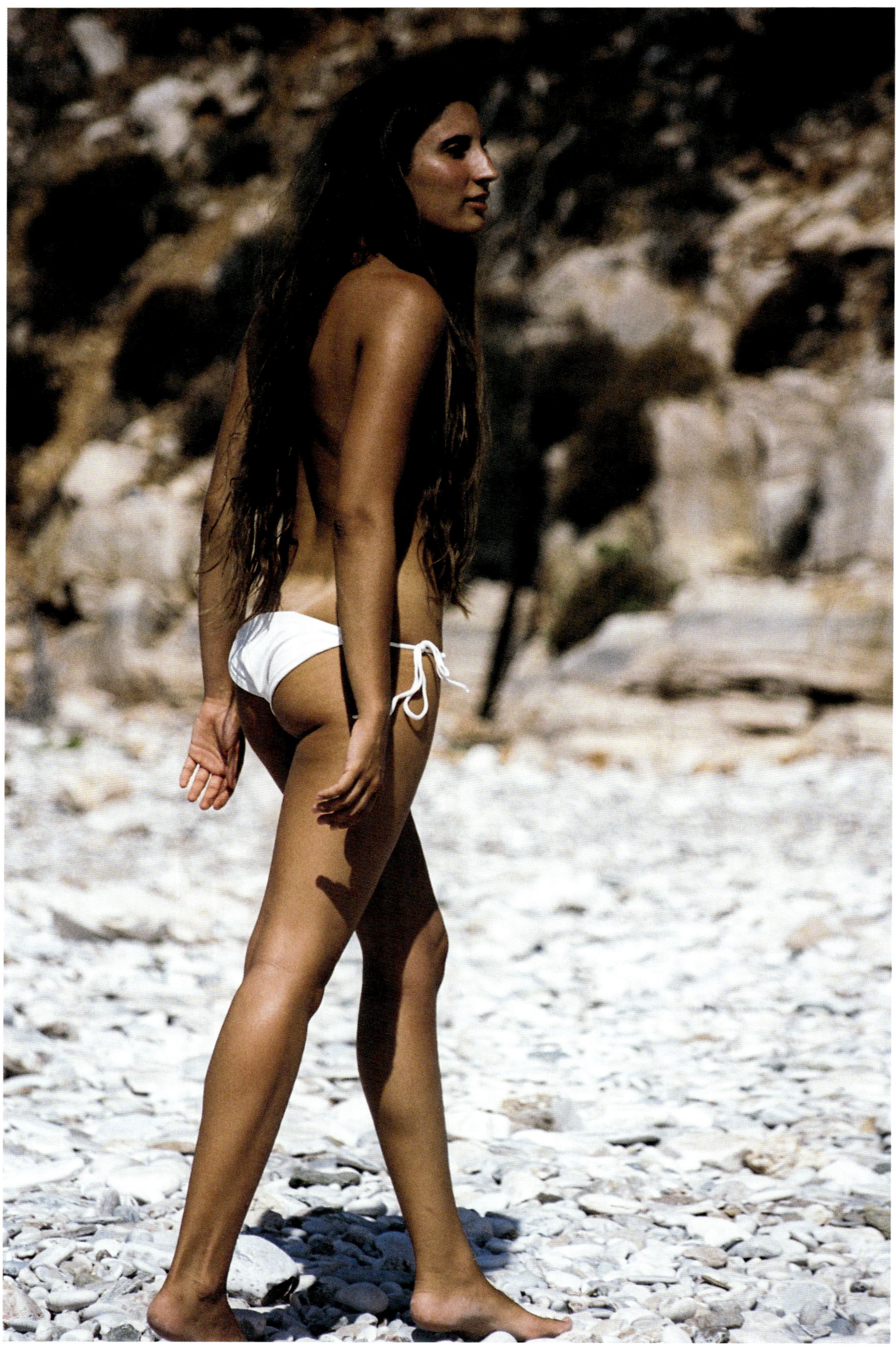

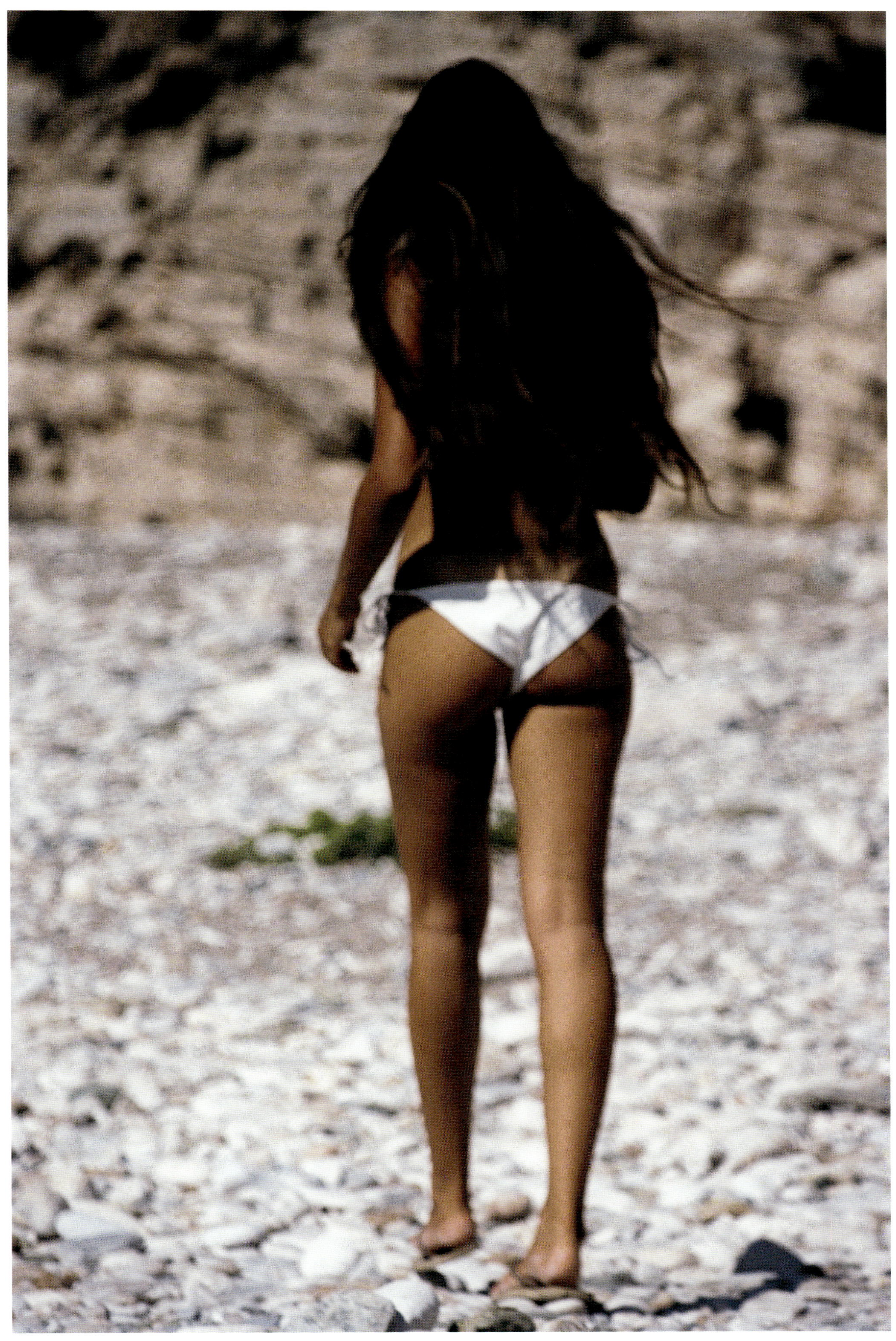

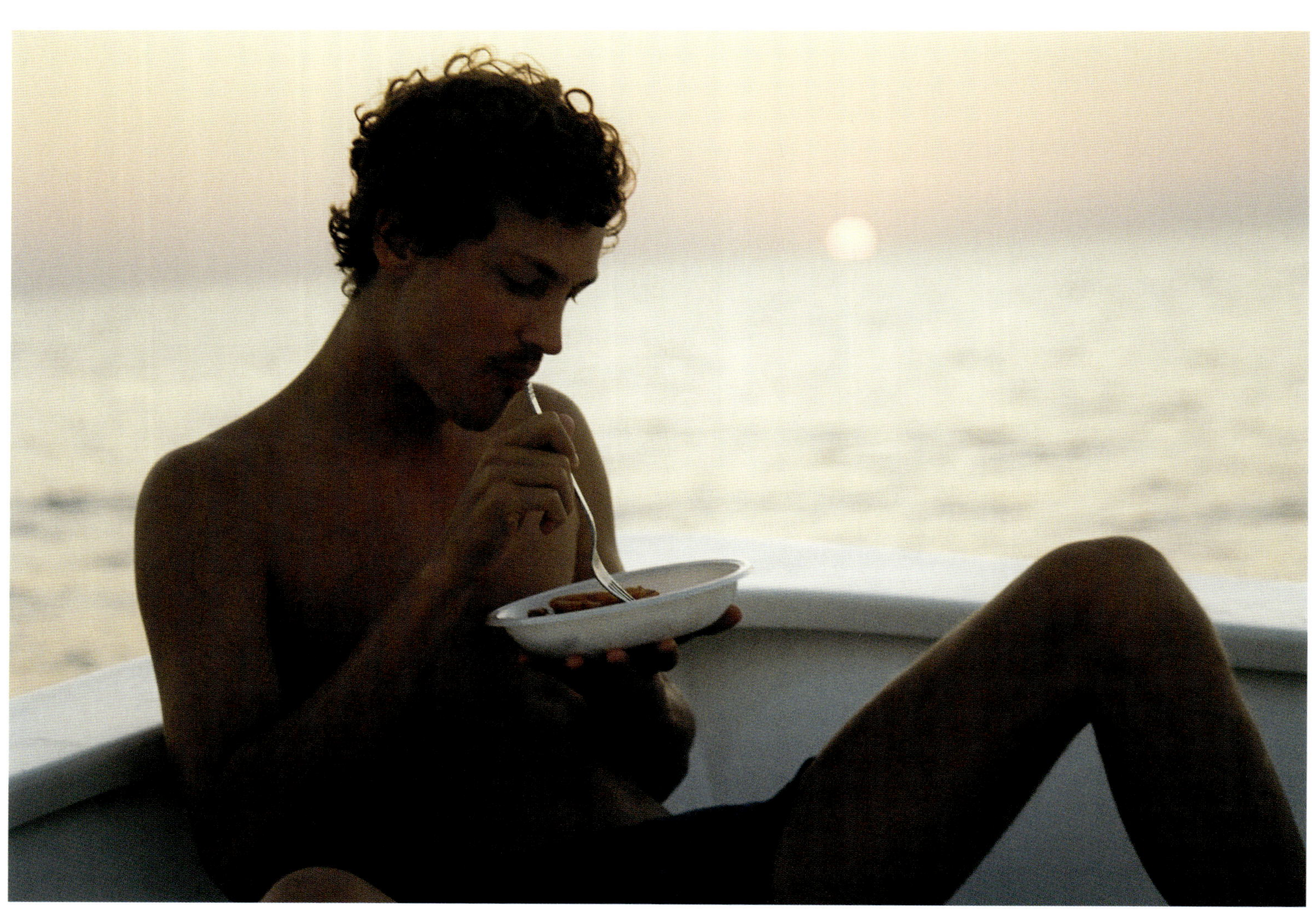

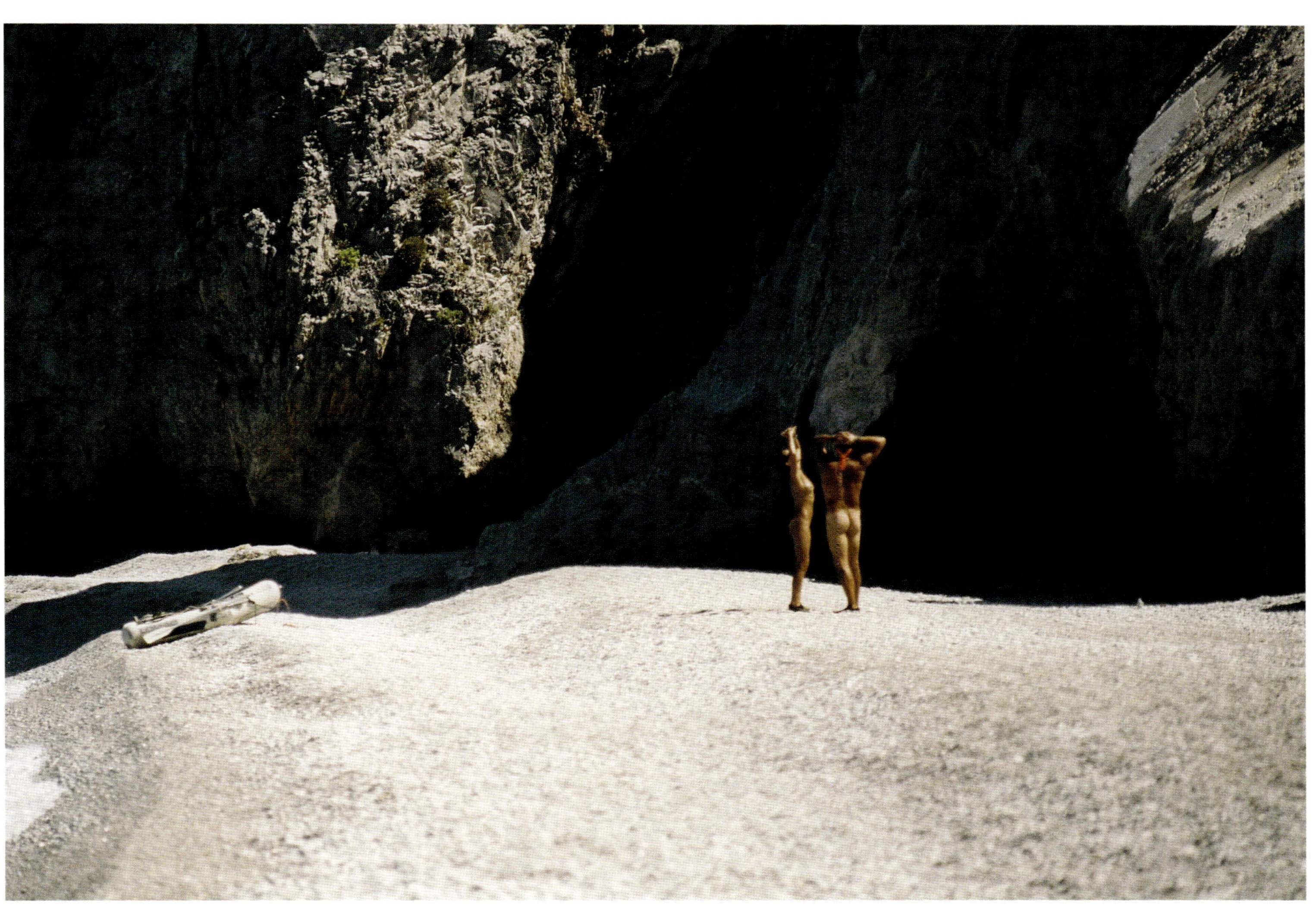

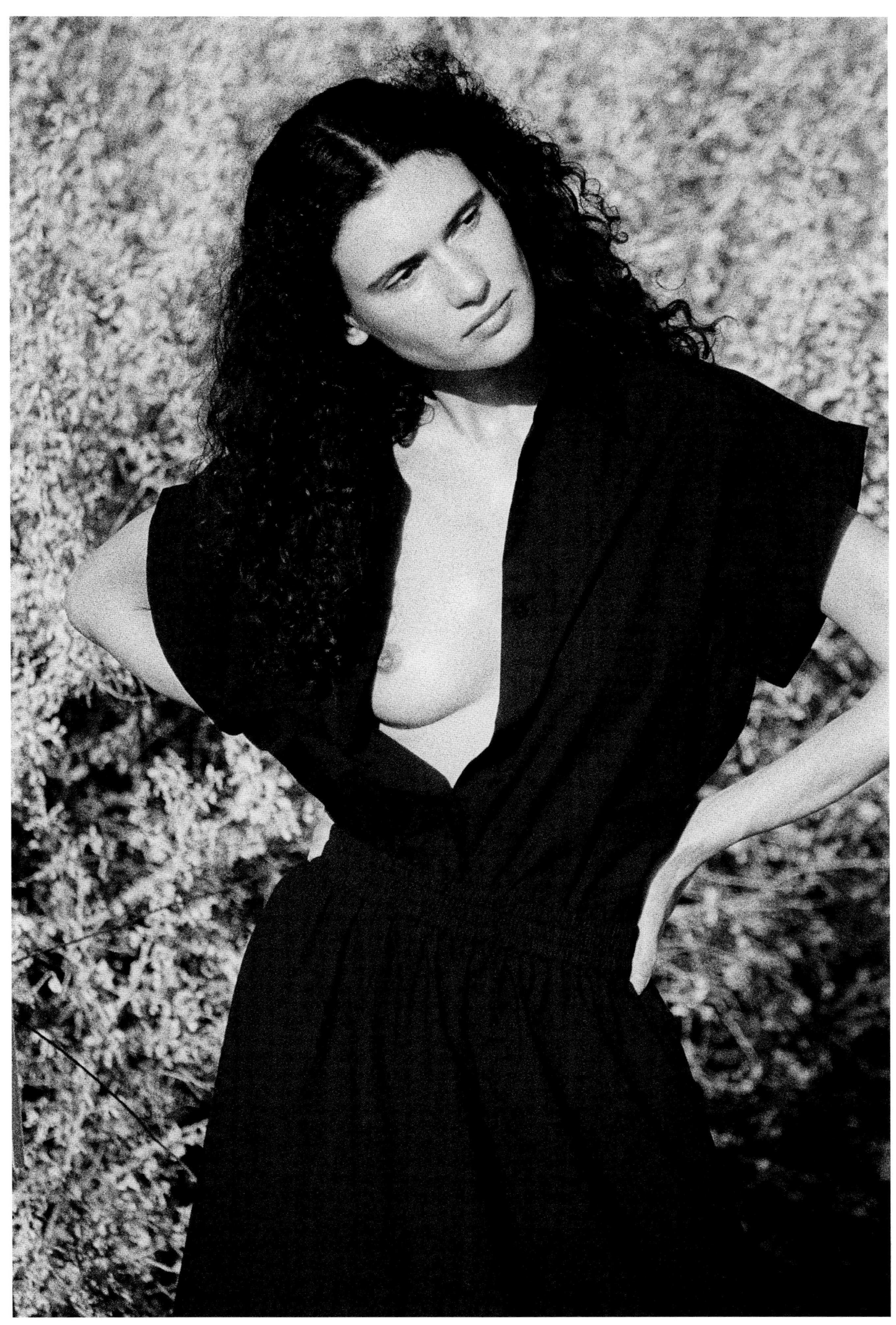

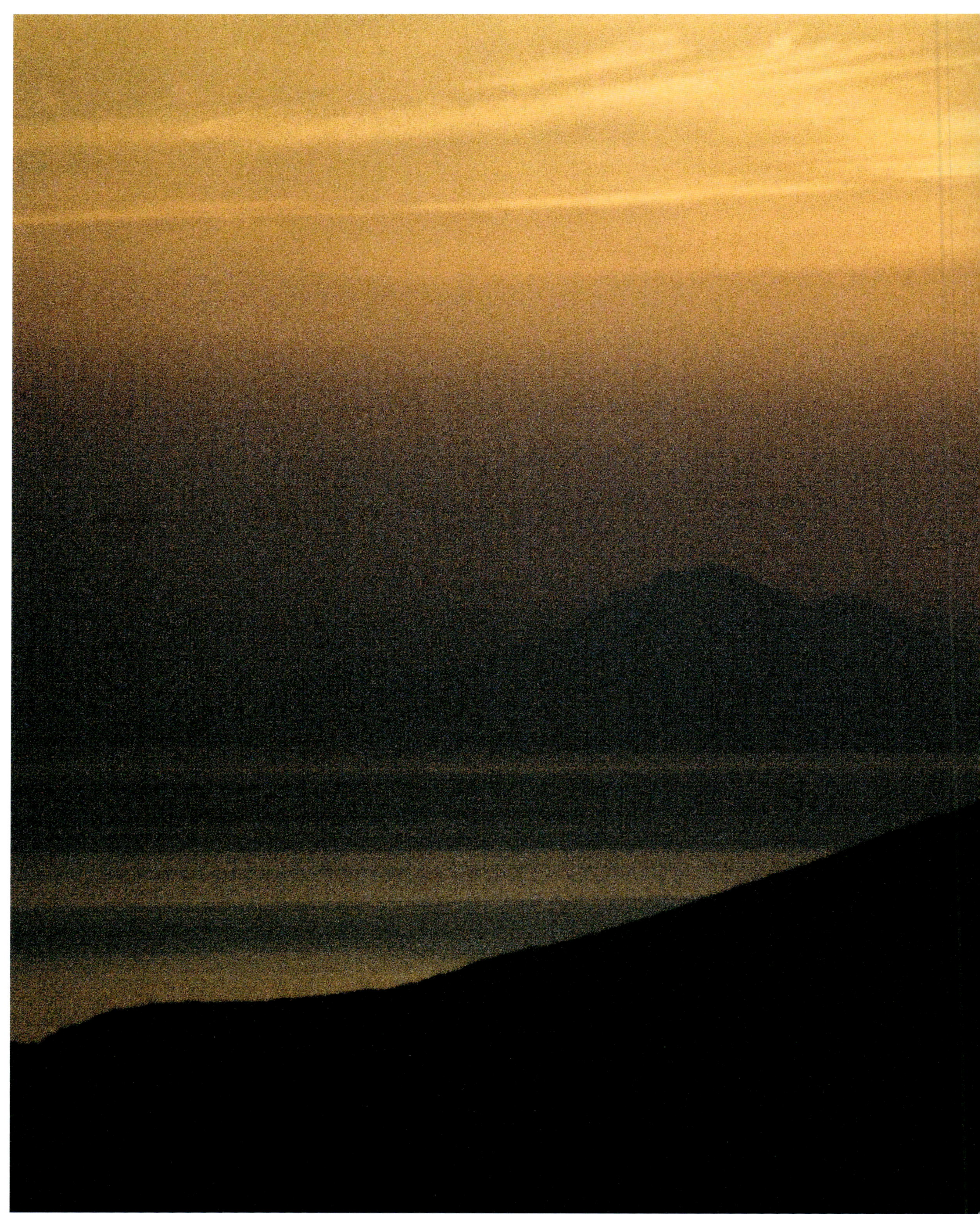

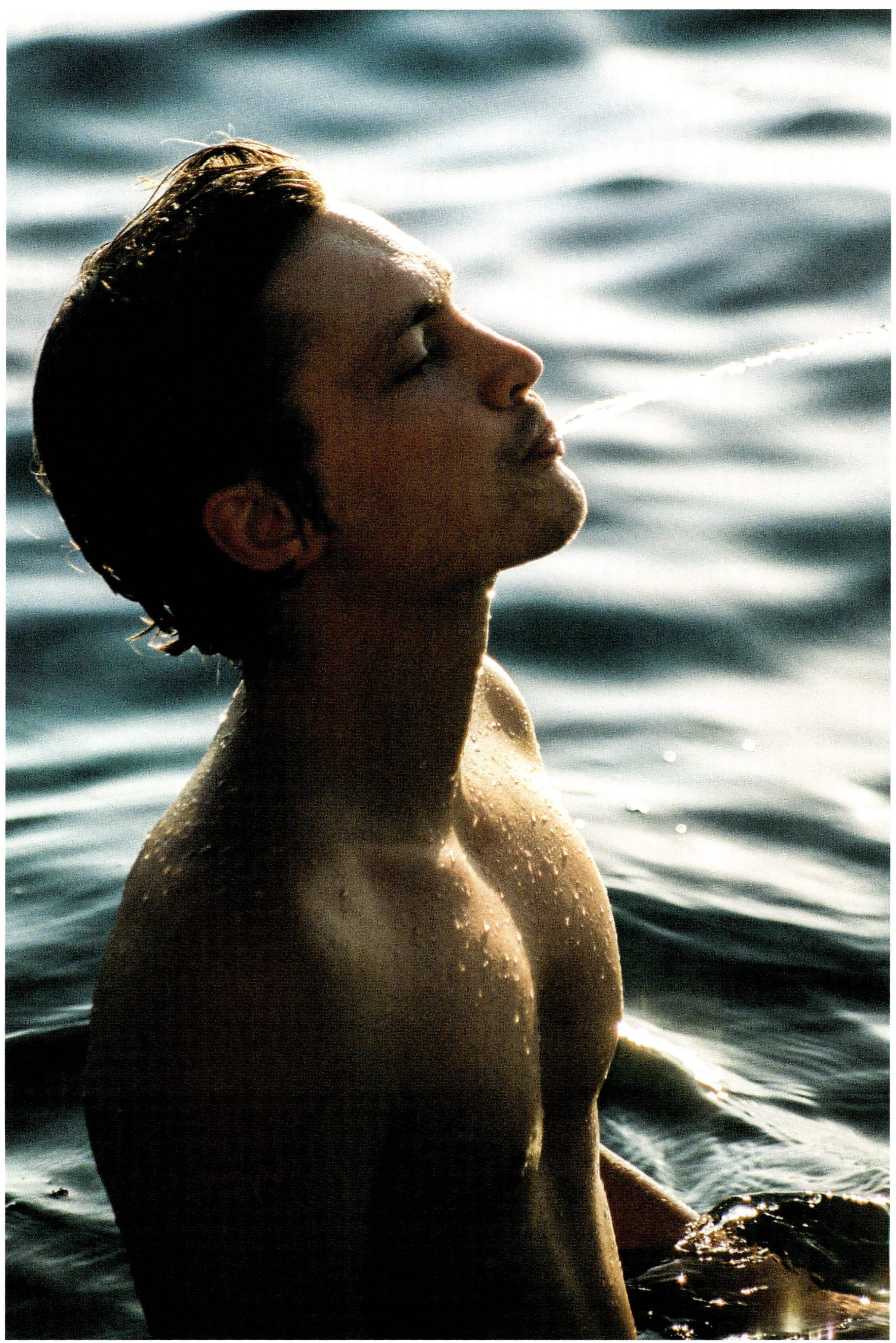

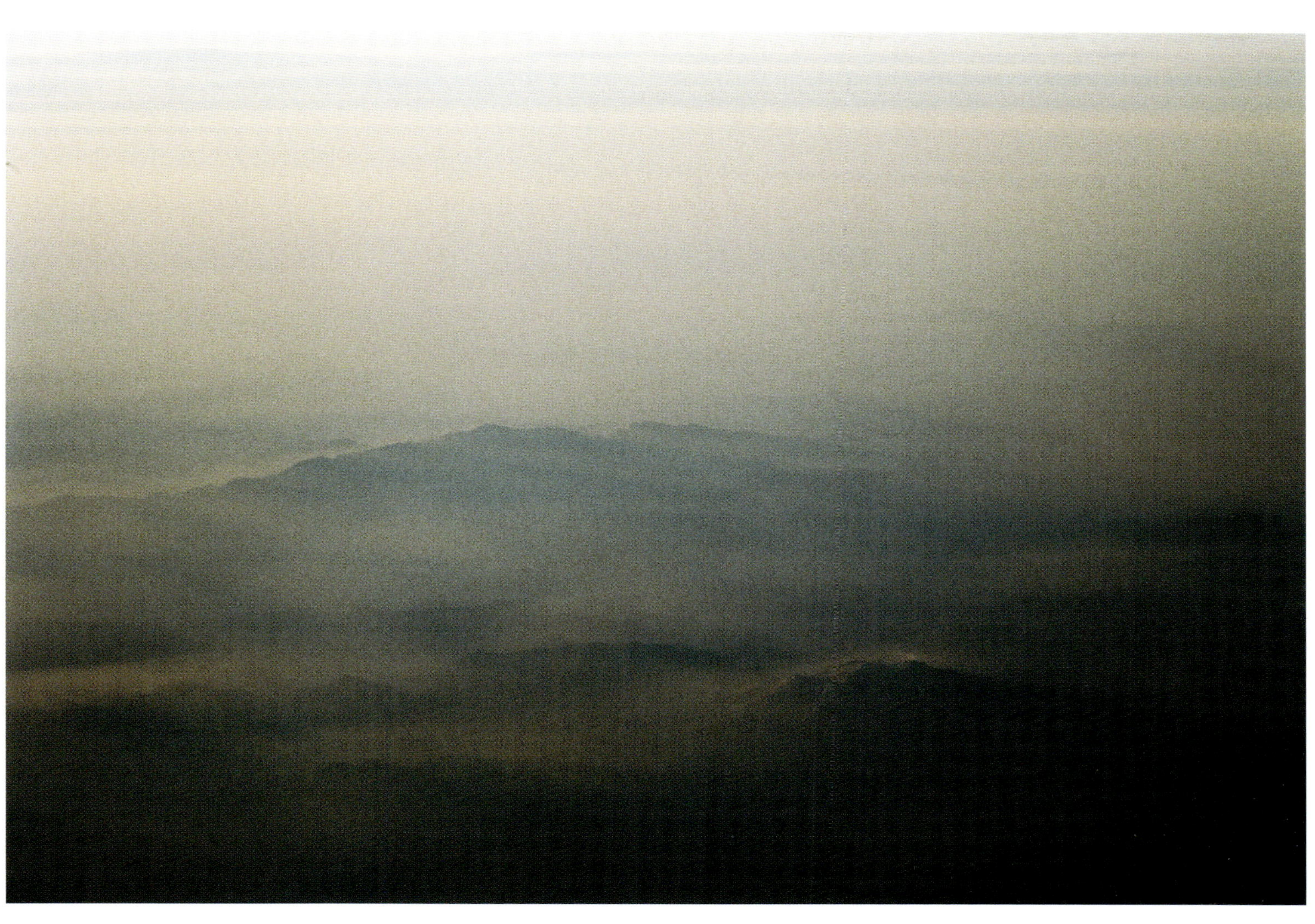

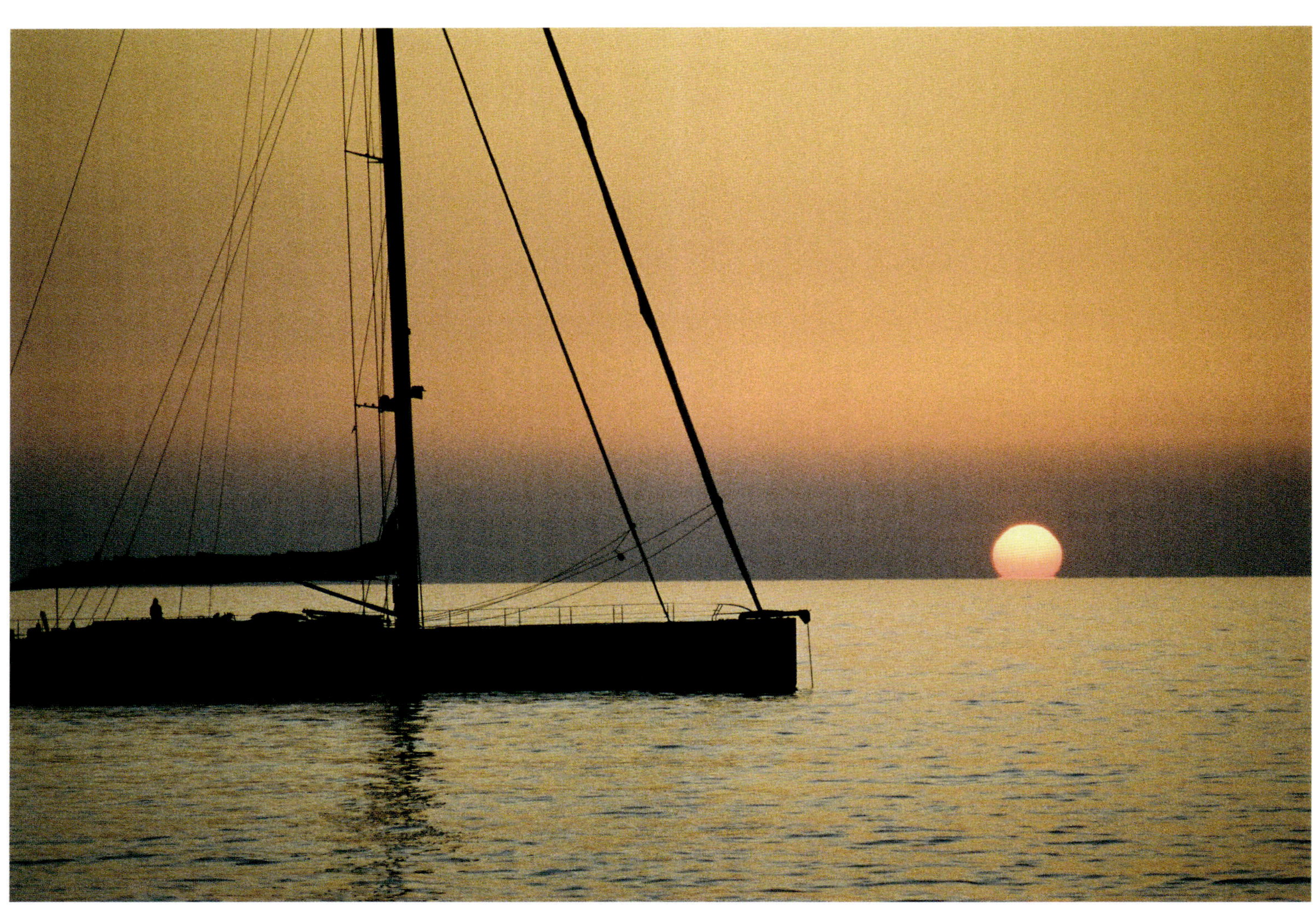

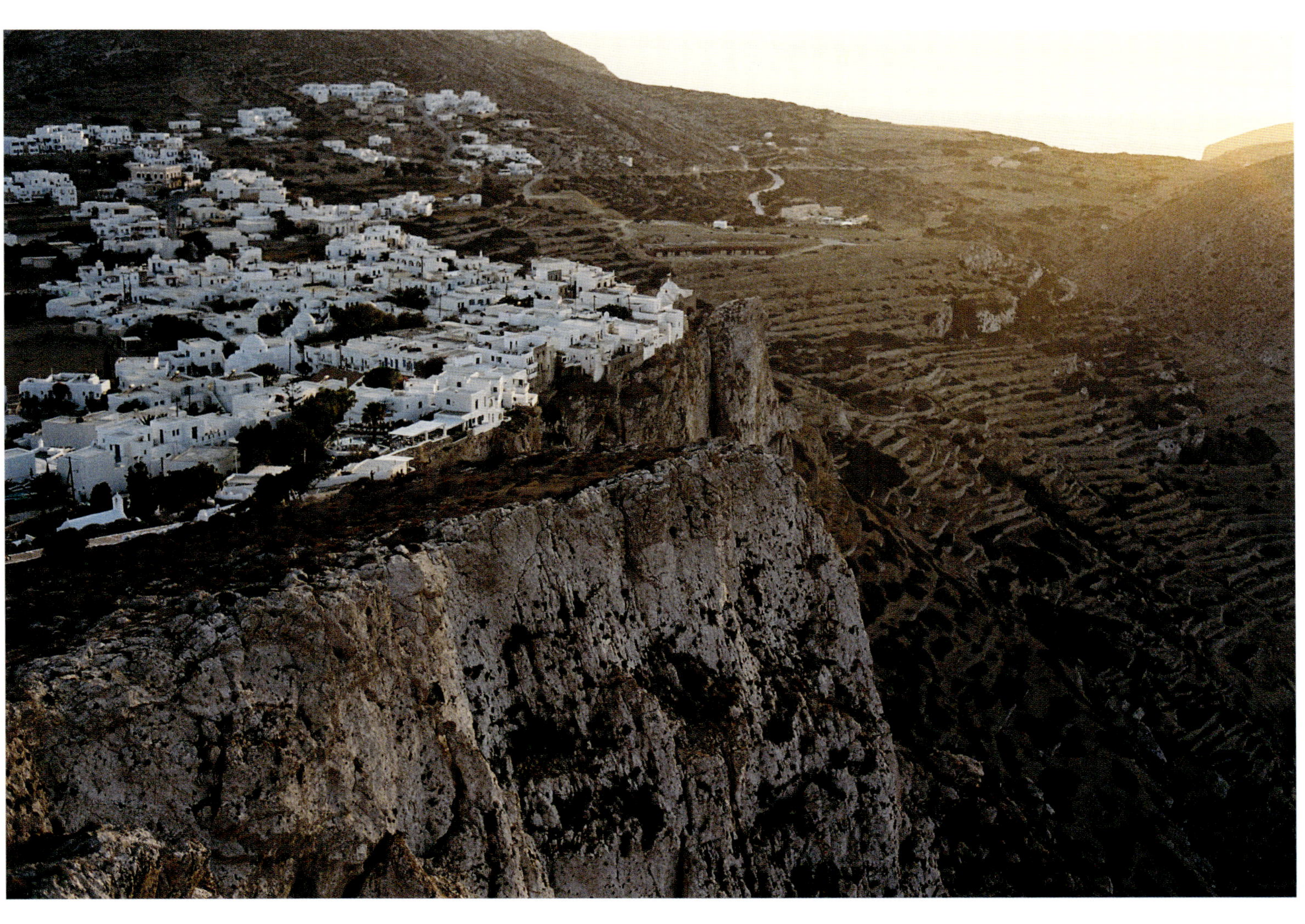

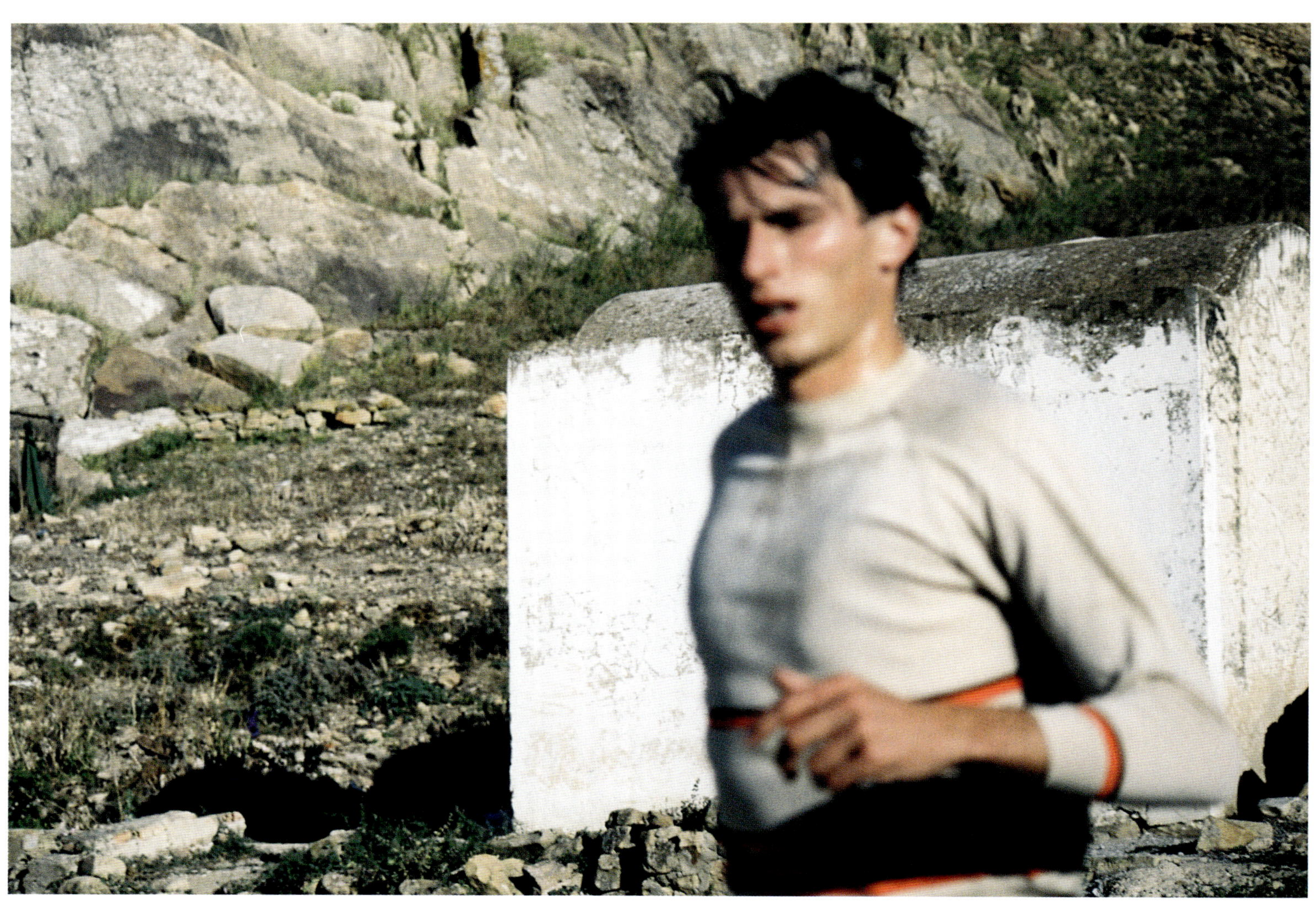

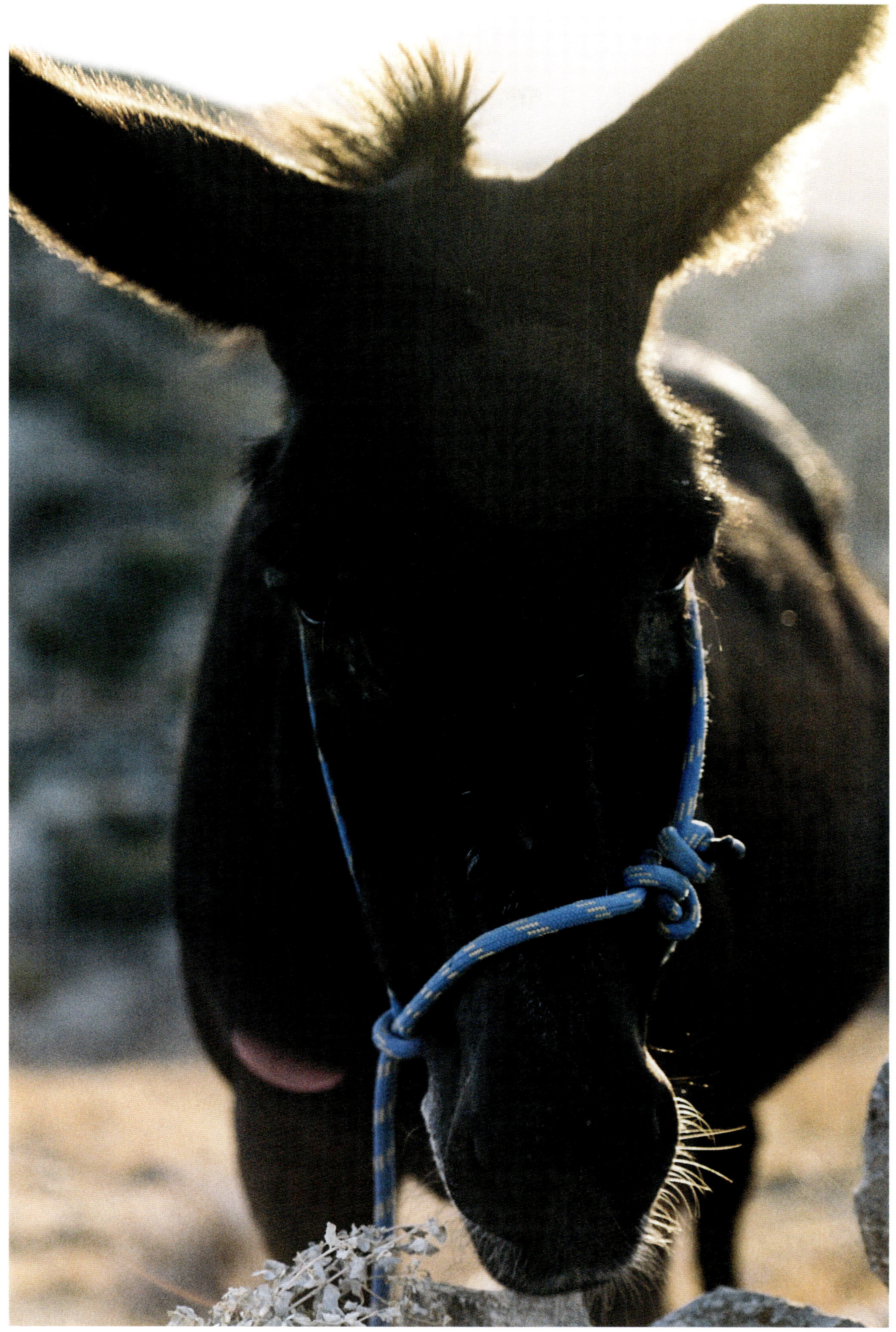

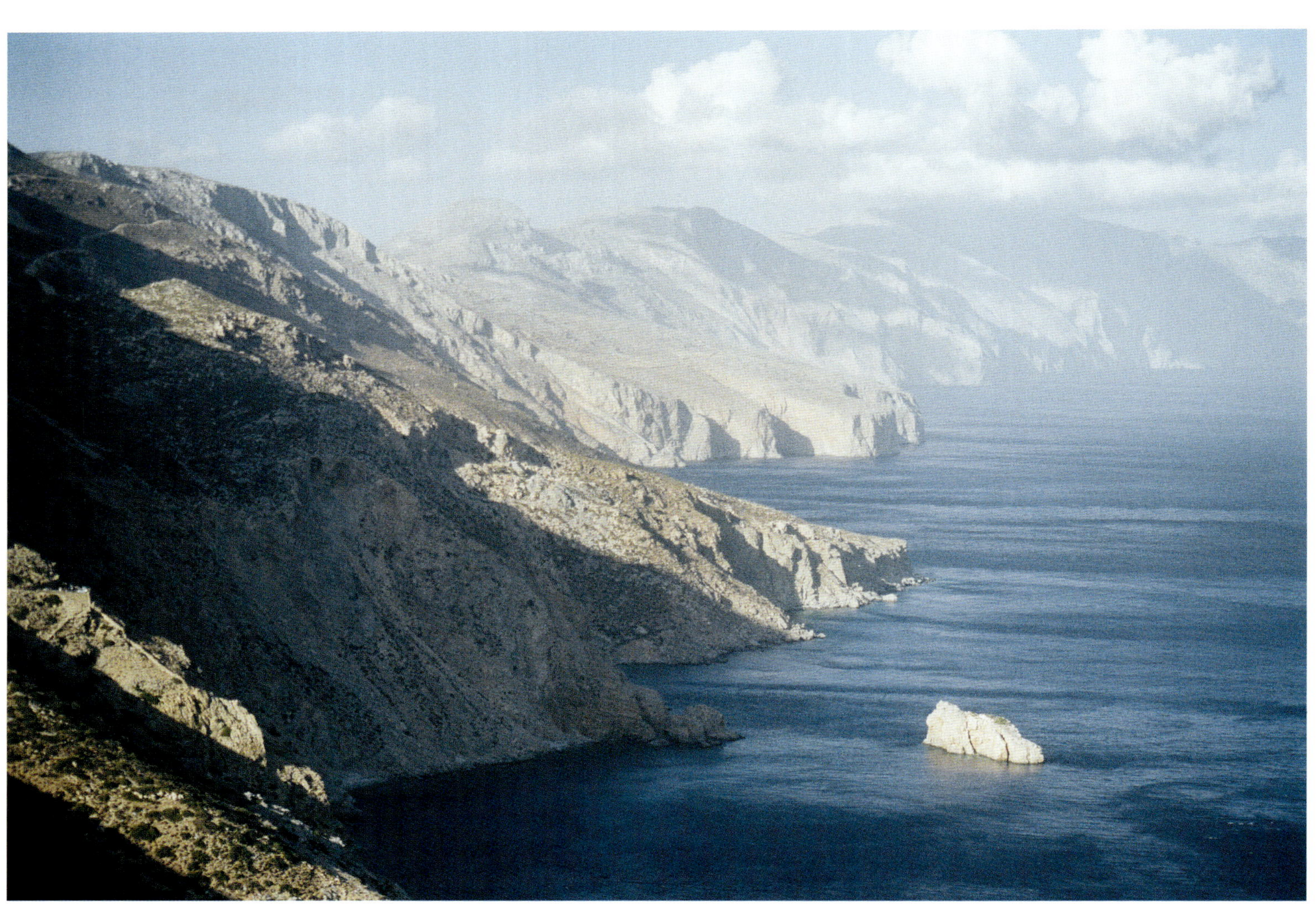

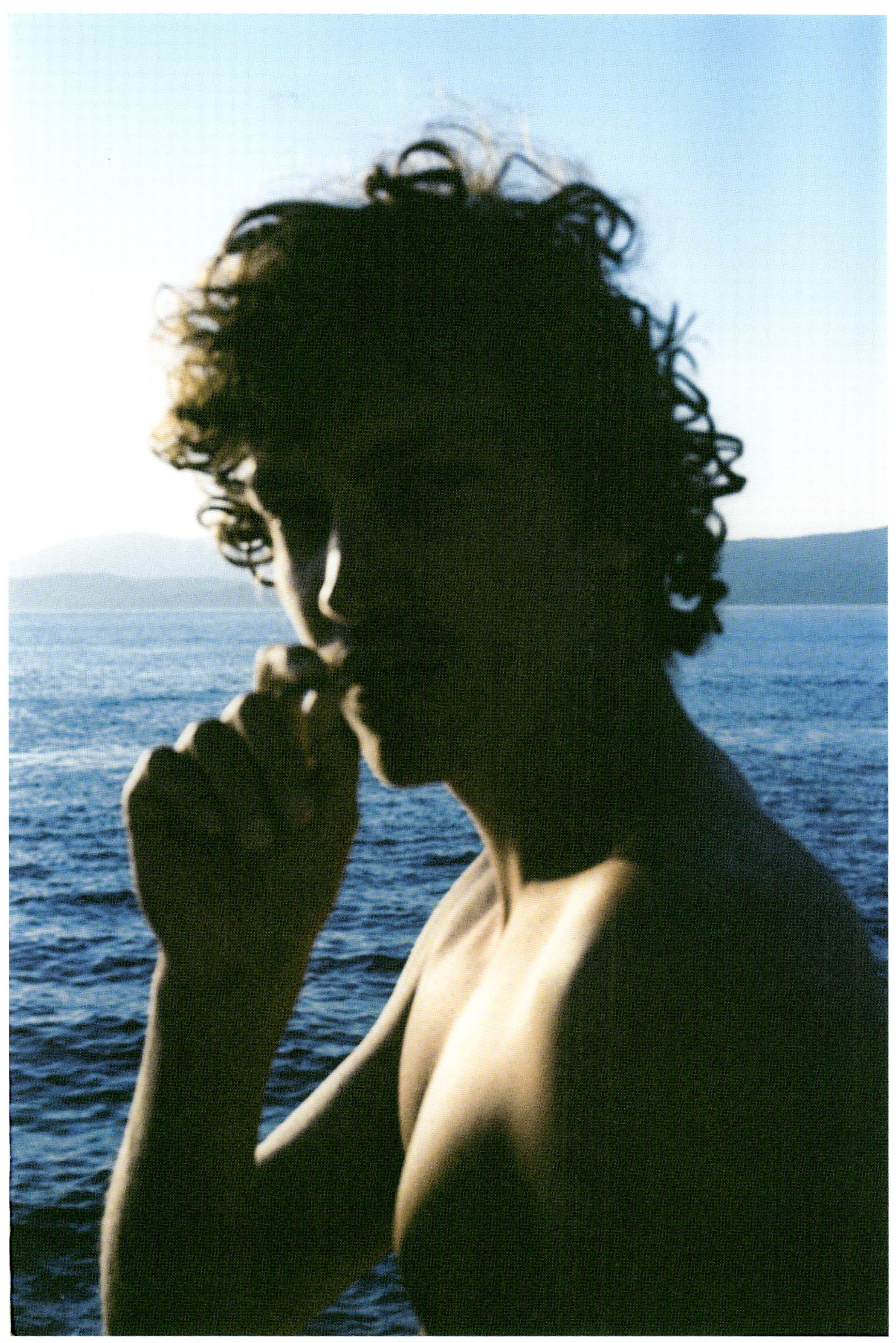

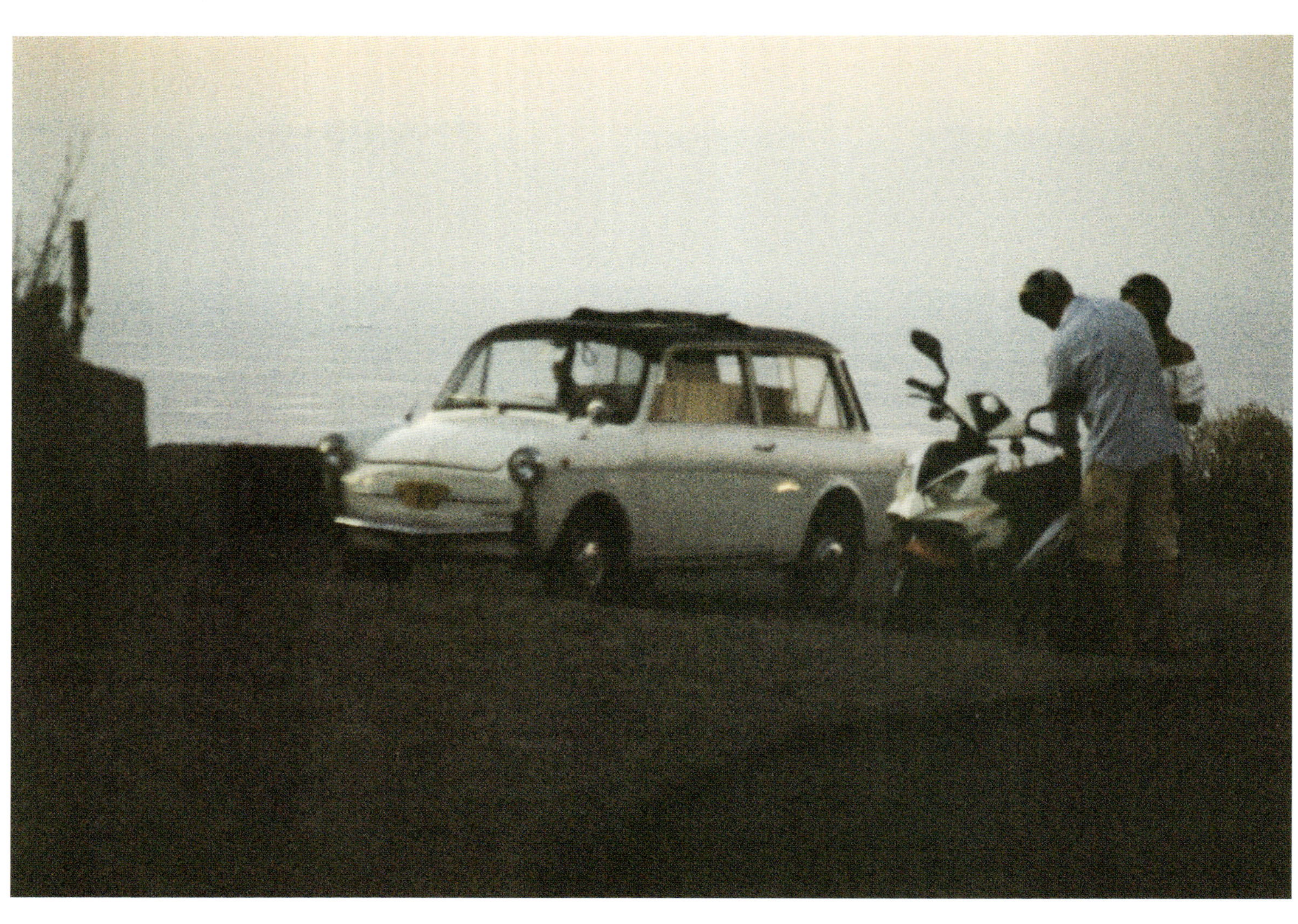

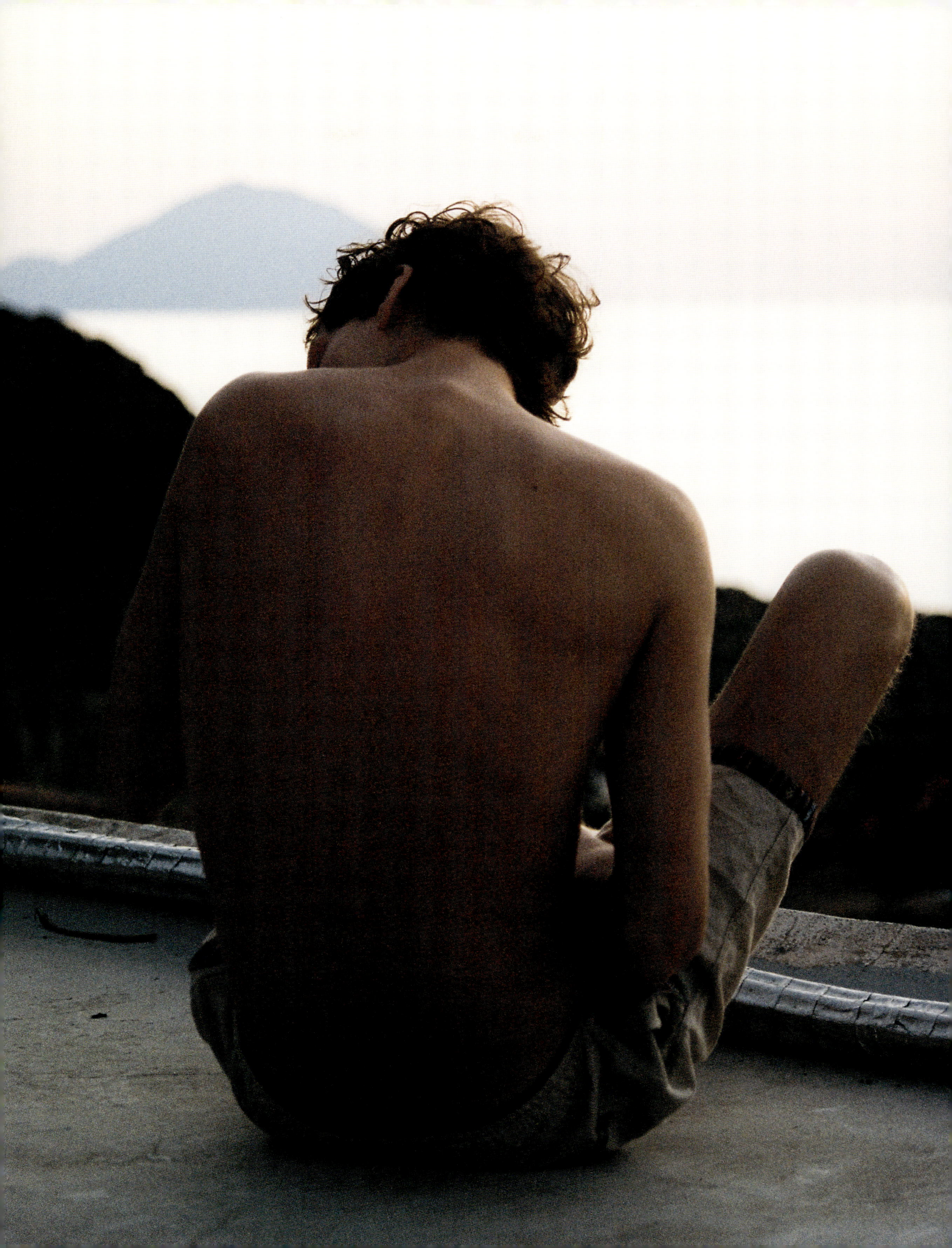

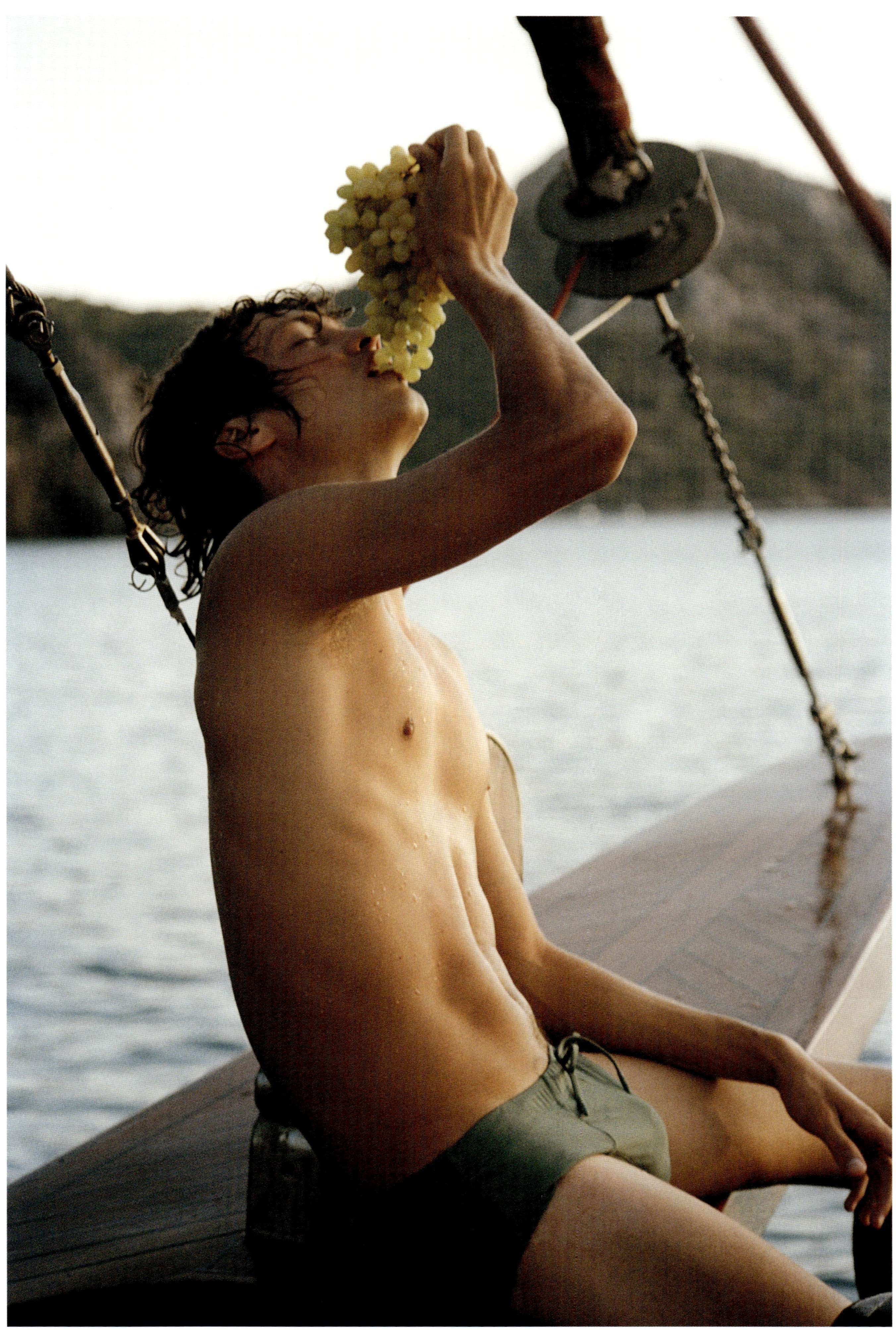

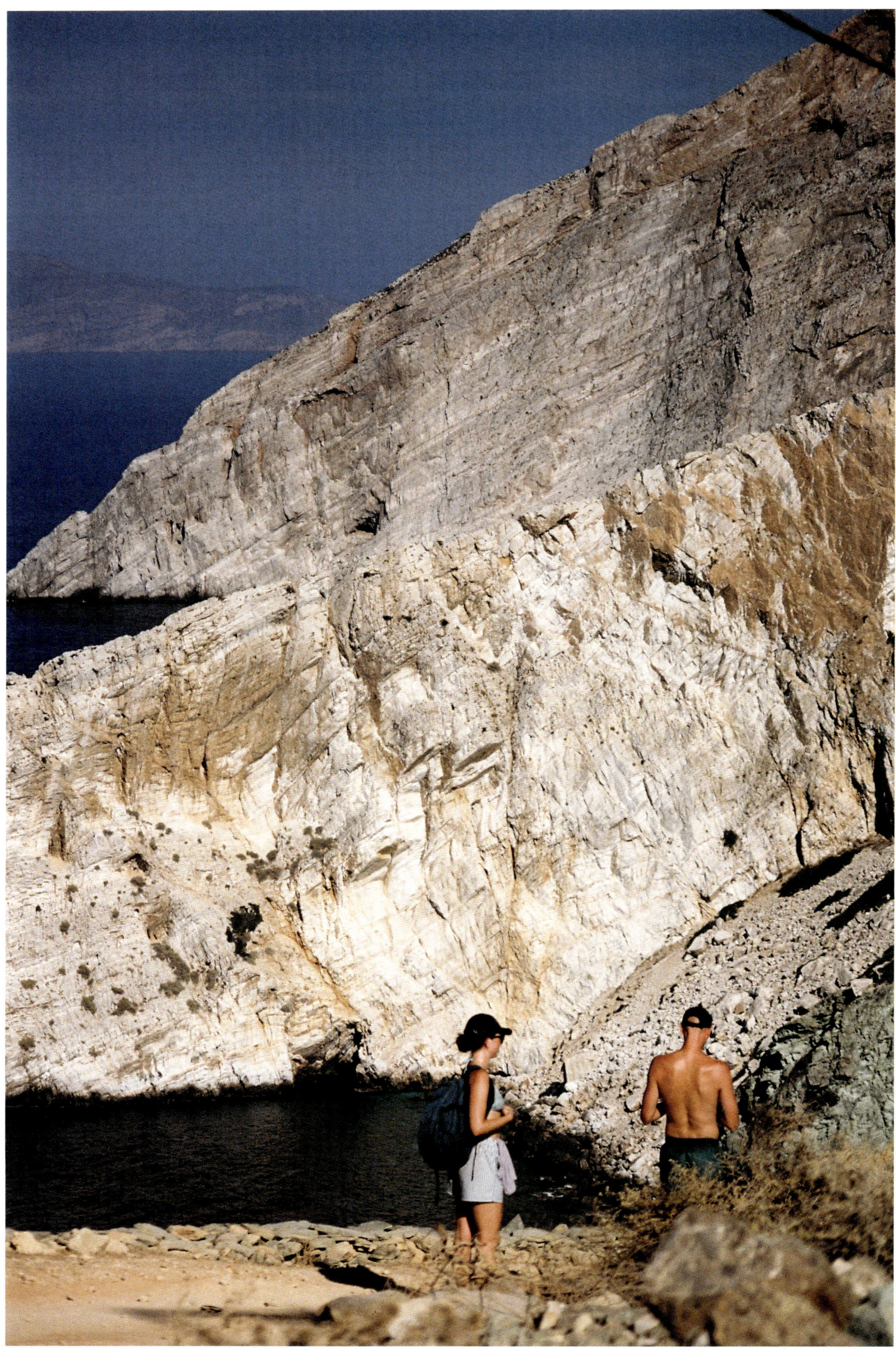

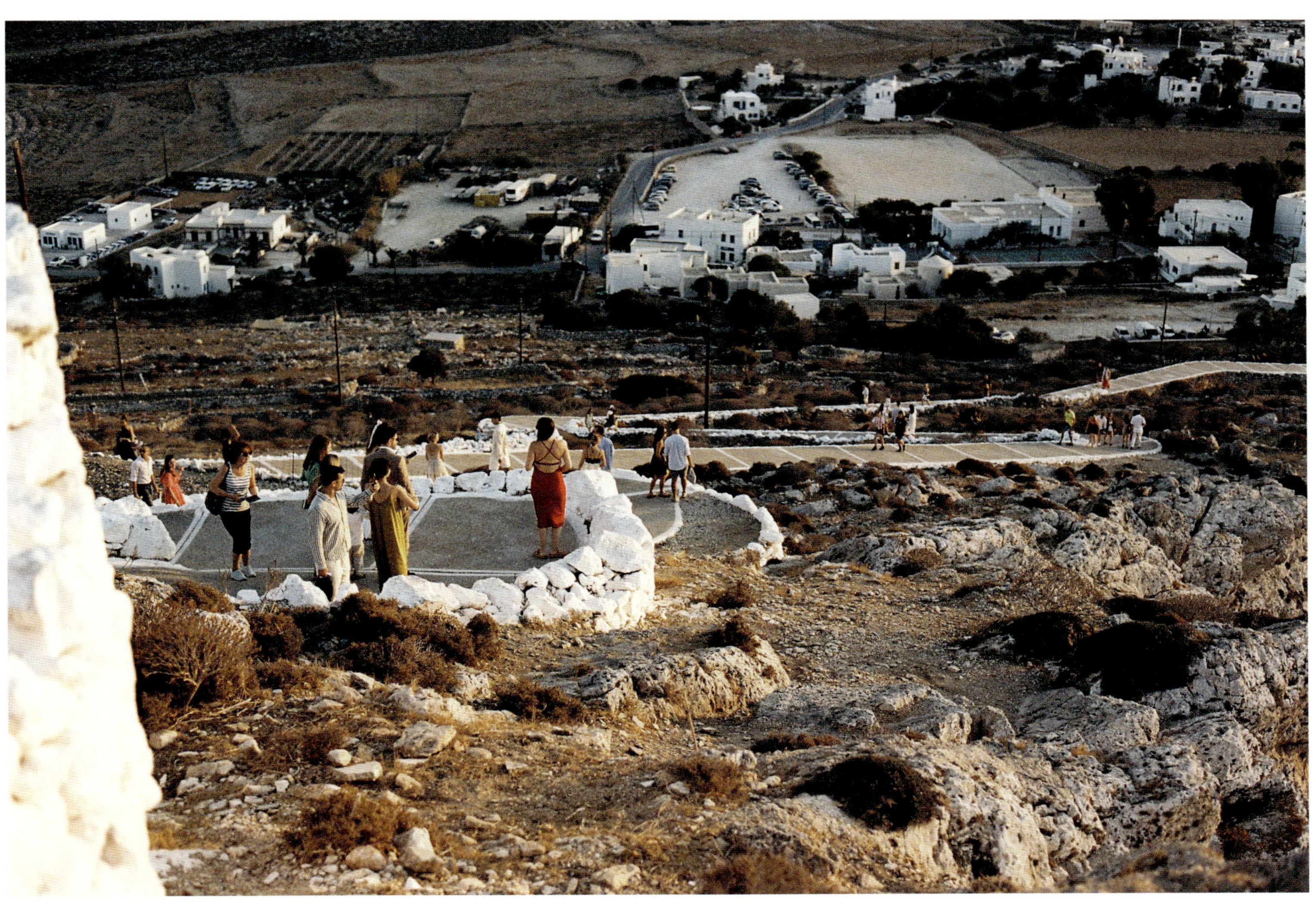

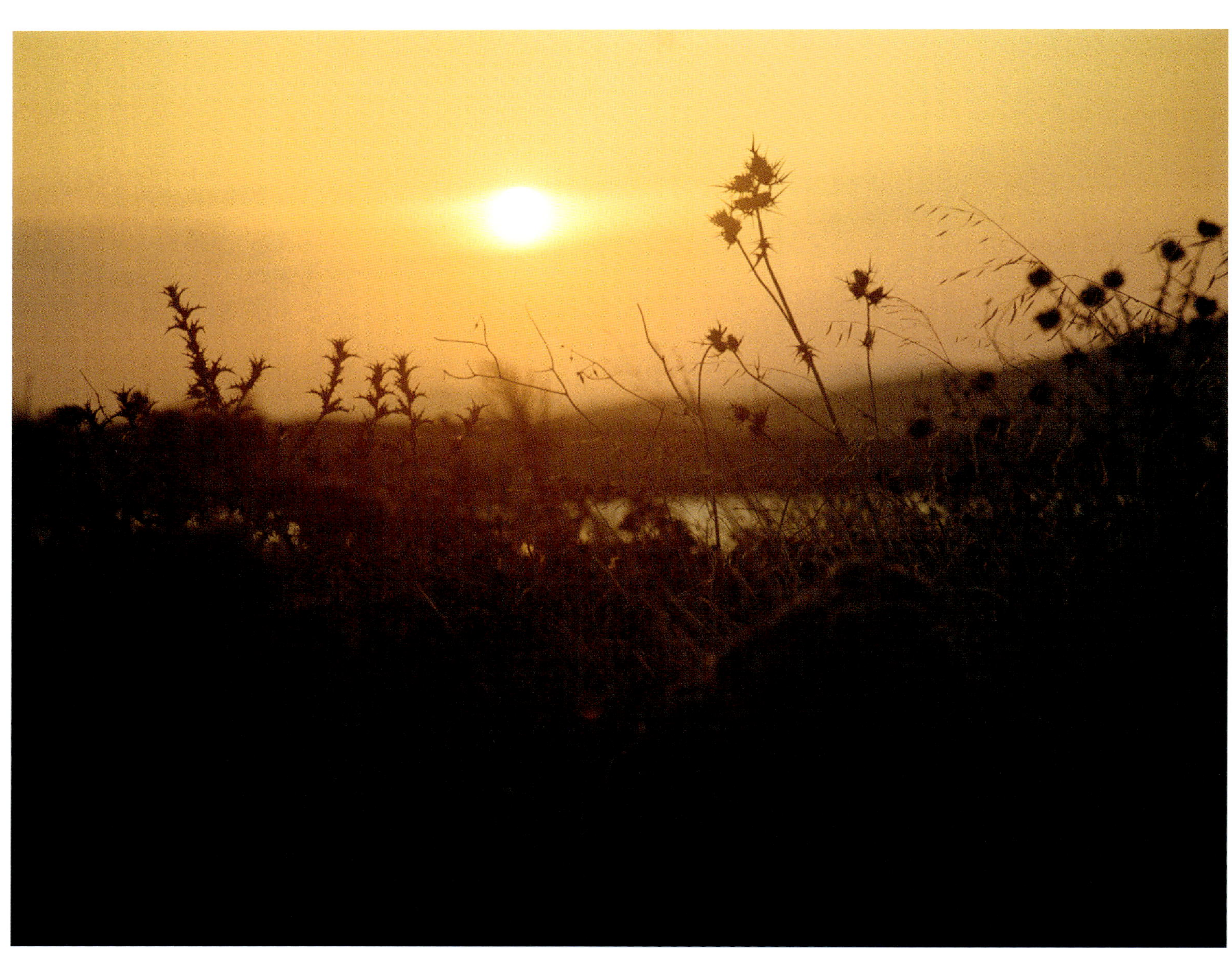

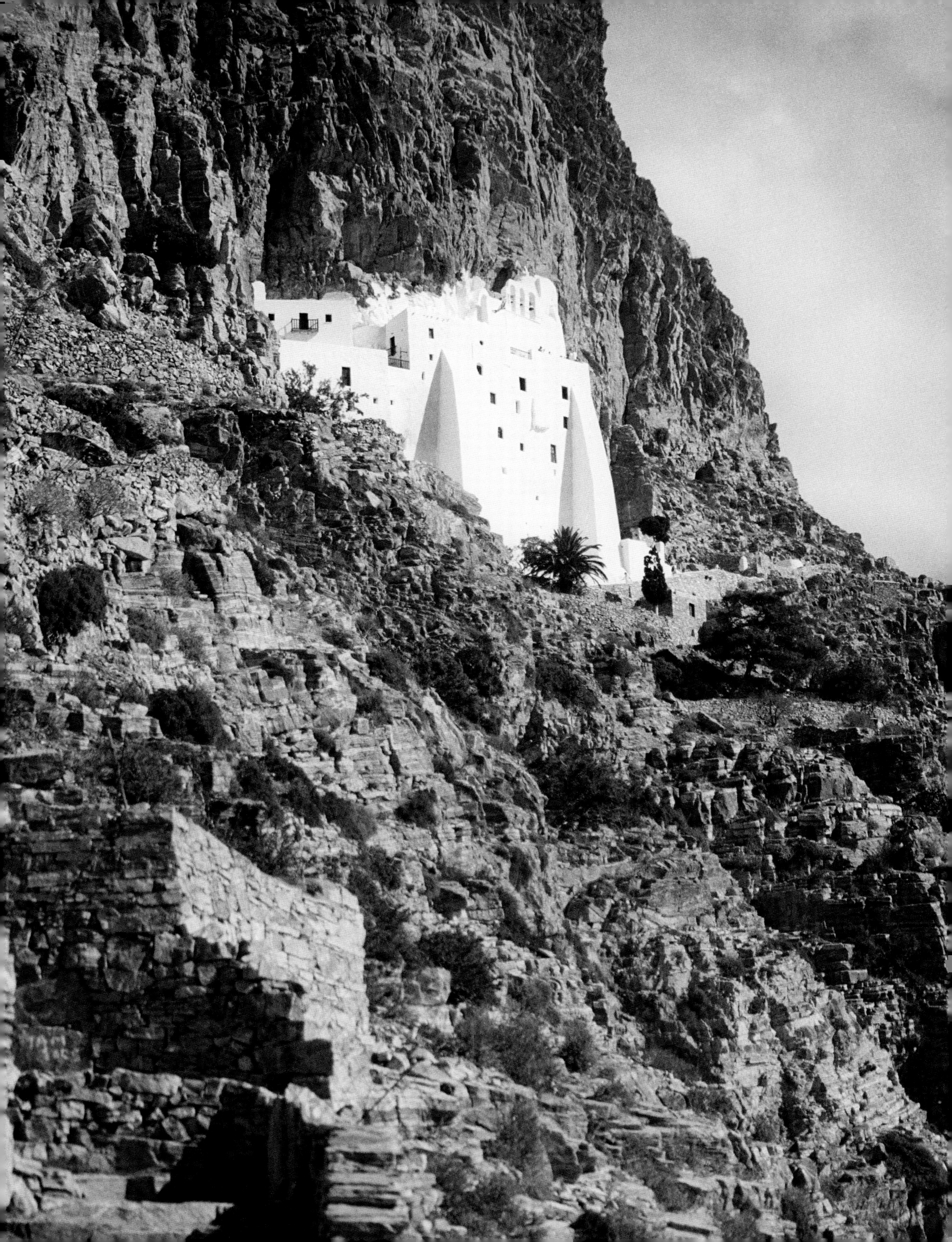

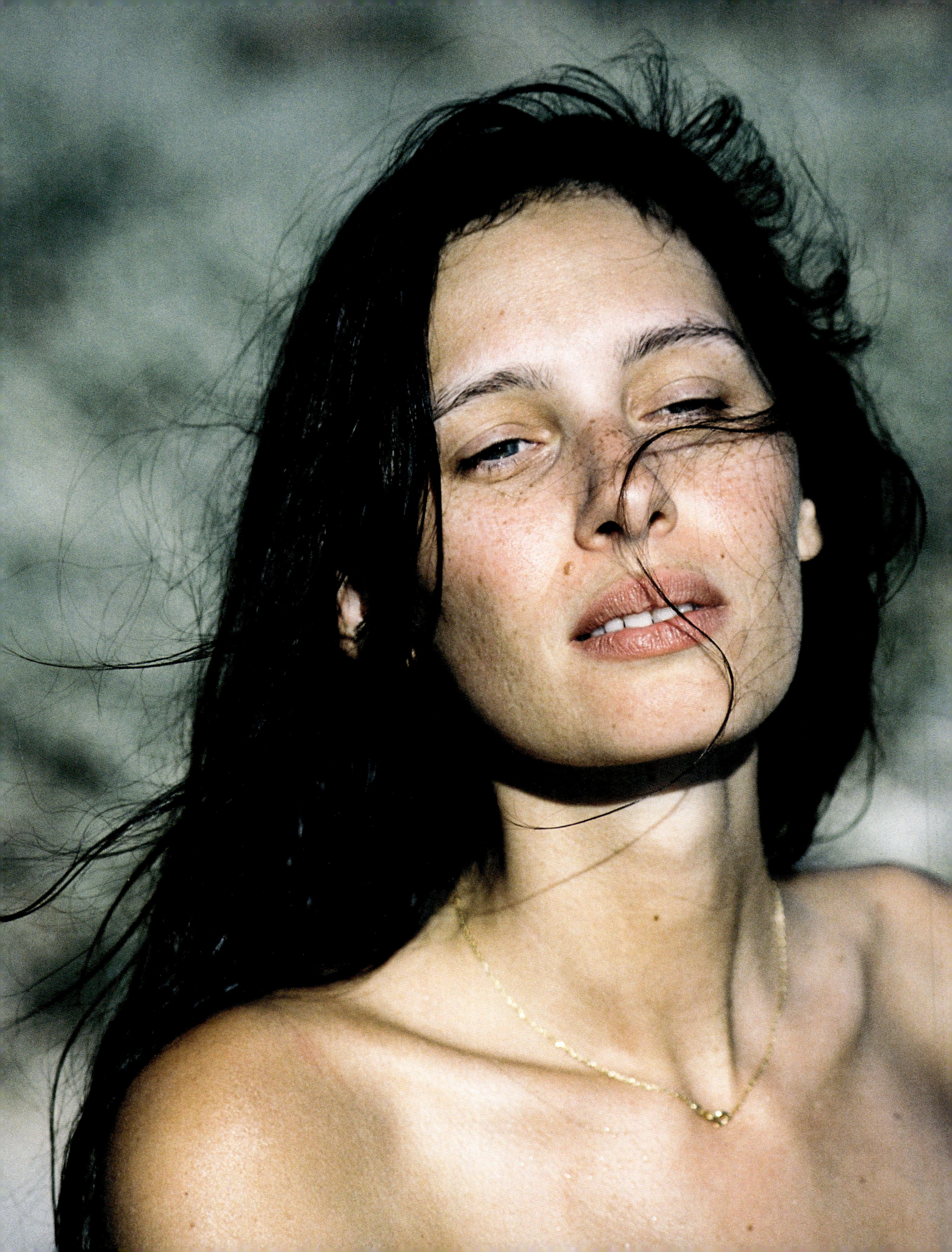

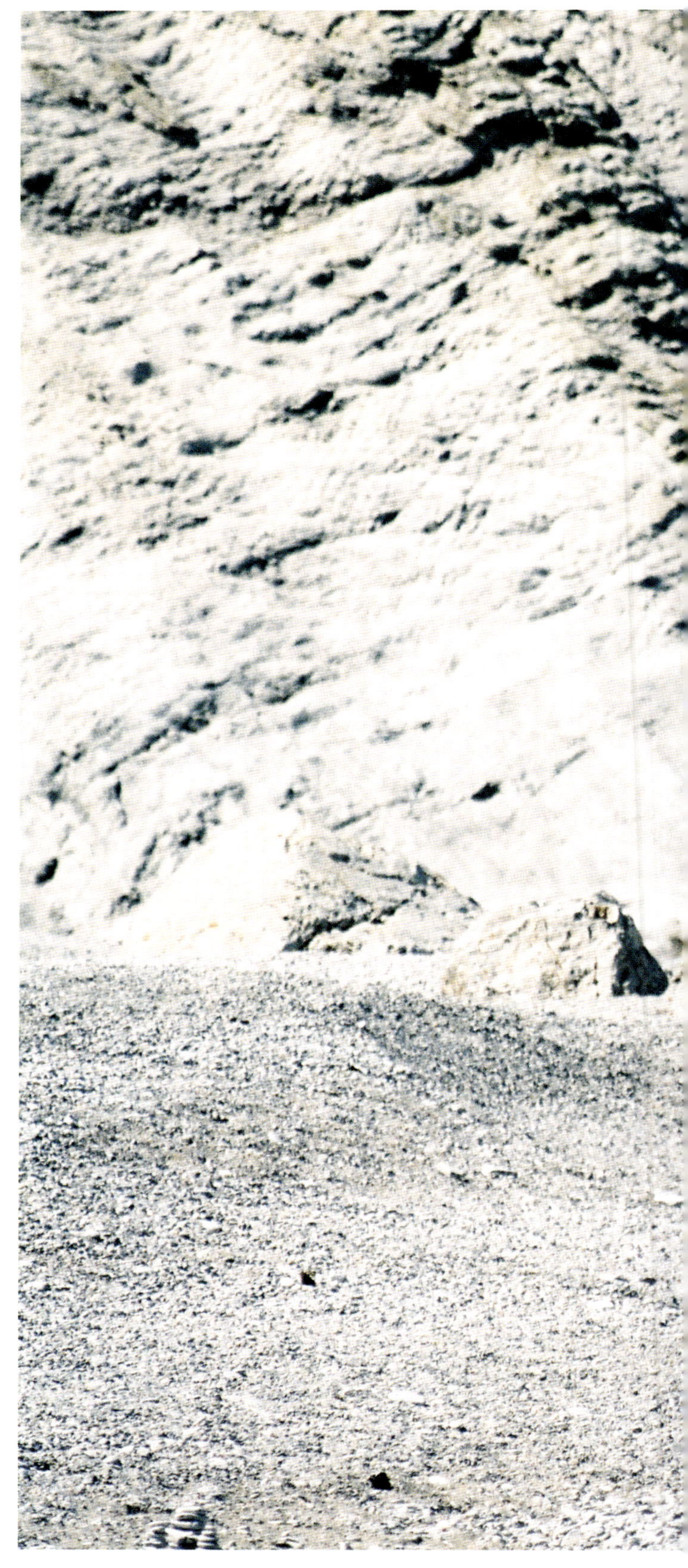

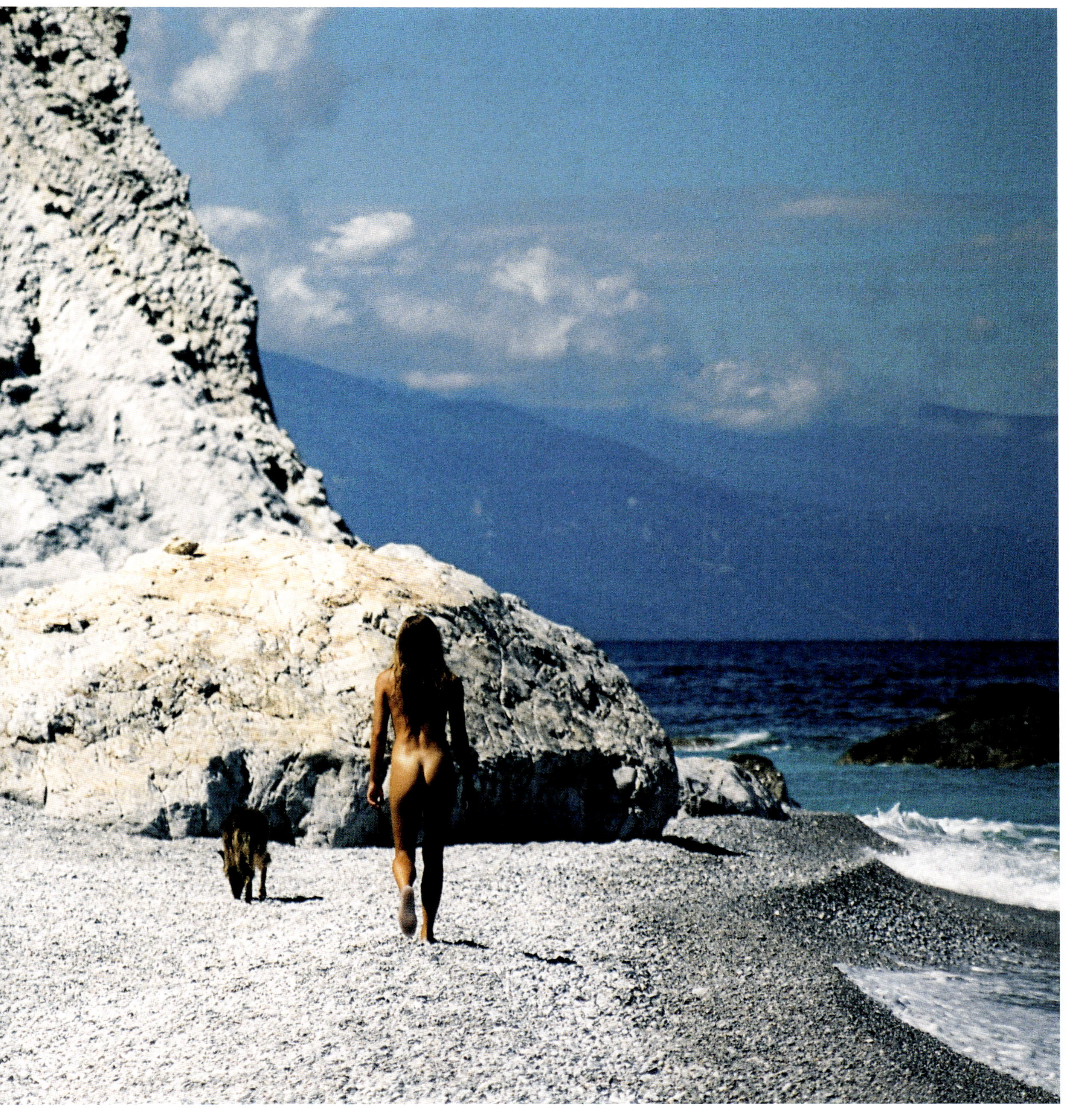

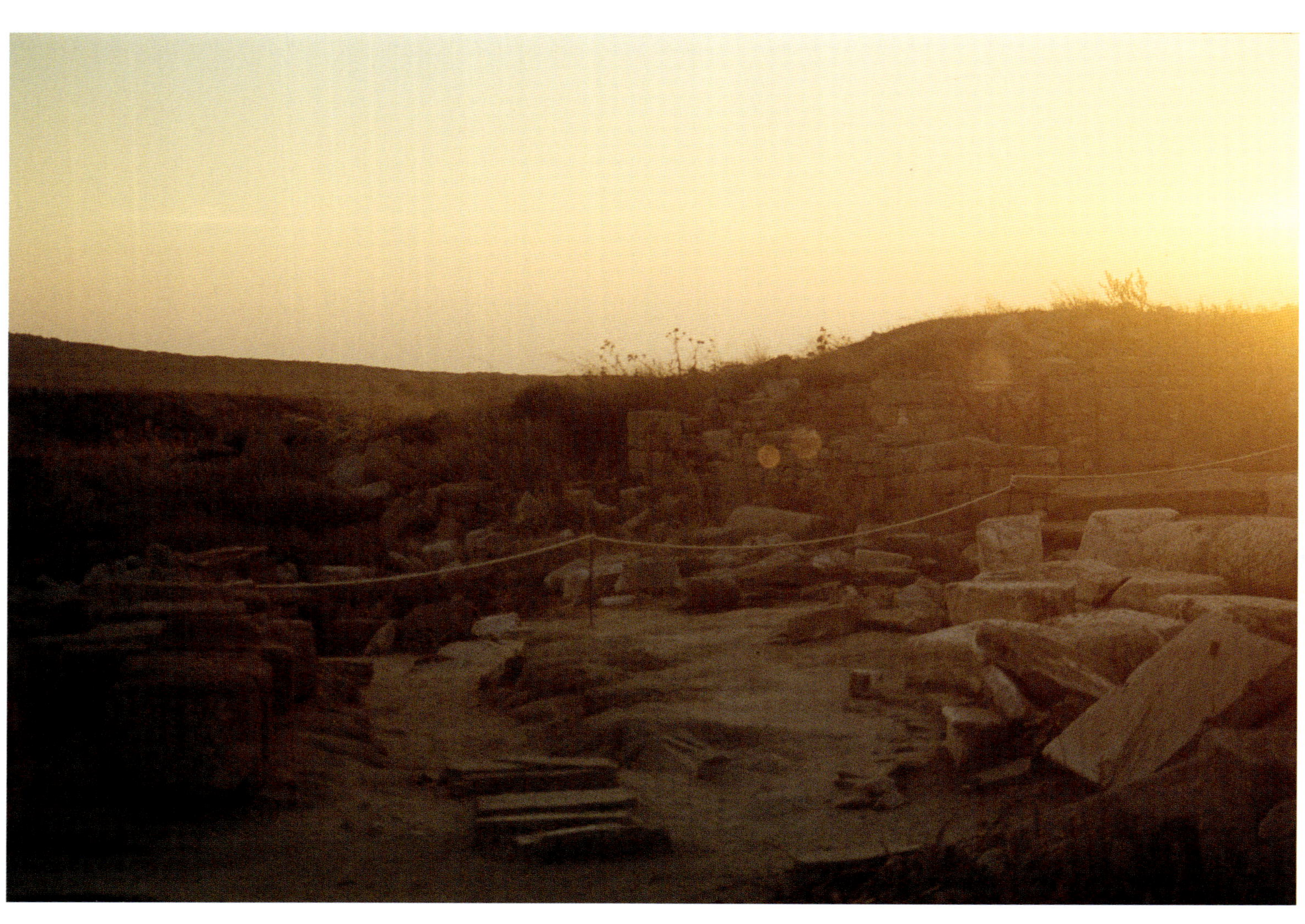

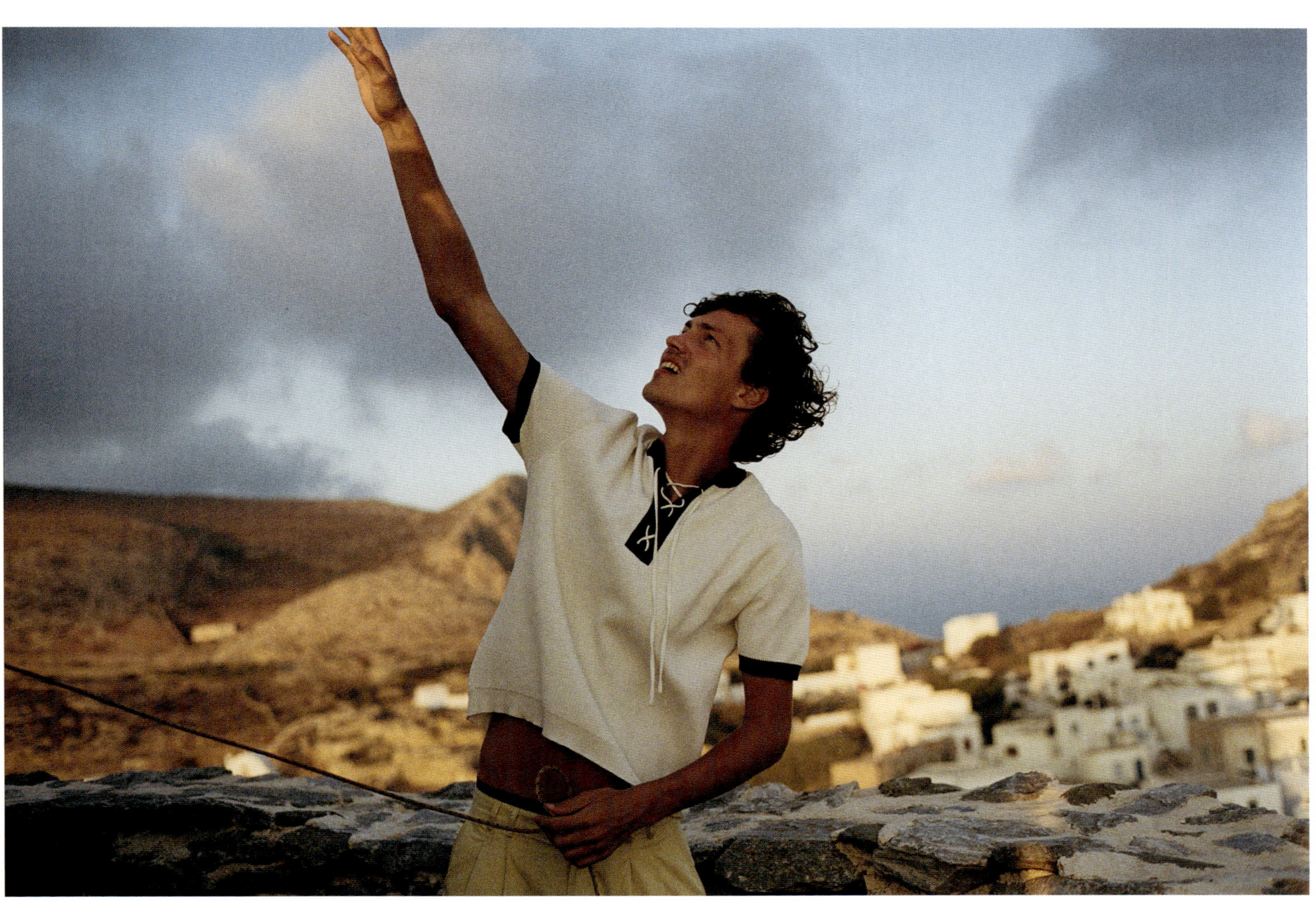

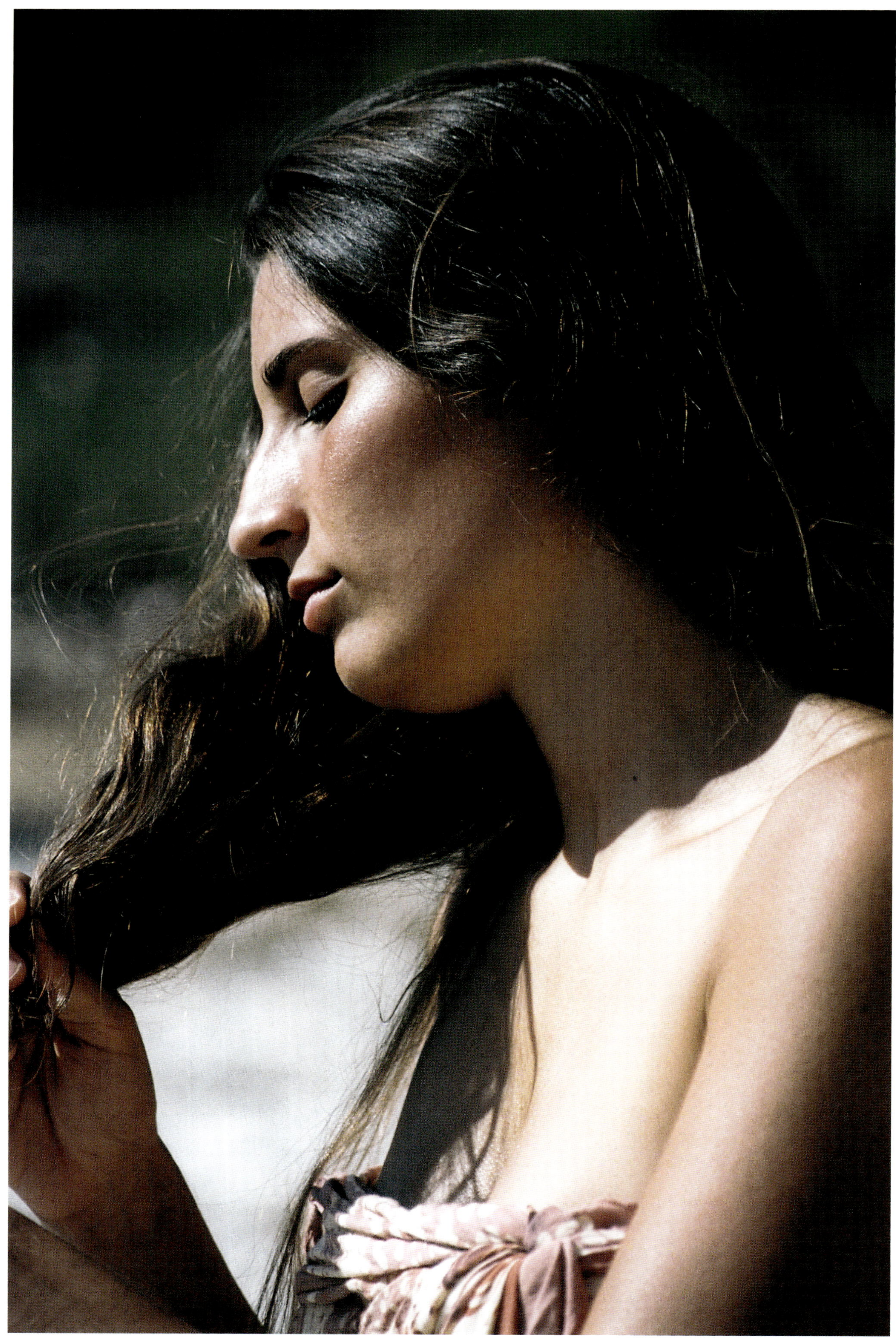

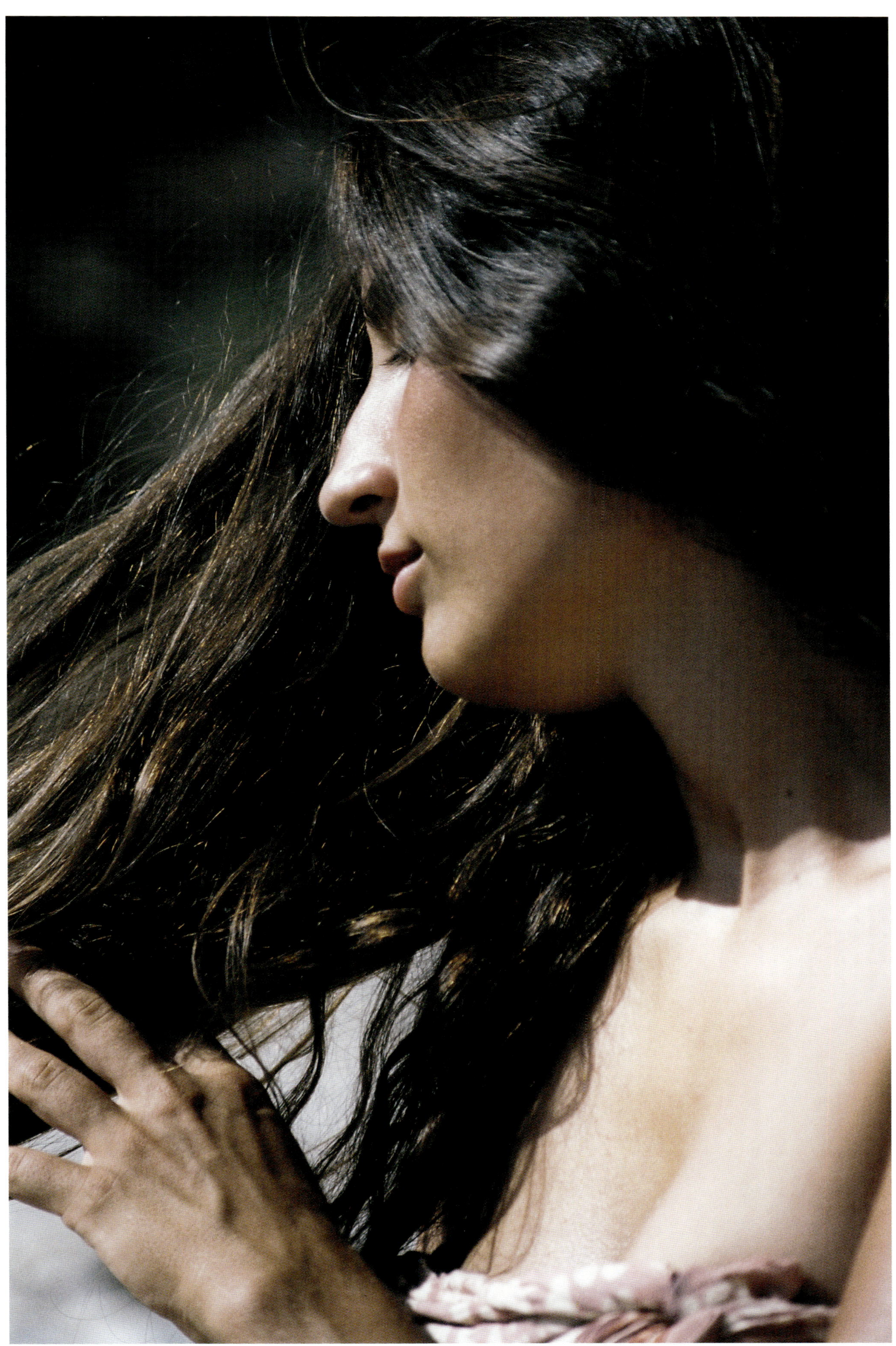

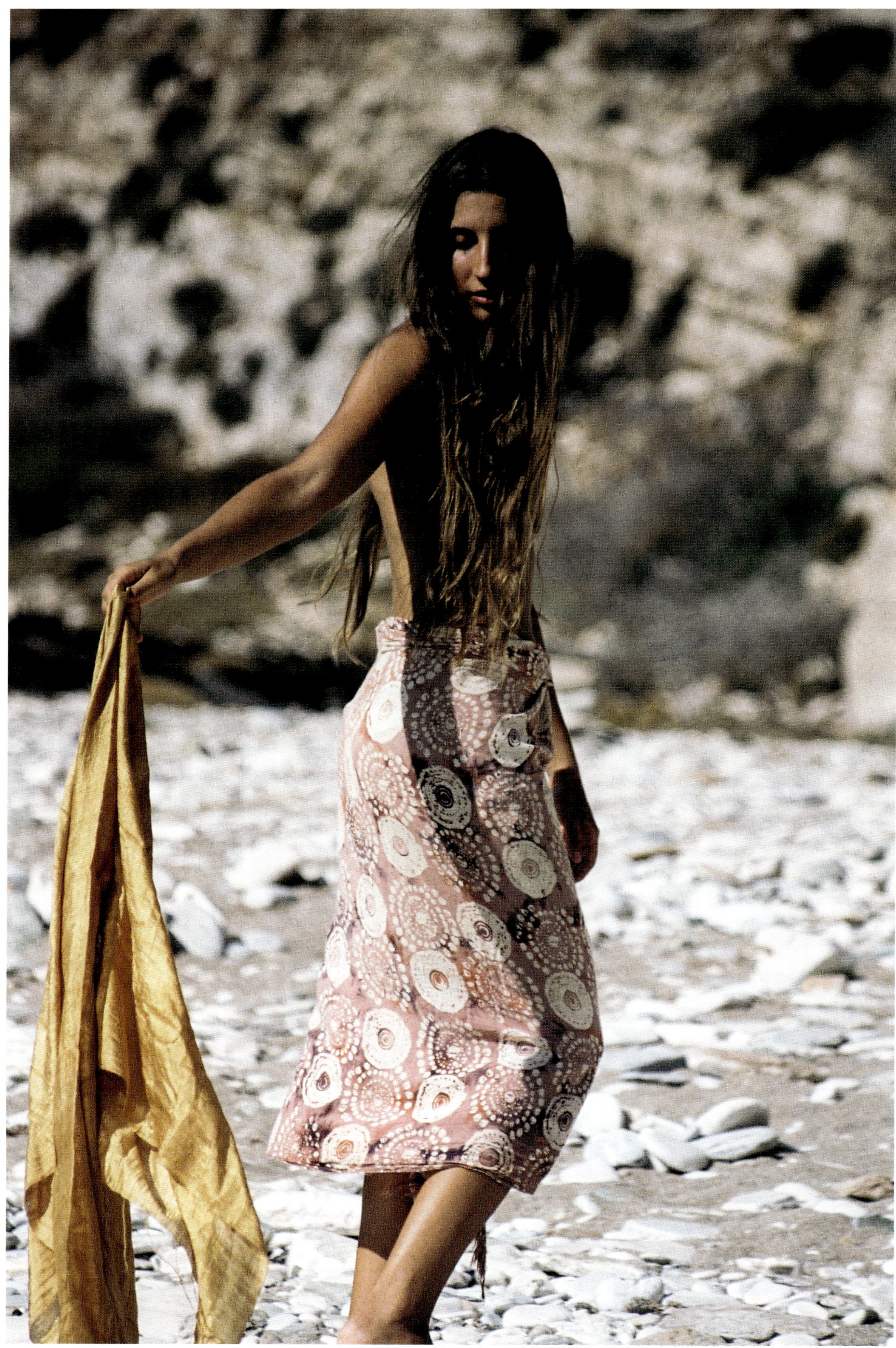

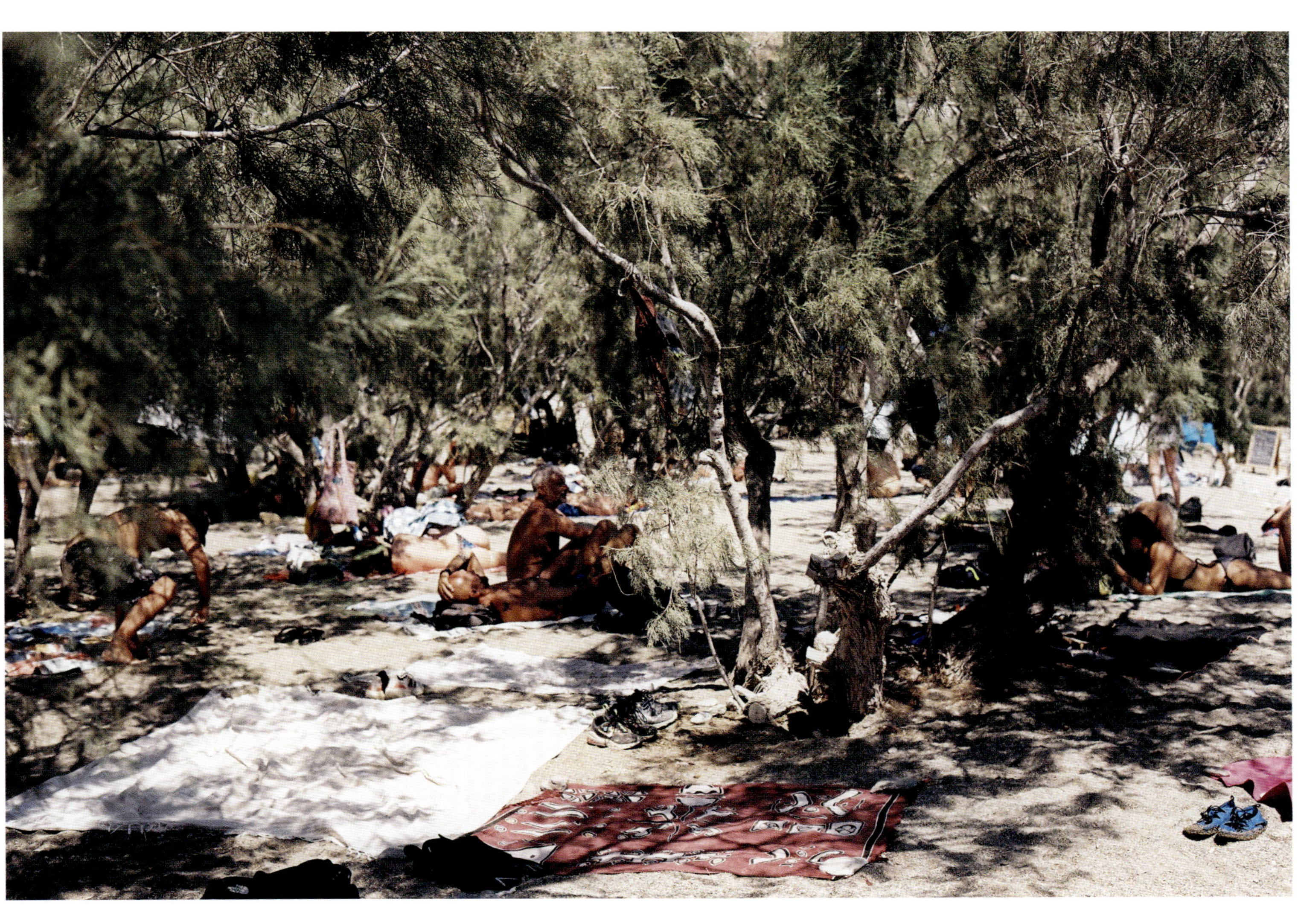

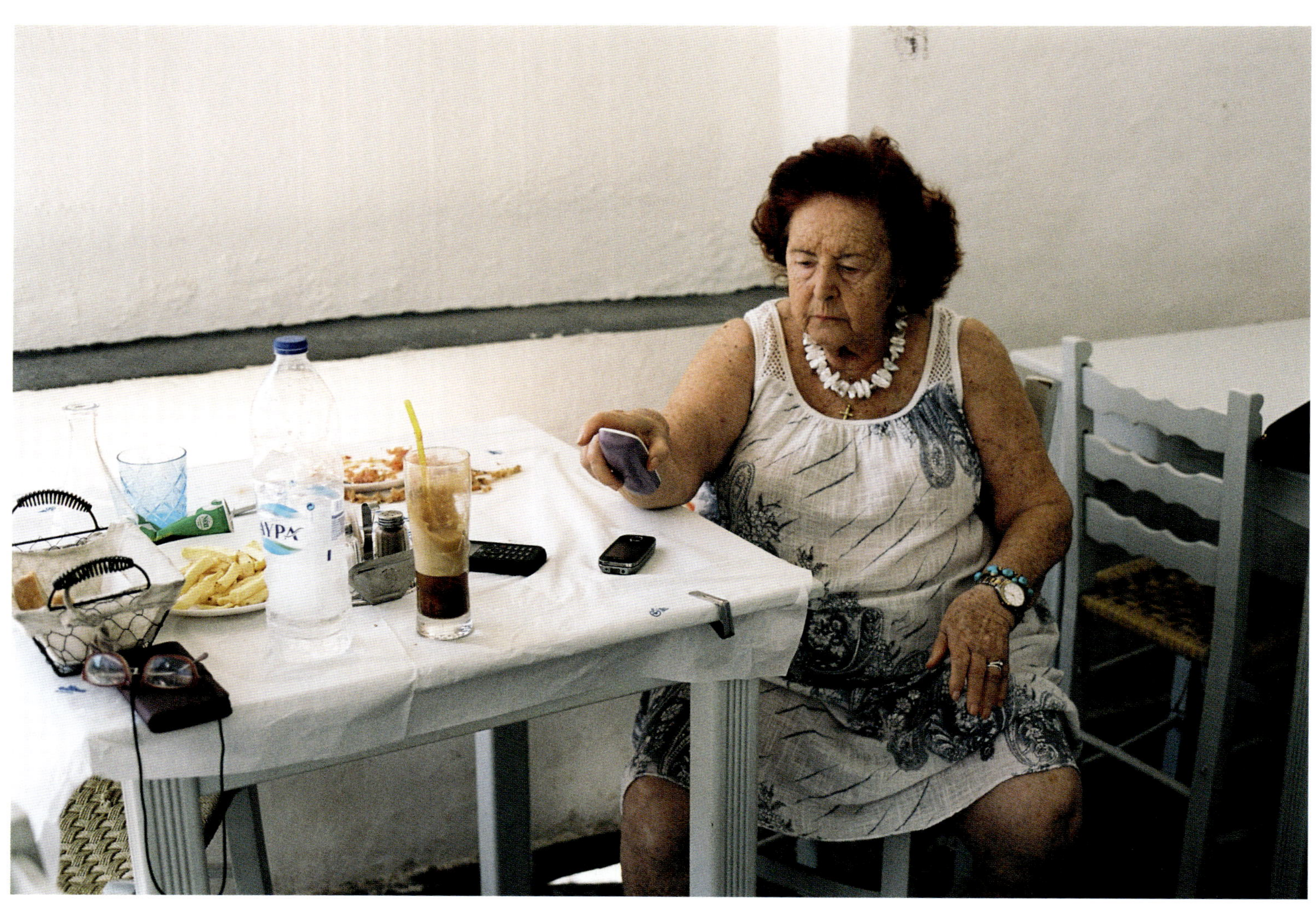

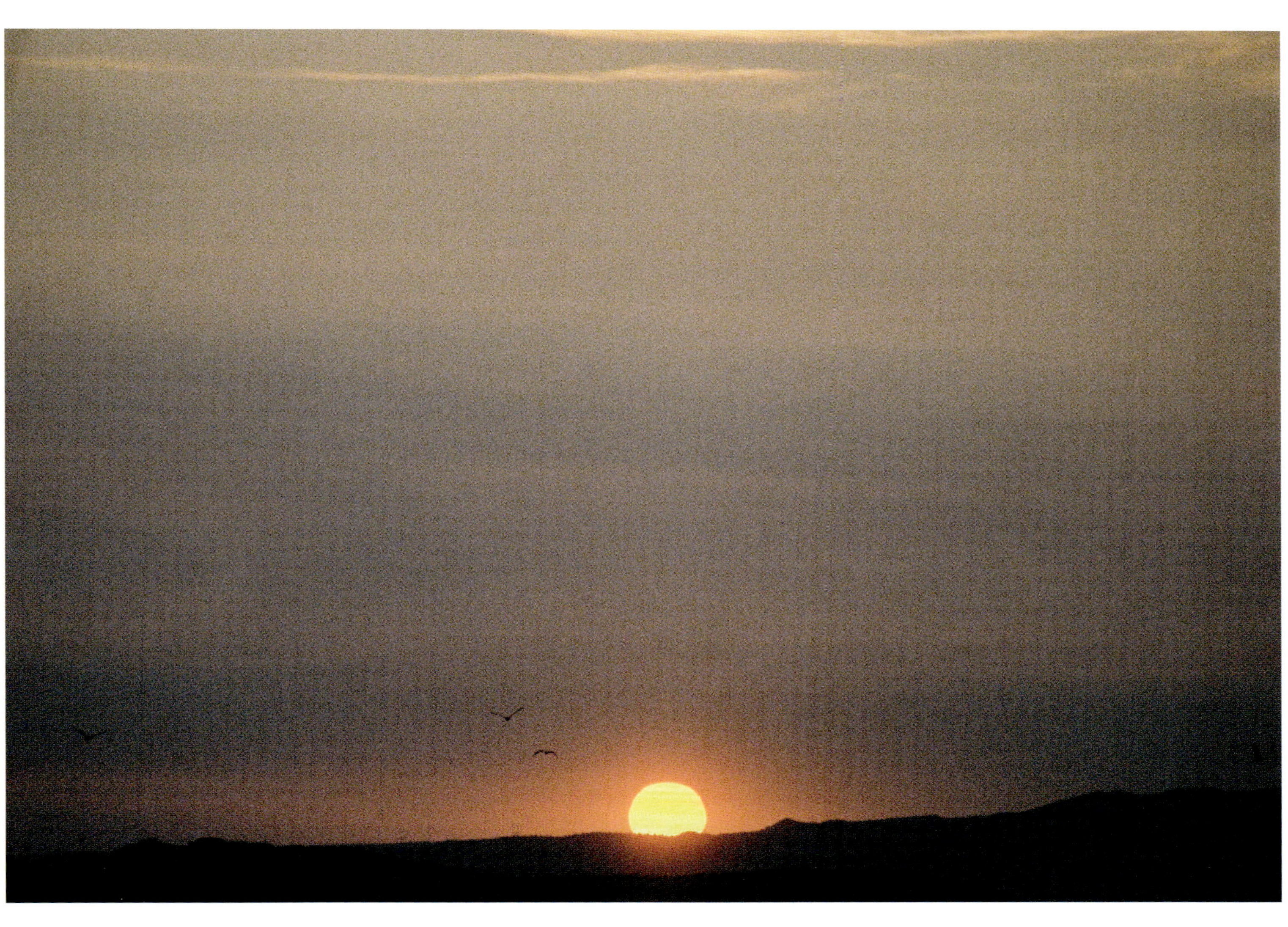

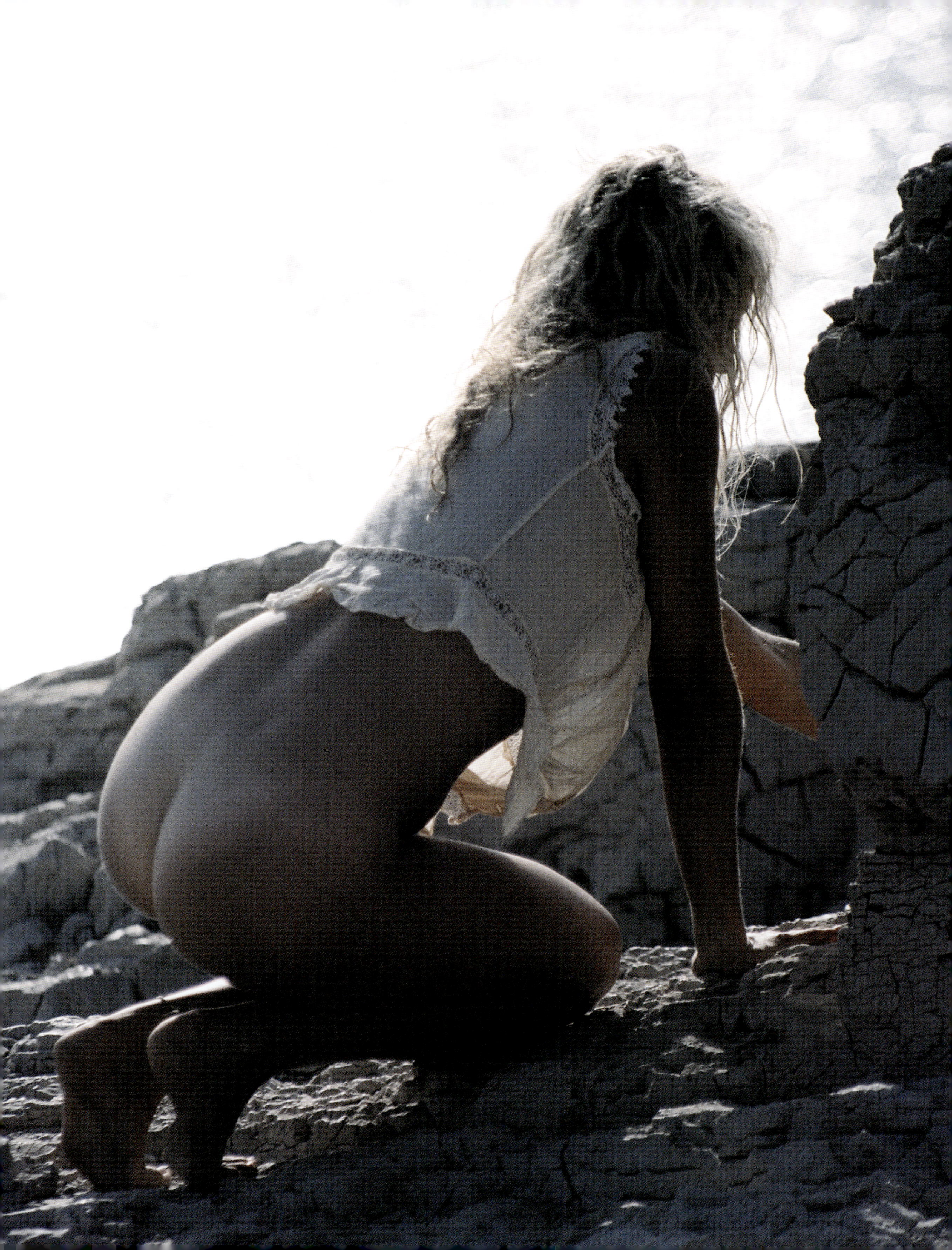

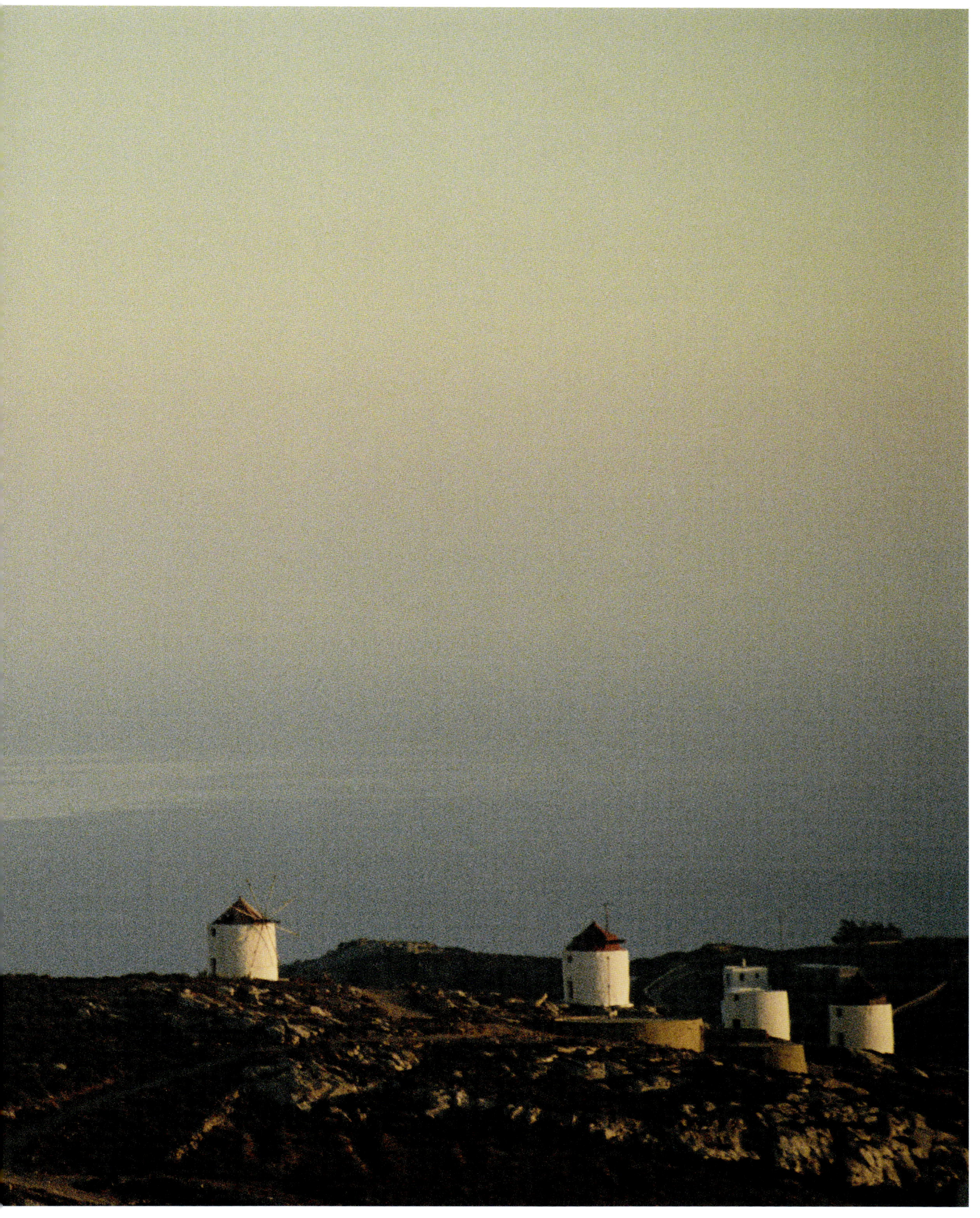

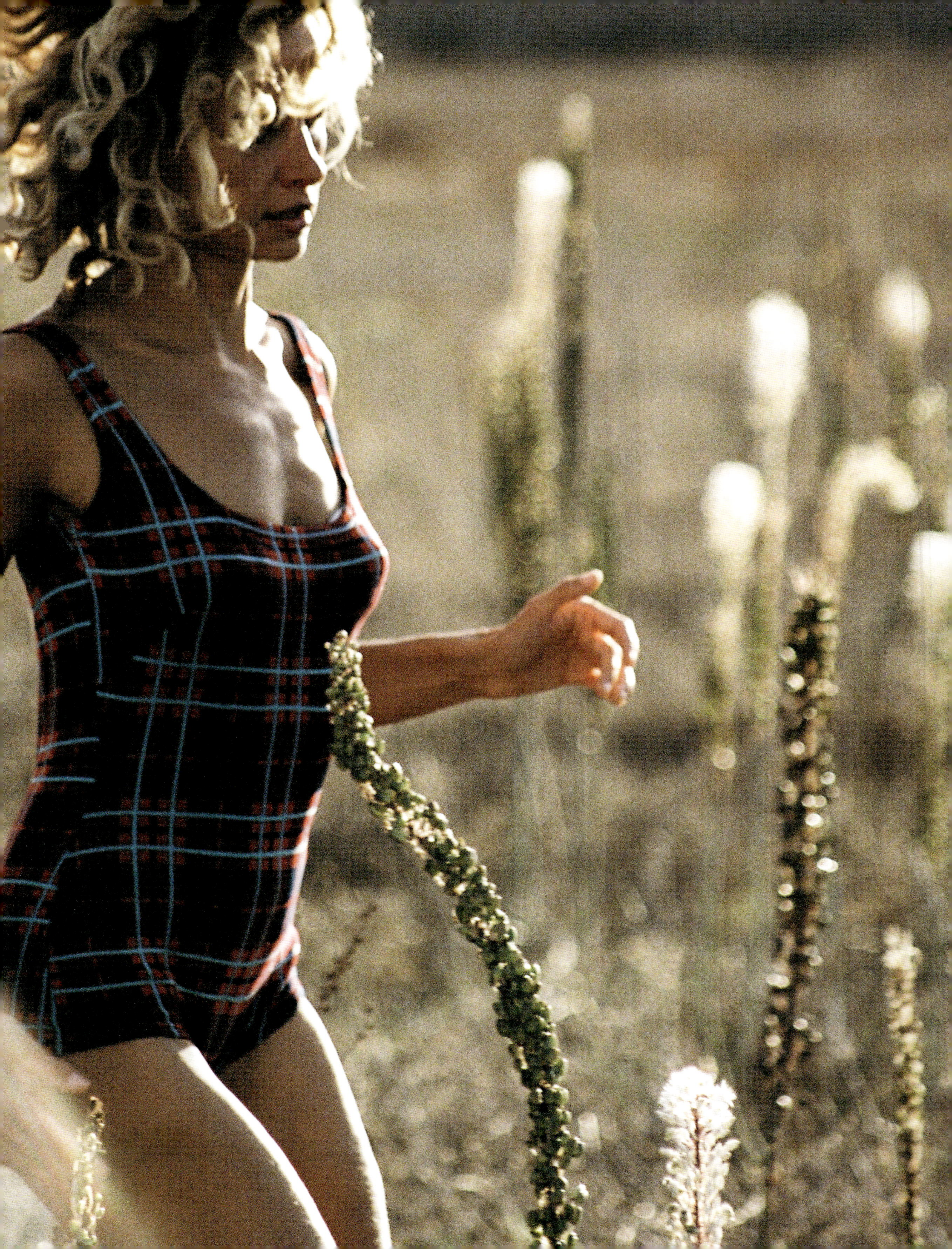

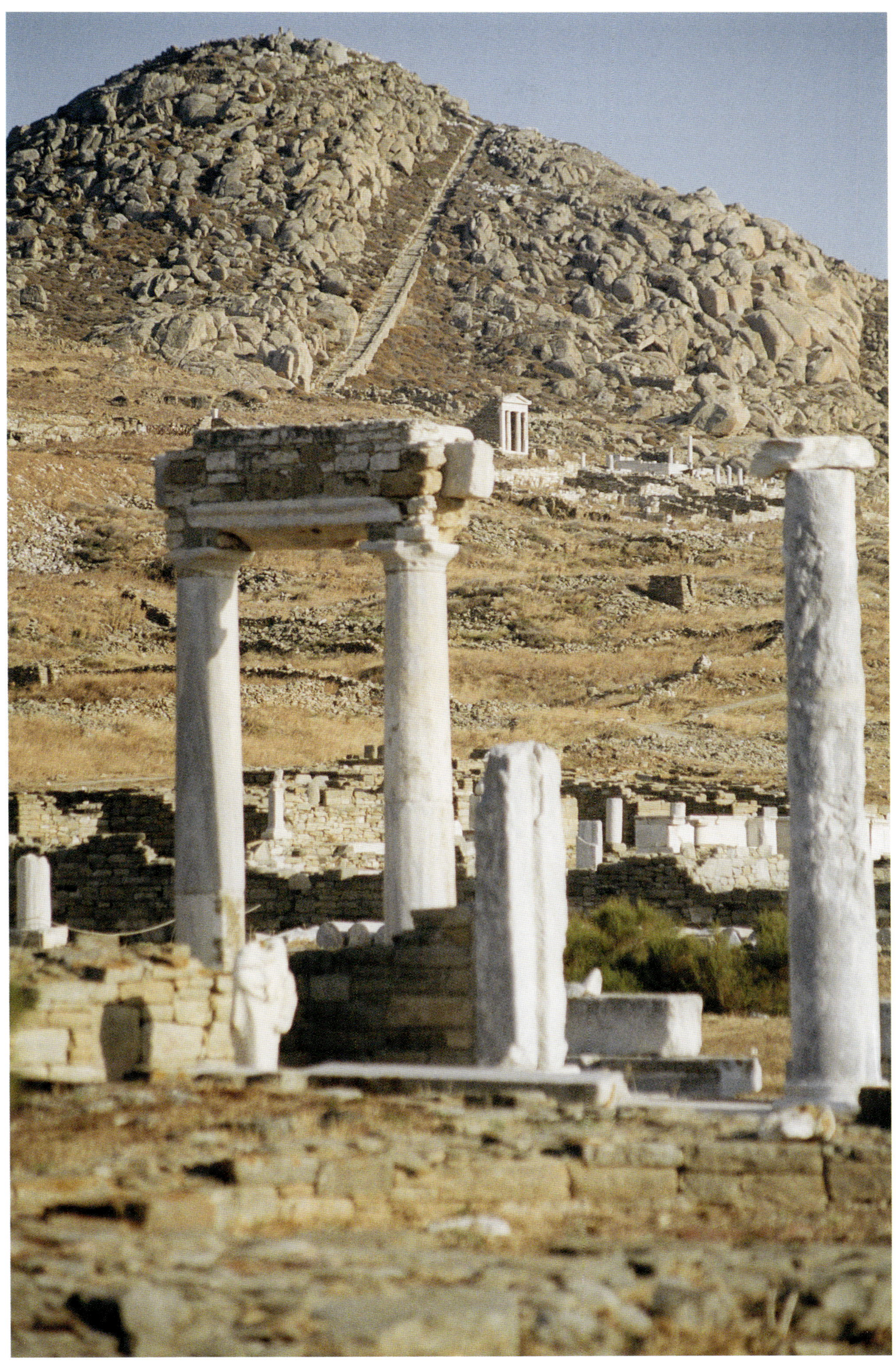

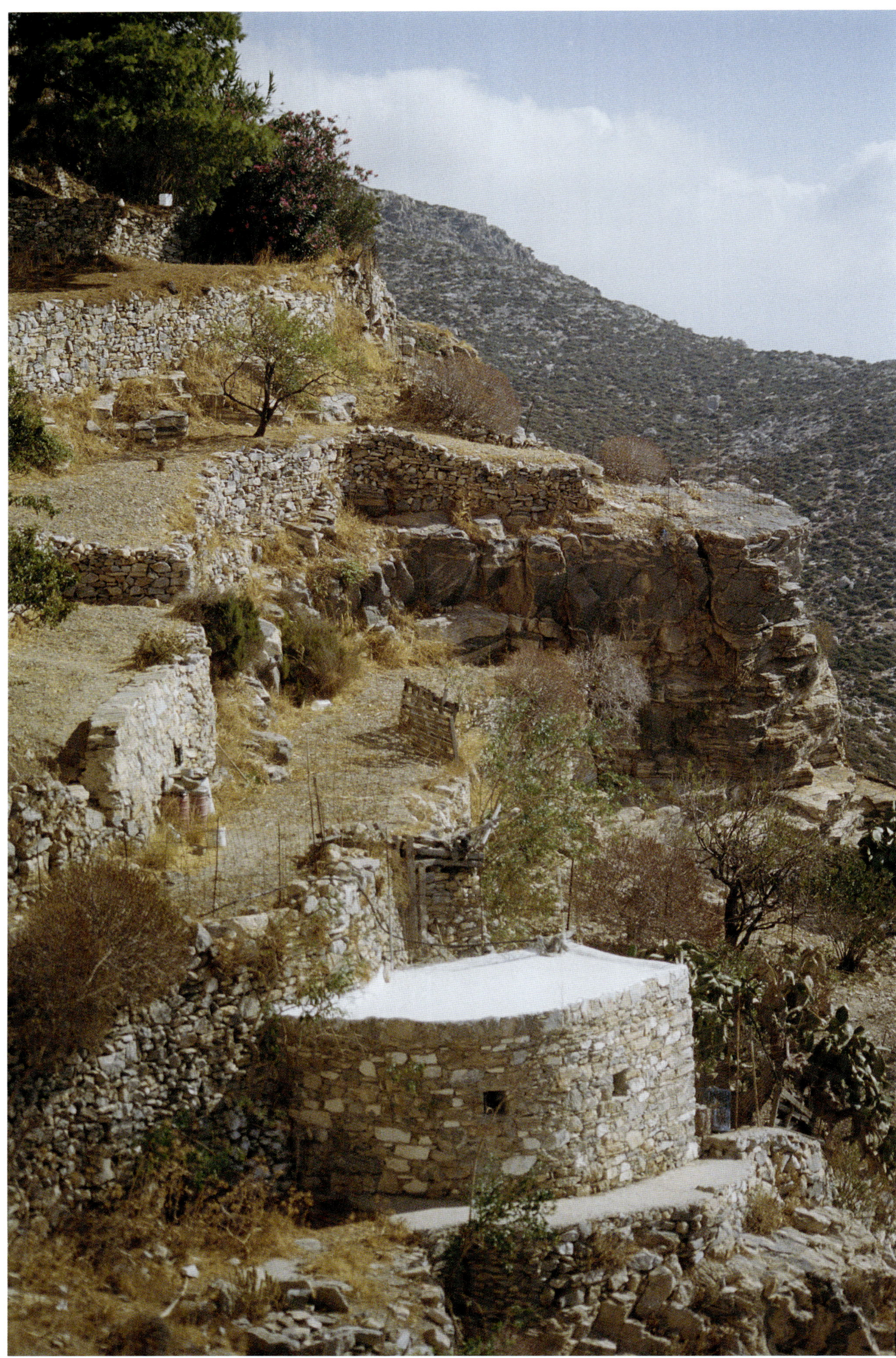

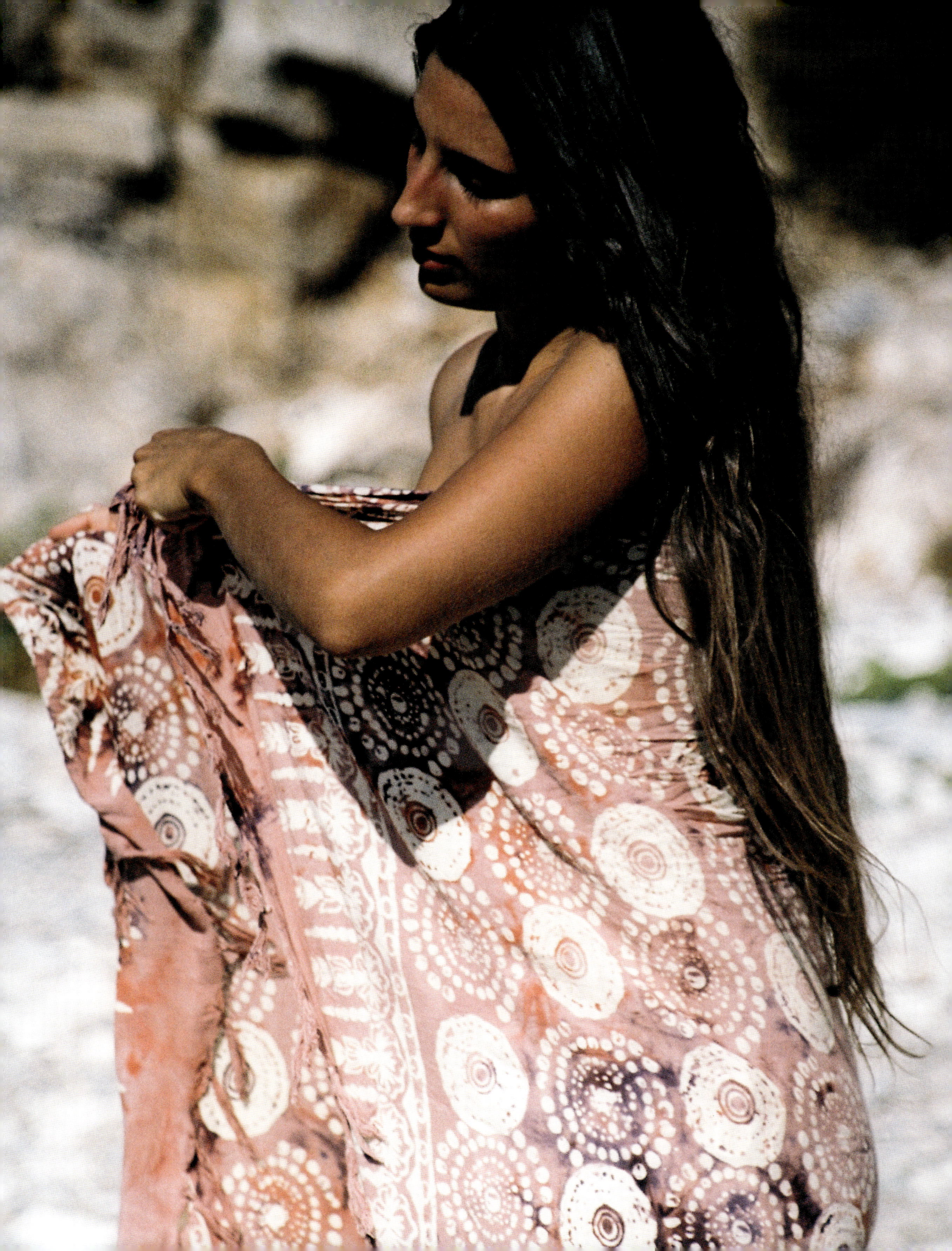

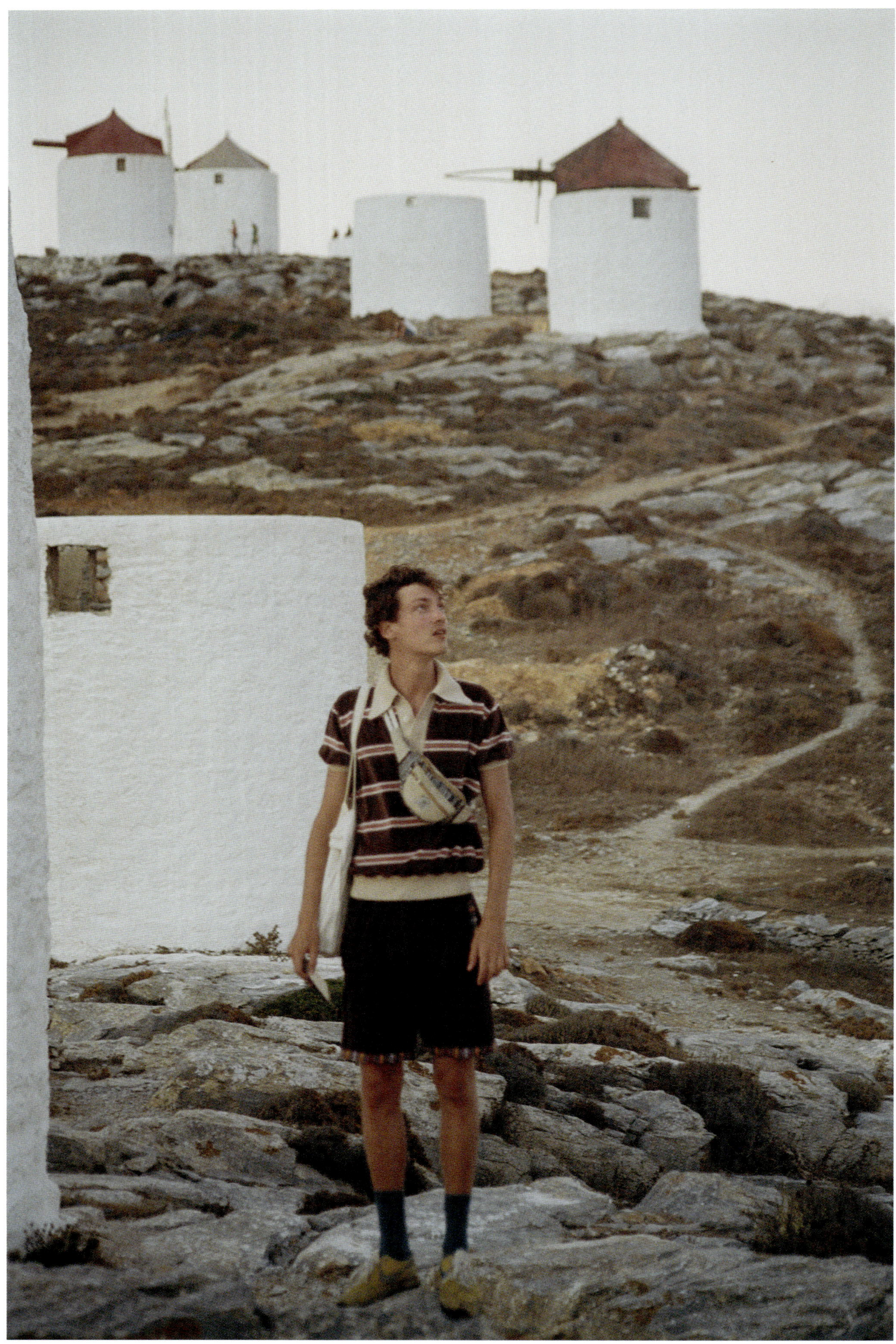

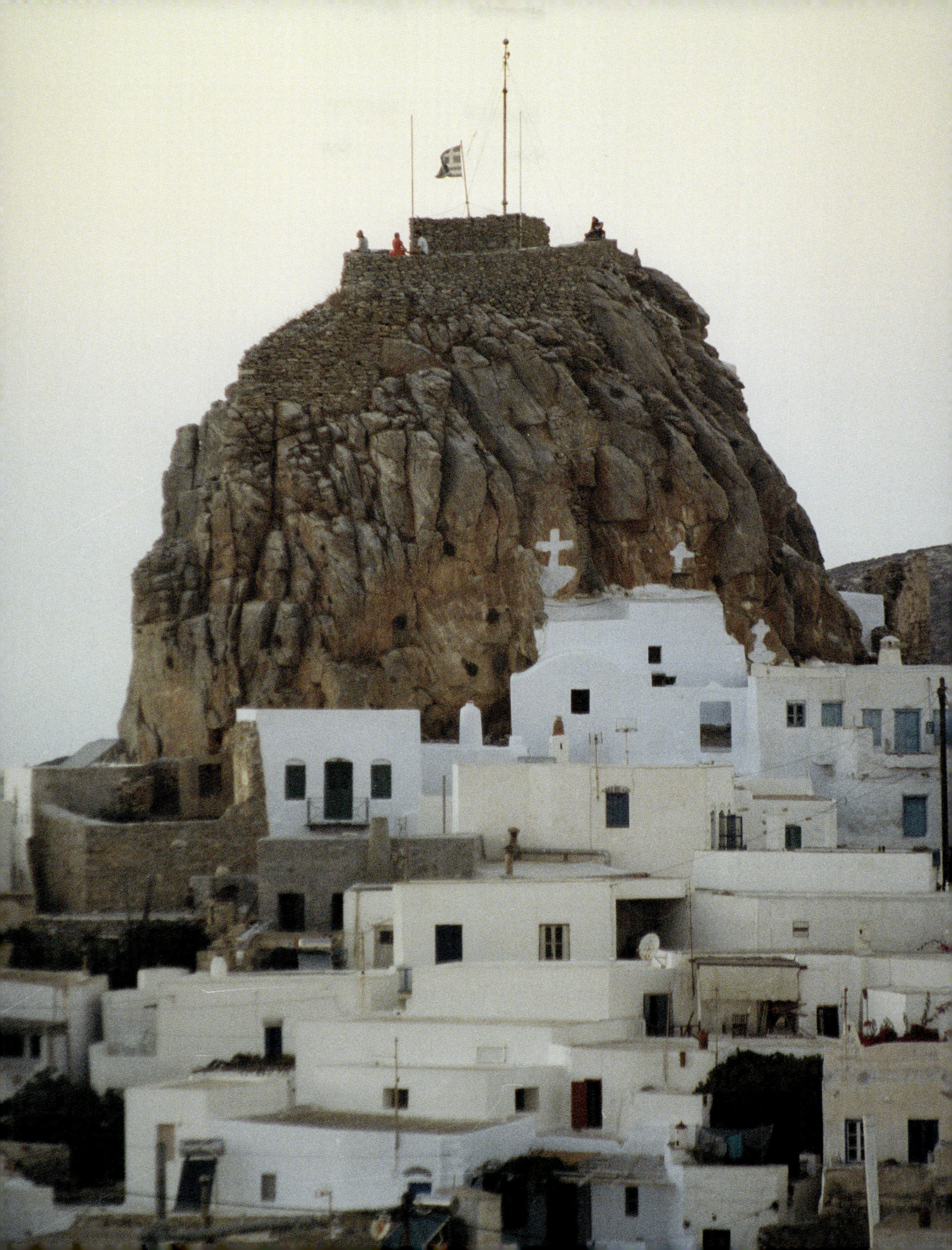

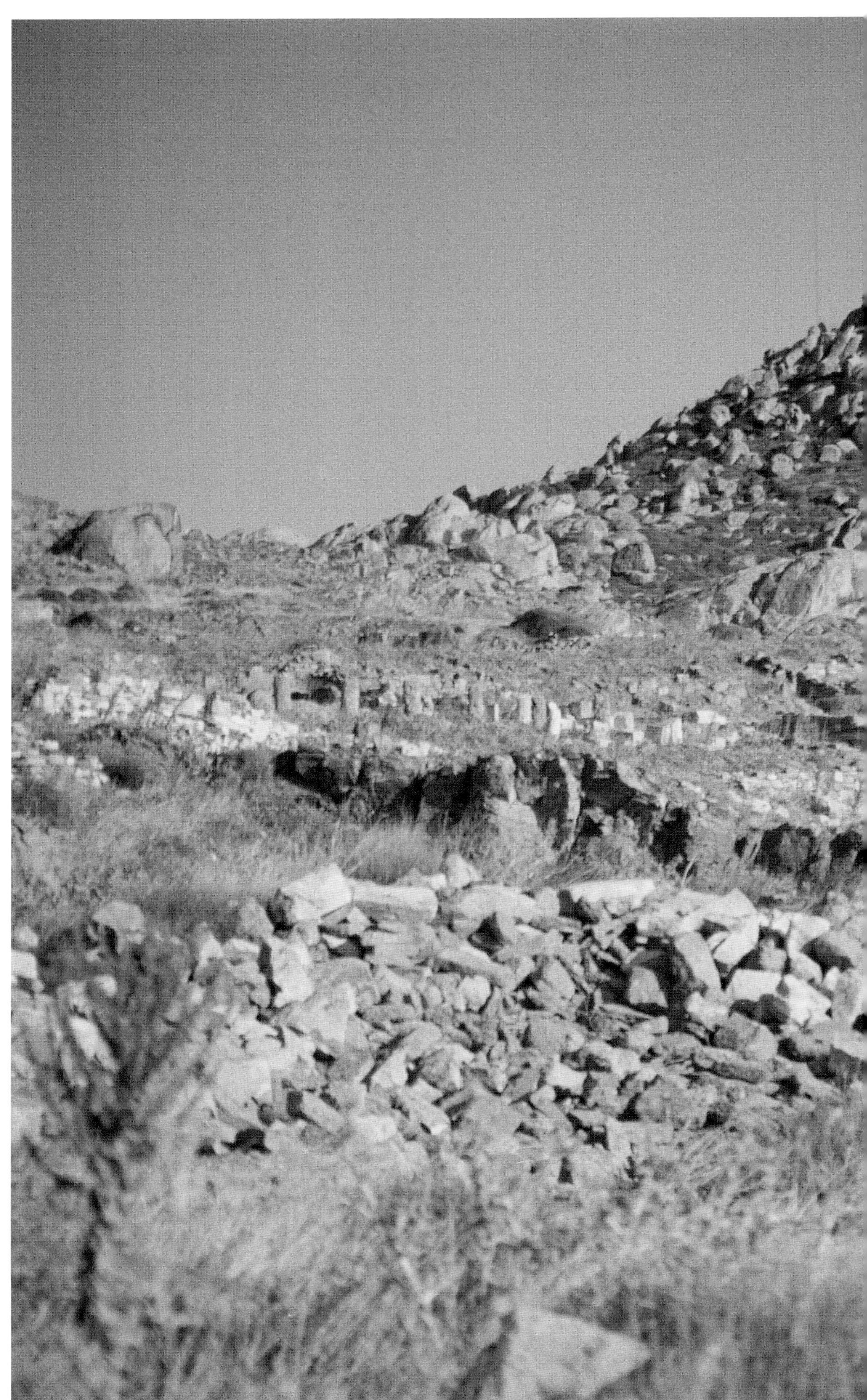

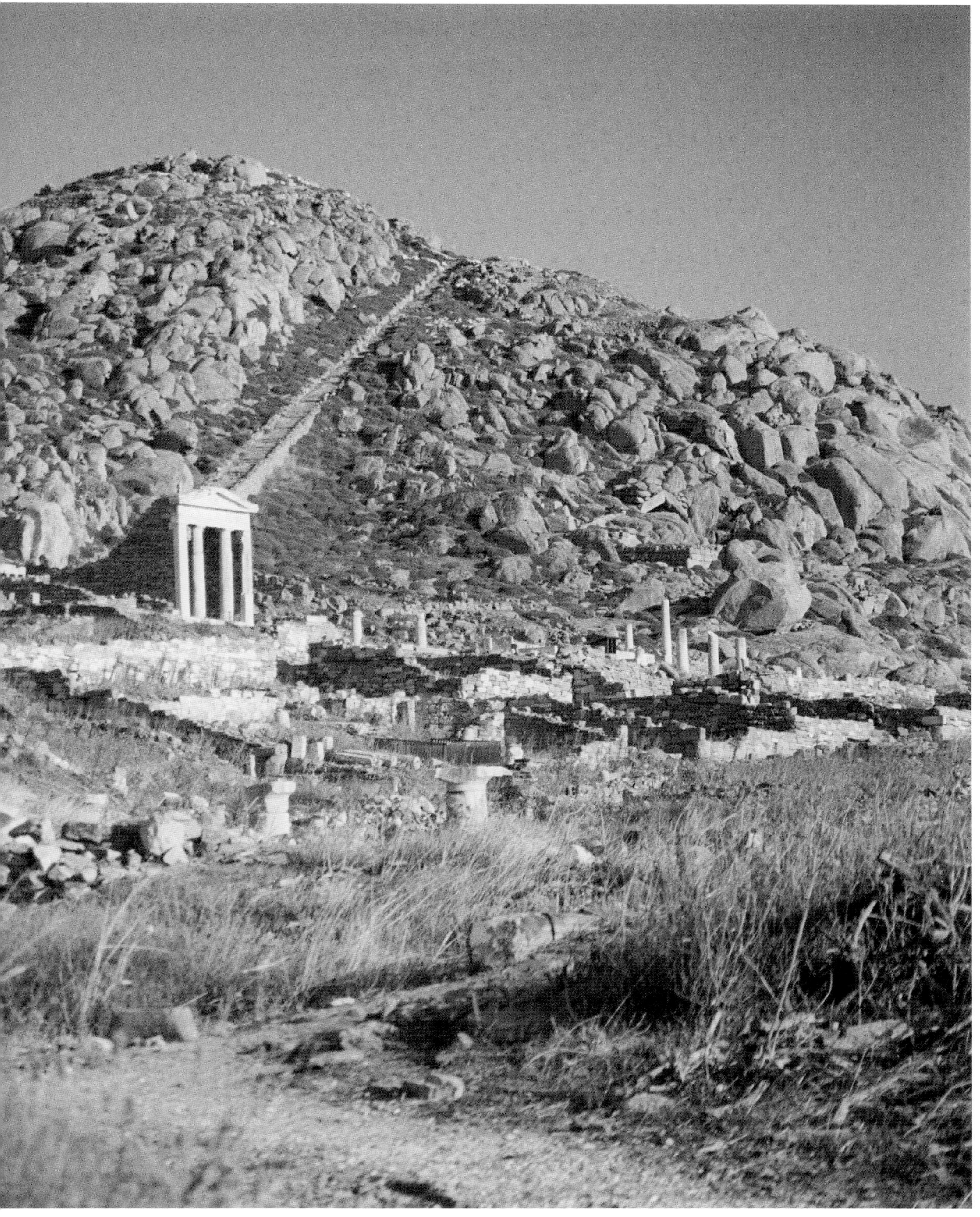

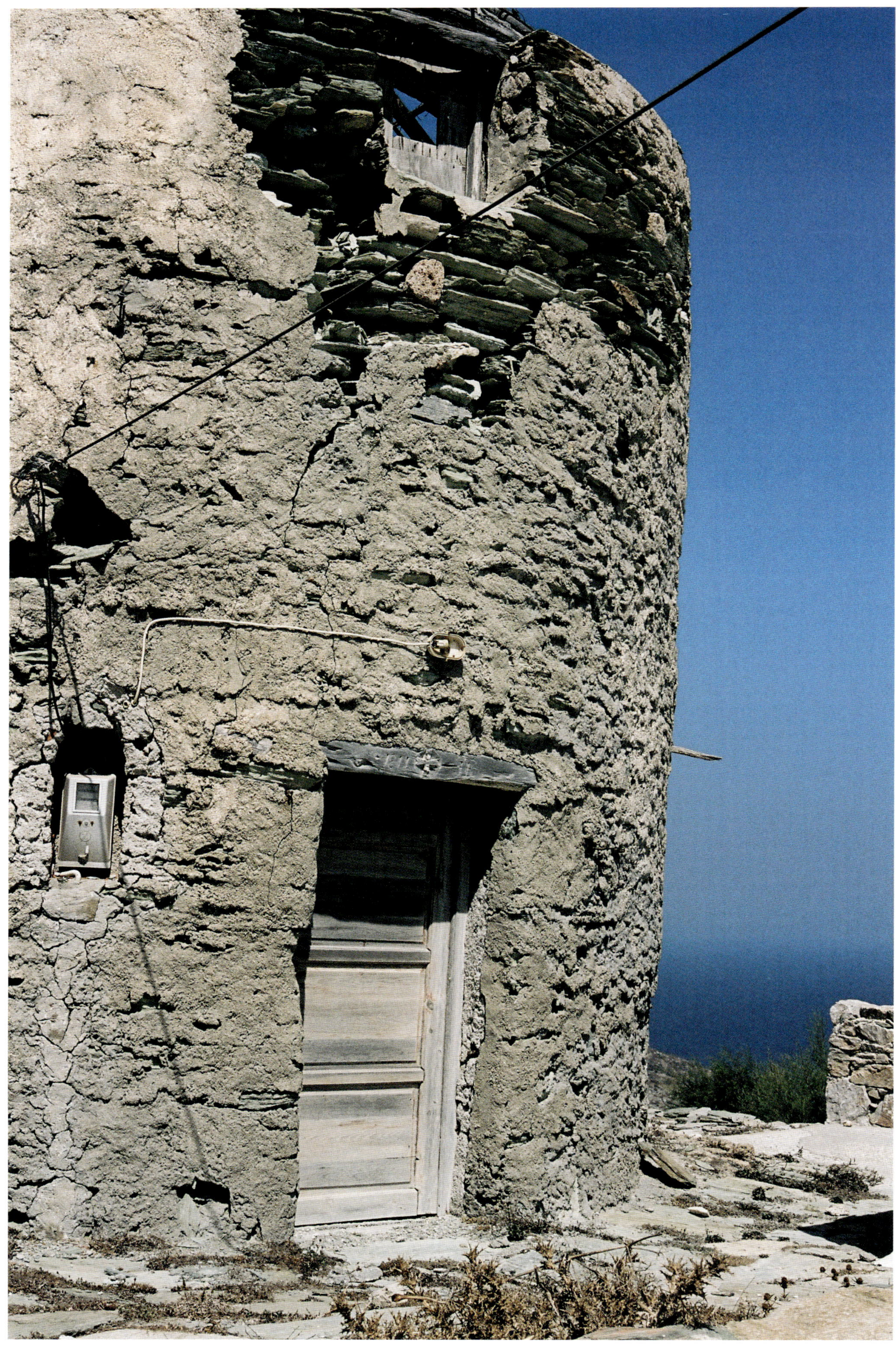

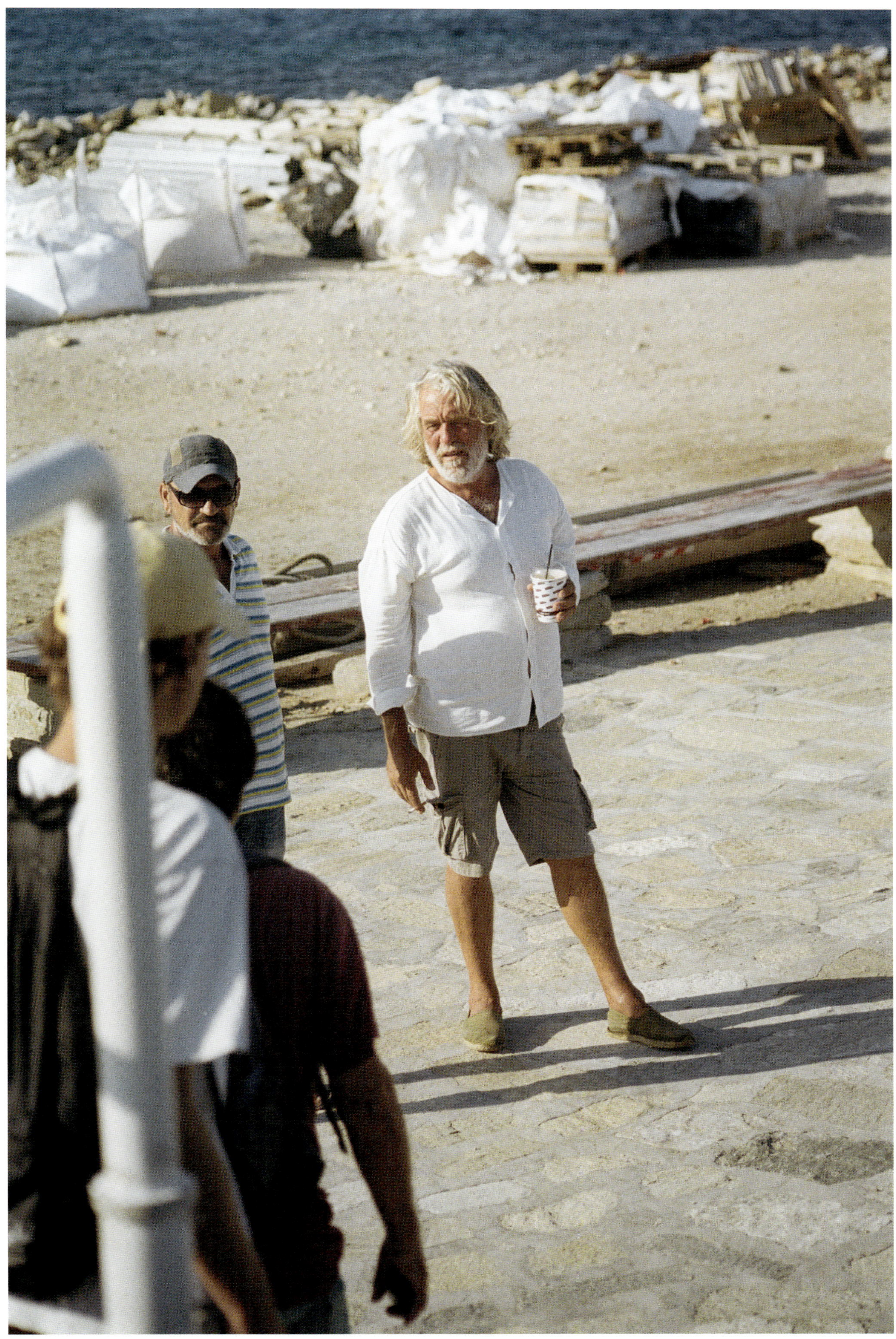

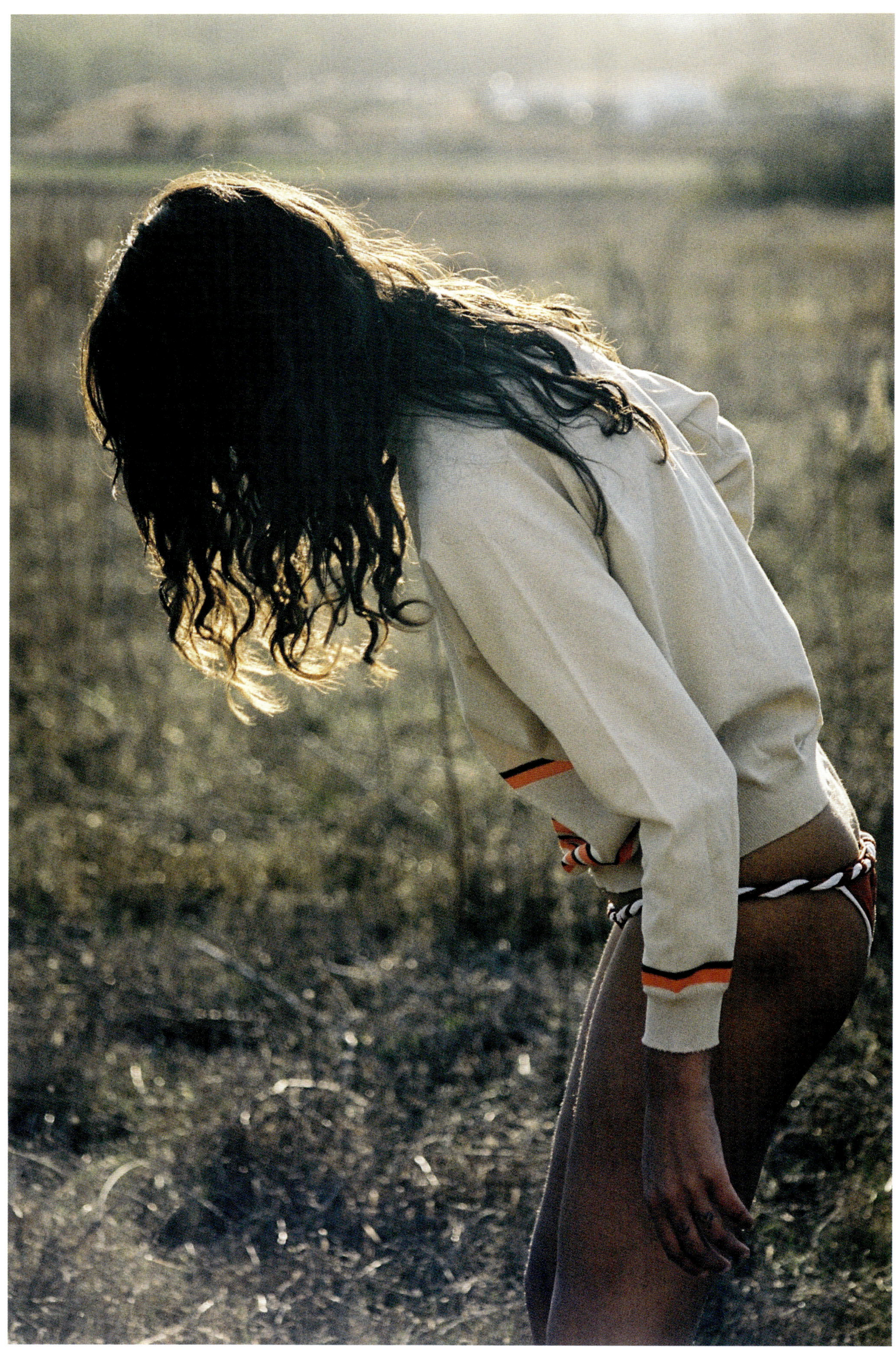

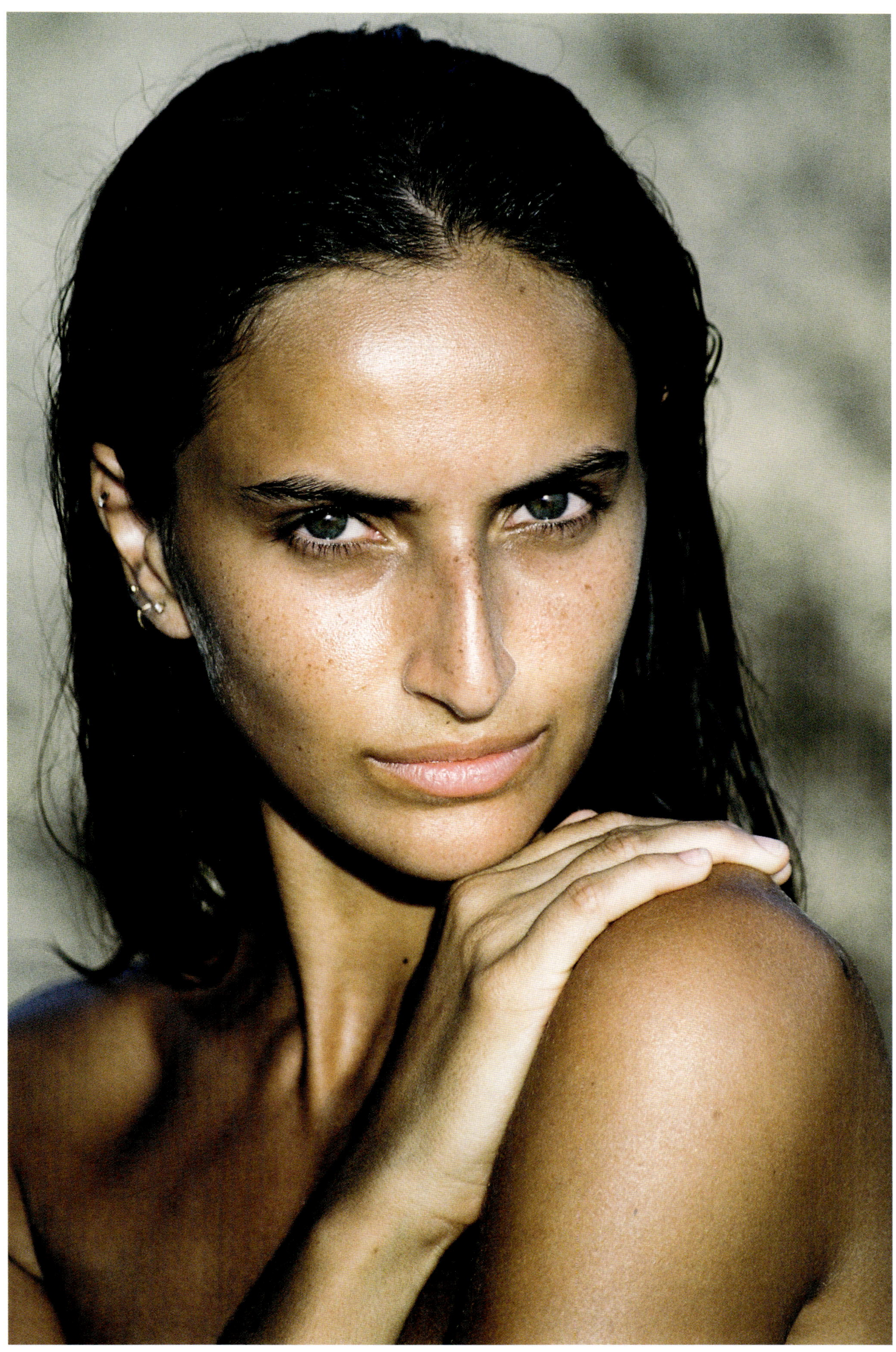

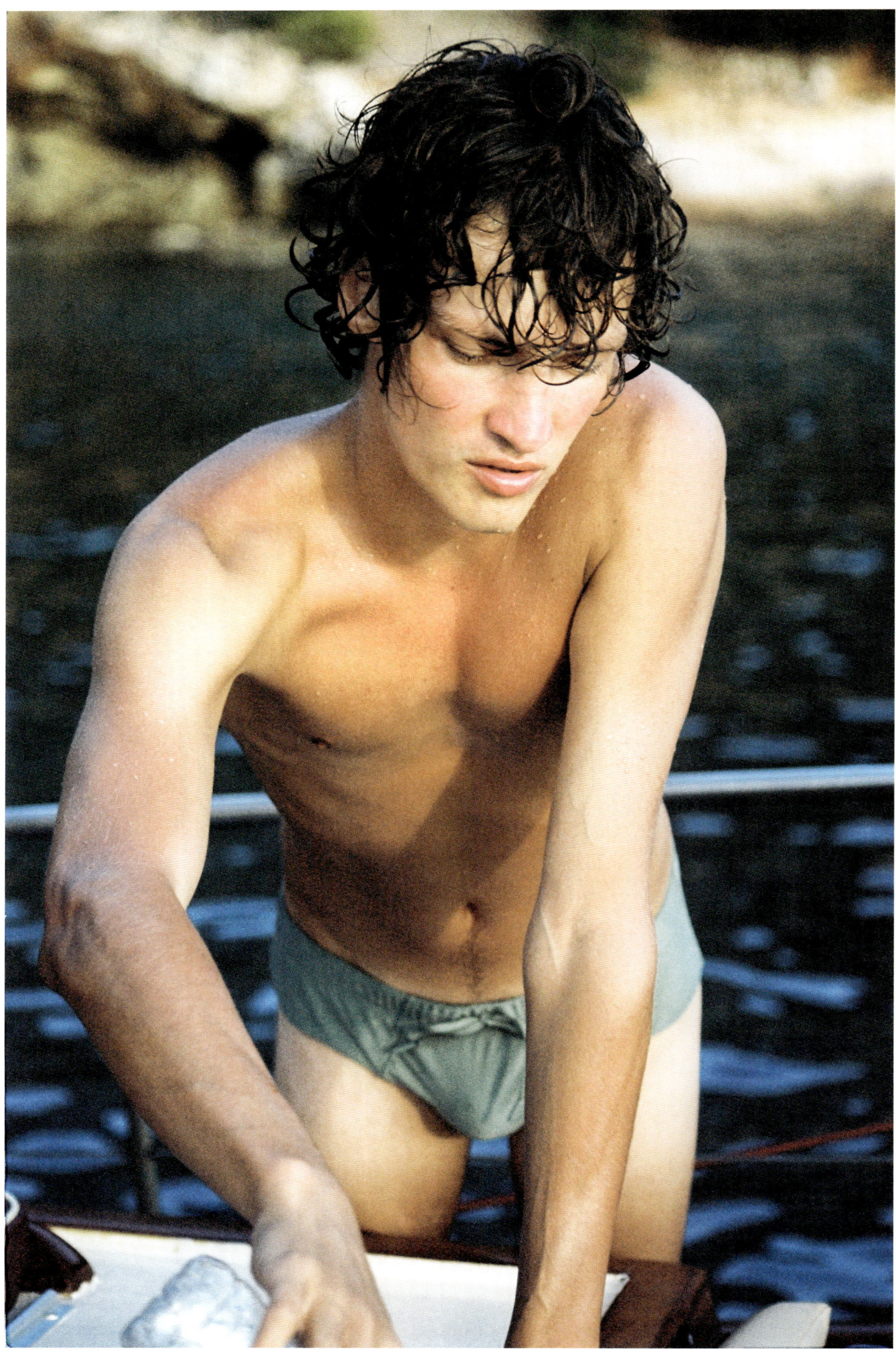

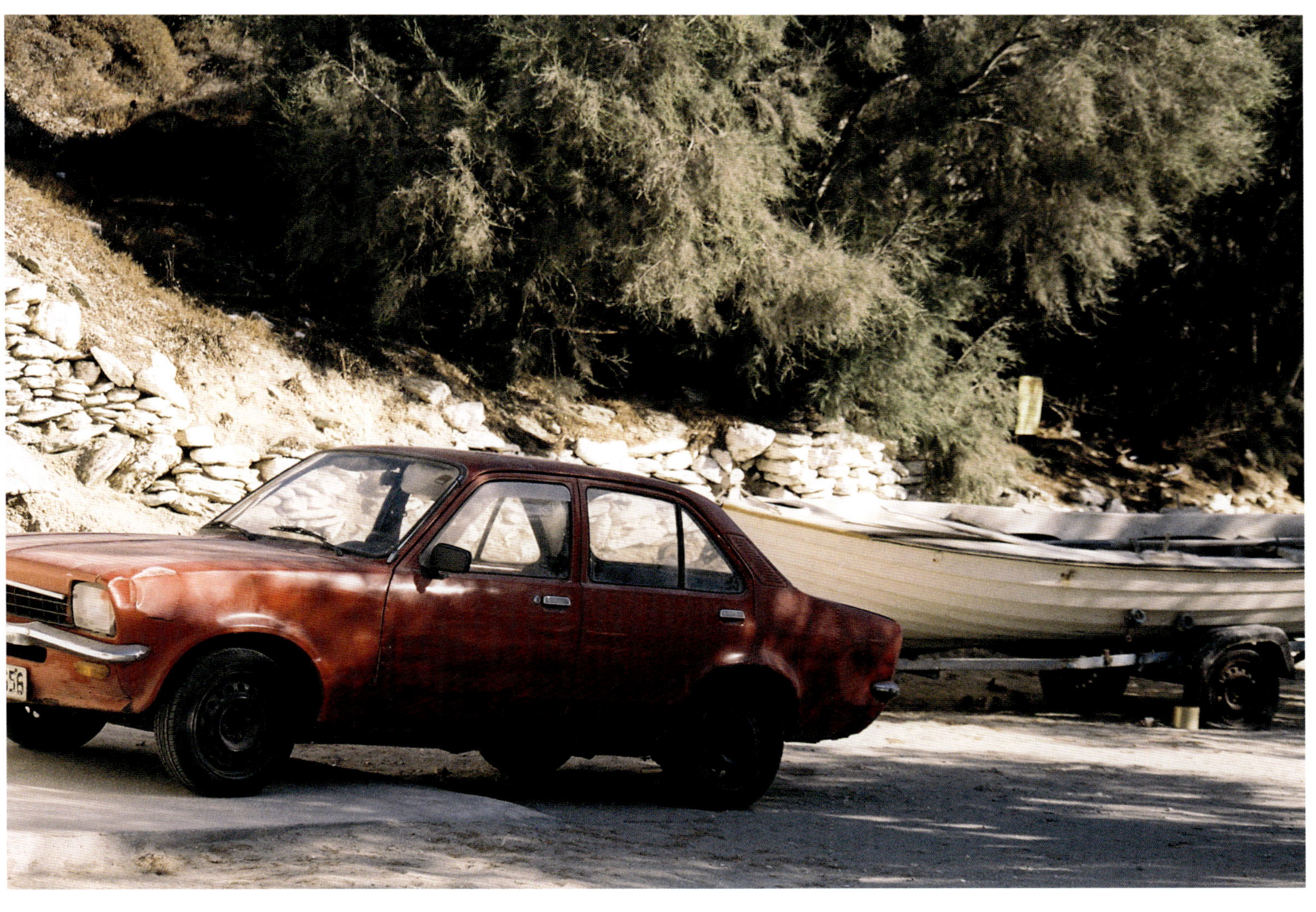

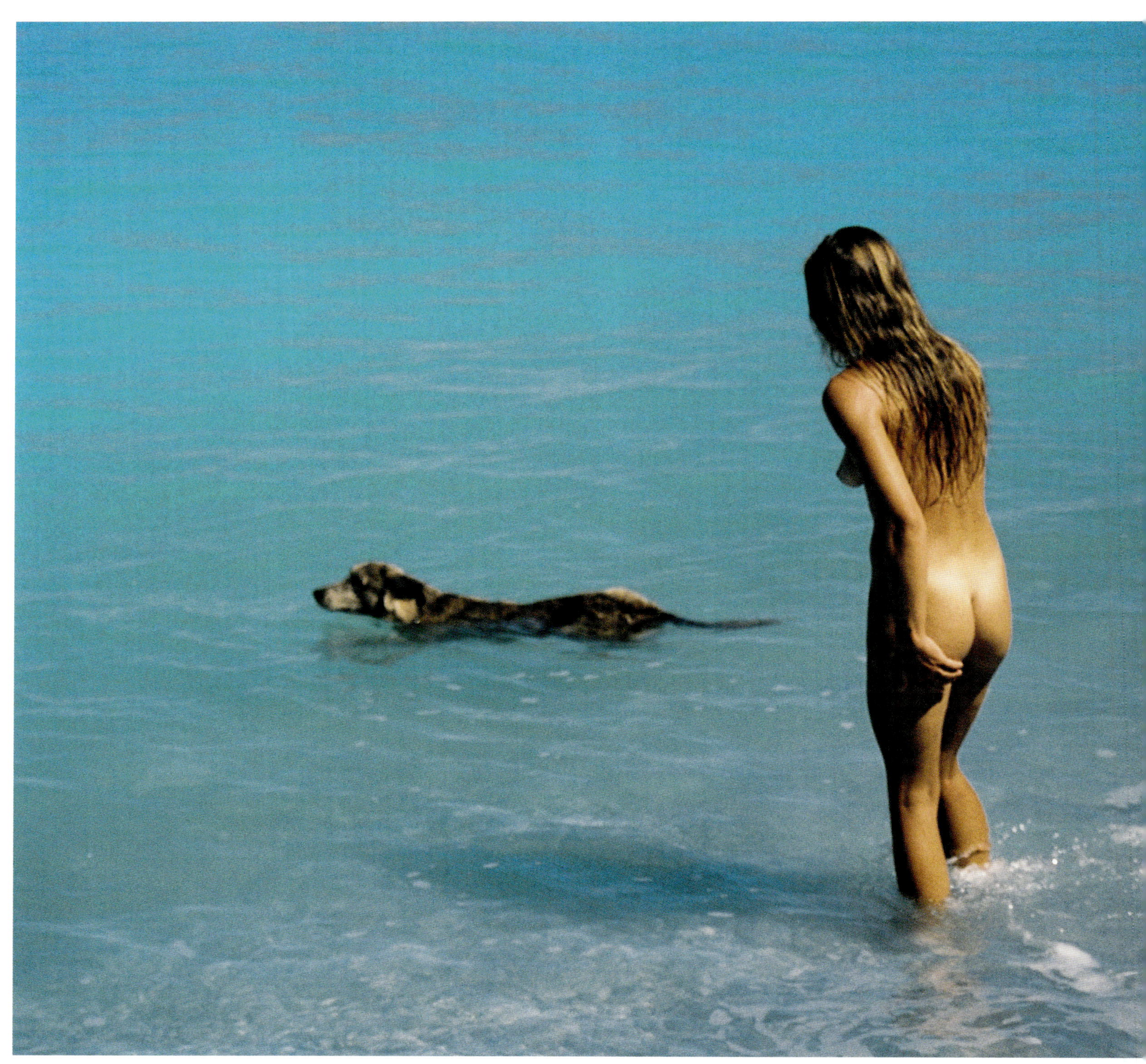

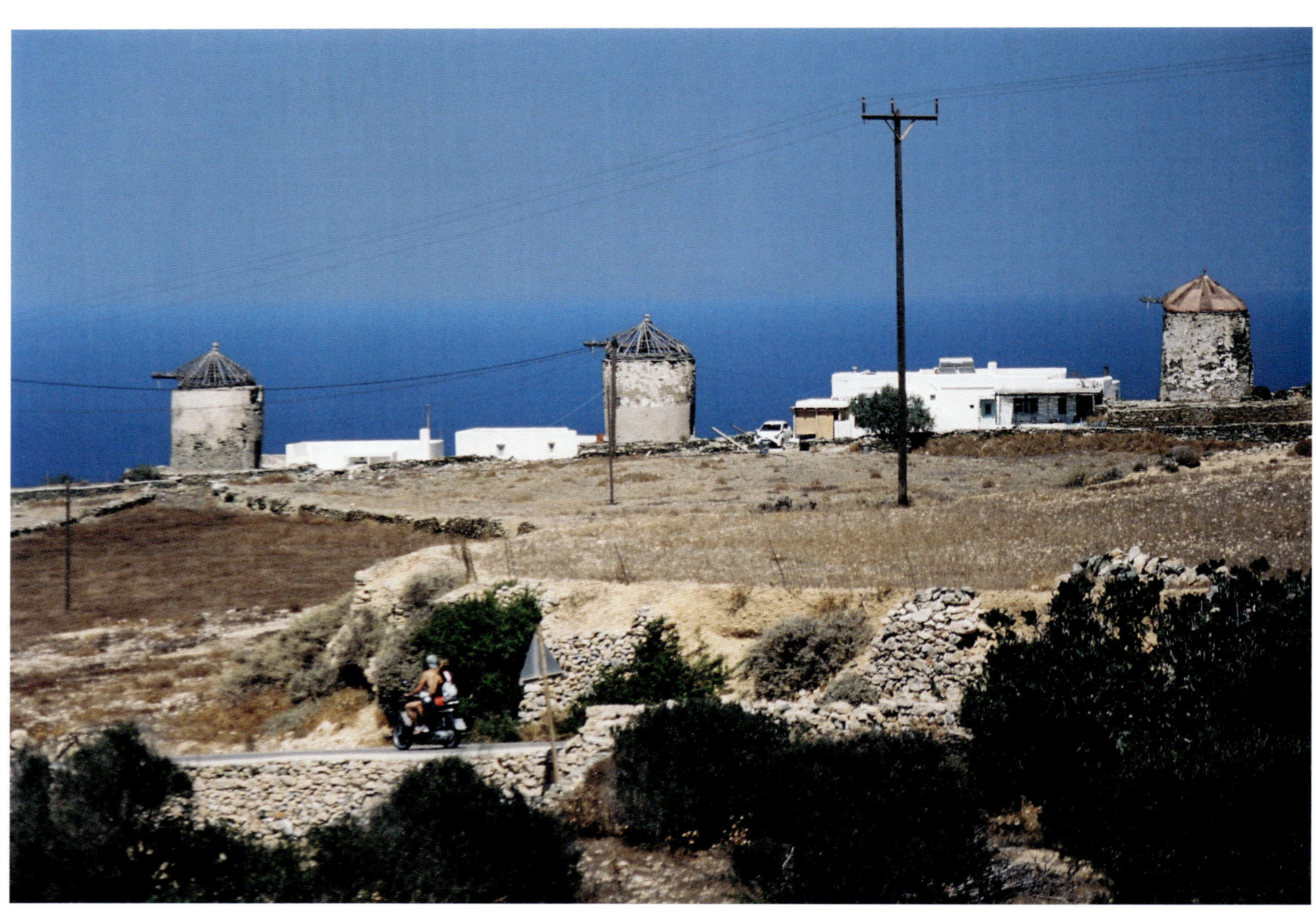

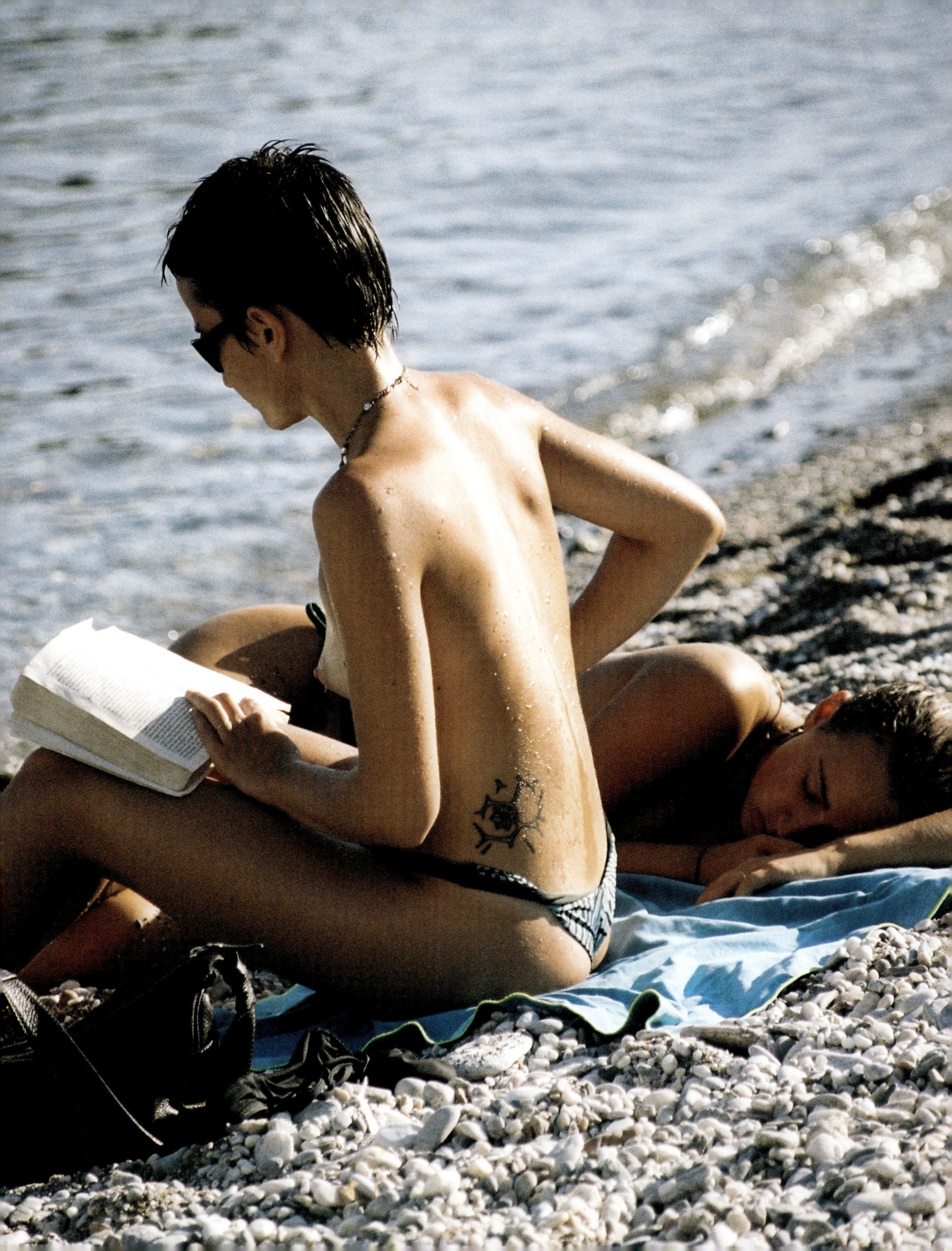

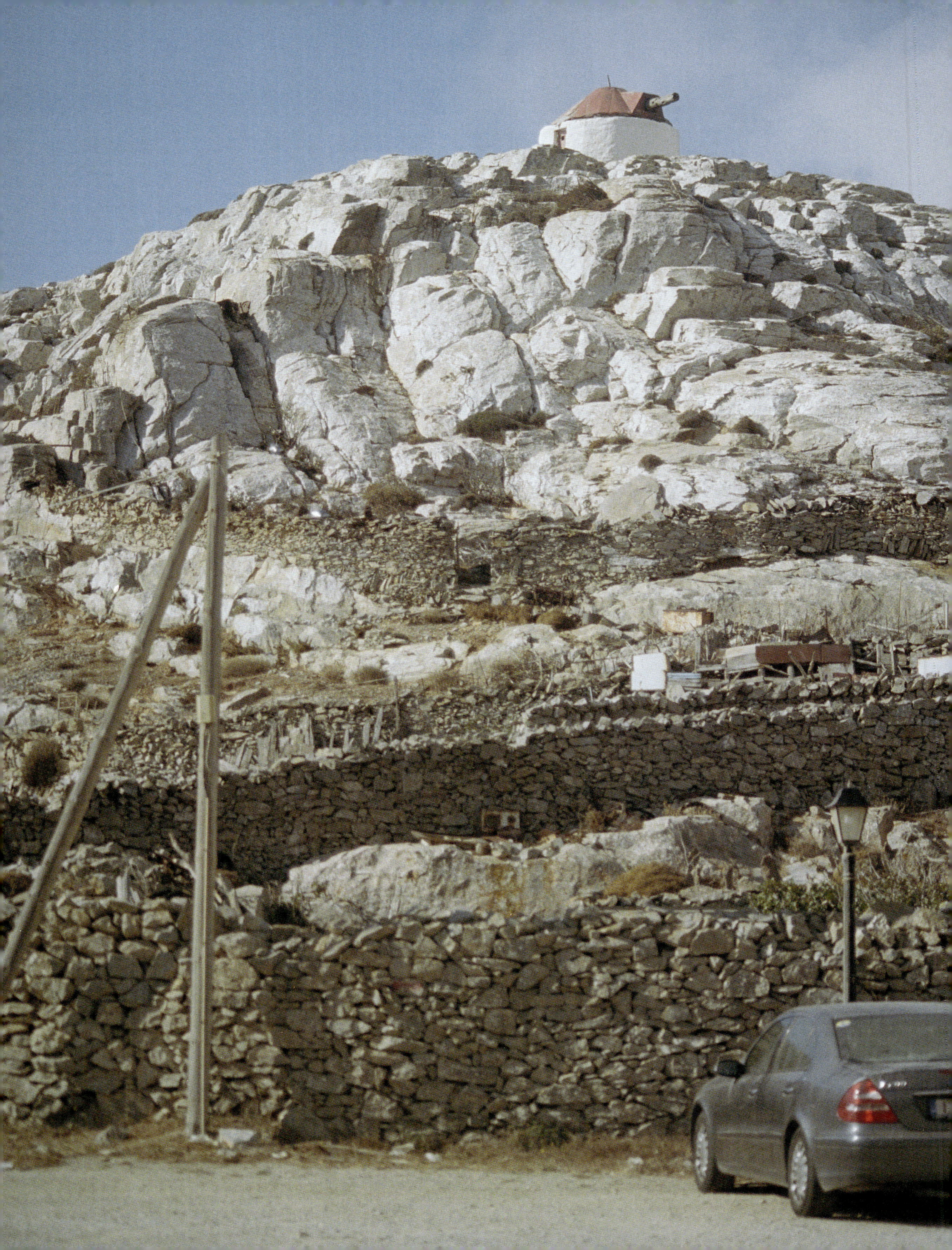

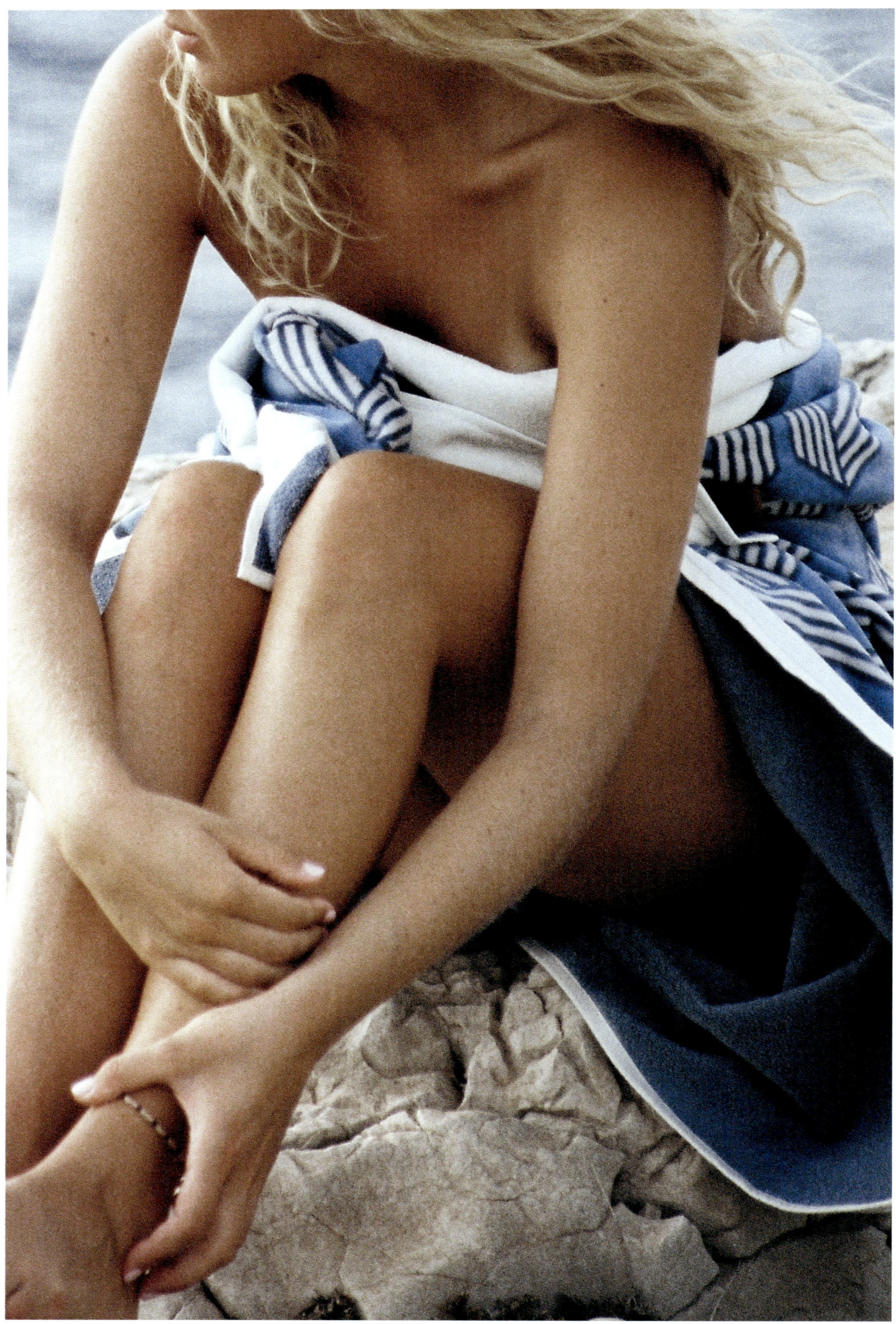

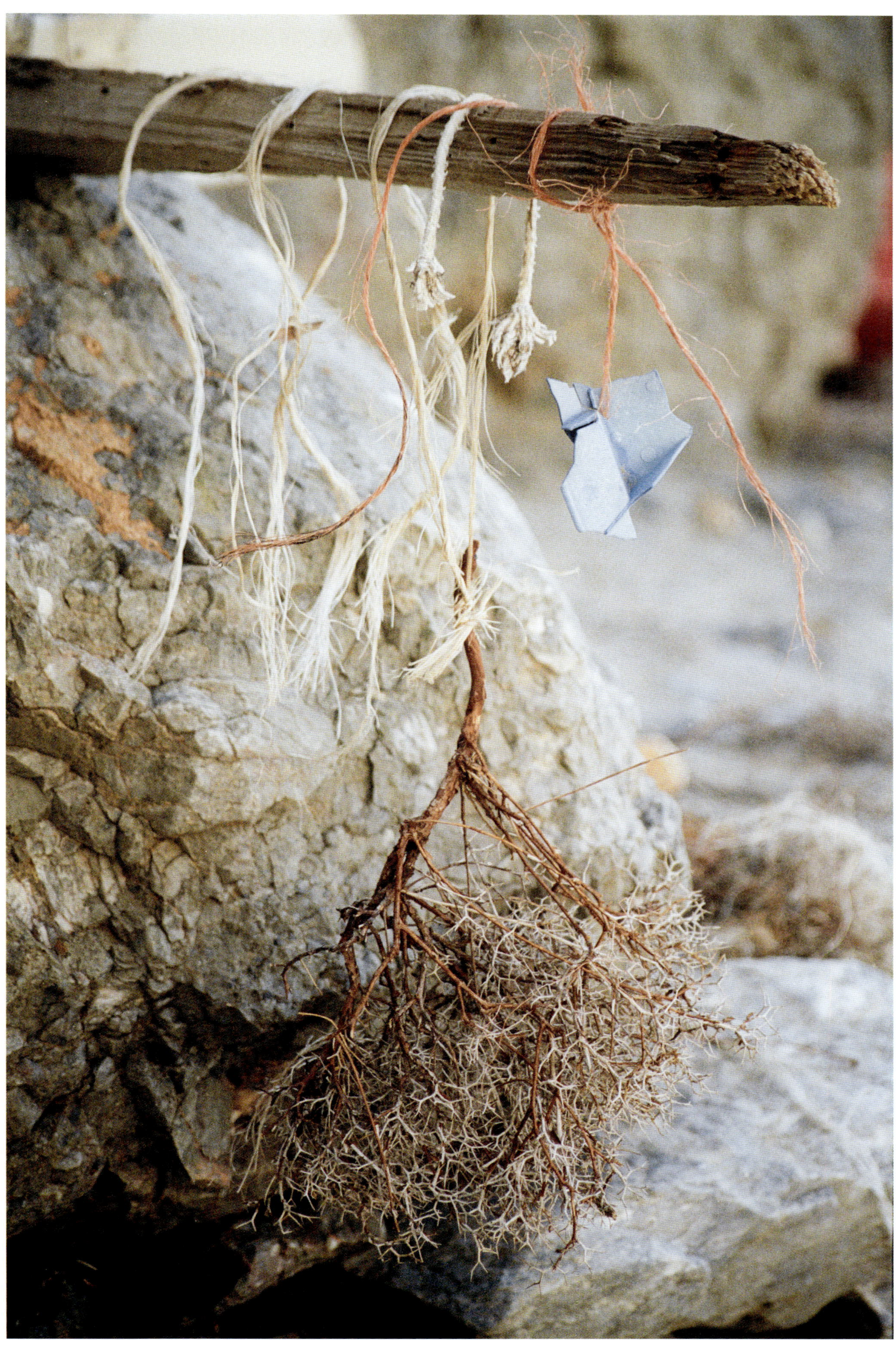

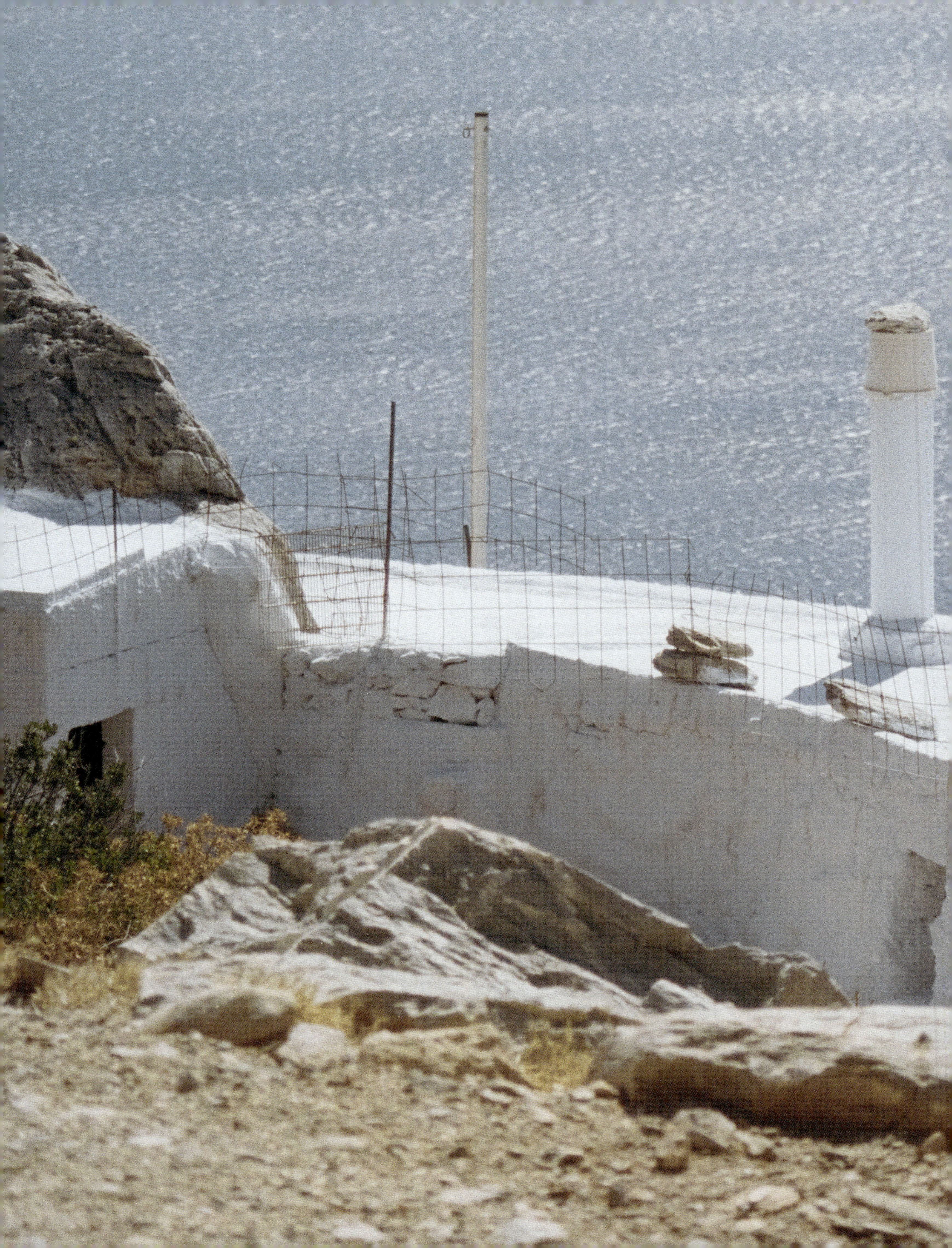

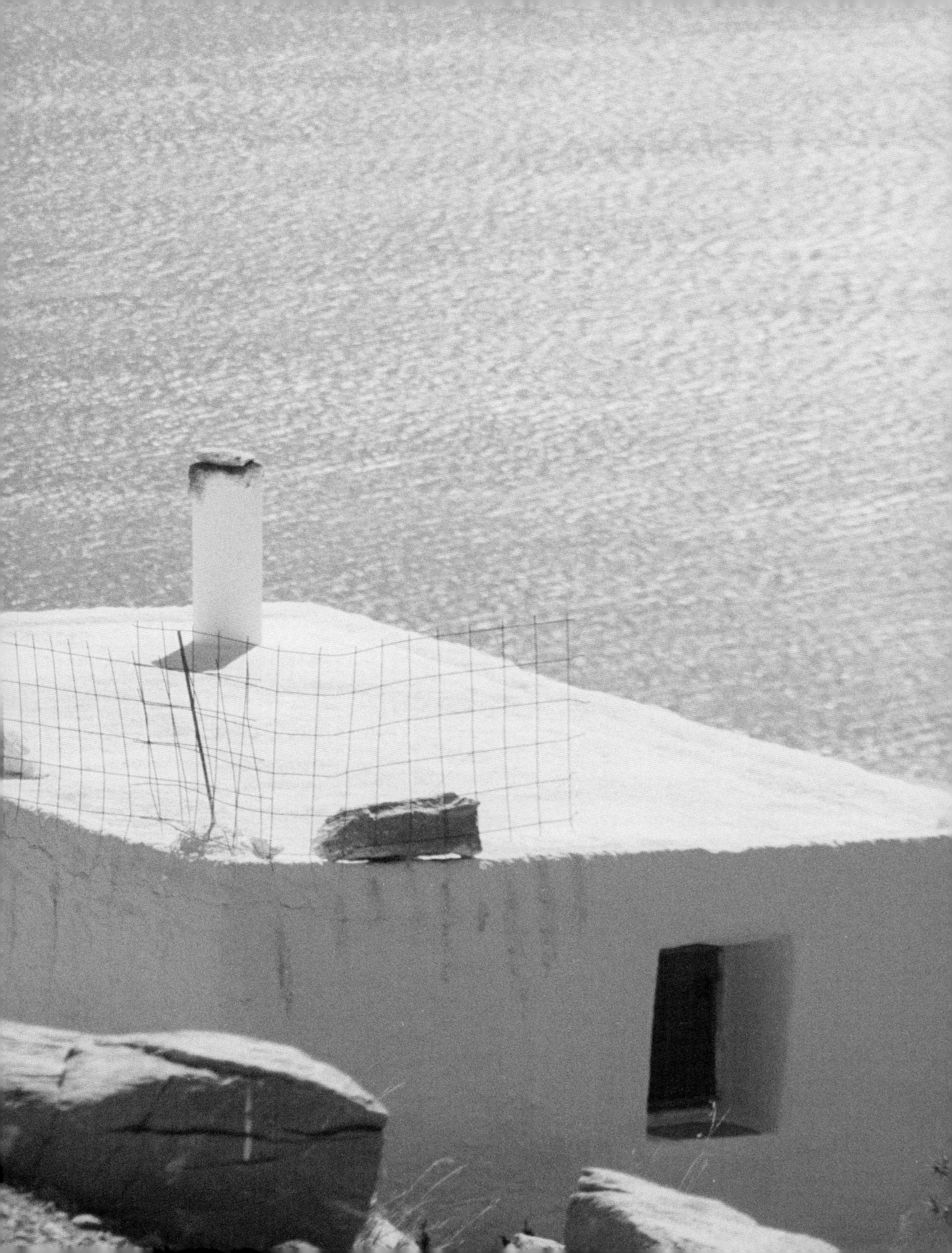

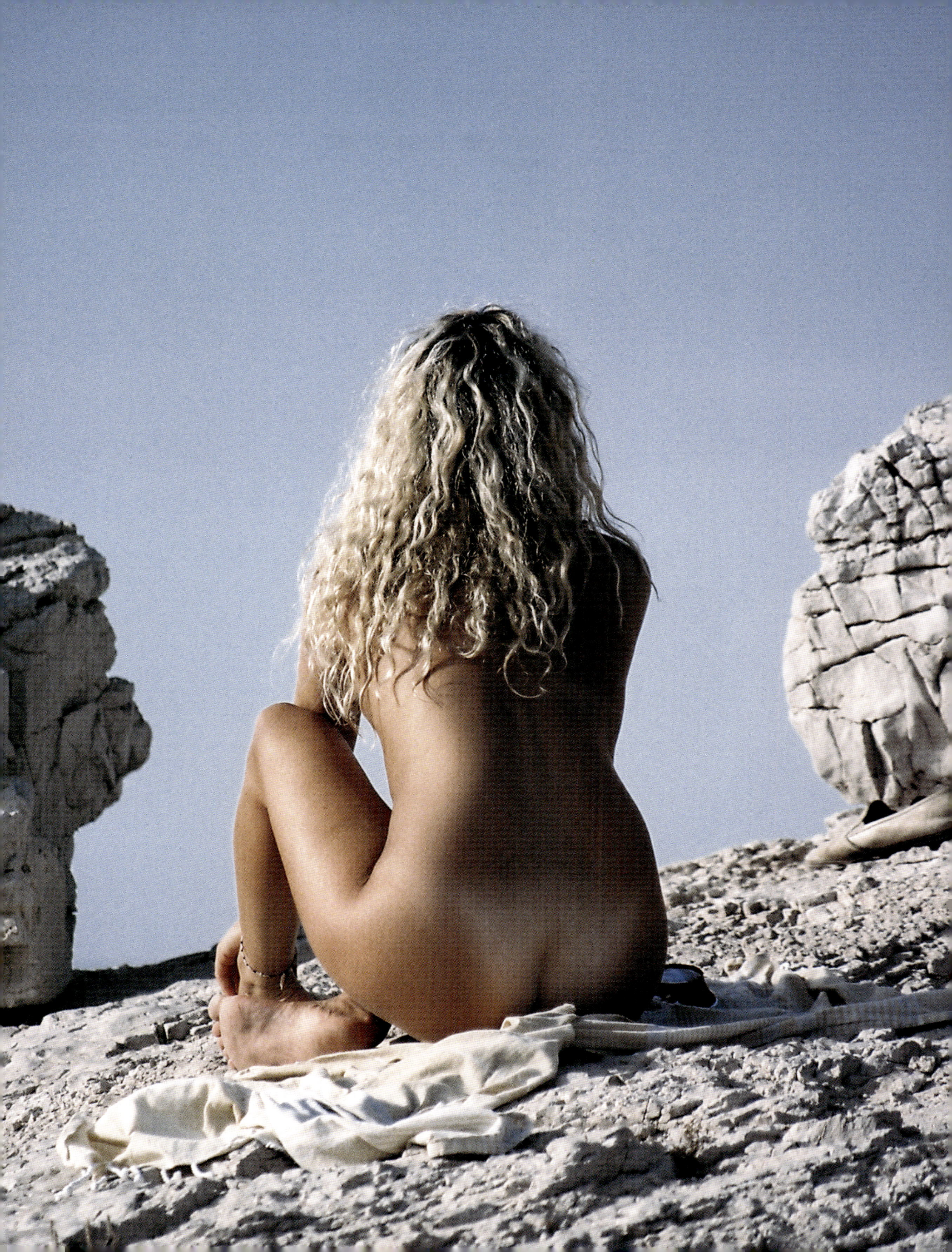

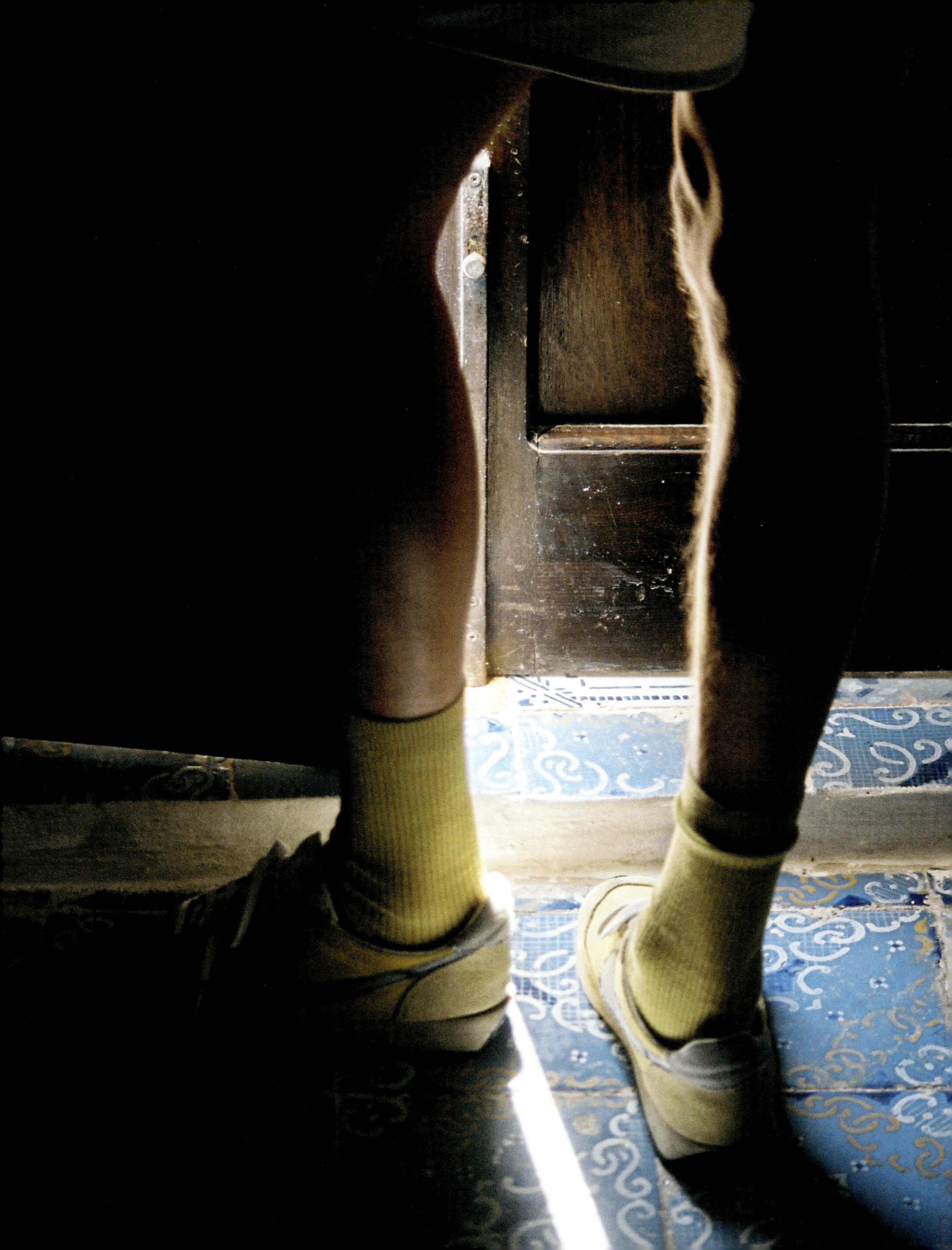

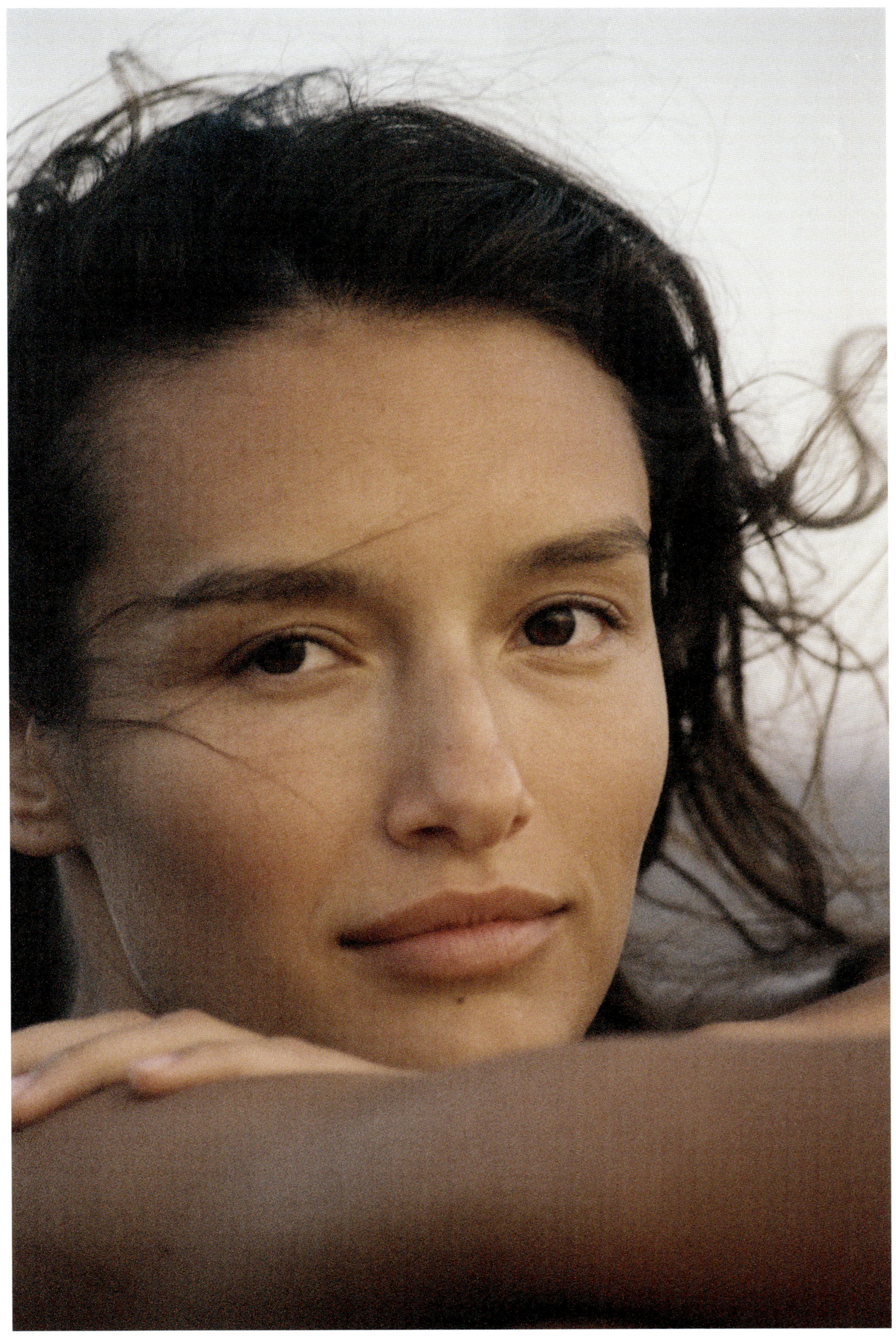

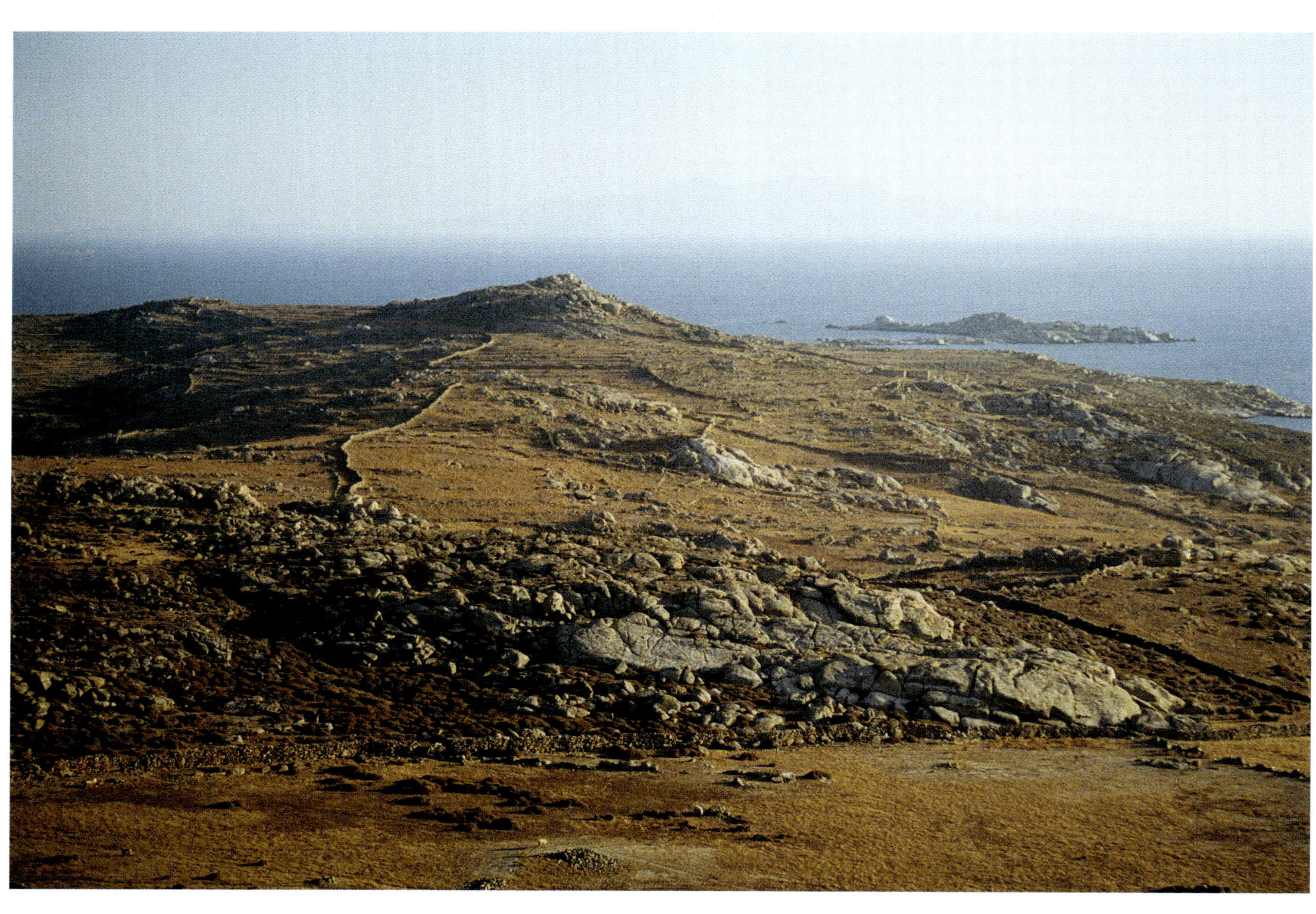

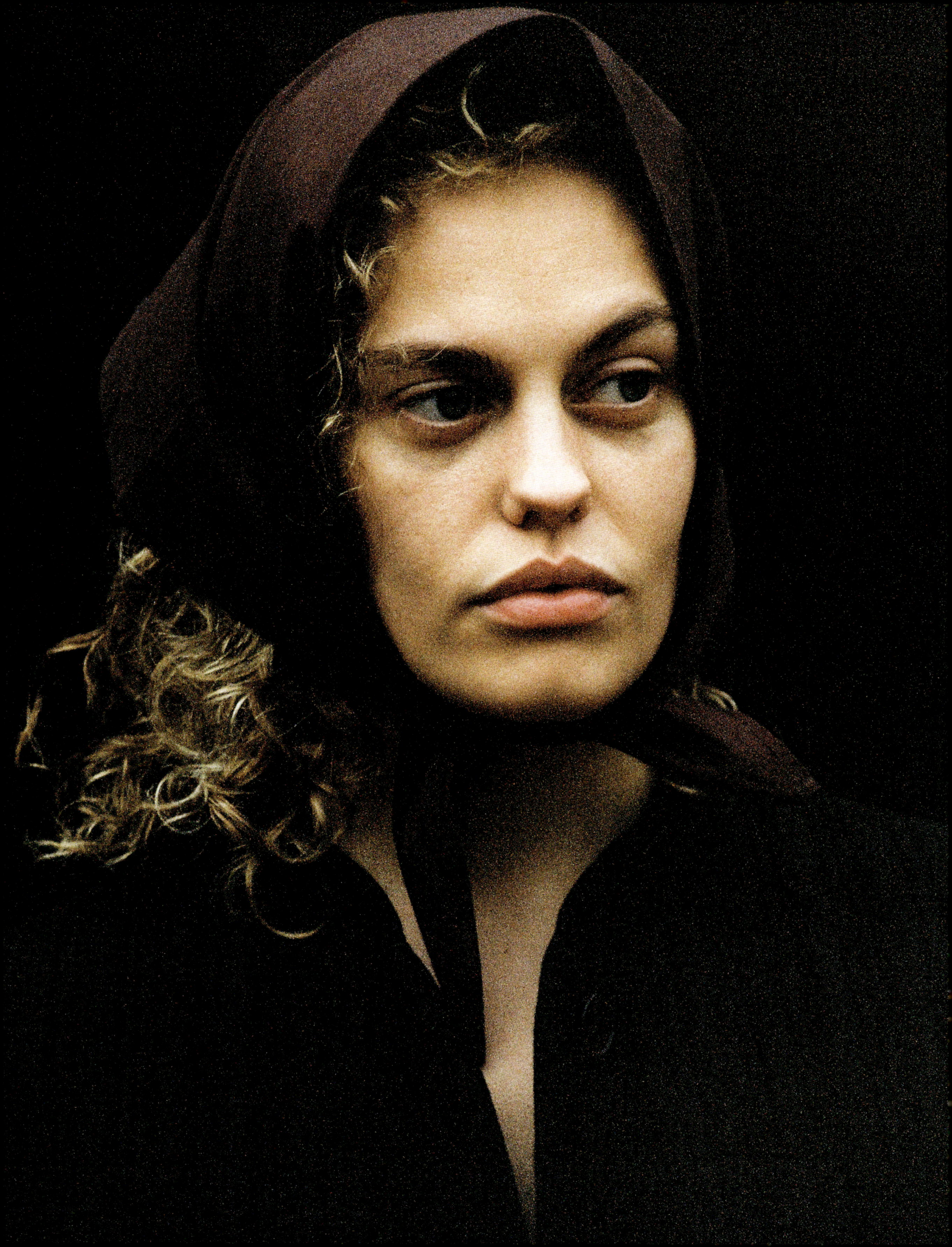

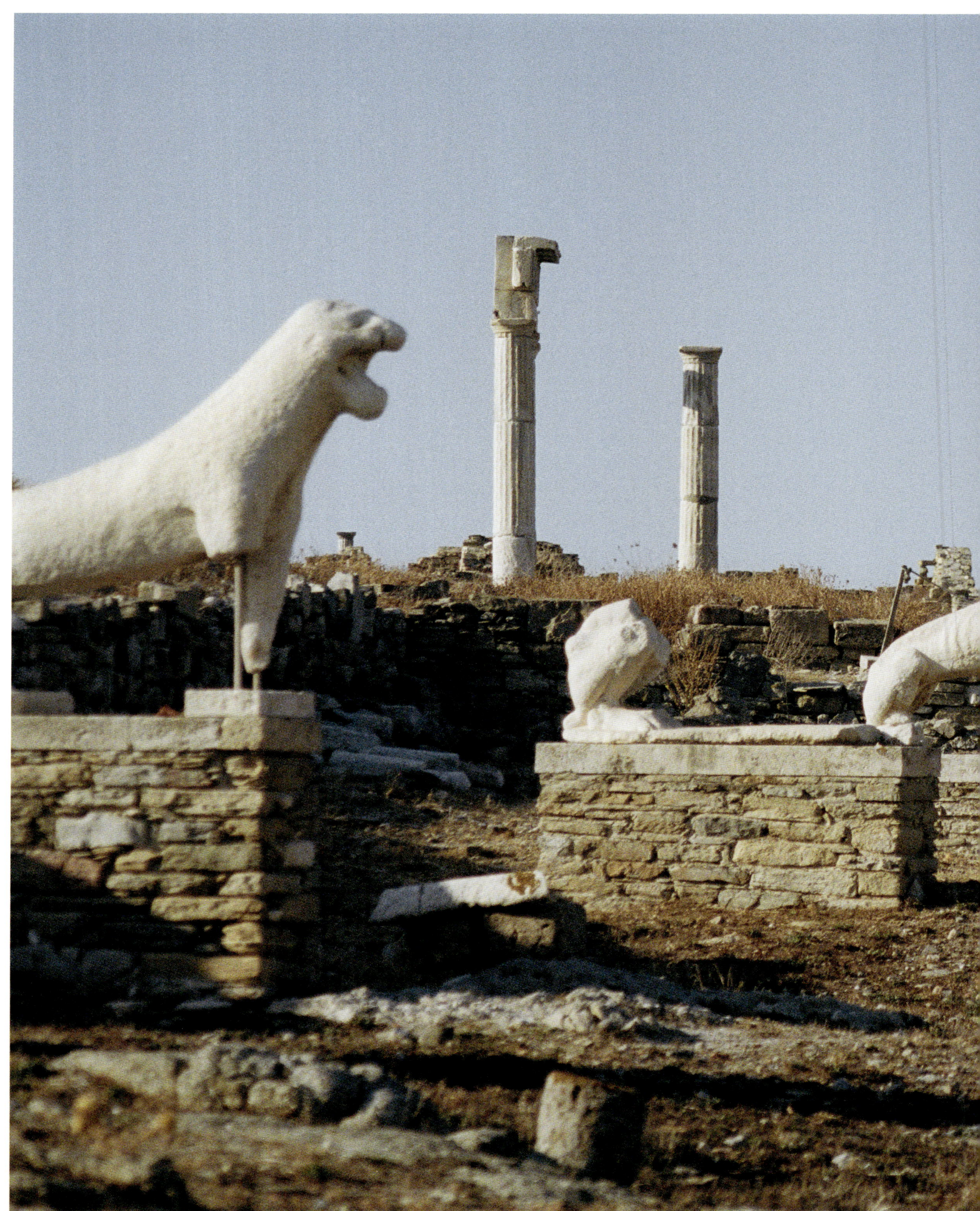

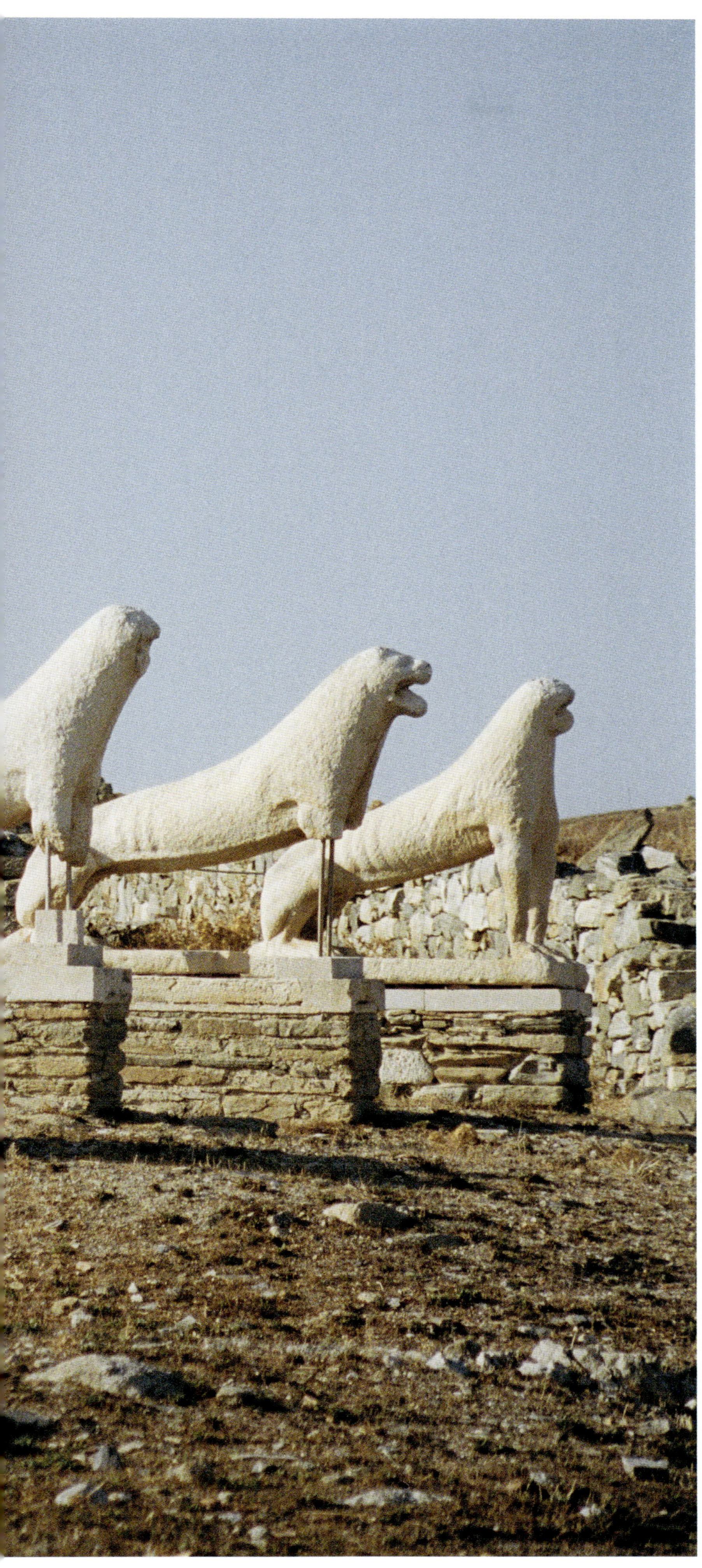

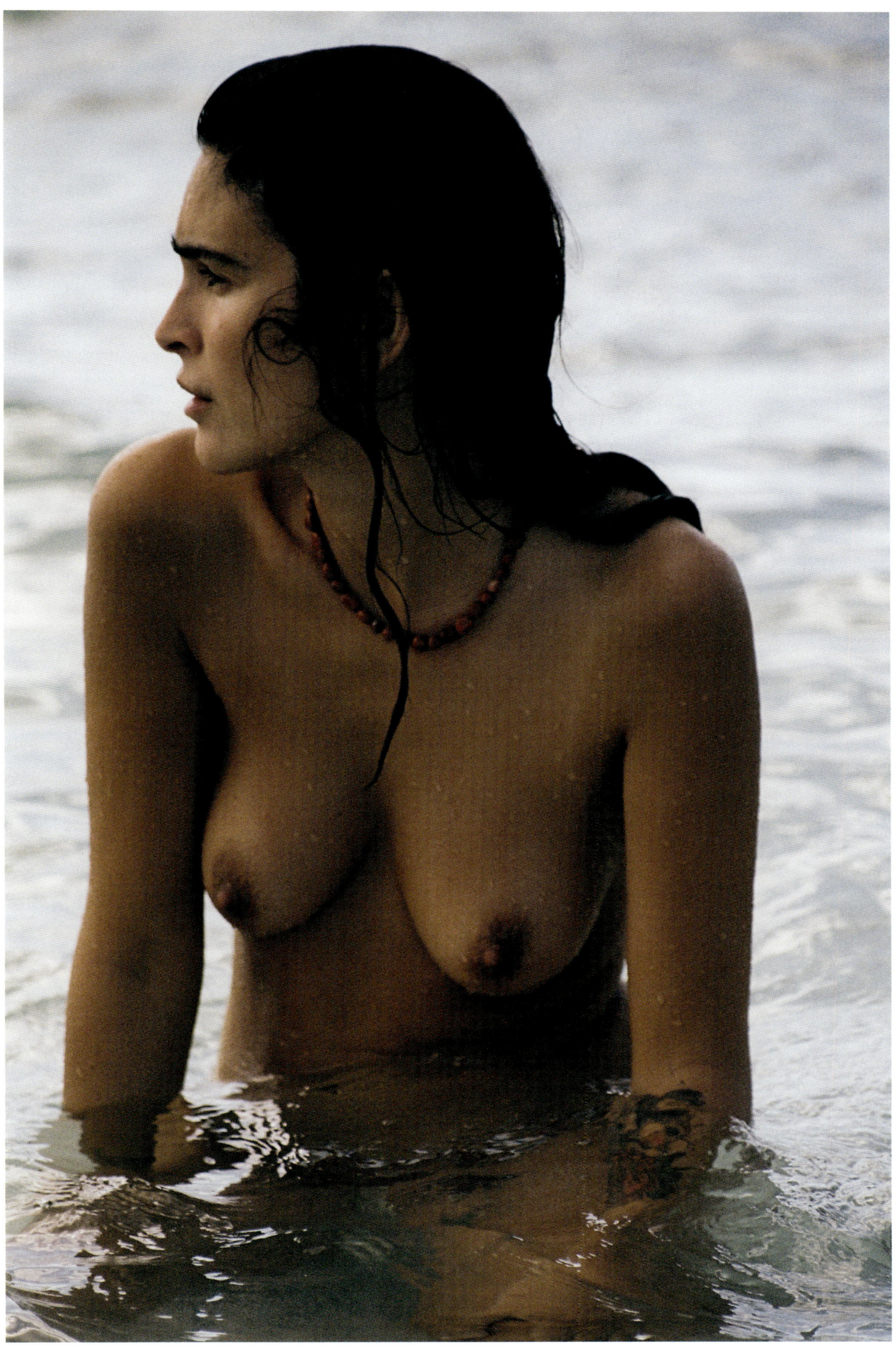

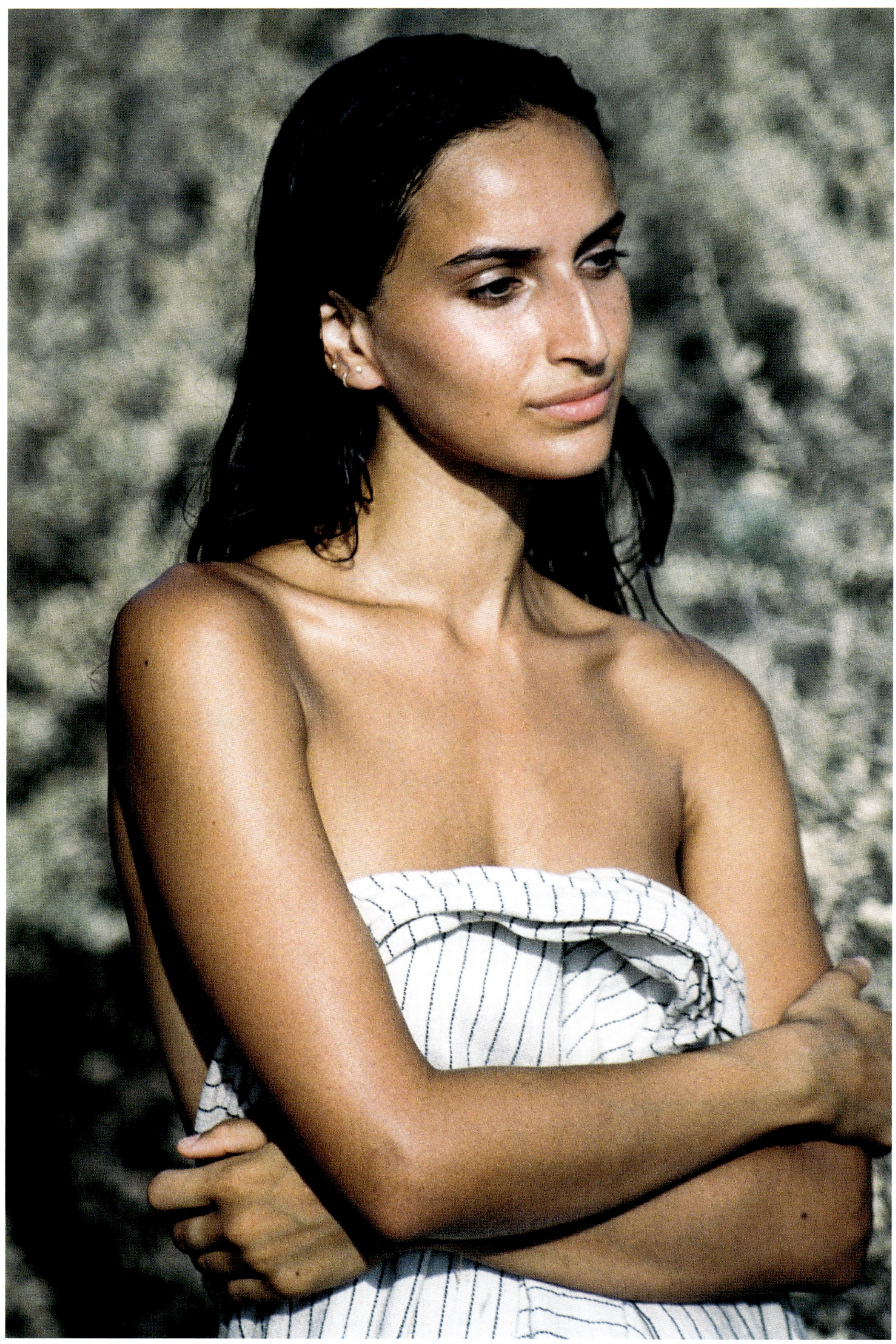

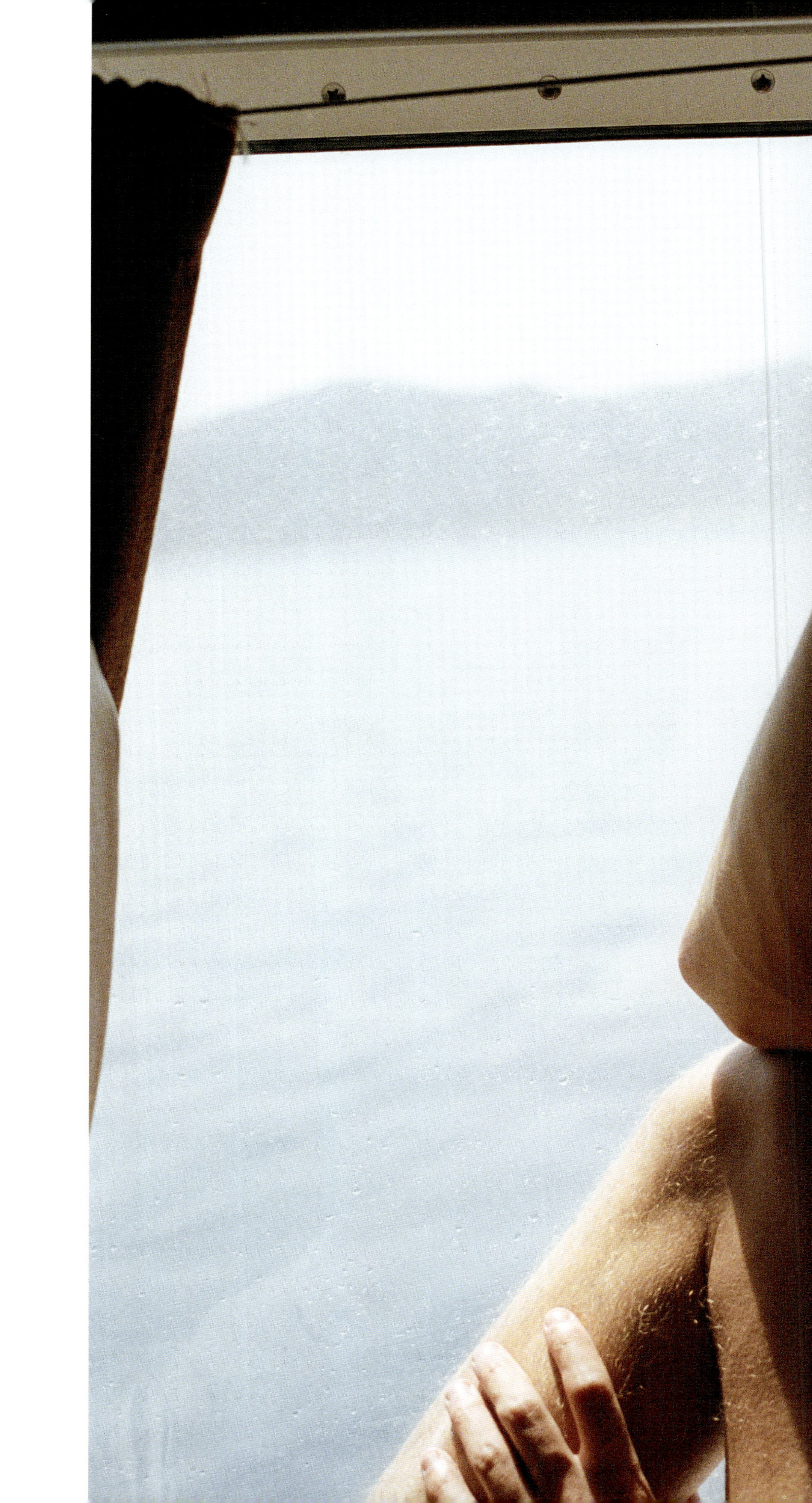

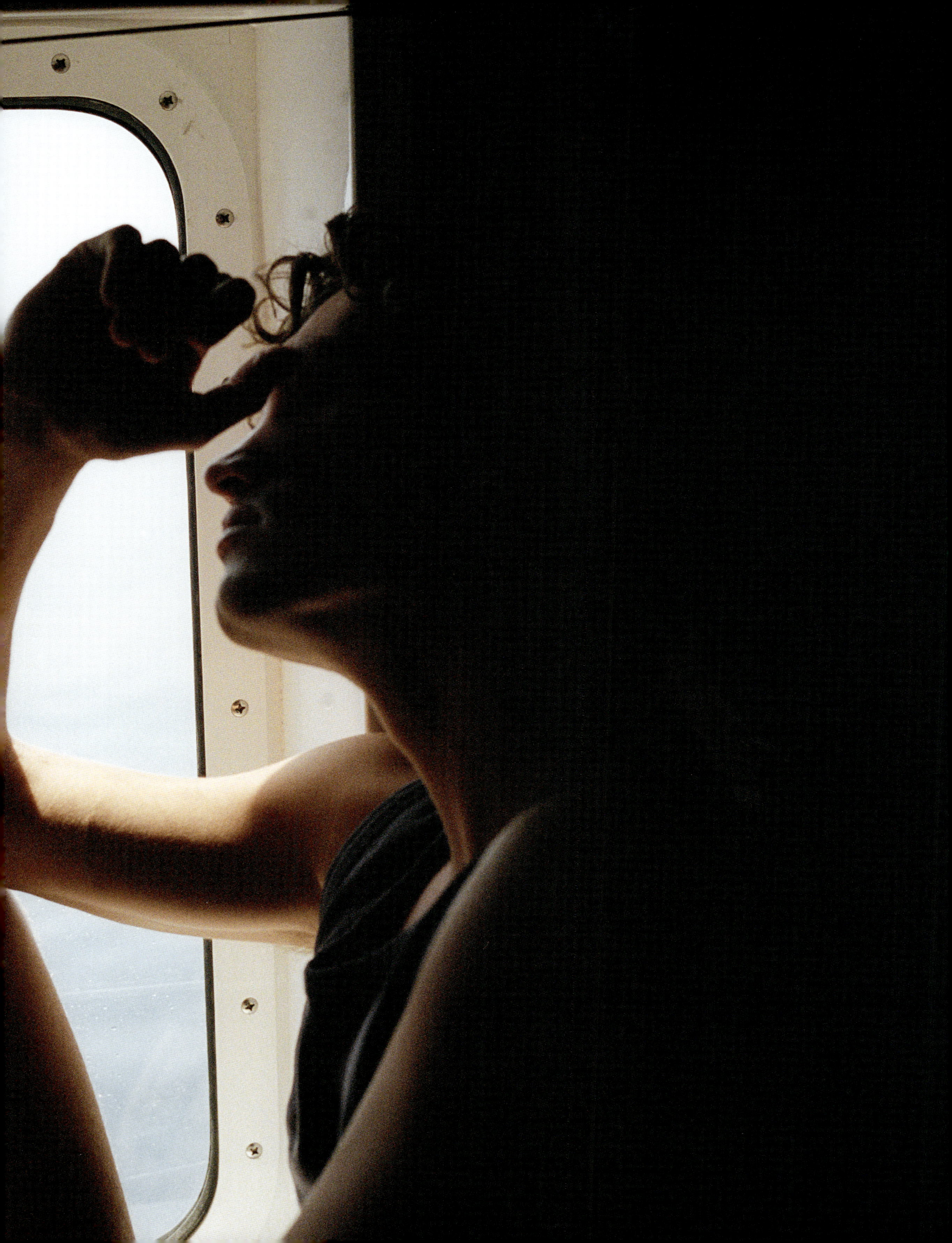

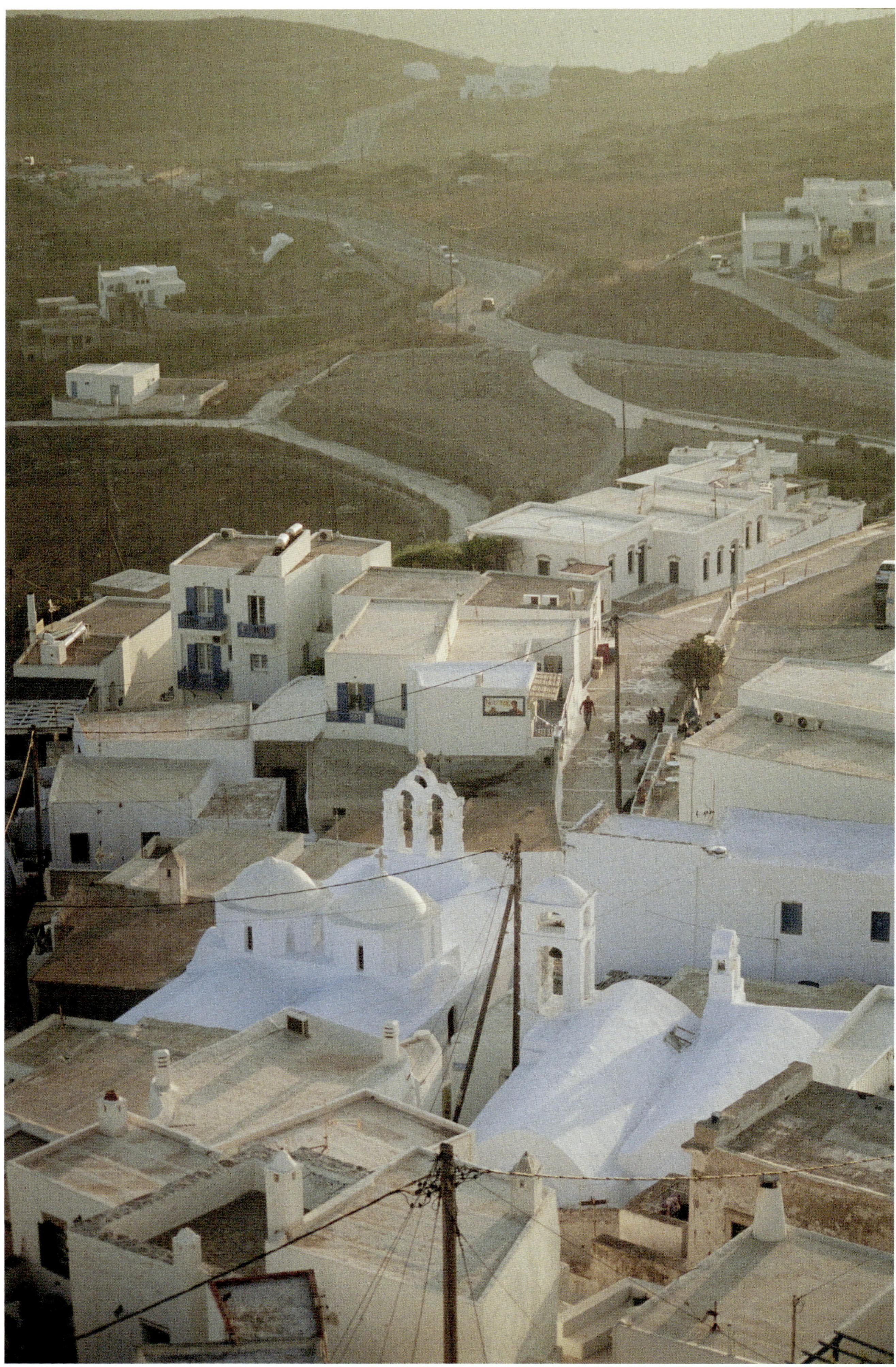

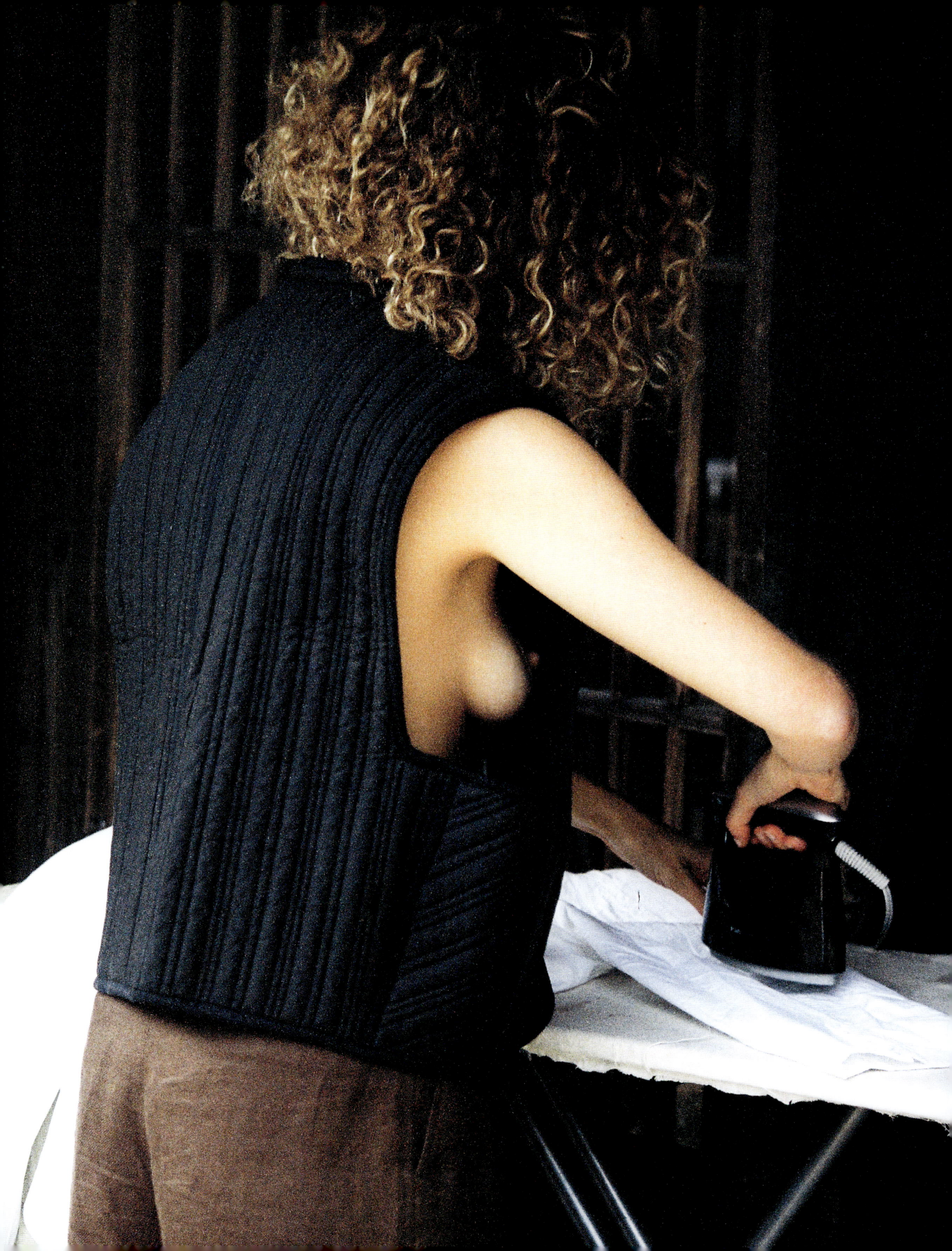

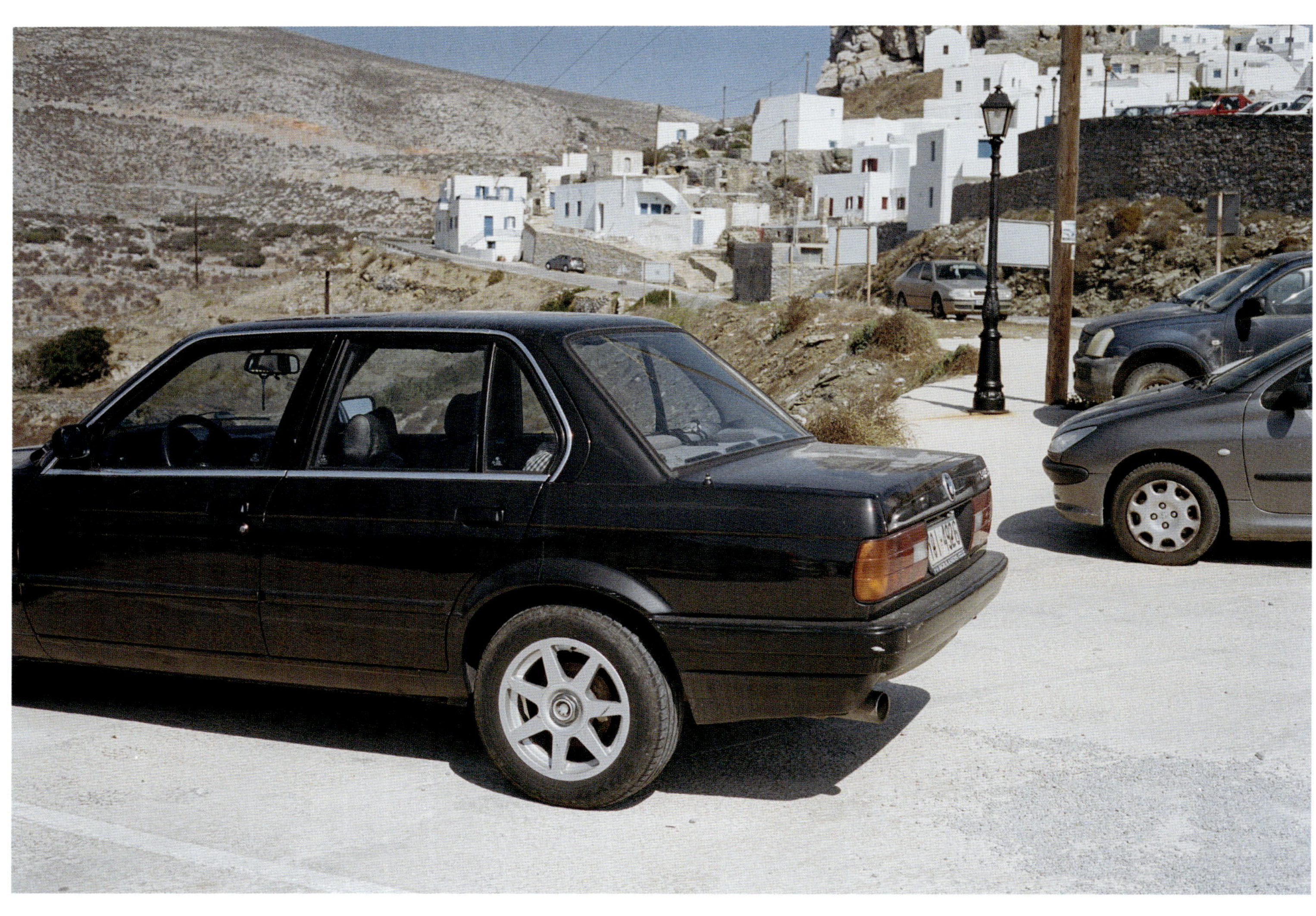

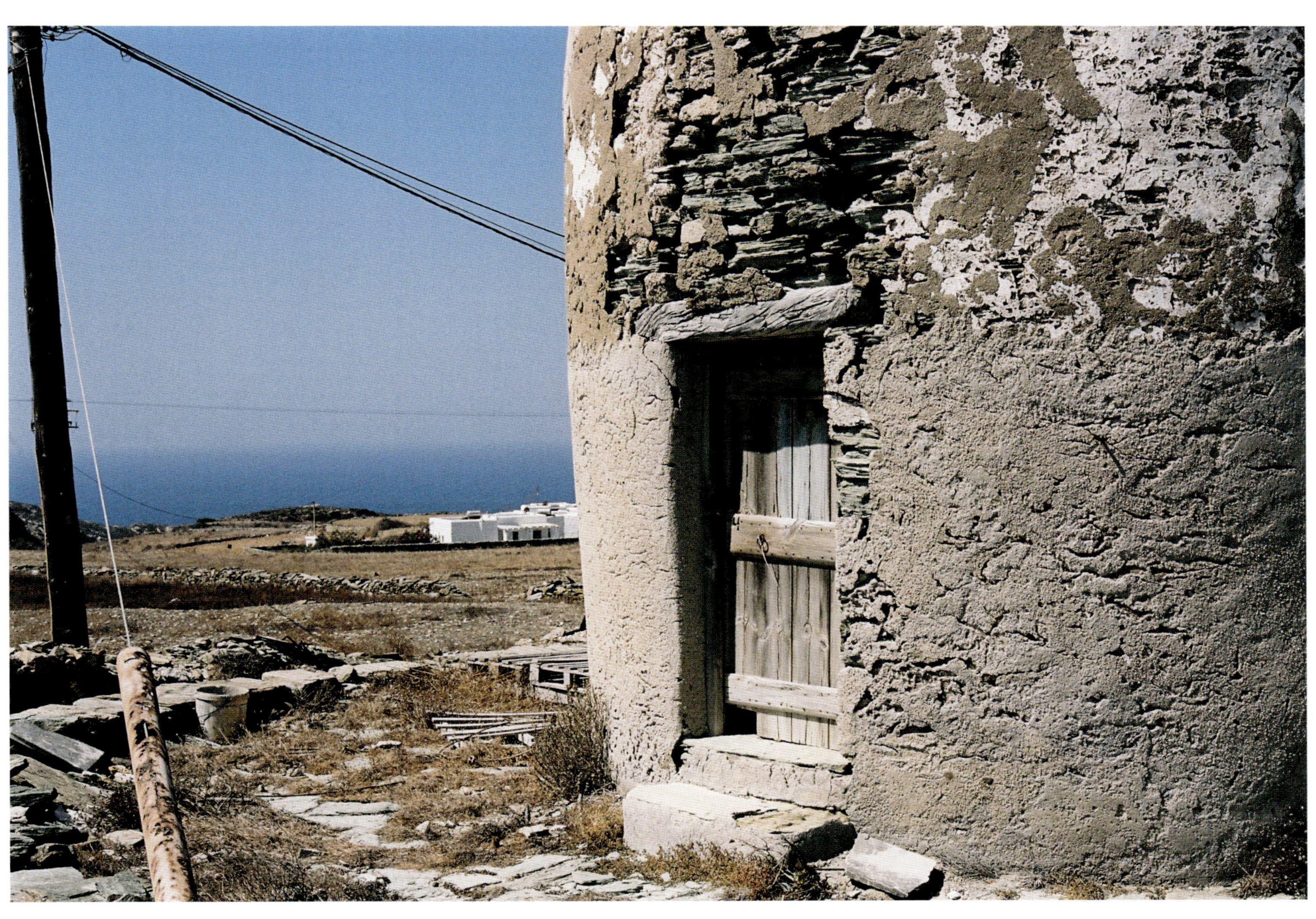

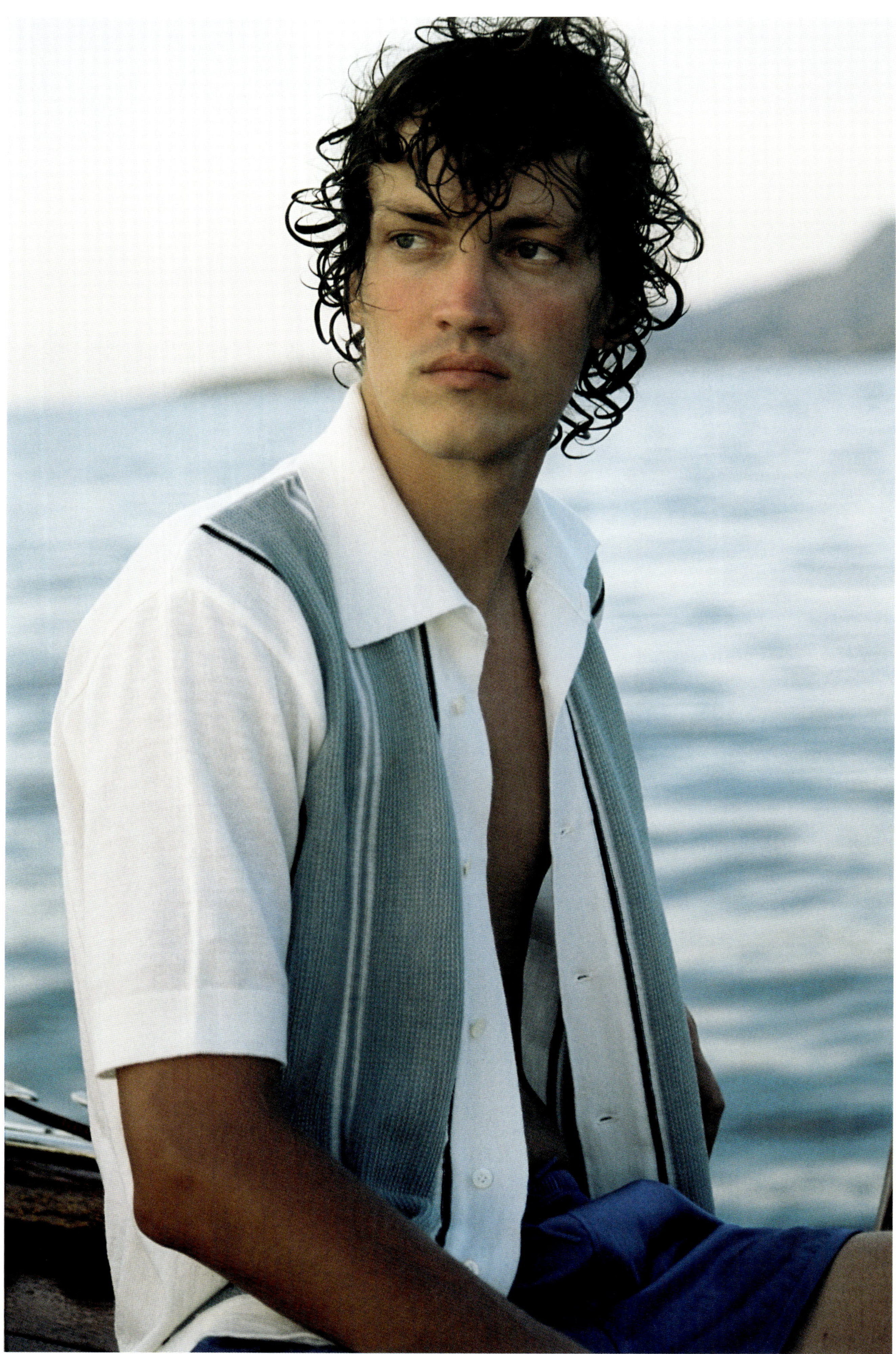

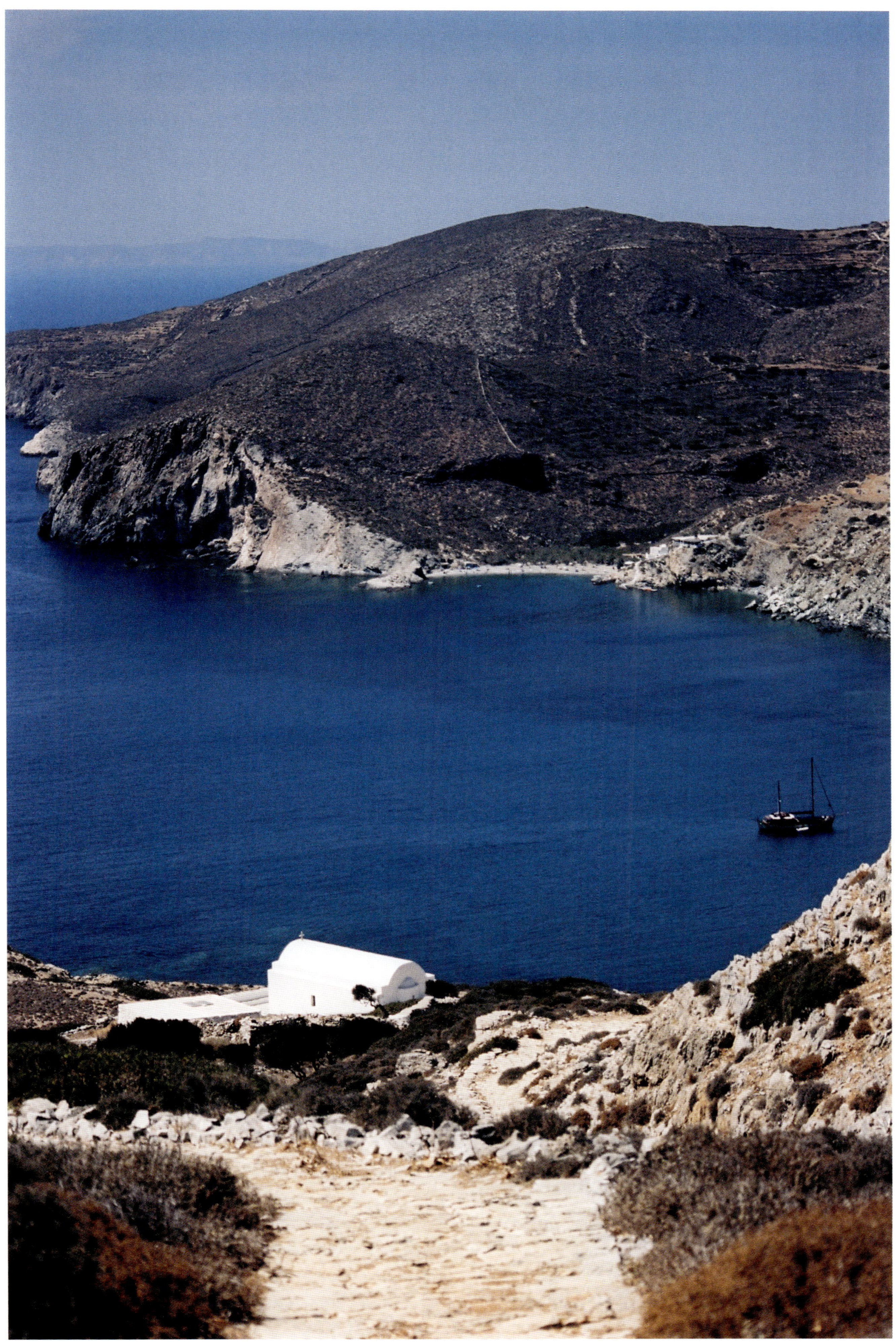

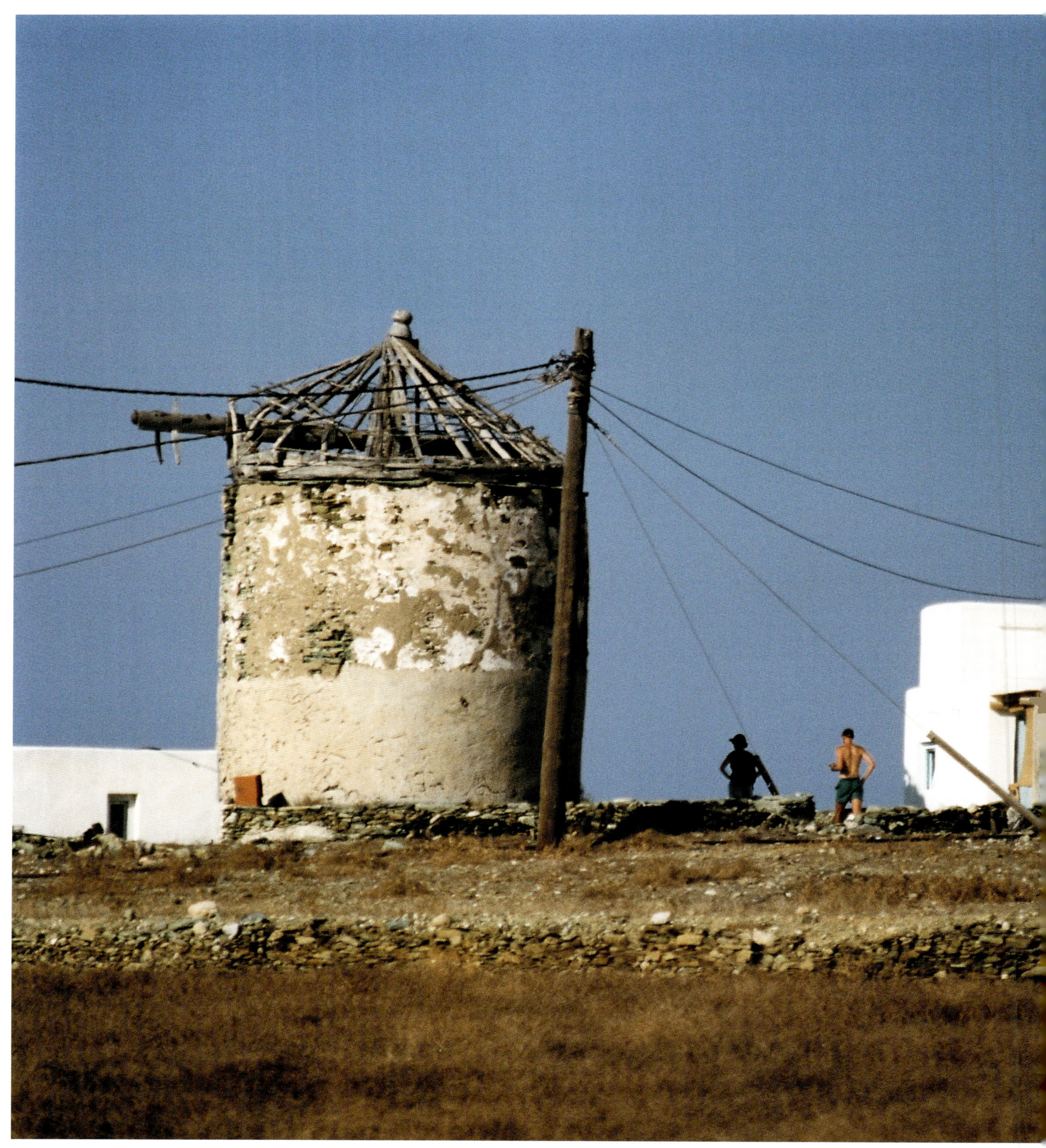

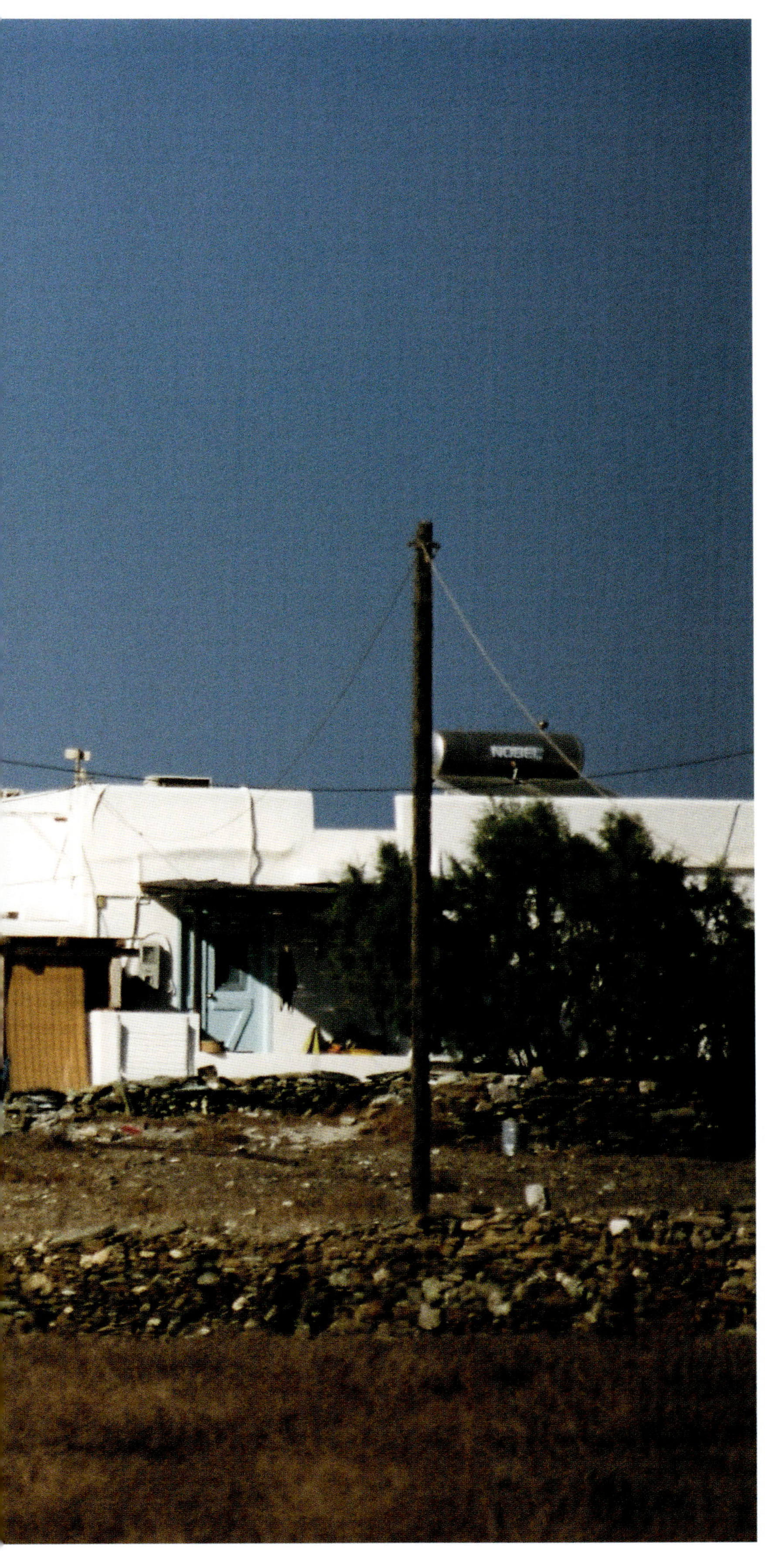

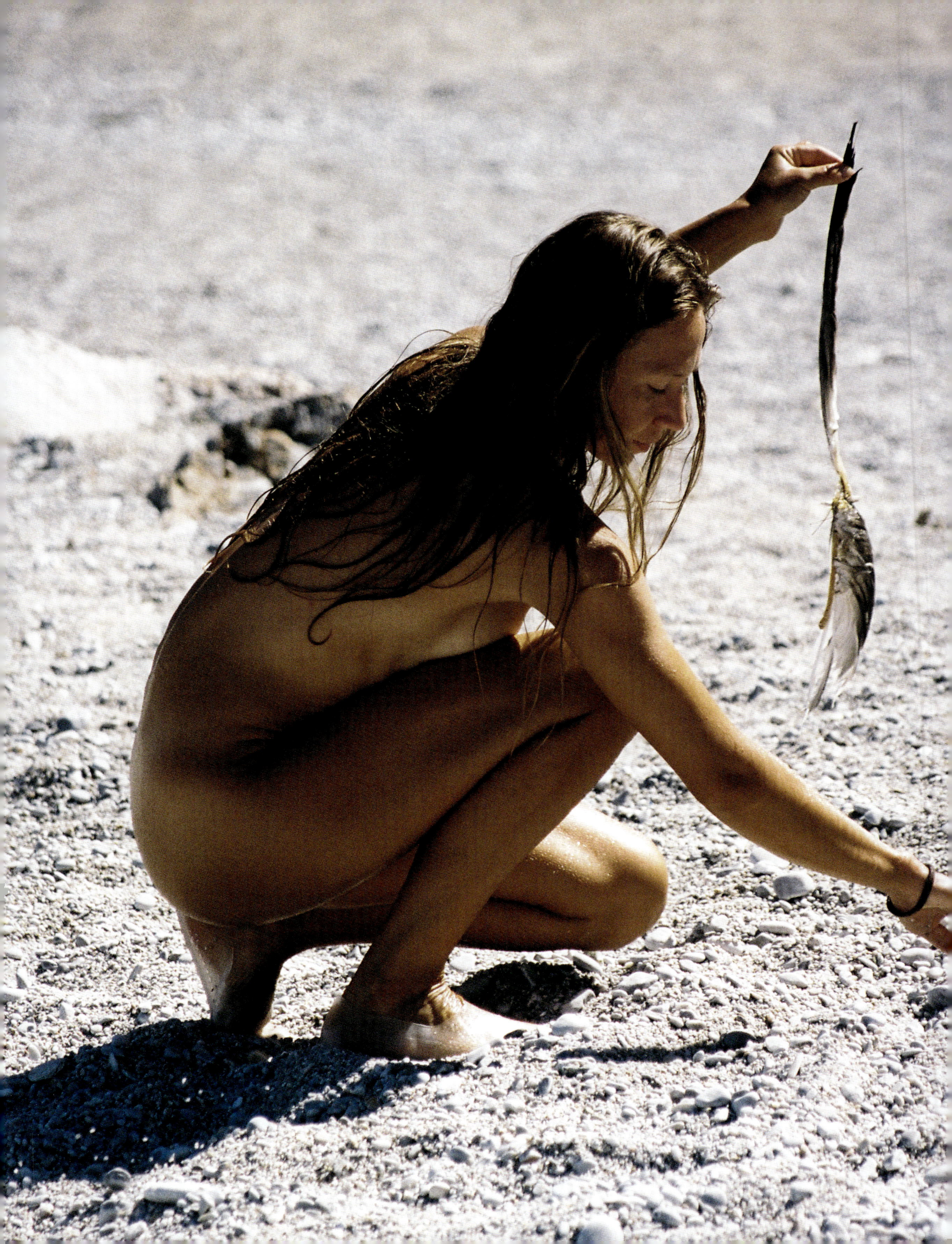

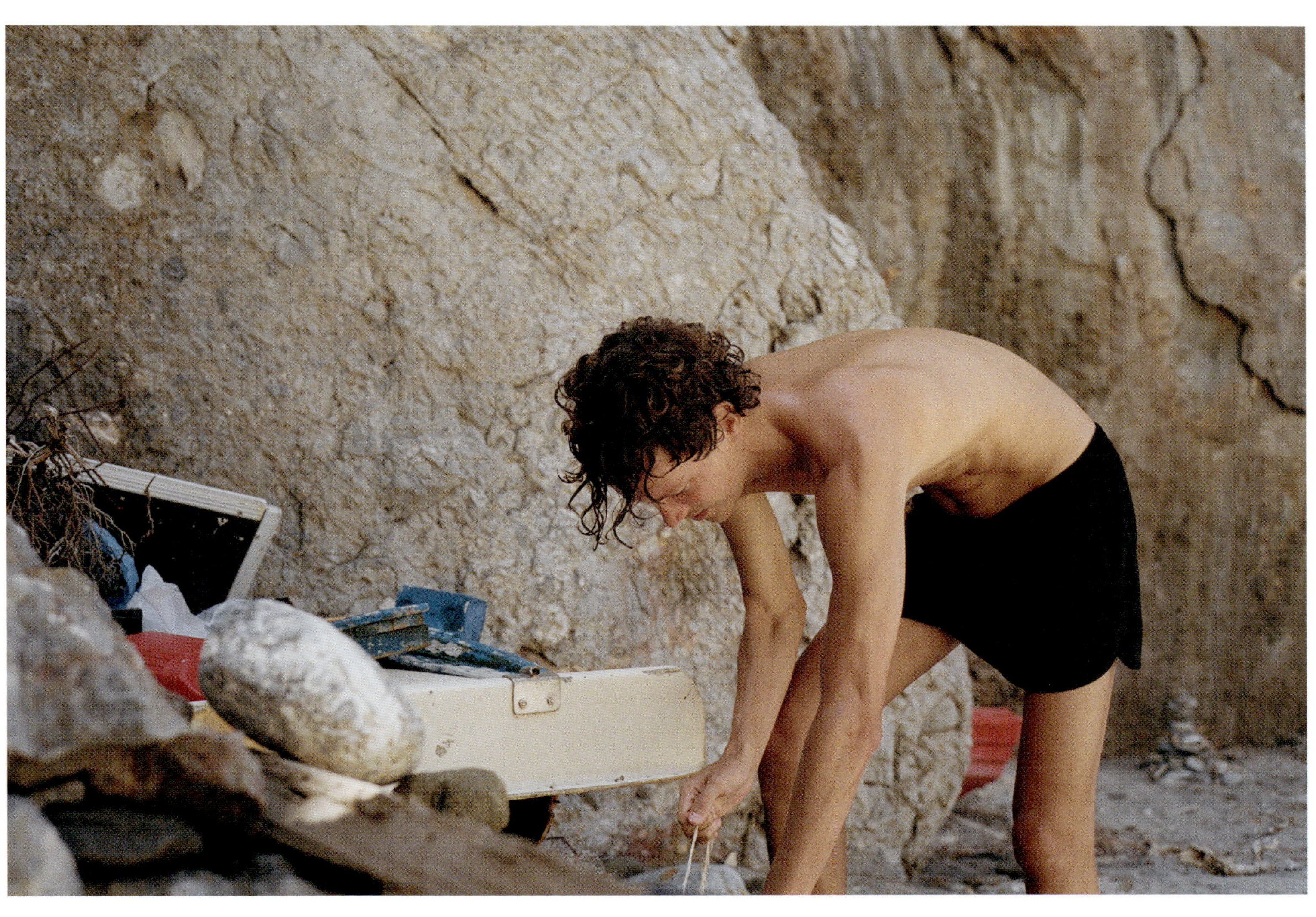

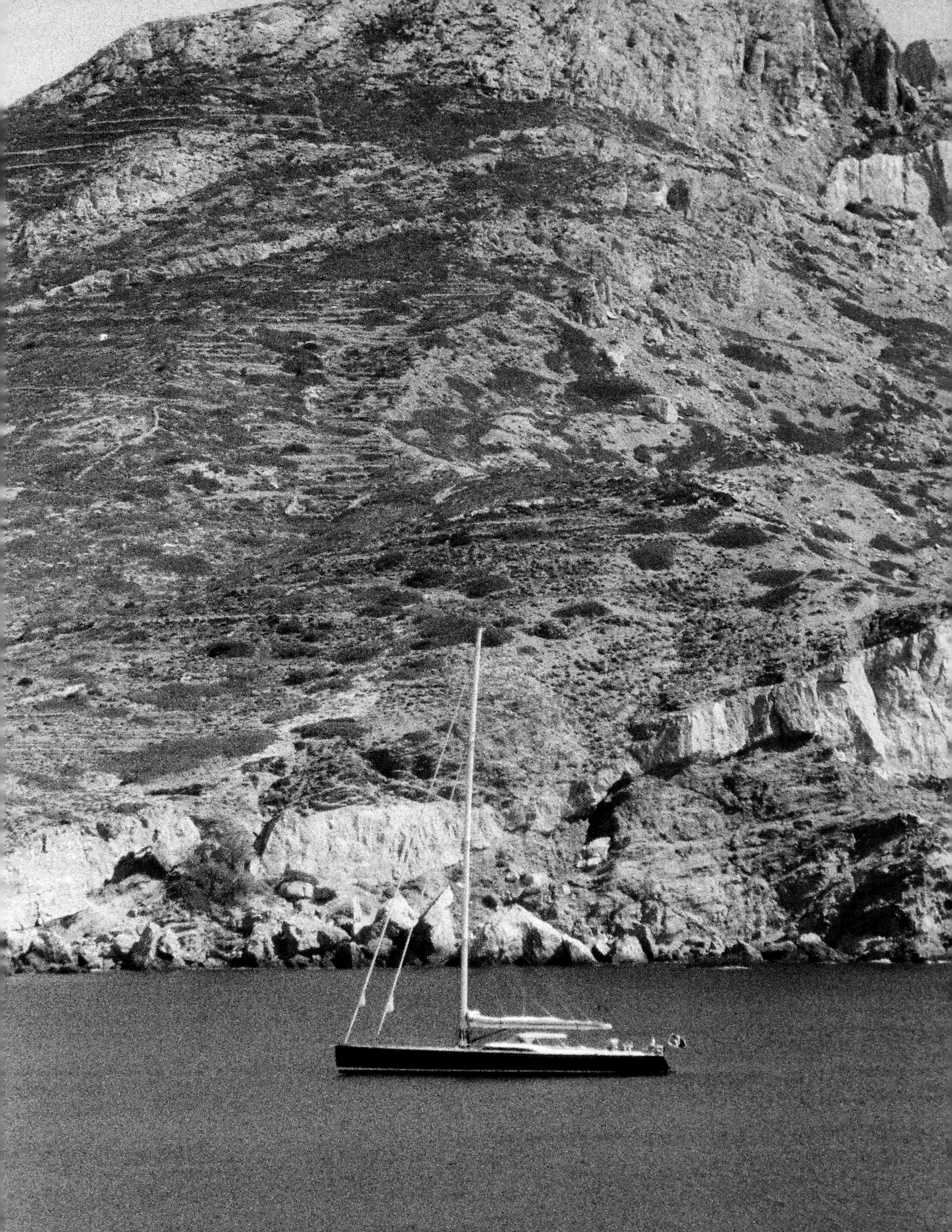

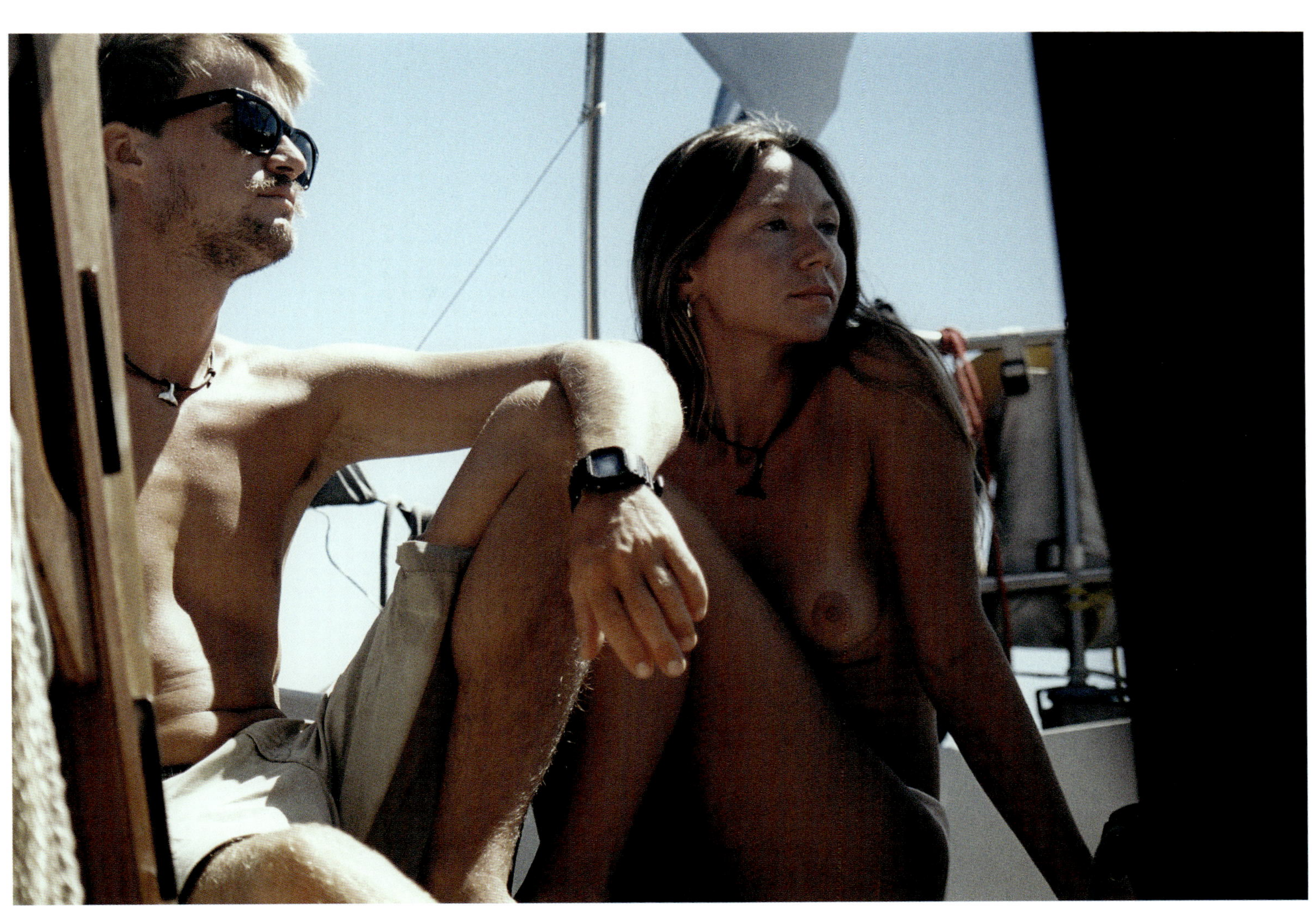

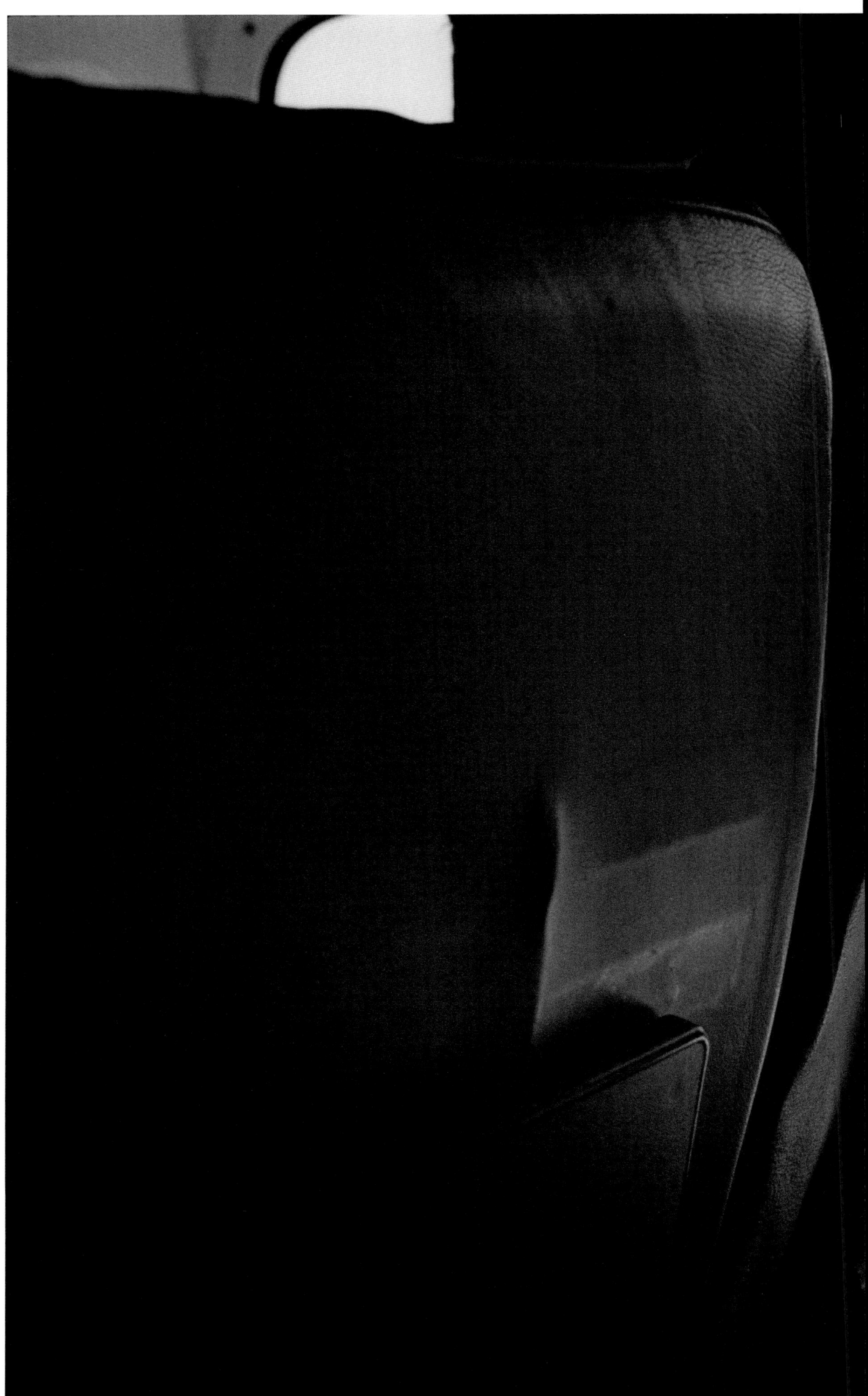

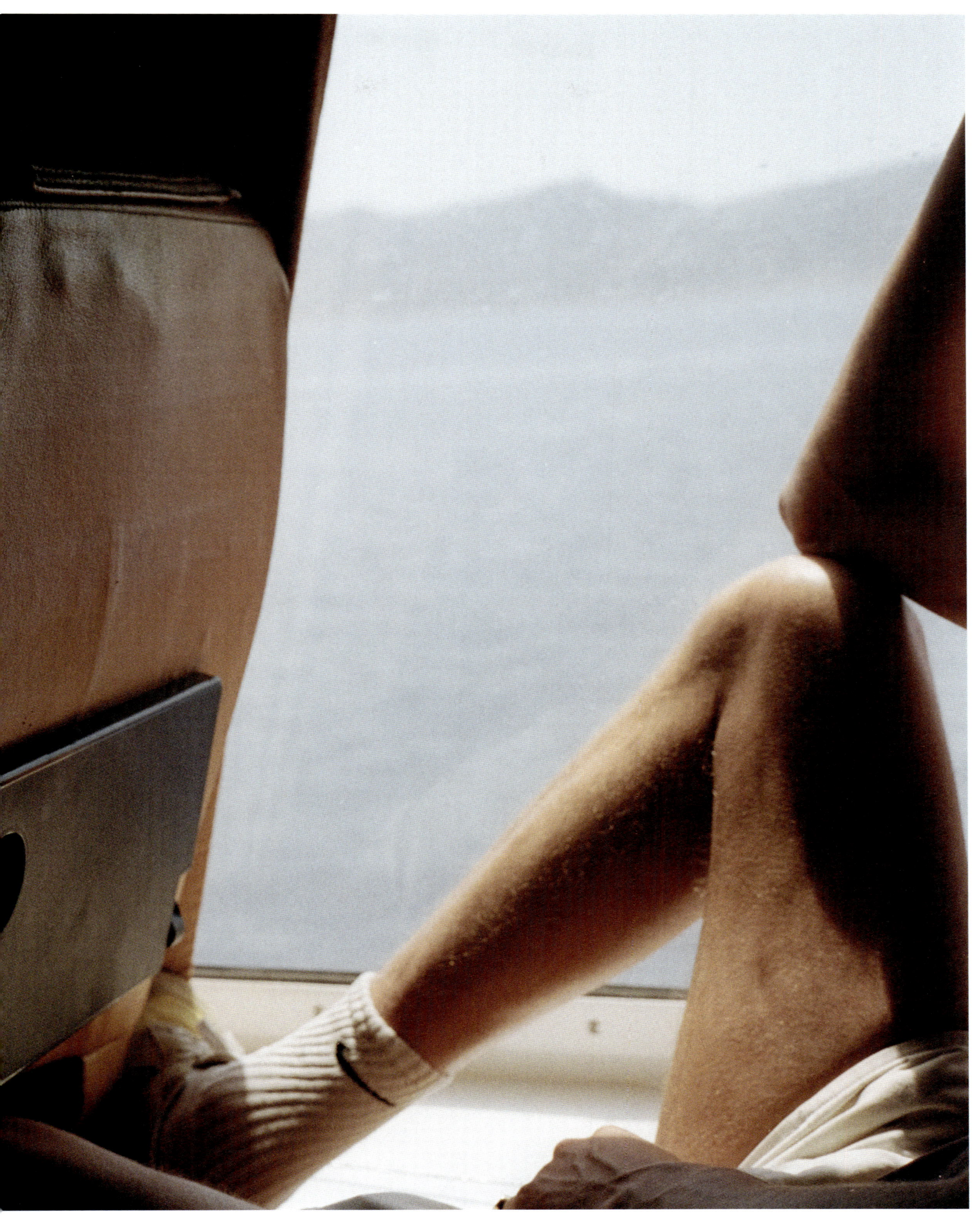

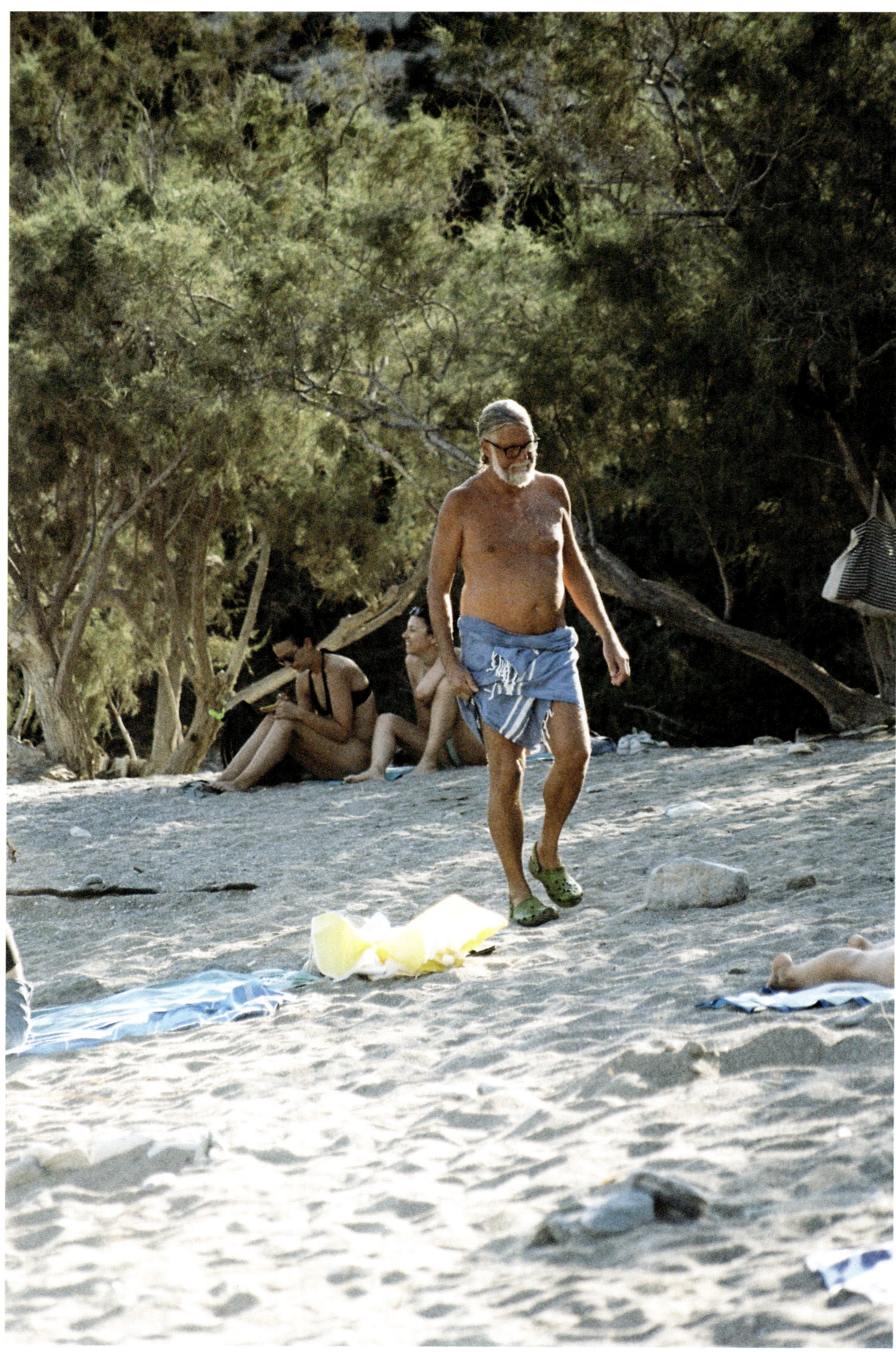

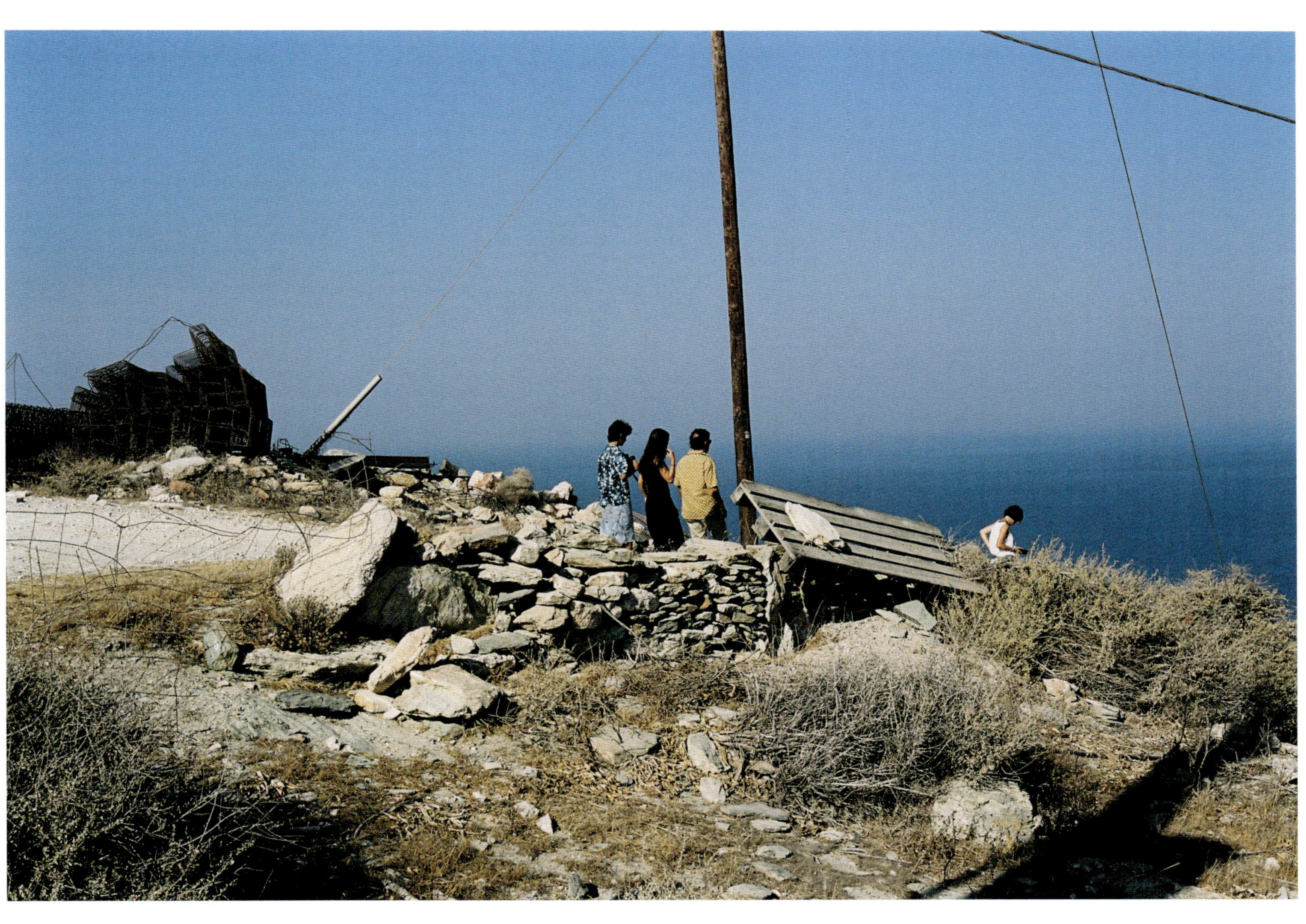

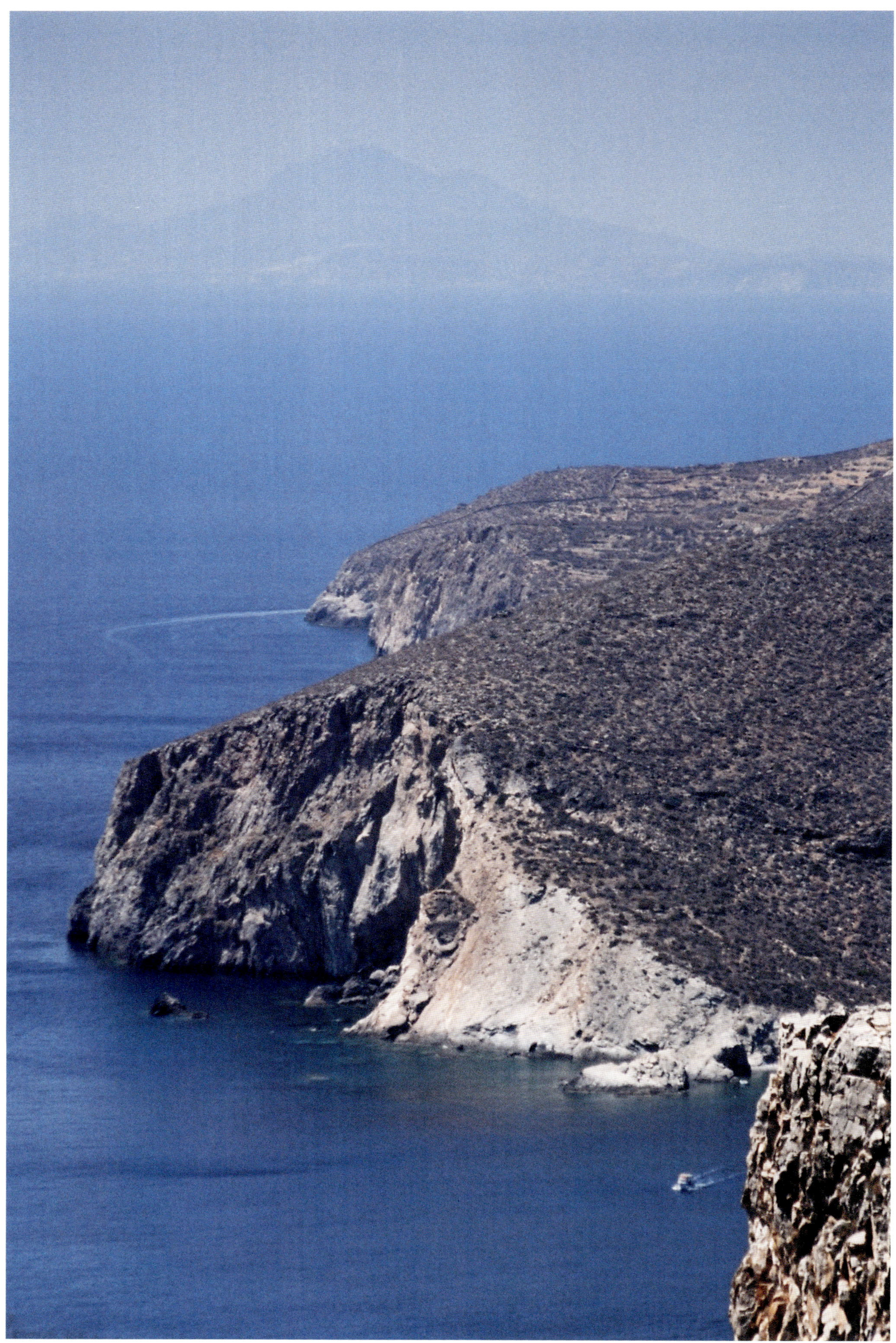

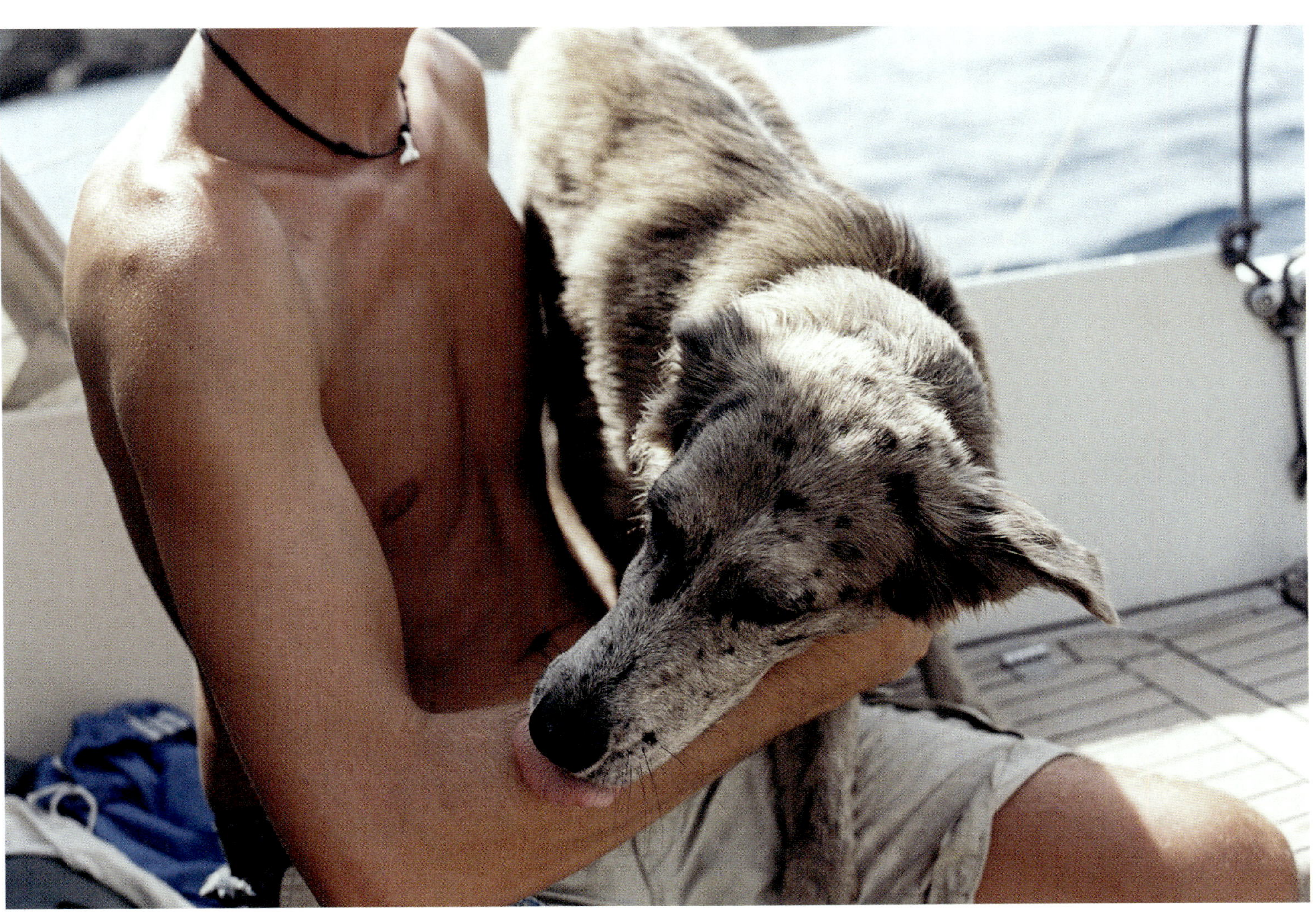

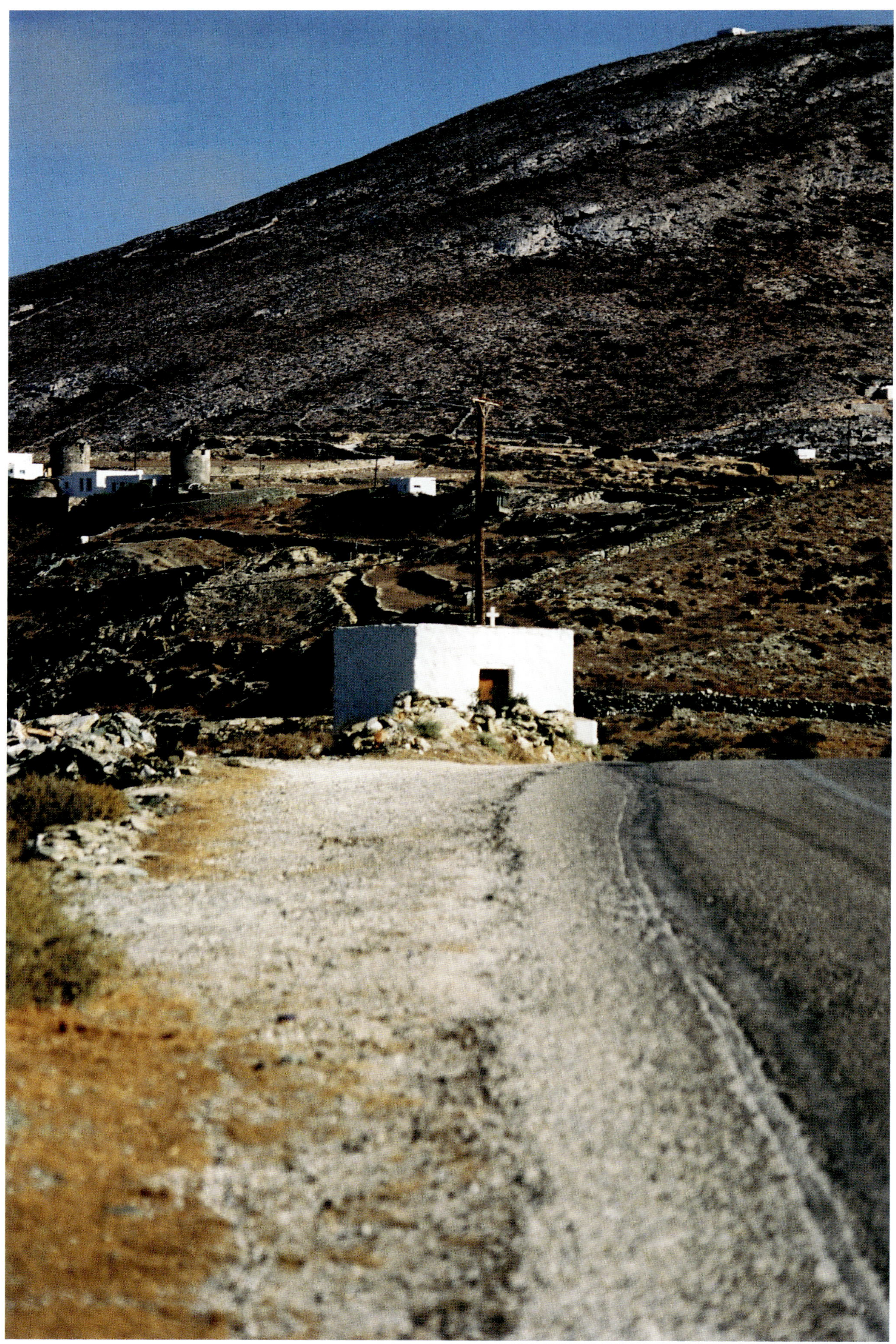

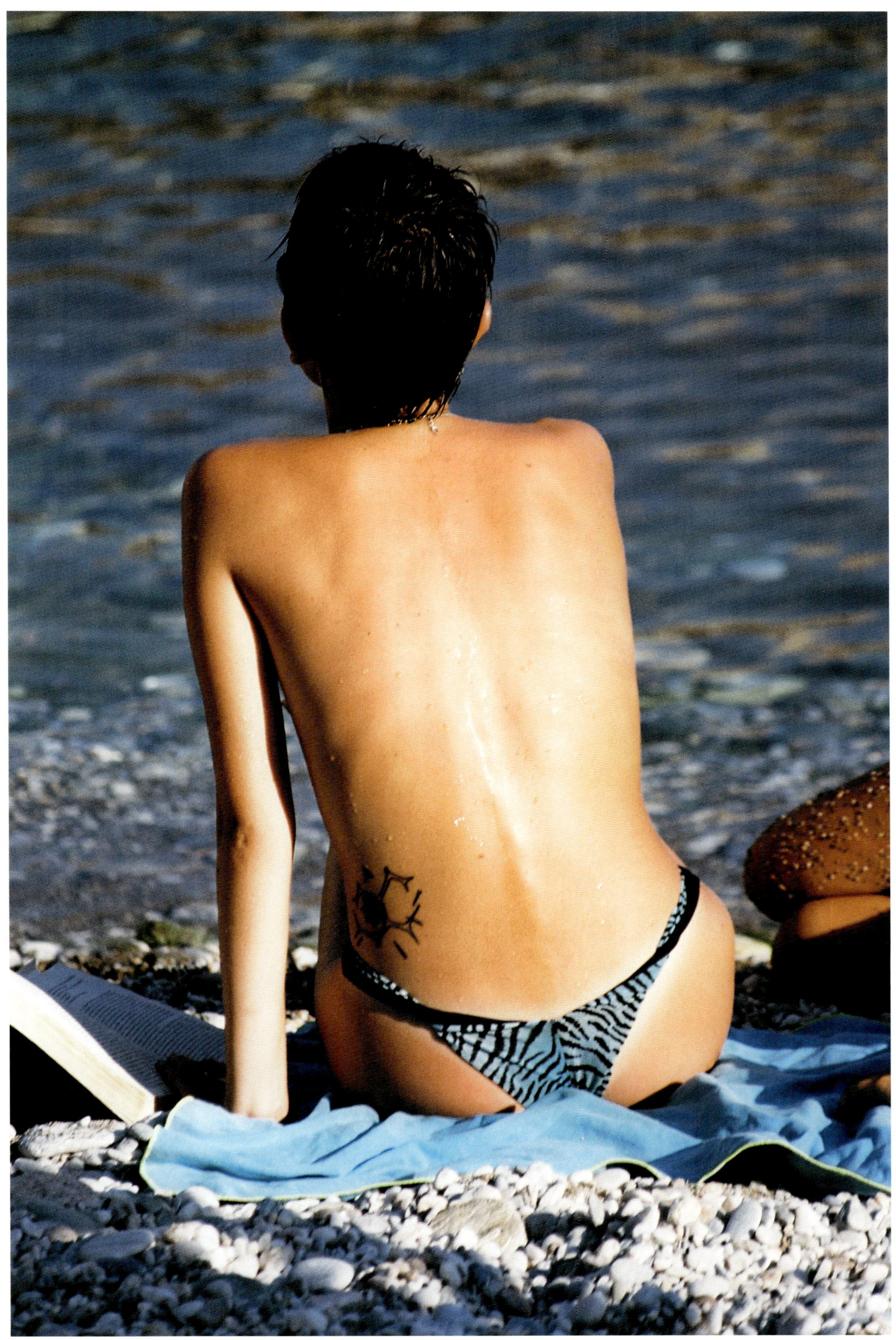

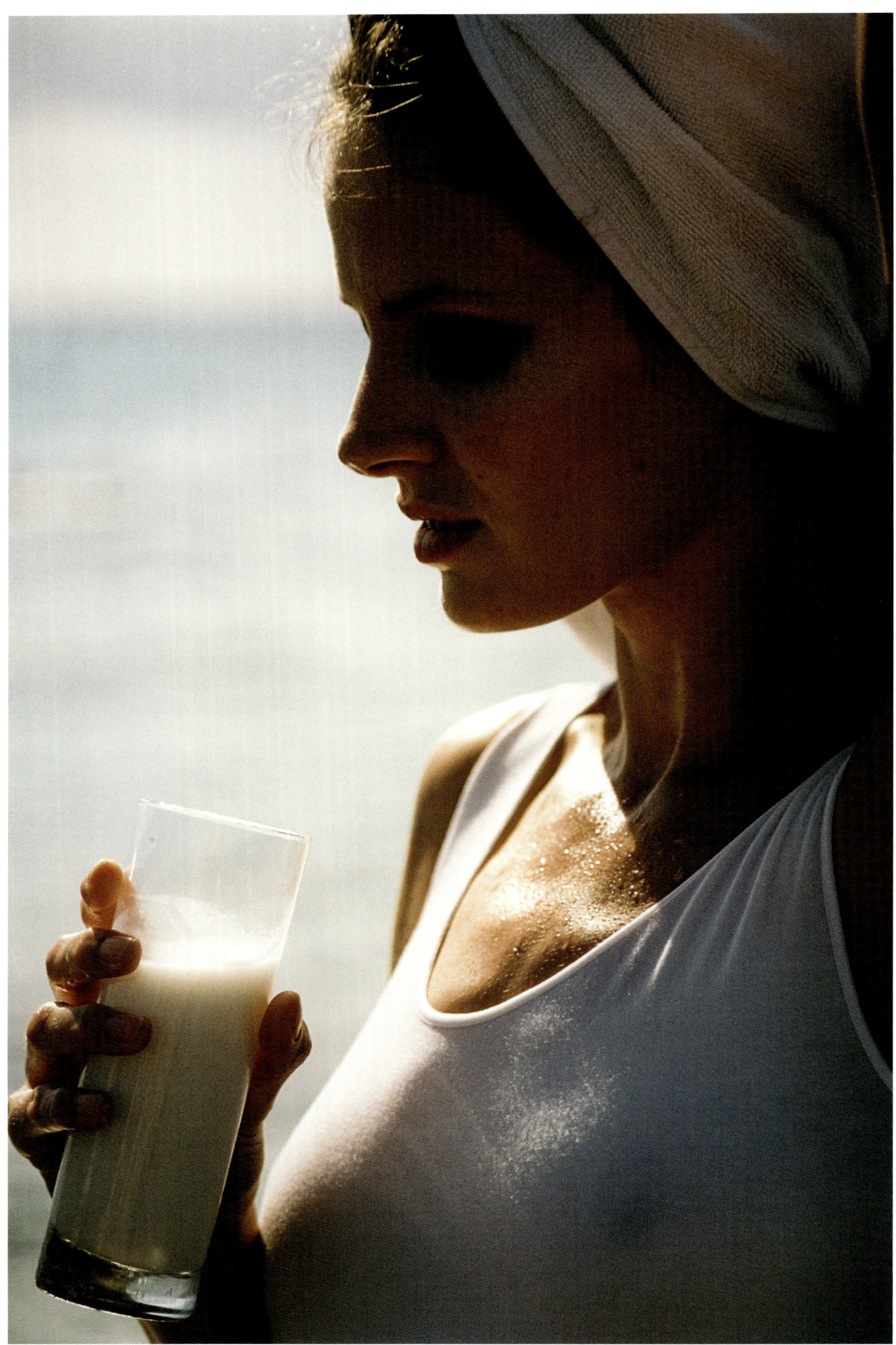

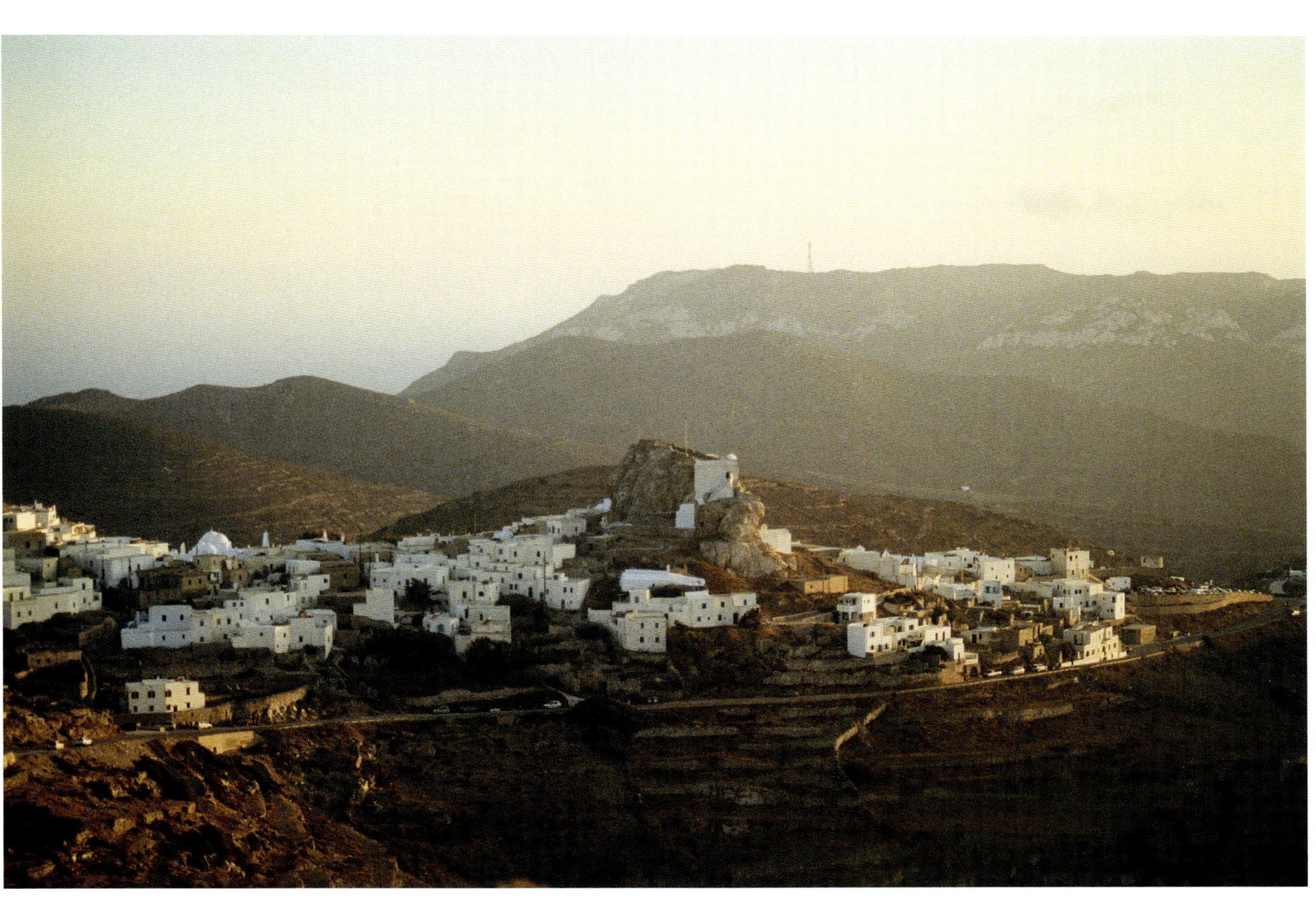

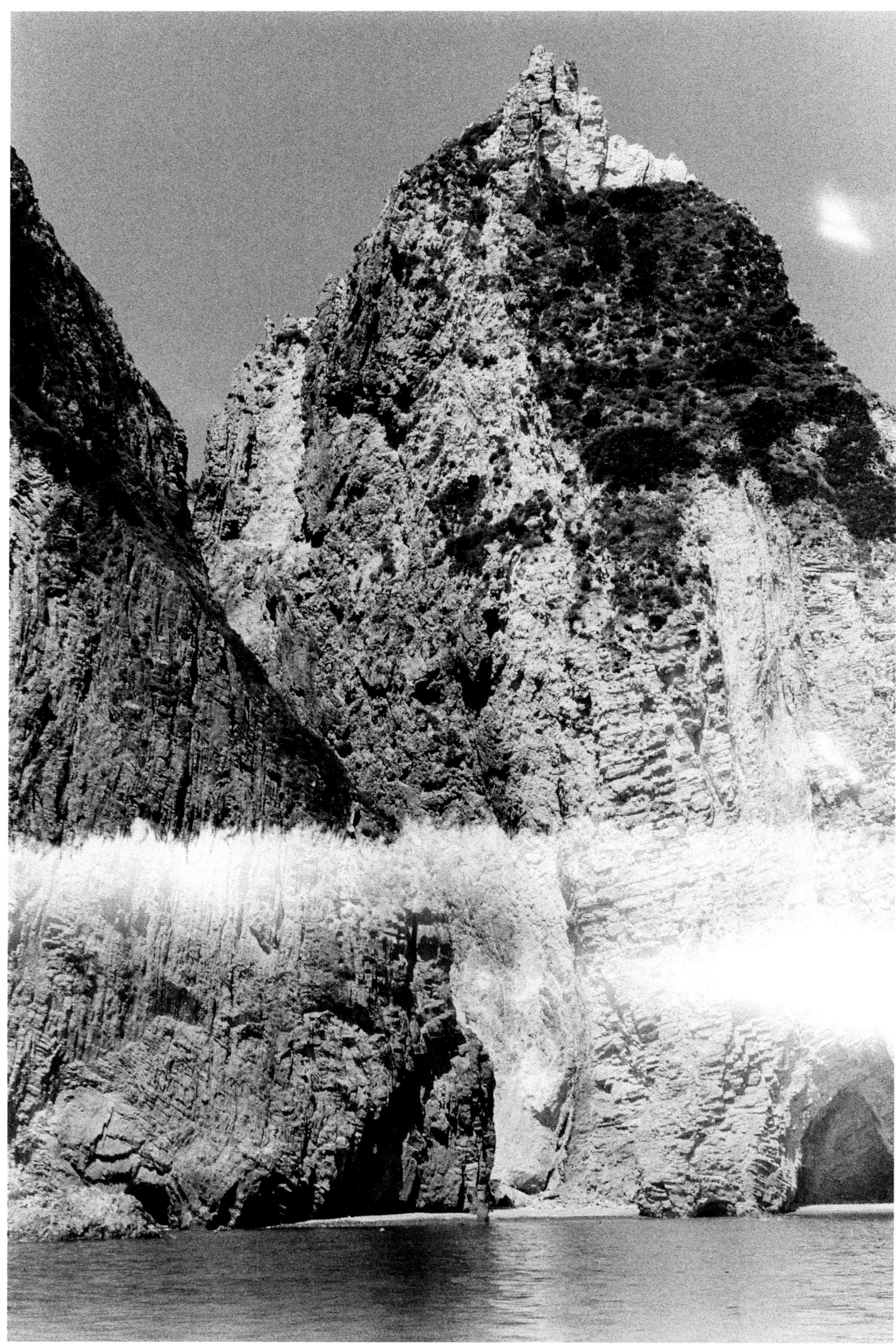

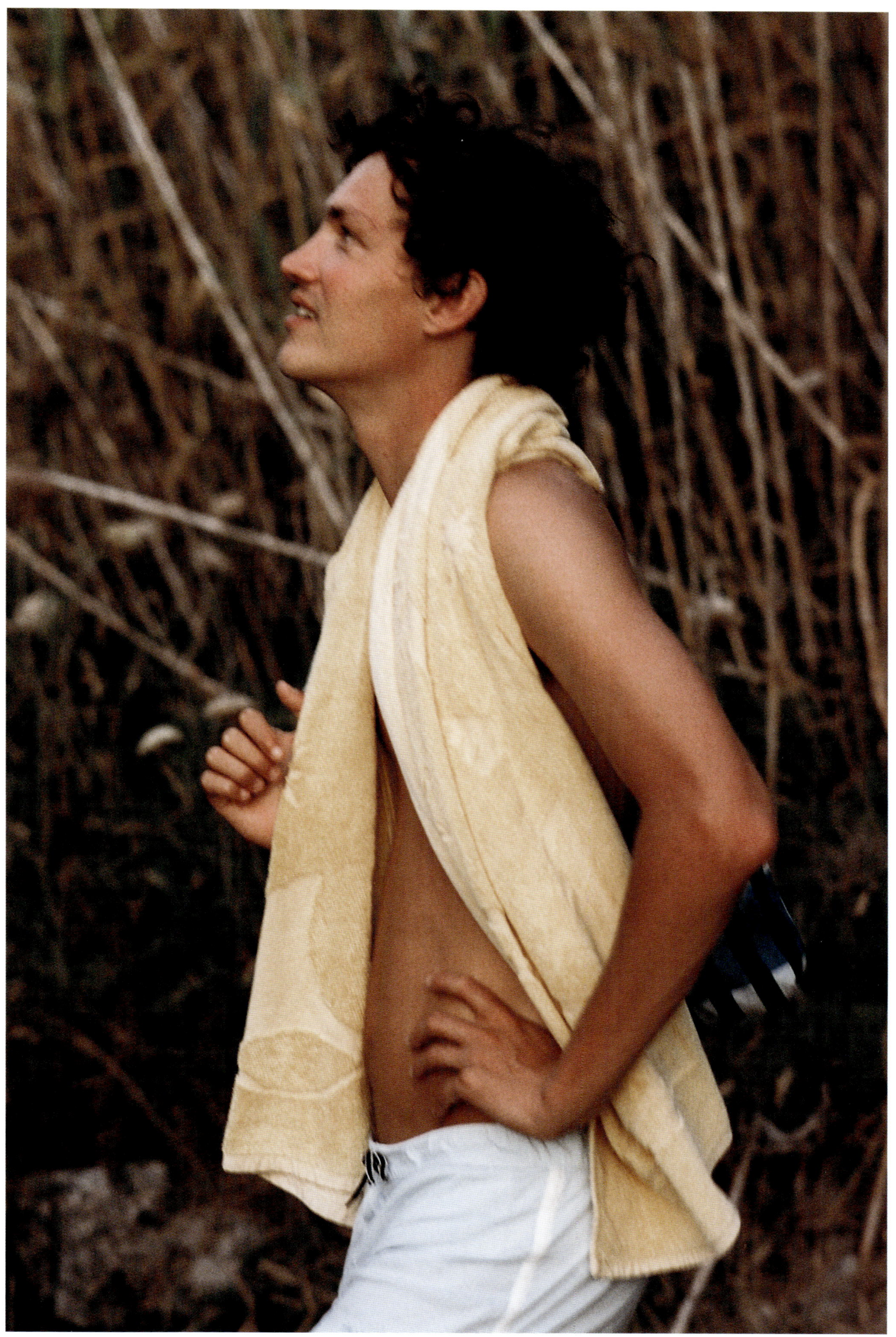

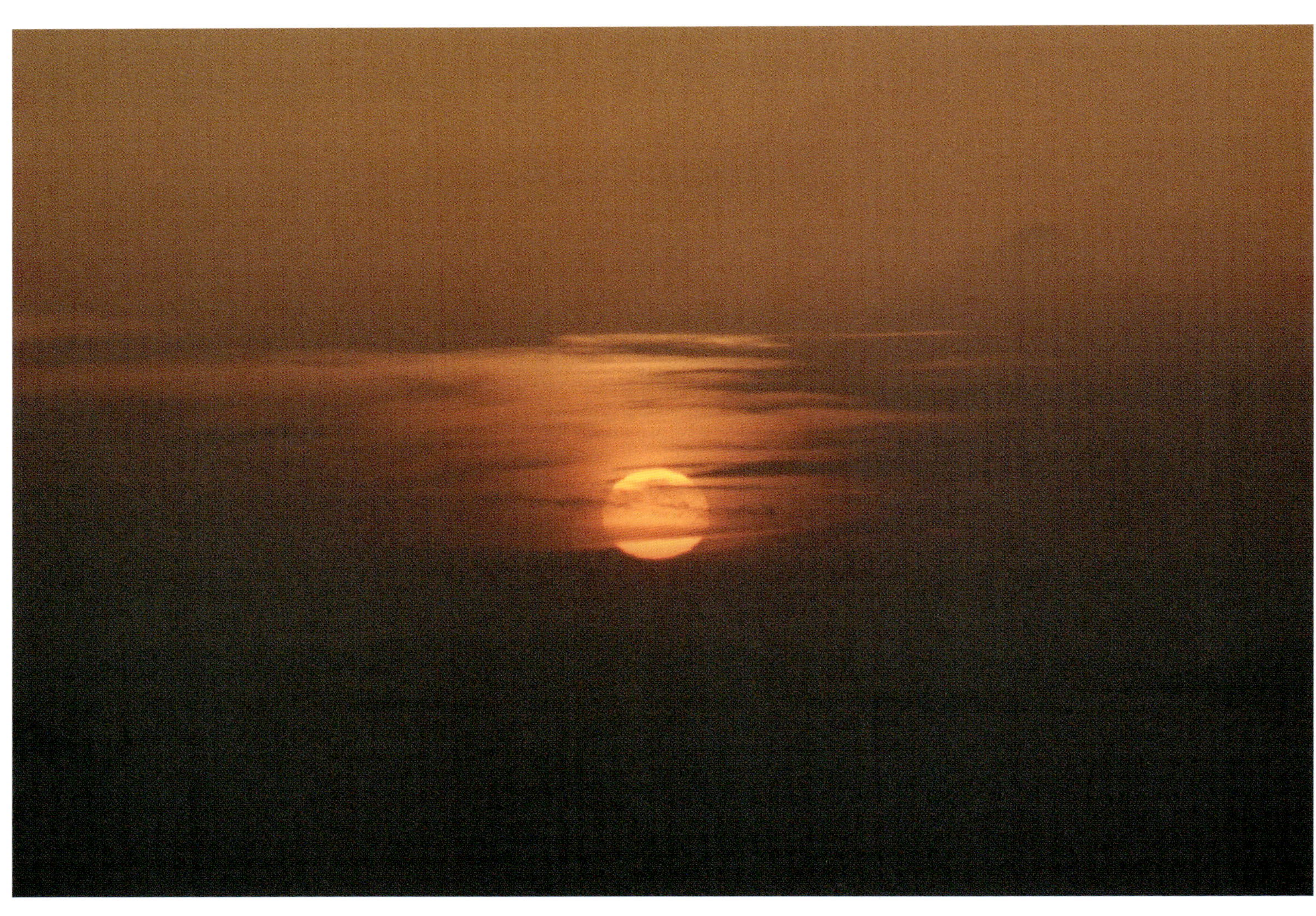

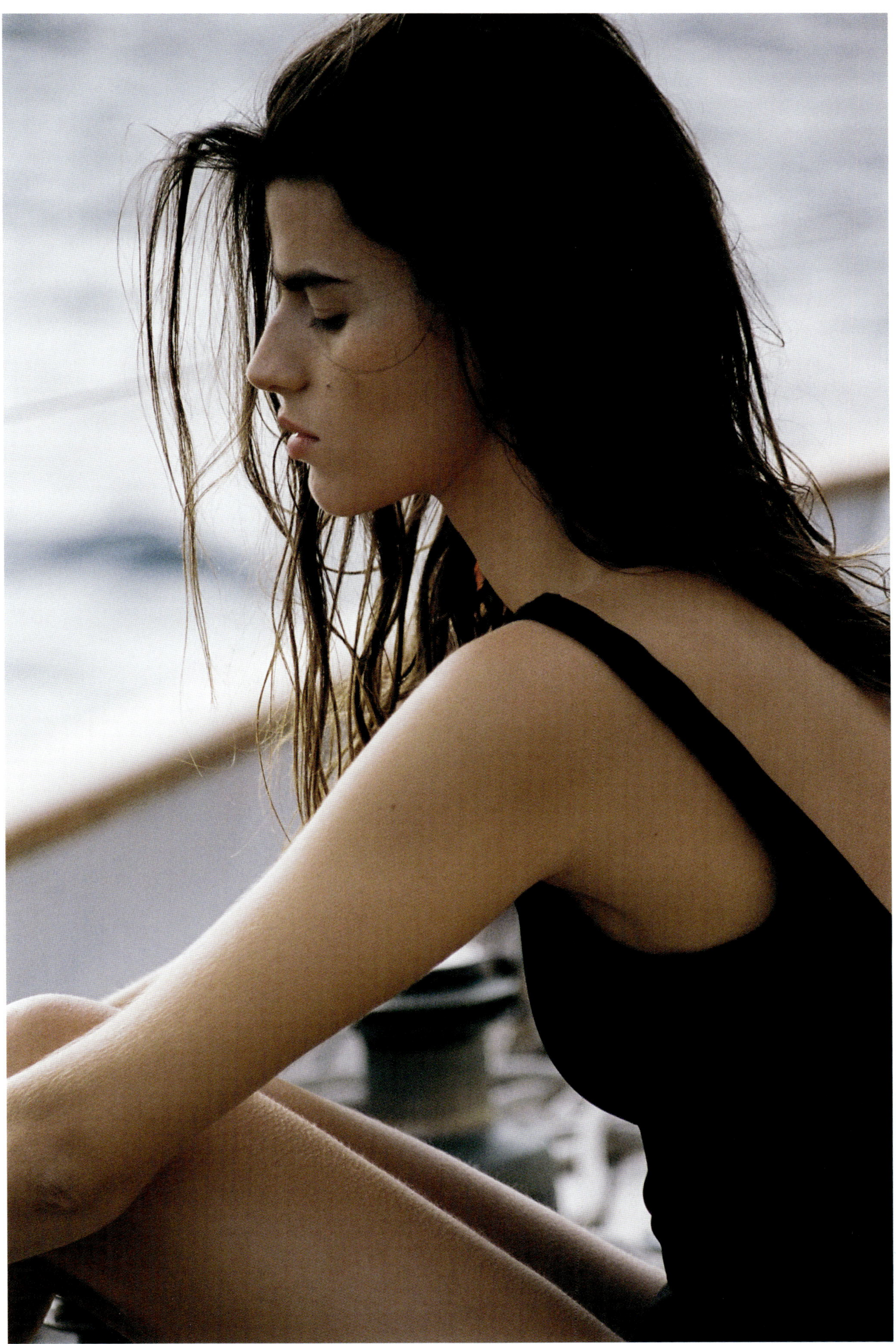

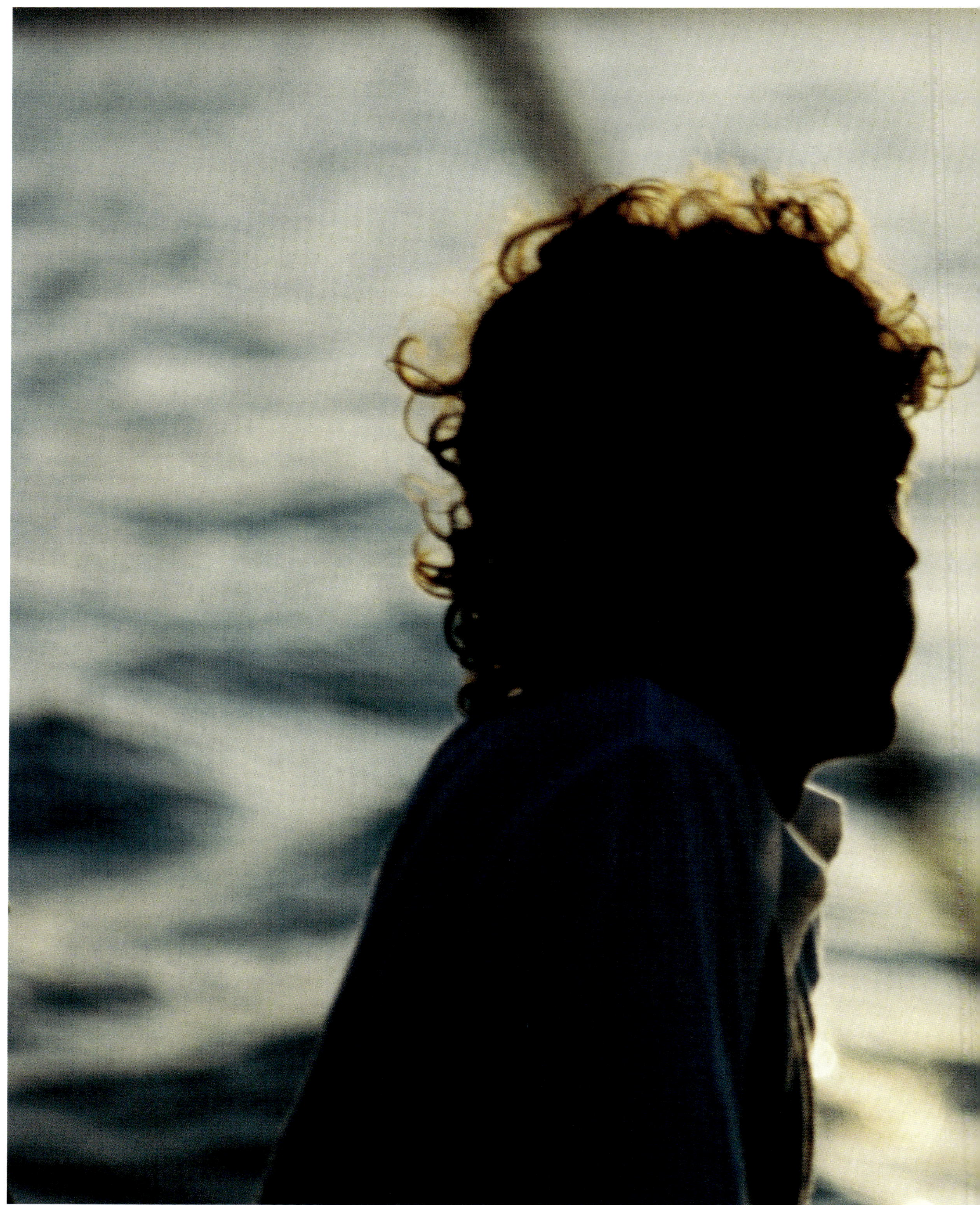

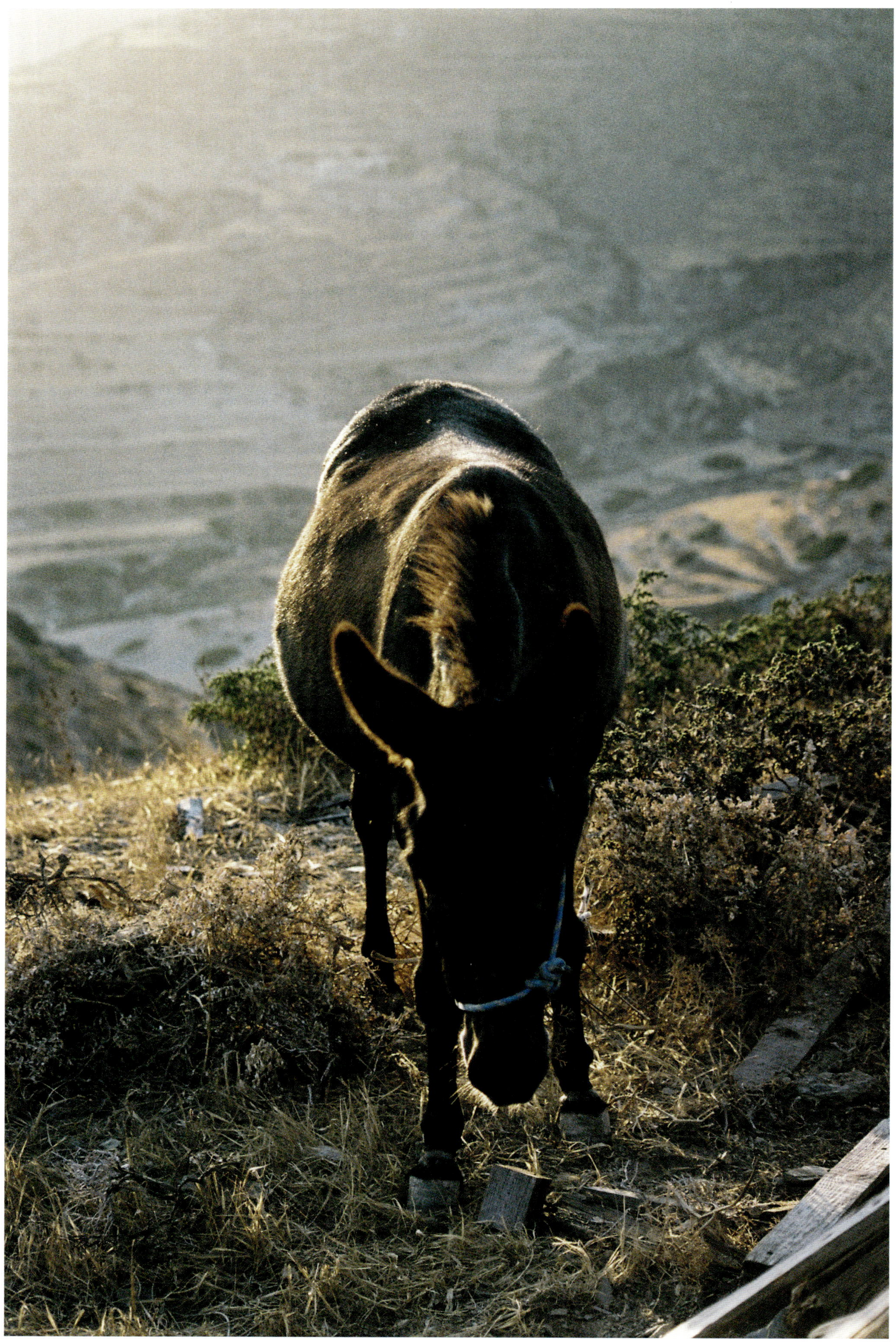

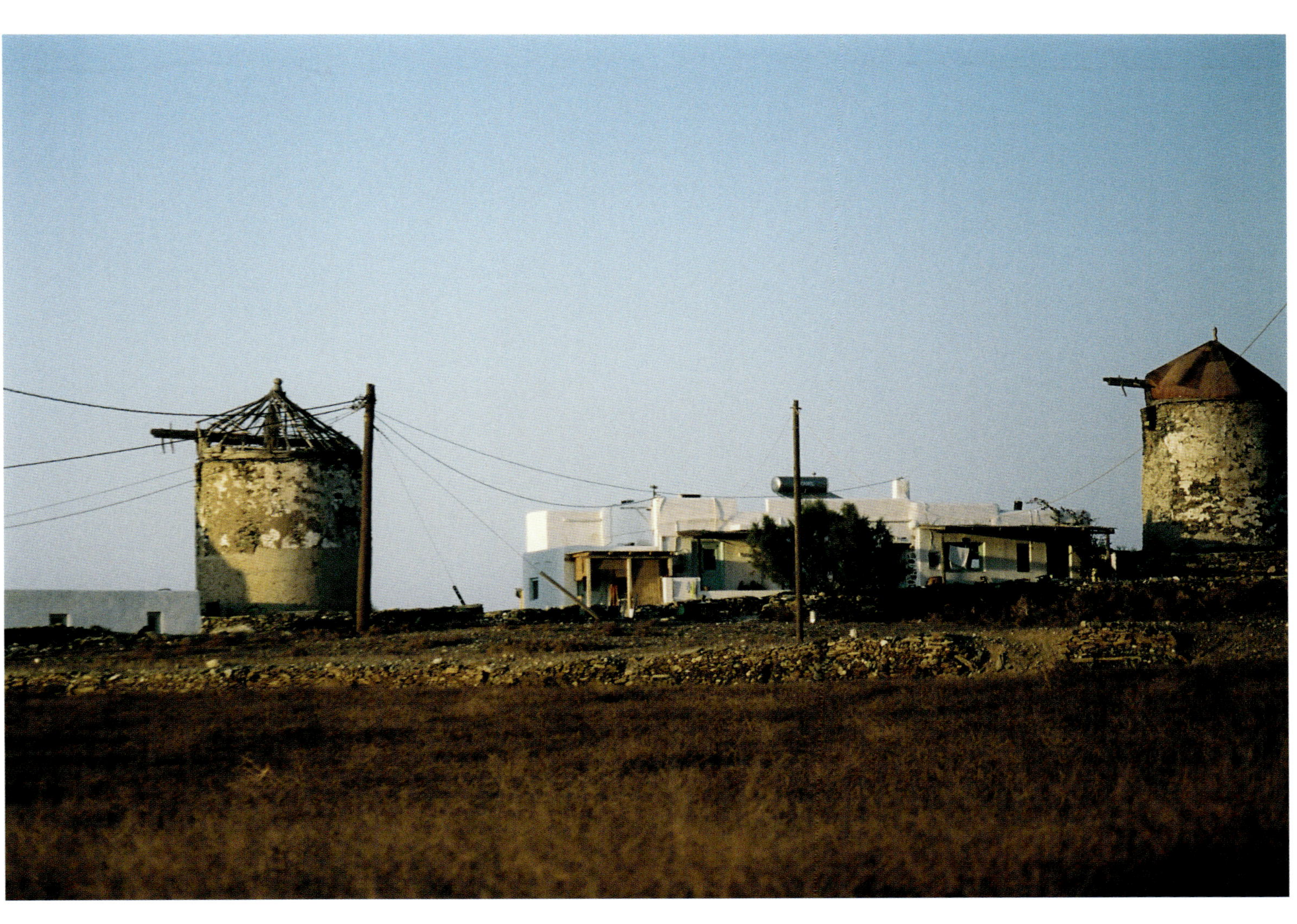

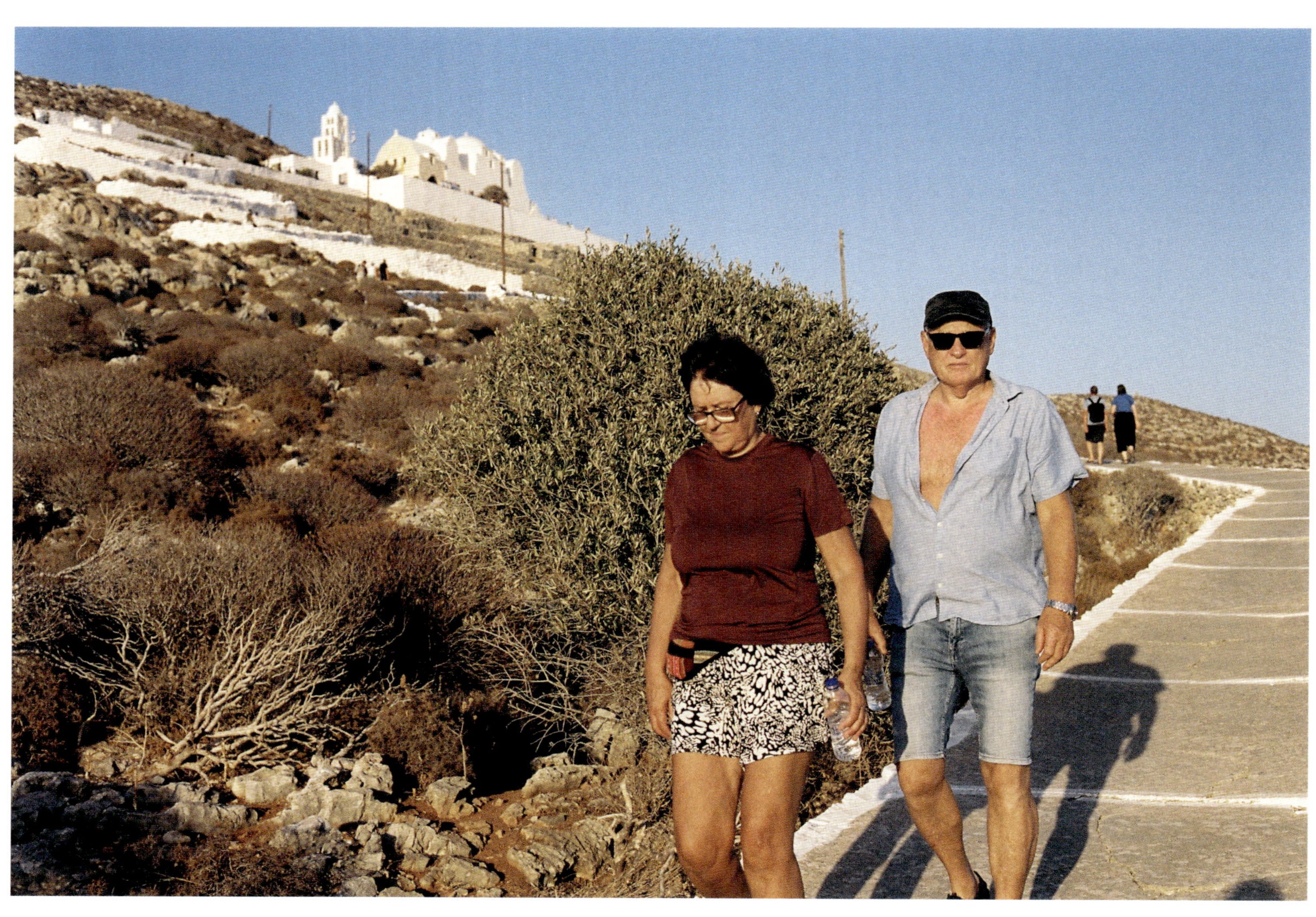

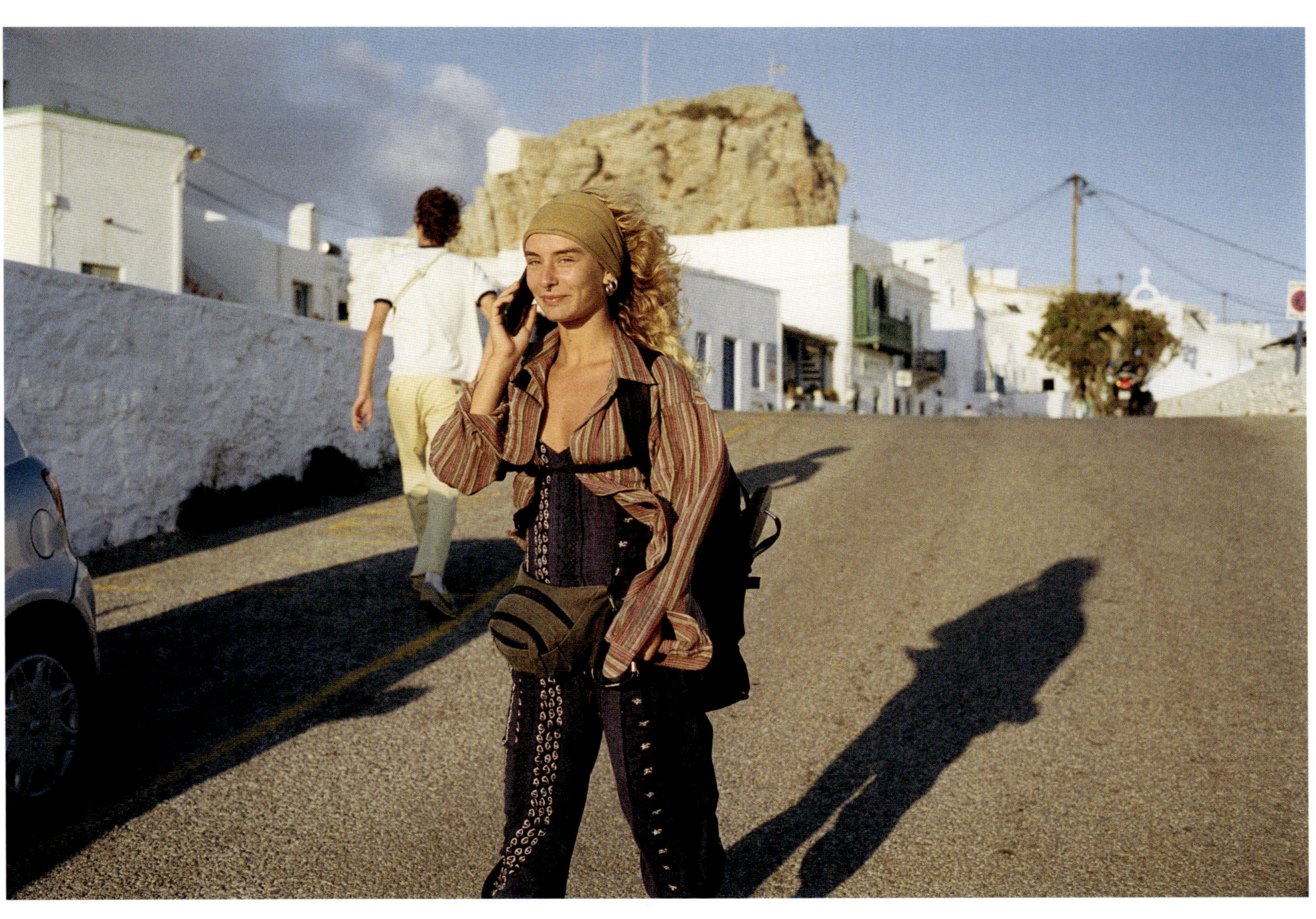

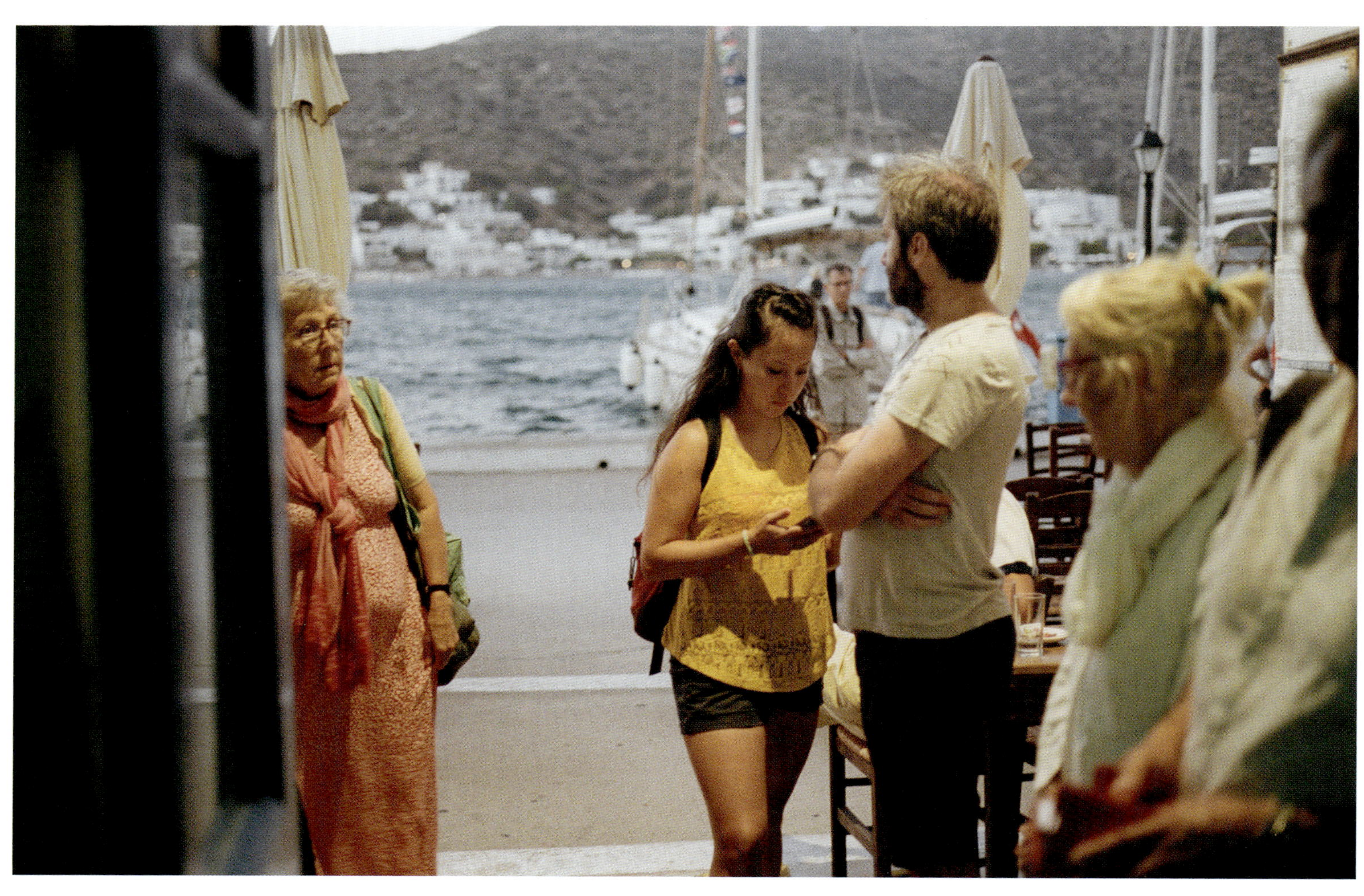

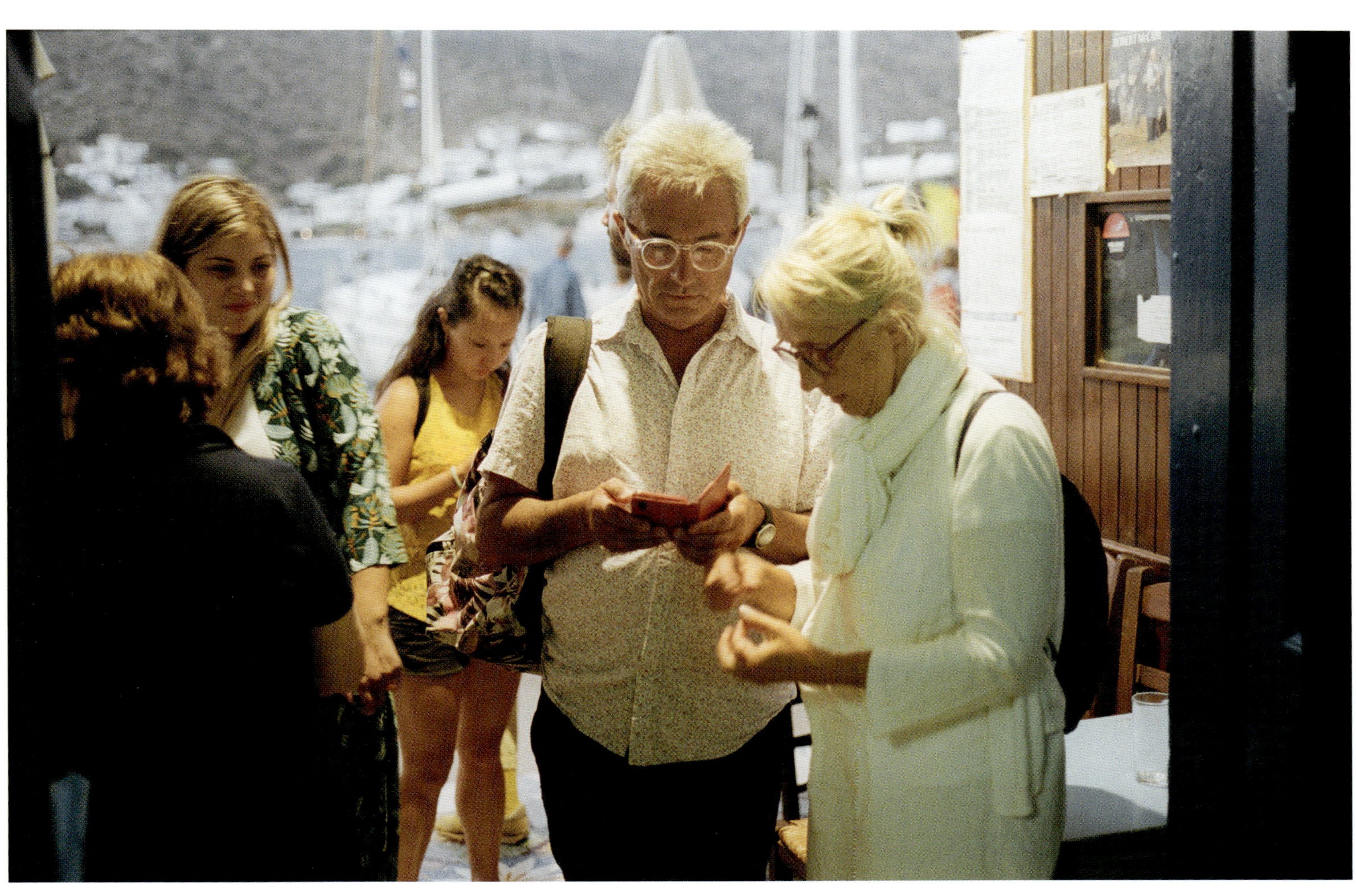

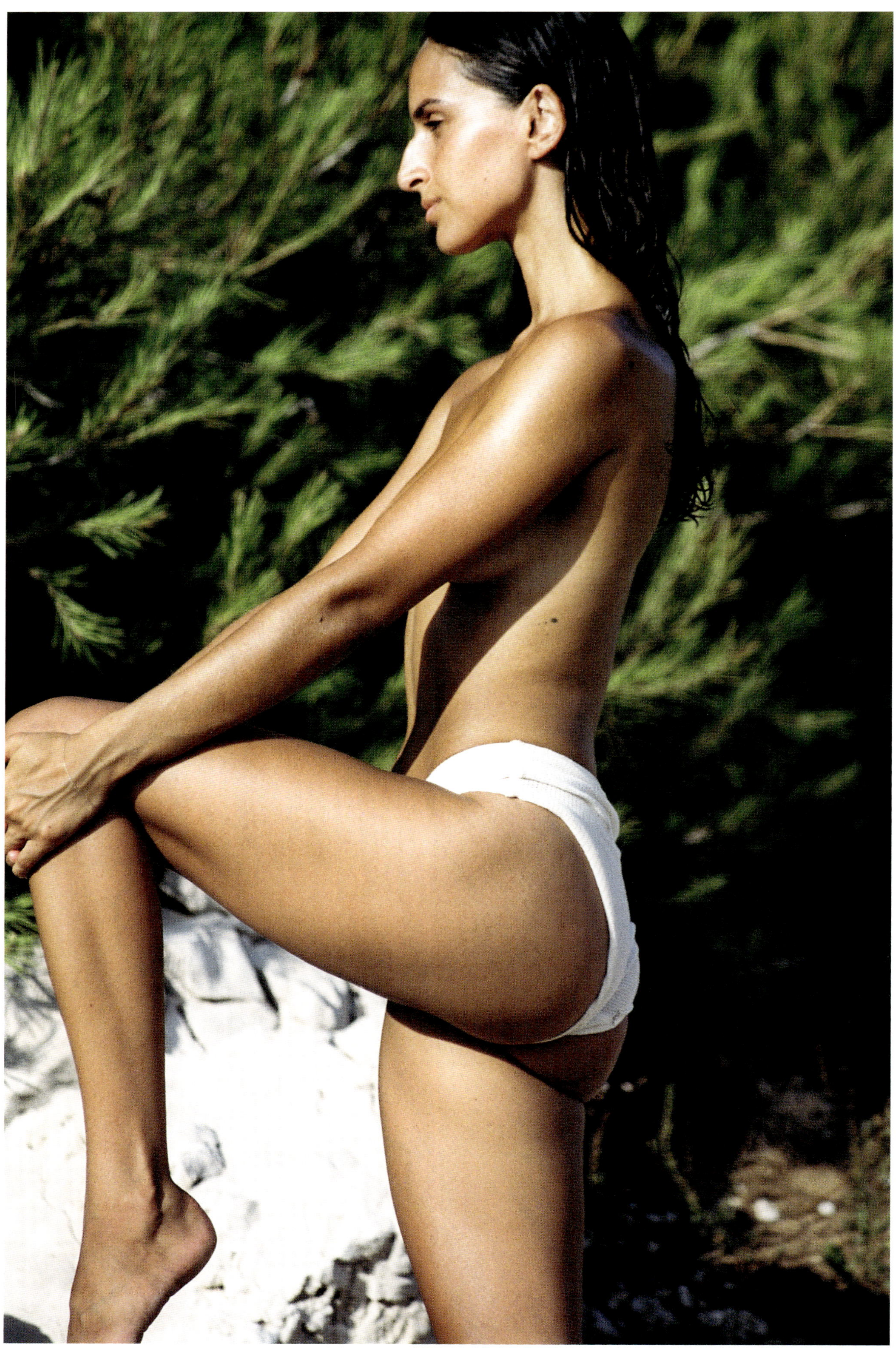

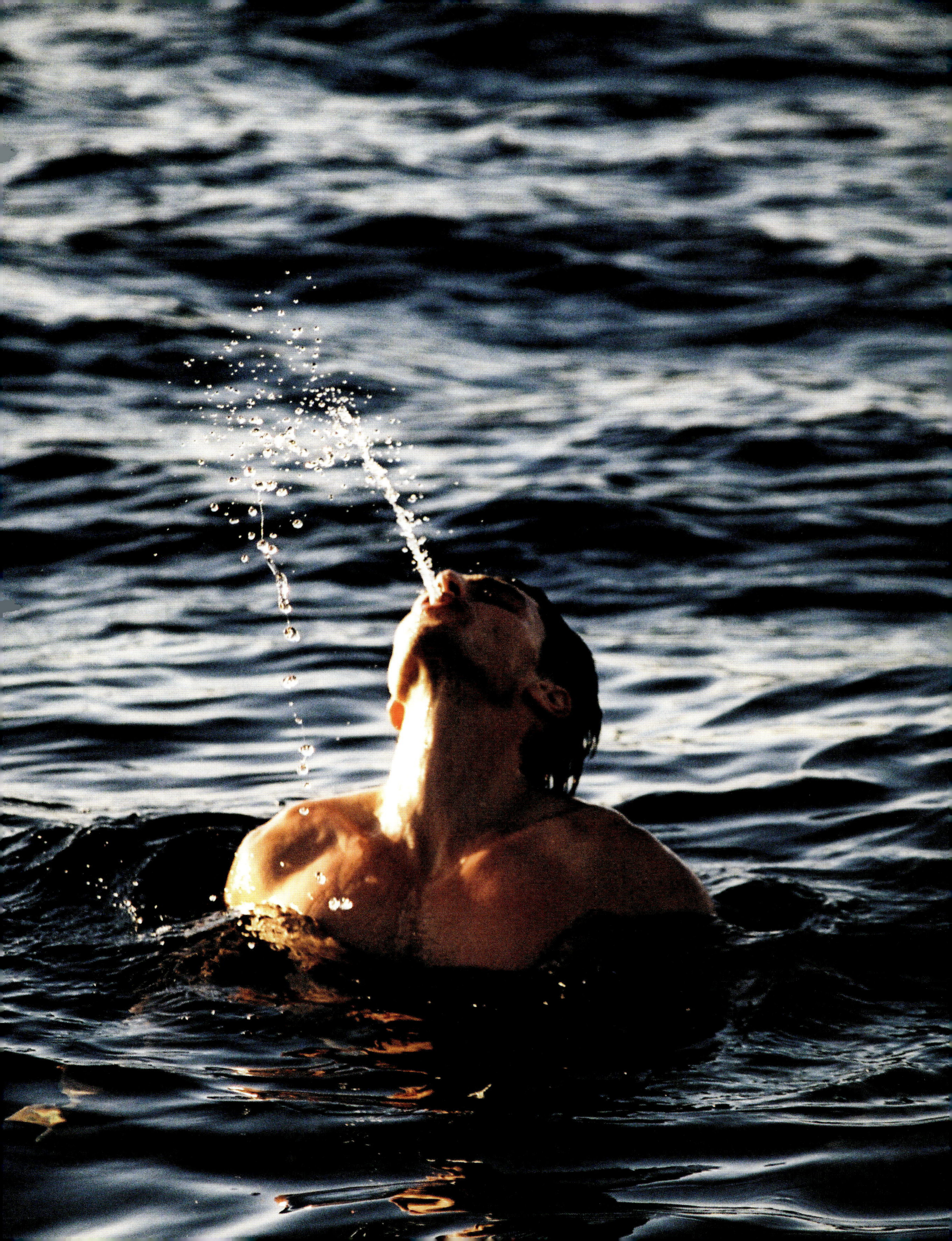

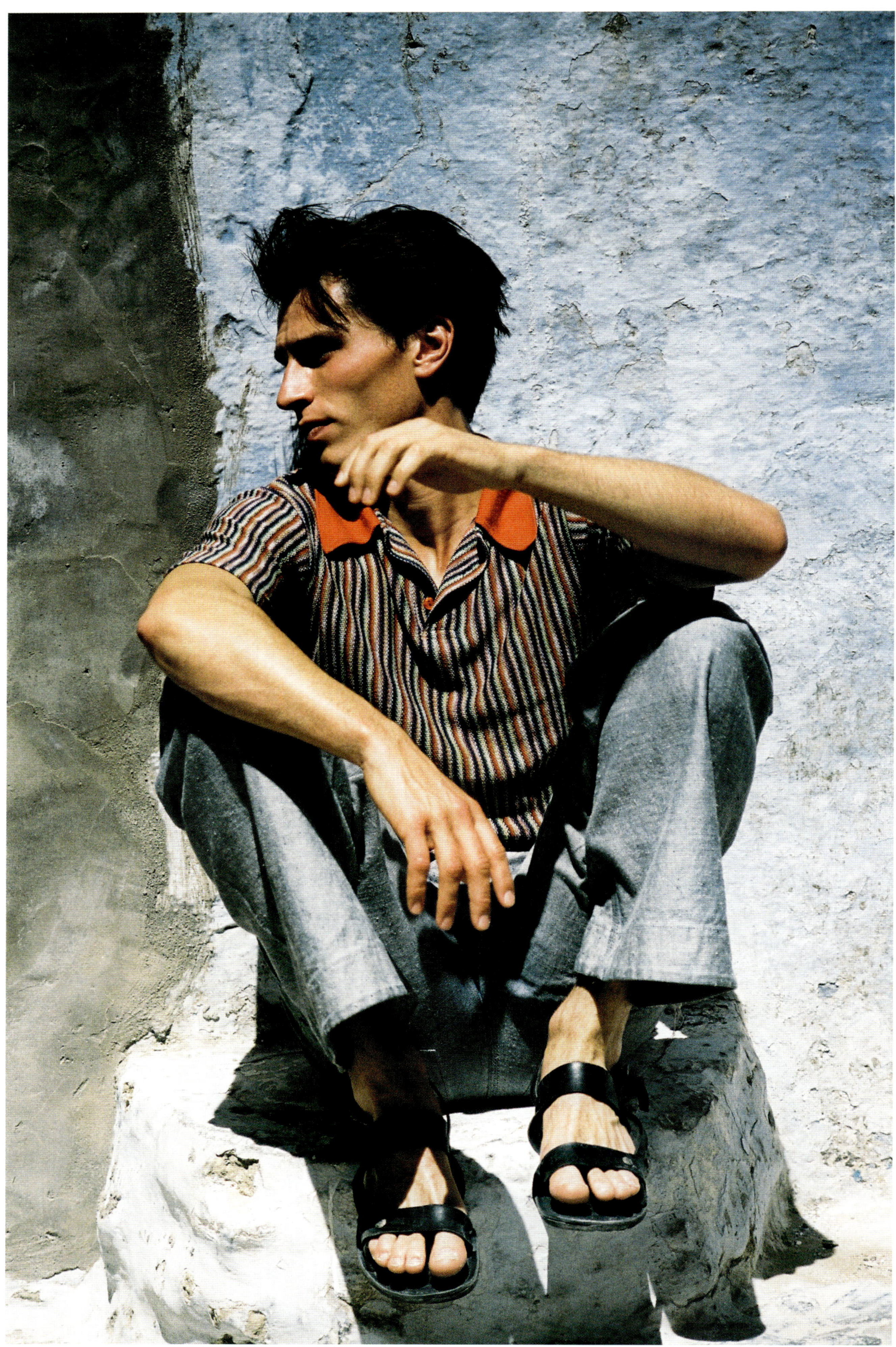

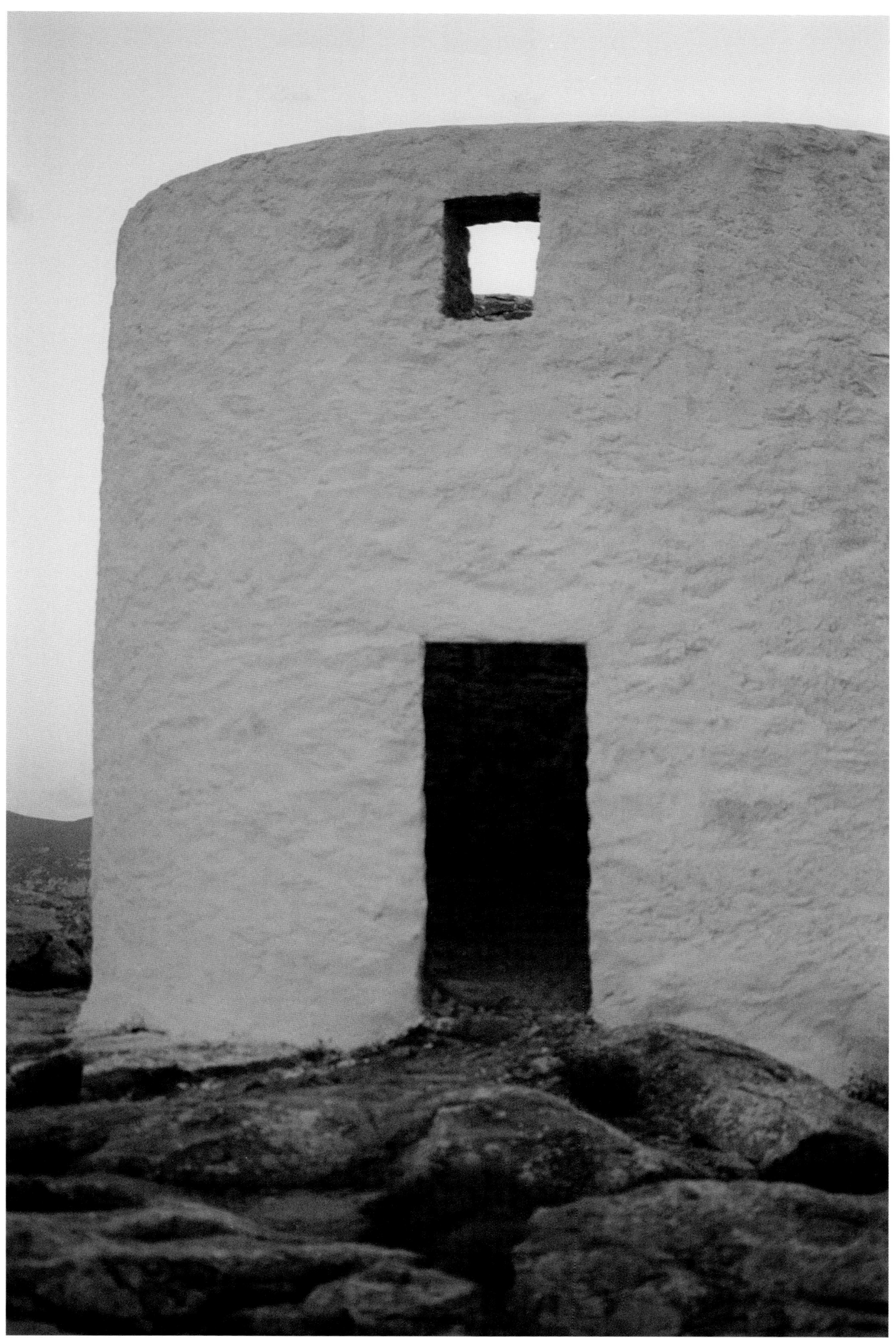

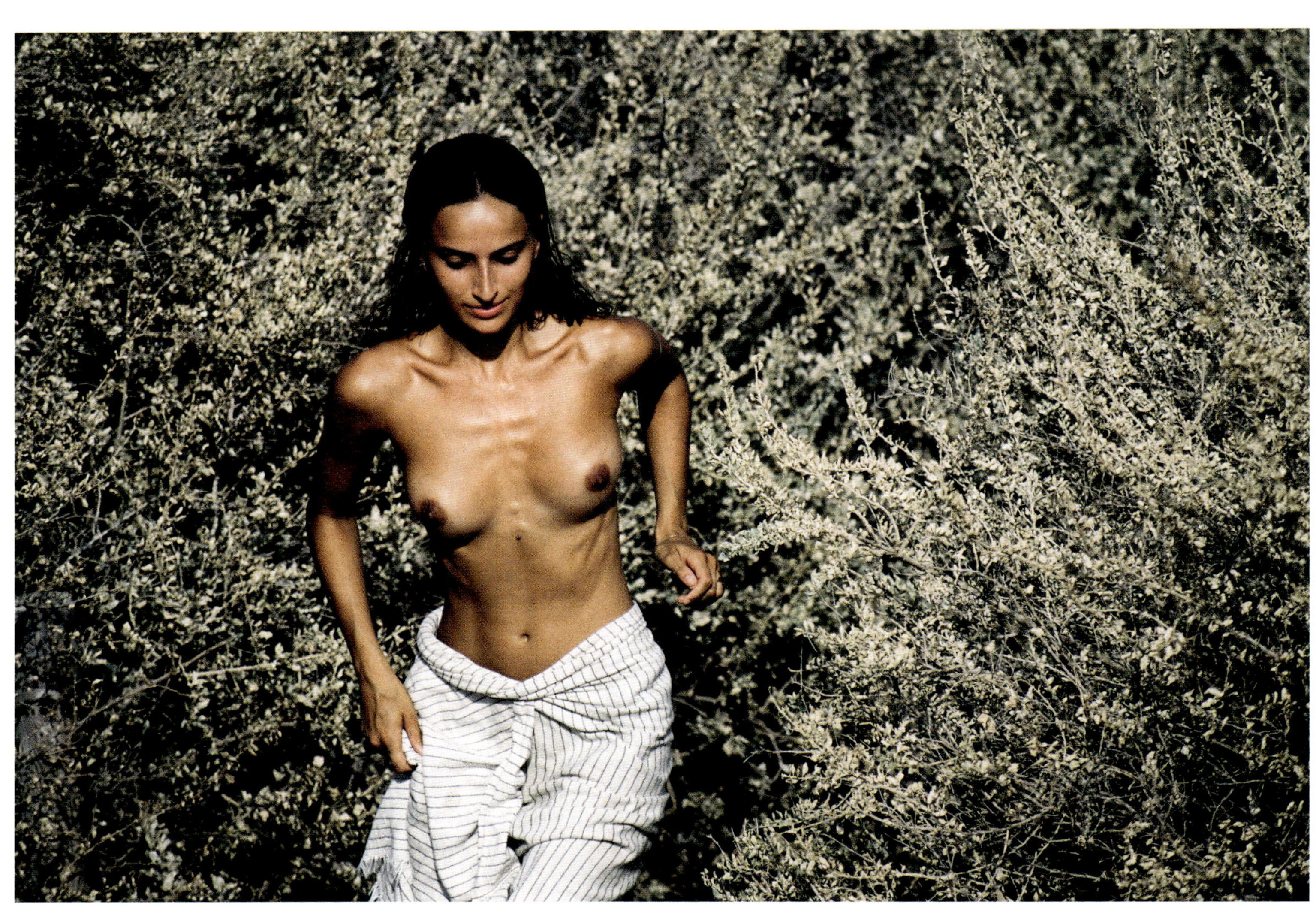

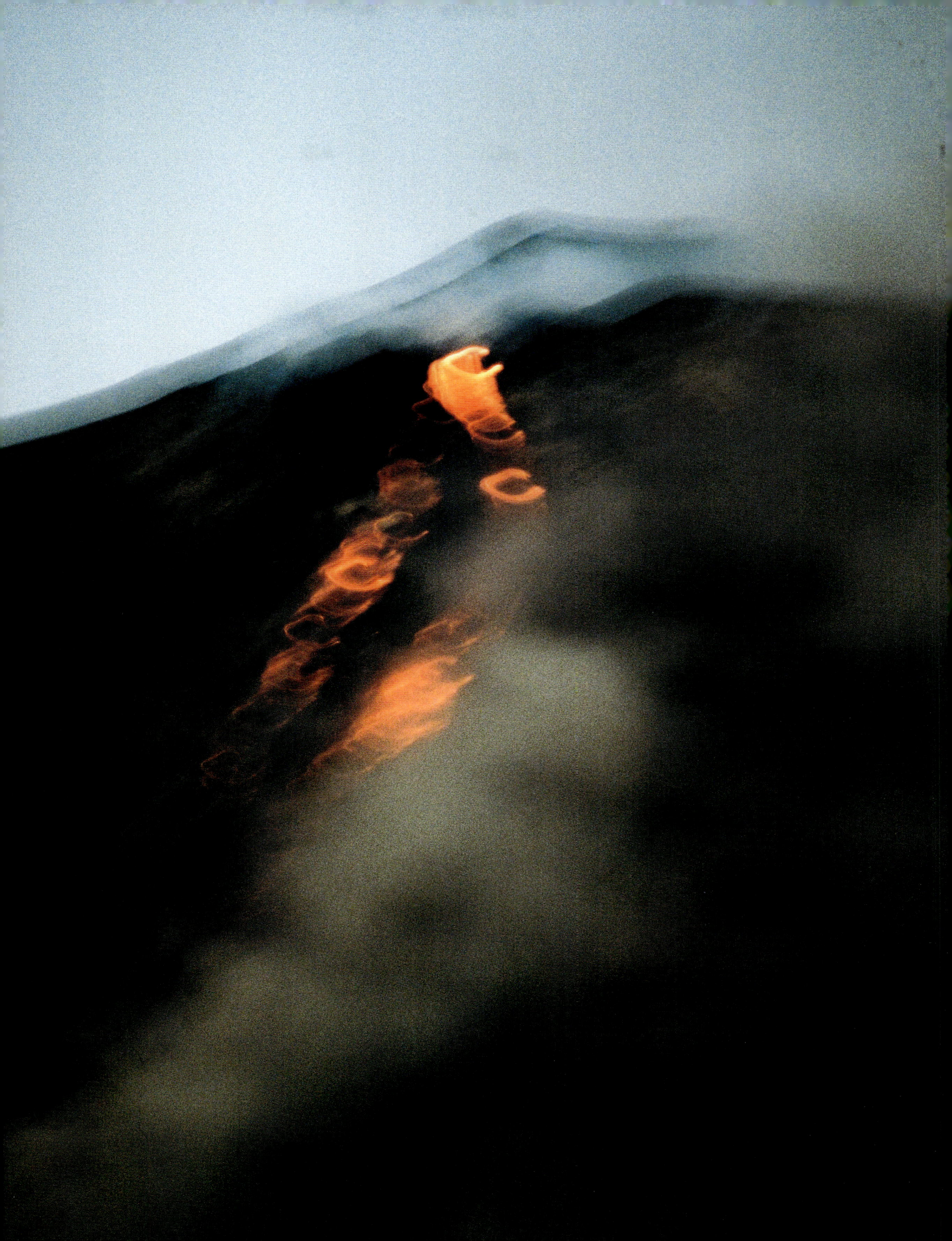

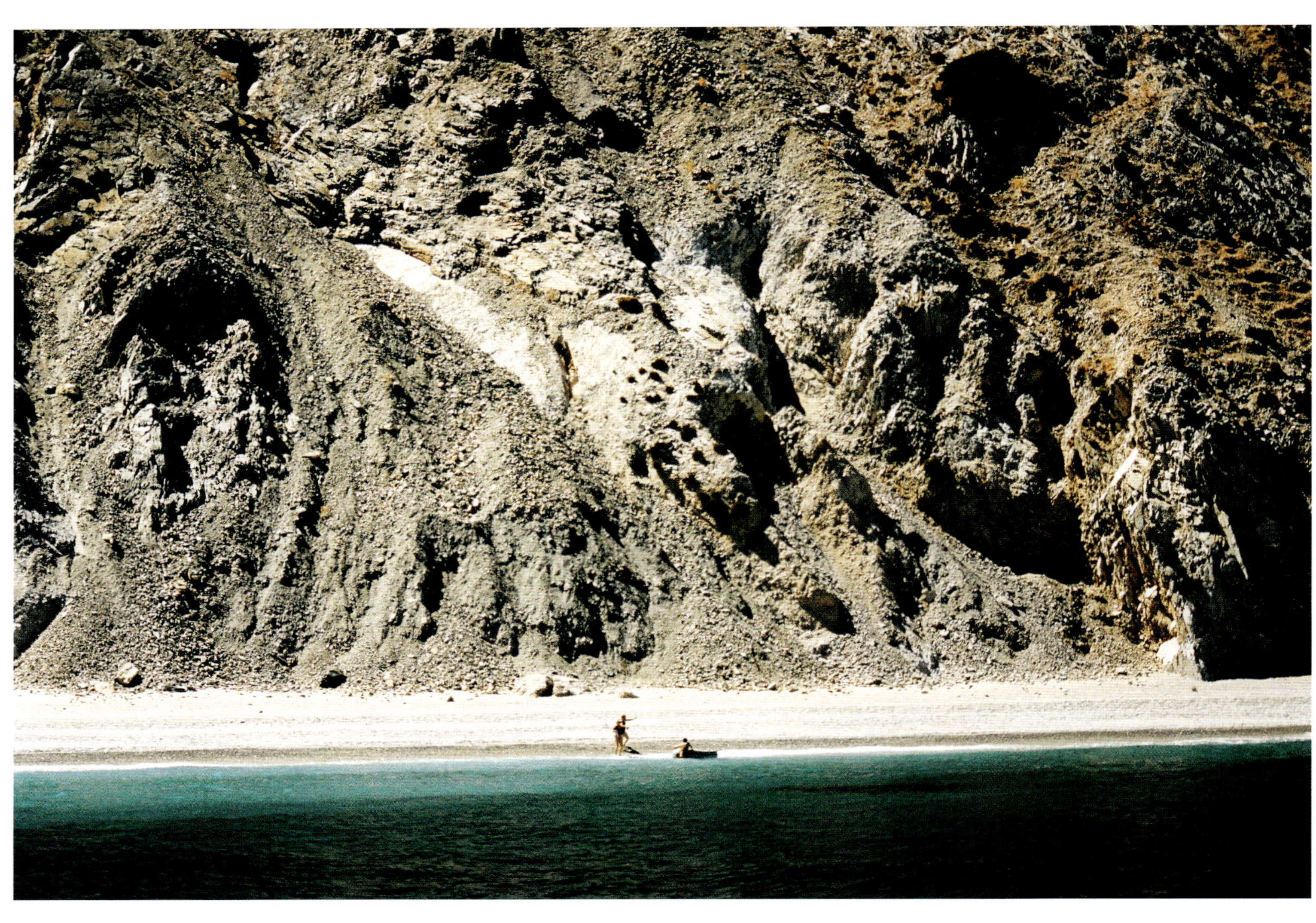

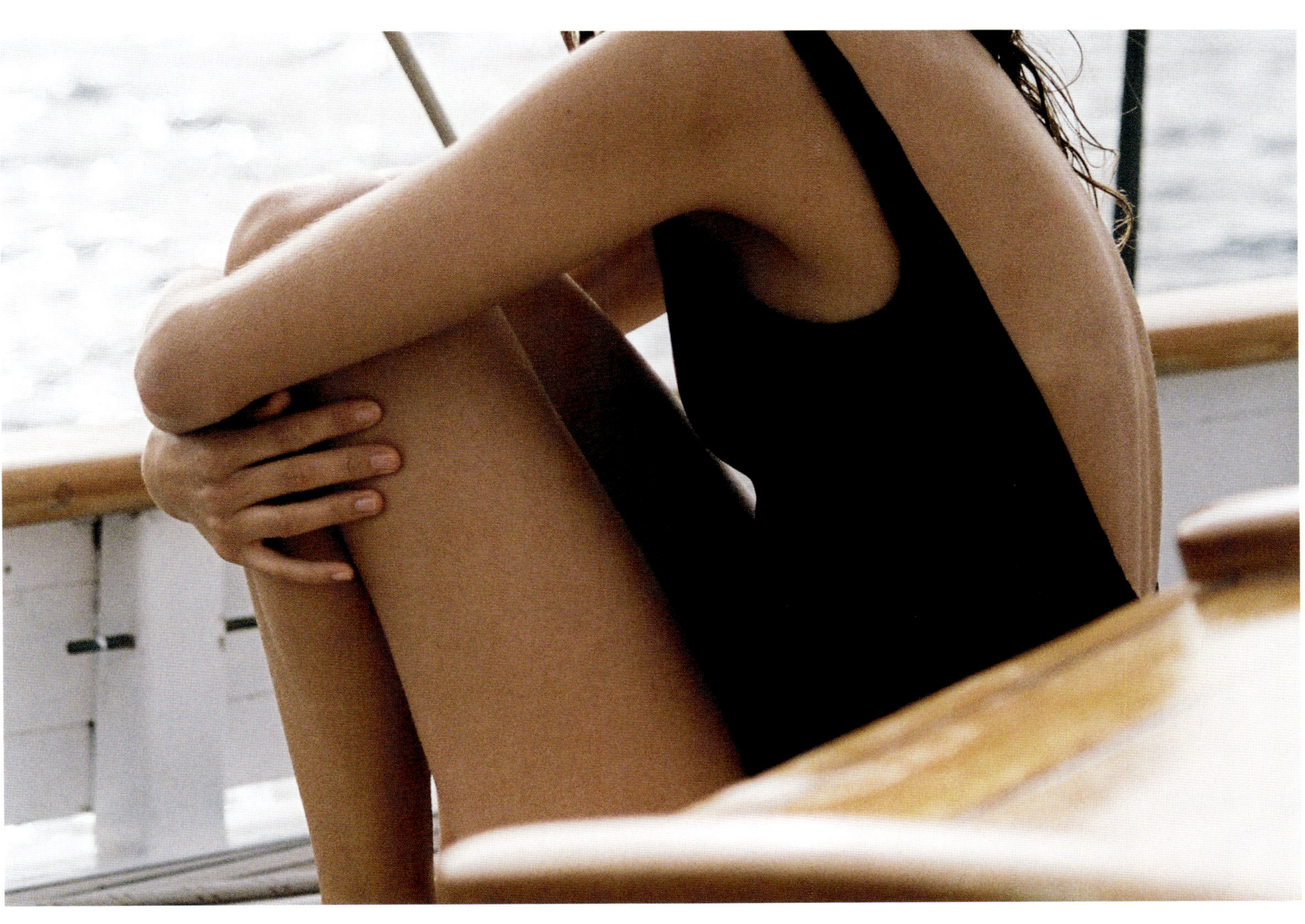

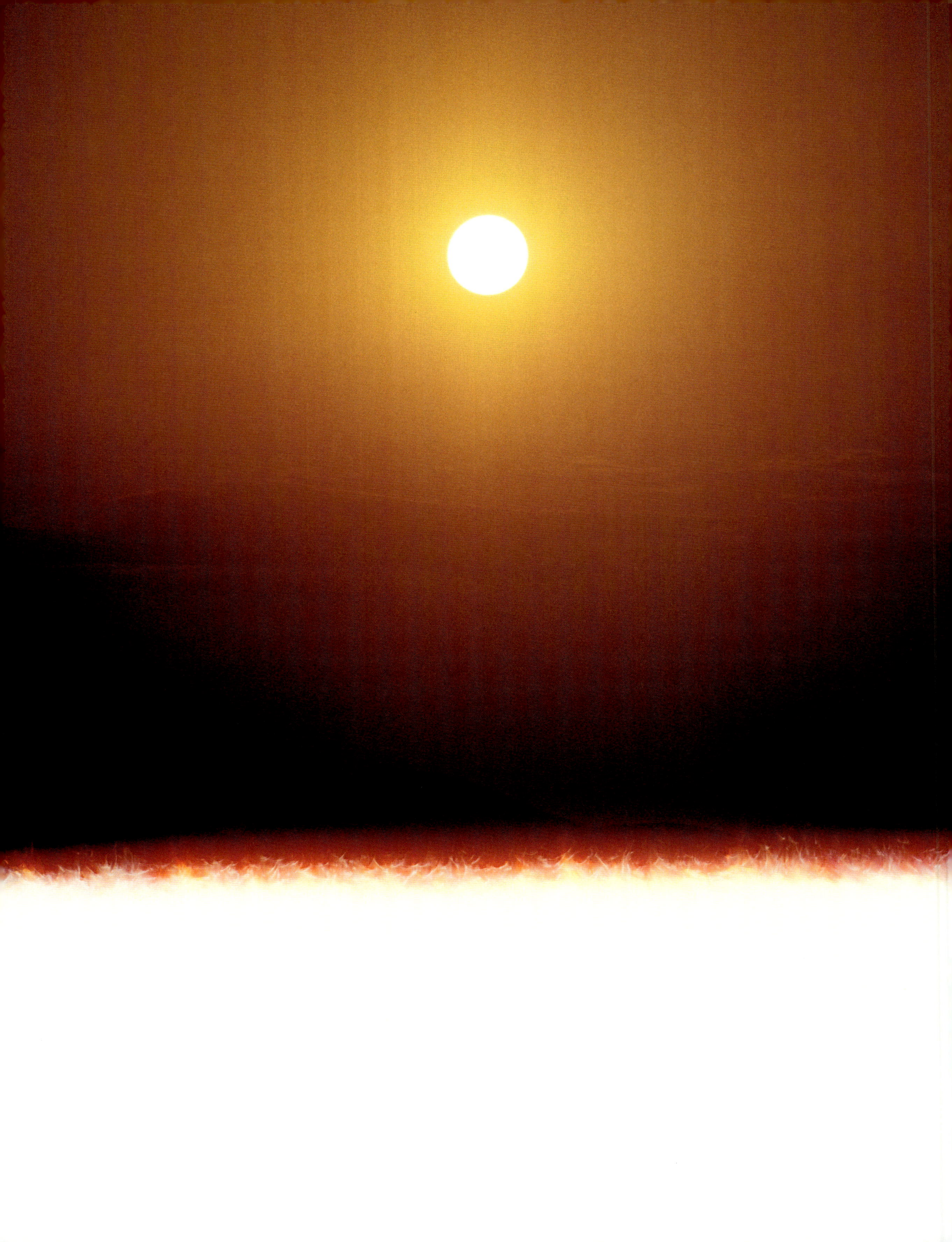

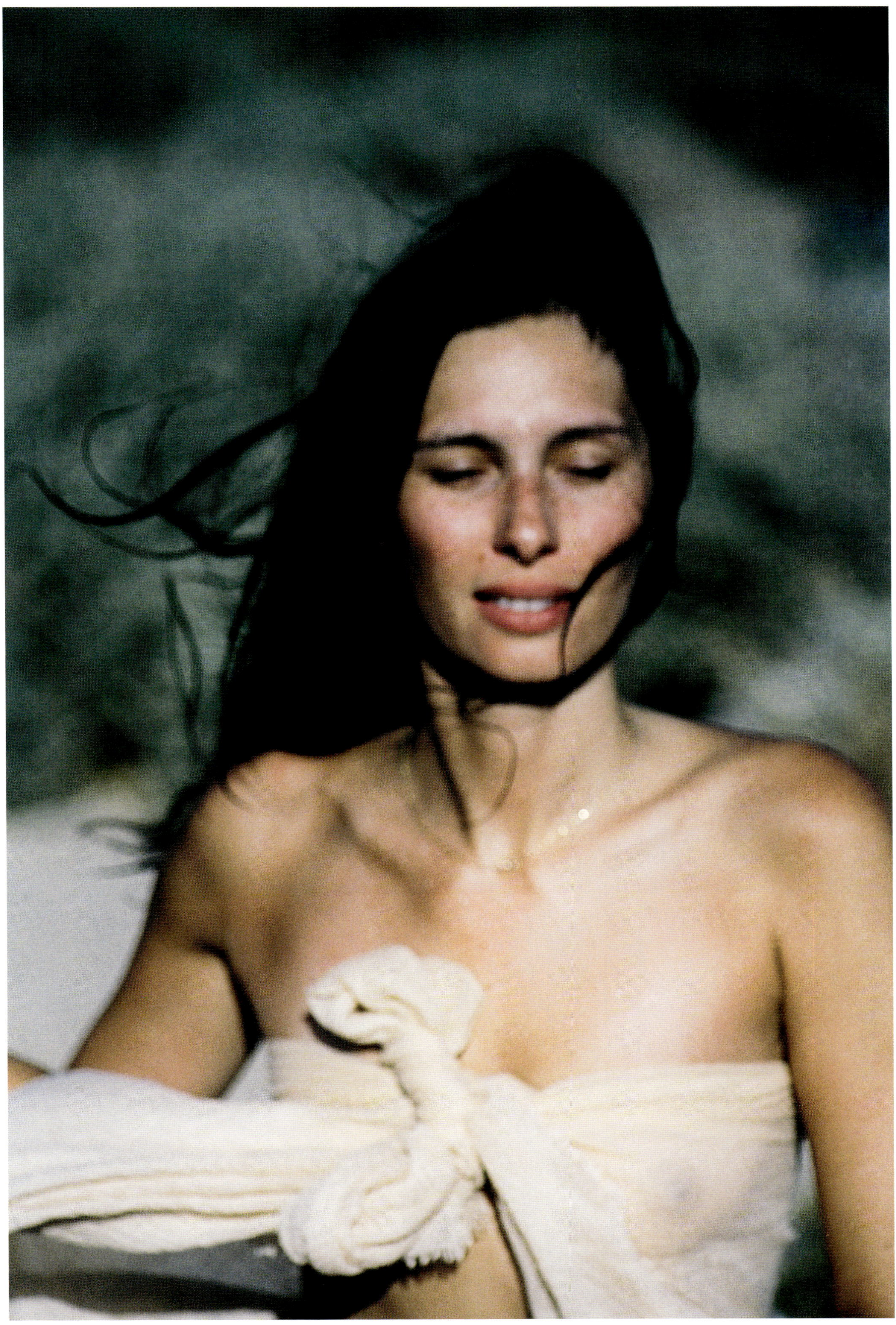

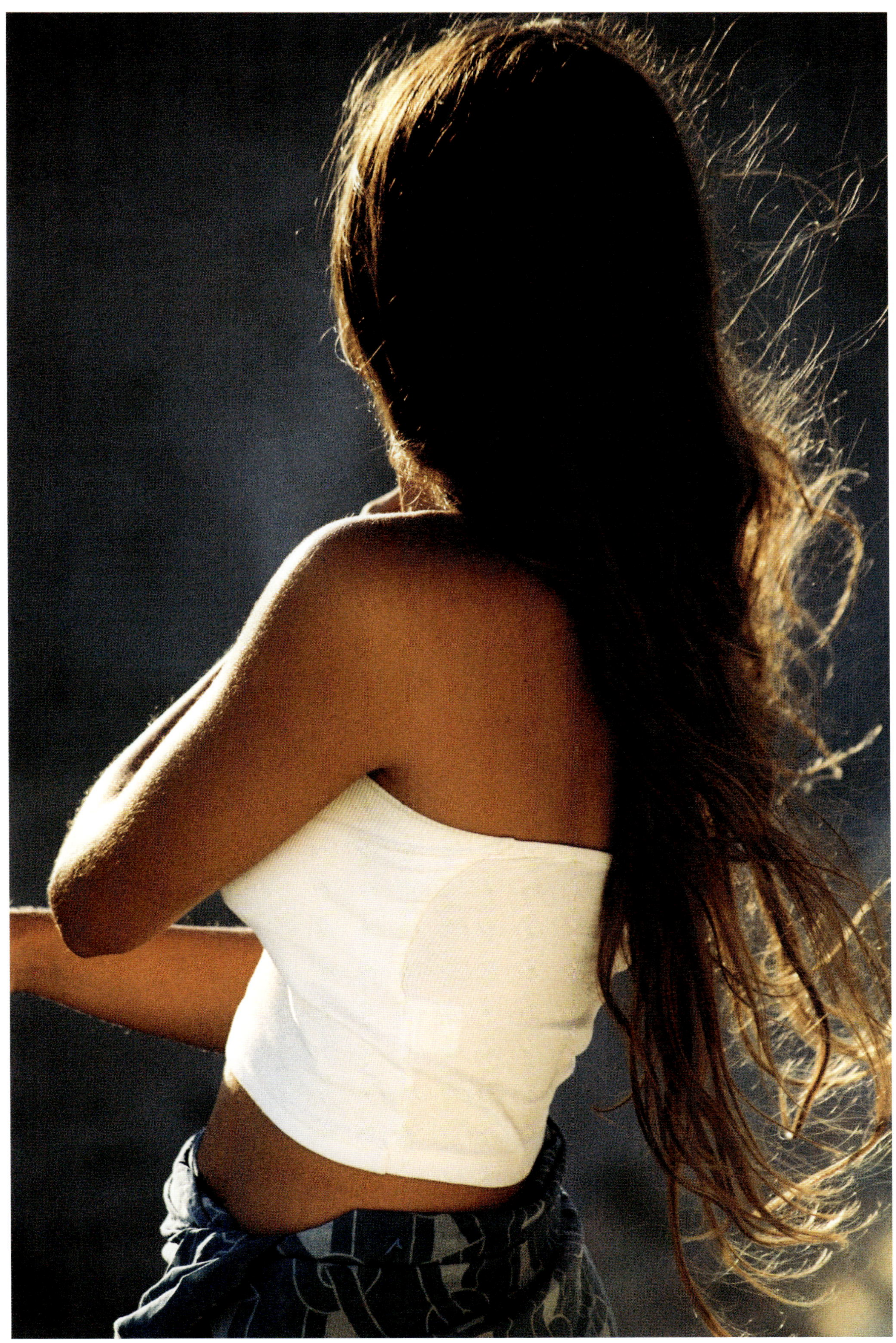

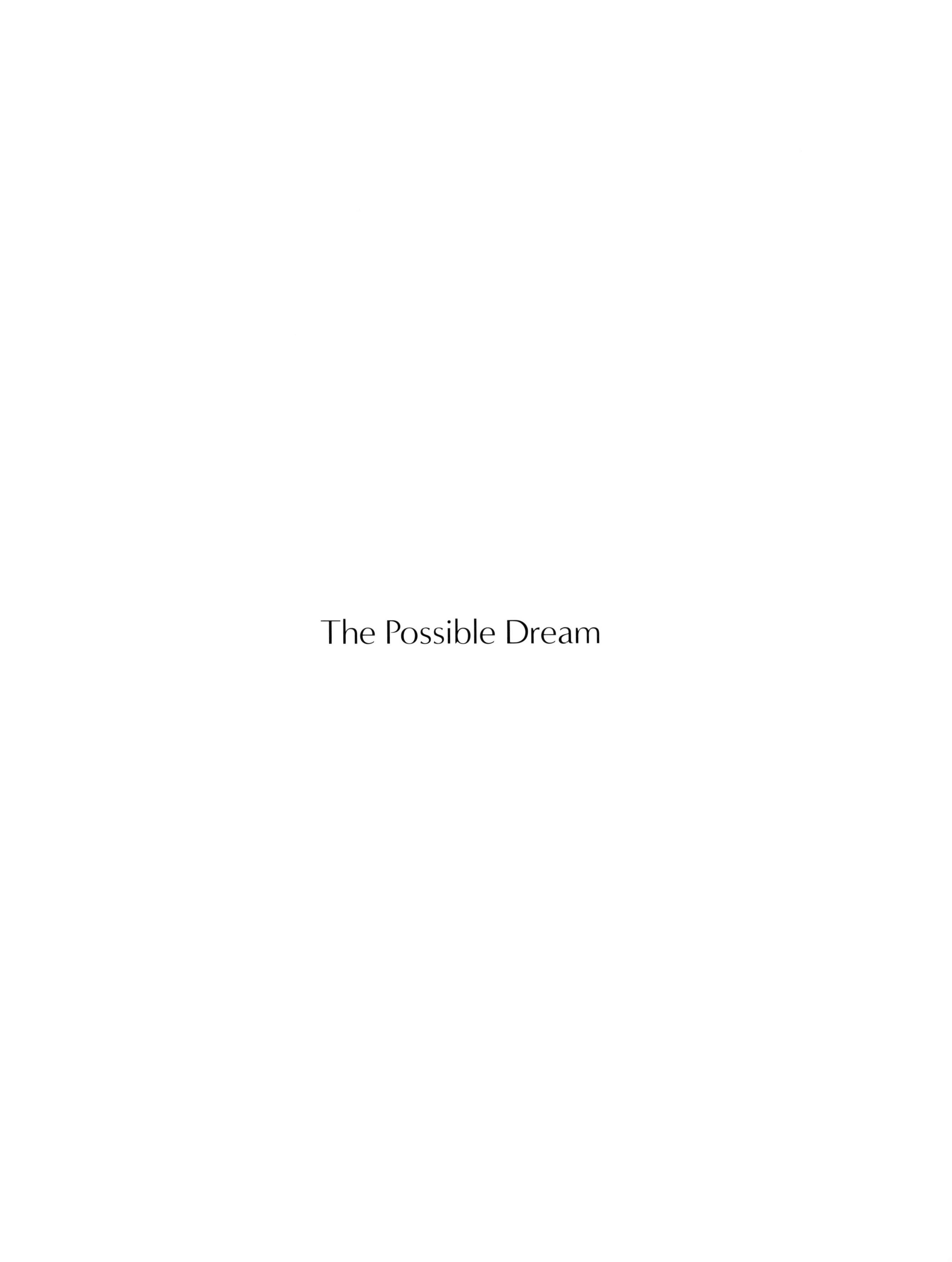

The Possible Dream

WE CALL IT PROGRESS when bridges leap across rivers, when tunnels bore through mountains for kilometres, when glass towers rise higher every year. From the window of a car or a plane, these structures pass like proof of a species determined to build against its own mortality. The same impression arises in front of a glowing computer screen, a television or a phone. Beneath their smooth, luminous surfaces lies an entire universe of invisible gears, fibre optics, liquid crystals, code and micro-components perfectly interlocked to make the miracle of contemporary technology possible – projects that require years, the labour of thousands of people, materials extracted from everywhere, endless construction sites.

Industrial and post-industrial civilisation is often celebrated as a triumph of progress. Do we truly need all of this? As time goes on, the feeling grows of an unstoppable inflation of what is considered "necessary". Every new function, every new object, every new service is presented as indispensable. Layers of complexity pile upon layers and are named "evolution", "development", "the future". But the final purpose of this movement becomes increasingly blurred.

This is not an argument against technology. The contemporary world is also an entertaining one – in the original sense of *devertere*: to divert, to turn away, to entertain. A universe offering endless distractions and escapes from oneself. All this matter, all these stimuli and devices seem to serve a psychological function too: filling the void, soothing the fear of looking inwards, of remaining alone with one's own questions. Yet if the background noise is suspended even for a moment, an essential question resurfaces: what kind of life is actually being lived?

It is a life spent on concrete, in saturated and often polluted air. A life of exhausting workdays, wages chasing inflation, widespread precarity – one that often resembles organised survival more than full existence. In the urban landscape, people at the margins – on pavements, under arcades – are systematically ignored: their presence cracks the optimistic narrative of normality. What kind of humanity is visible in this picture?

The contrast becomes clear in places where time follows another rhythm: rural landscapes, hills, small towns where the pace is slowed down, neighbours greet one another, conversations happen spontaneously, the fireplace marks the seasons. No urgency to show off, no pressure to dress well in order to belong. The essential is enough. This is not mere nostalgia for the past, but the concrete perception that a different way of inhabiting the world exists – one that relies less on accumulation and more on experience.

Here, a widely misused yet deeply necessary word comes into play: minimalism. Minimalism is not simply an aesthetic of clean interiors and white surfaces, but the instinctive reaction of a weary age. Ours is still the era of maximalism: the overproduction of goods, information, images, noise, opinions. Every space is occupied, every moment filled. Quantity has devoured quality. Minimalism arises from this collapse. When matter and language reach saturation, the opposite desire emerges: rarefaction. Minimalism is the choice to subtract in a world that never stops adding – a gesture of those who, faced with too much, decide to reduce, select and focus on what is essential.

The environmental crisis is the physical trace of maximalism. Wars, political polarisation, resource depletion, climate catastrophes: all are variations of the same illness – excess. It is the legacy of a modernity that, from Francis Bacon onwards, has interpreted the world as something to dominate, measure and exploit. Nature as raw material, the human being as producer-consumer, the planet as a vast machine. Now that this model begins to show its limits, a need emerges for a different measure: subtractive, selective, essential. Not adding more, but stopping. Not filling every space, but leaving one empty so that breathing becomes possible again. Reduction becomes perhaps the last possible form of elegance in a landscape that can no longer bear further additions.

It is in the light of these questions – about progress, excess and the desire for less – that Akila Berjaoui's work can be understood. Her photographs, far from being mere images of bodies and landscapes, appear as a visual response to this need for subtraction, an attempt to return to a simpler and truer way of being.

The first impression before one of her images is not that of a photograph, but of a memory: the memory of a summer perhaps never lived yet strangely familiar. A body that does not pose, a shadow falling like an omen, the sea breathing louder than the subject. Above all, what strikes the viewer is the silence – a silence not empty but dense with truth. Akila's work does not merely ask to be looked at; it asks to be listened to.

To understand these images, one must imagine a young girl who always swims further out than anyone else. A girl unafraid, challenging each wave as if it were a border to cross, a passage towards the infinite. This is Akila in the Queensland waters of her childhood spent in Australia: always the furthest out, always the freest, always the most alive. That courage, that persistent search for the horizon, is the invisible matrix of this book.

And yet this freedom, today, carries the taste of a return. Before that ocean came war. Before the young girl who challenged the sea, there was another child learning too early the sound of bombs, the feeling of fear and precariousness. And as life continued, further forms of control, constraint and violence followed. Each image in this book is born from the search for a space where fear no longer rules.

We live in a time that has "seen too much" – too much pain, too much destruction, too many images that cut into the collective psyche. The world is crossed by conflicts, from Palestine to other, less visible fronts. Our shared gaze absorbs daily amounts of violence that turn it into a traumatised organ. Creativity struggles to emerge when reality feels like a siege; digital noise crushes, speed devours, representation replaces presence.

Many of the photographs in this book were taken in Greece. This is not accidental. It is sometimes said – half joking, half cynical – that the Greeks built the Acropolis and then nothing more. Today Athens often appears as an urban tangle, a confusion of concrete, wires and clustered buildings, as if everything worth doing had been done and what followed was only a long, disordered tail of history.

But this is only half the story. Greece is also the symbolic cradle of what is called Western civilisation. Long before our current crises, Greek thinkers wrestled with the same questions that resurface today in new forms: What is the world? What is its principle, its origin, its *arche*? Thales of Miletus found it in water – the simplest, most mobile, most essential element. Anaximander found it in the *apeiron*, the indefinite, as if sensing that every rigid form is only a temporary crystallisation of something vaster. Heraclitus recognised it in fire and flow, in *panta rhei*: everything flows, nothing remains the same. Order is never final; the world is movement.

The Greece in Akila's work is not the Greece of monuments, but of elements: water, rock, sun, skin. Her photographs step below the level of history and return to the zero point of thought: not the world as something to dominate, but as something to inhabit, cross and contemplate without possession. In these images, Greece becomes an eternal present of light and truth – a place where things do not need justification. Light knows no irony; the sun allows few masks. Under such sky, pretence cannot survive long. In such a landscape, minimalism is not a style but a natural condition. One lives with little, desires less, listens more. Akila's photography emerges precisely from this subtraction. Excess would feel out of place, almost obscene.

Every choice is an ethical gesture: clothing reduced to the minimum; second-hand or vintage, no artificial production, no superfluous scenography – only light, skin, rock, wind, water. A primordial aesthetic that refuses to add new wounds to the environment: minimal footprints, an almost ritual fidelity to nature's rhythms.

This is a return to simplicity – not the polished simplicity of social media, but an existential one. A life measured by a few essential elements: the warmth of the sun, the freshness of the sea, contact with the earth, the presence of others. A life that proves unexpectedly sufficient. The body, in these photographs, is never a spectacle. It is a body in the process of liberation – from beauty standards, from patriarchy, from the implicit hierarchies of the gaze, from systems of control.

It does not perform; it simply is. Fragile and strong, often marked by its own contradictions. In many images, alongside the light, the shadow also appears – the "shadow" of which Jung spoke: the unintegrated part, what one prefers not to see yet which accompanies every identity. Sometimes it is a restrained gesture, a distant look, a subtle tension between two bodies. There is no indulgence in it, only honesty: no authentic freedom exists without acknowledging one's darker zones.

The period following the pandemic marked a clear evolution in Akila's gaze. If her earlier work was more hedonistic, nocturnal and populated, here prevails a need for quiet, for introspection. In a politically and economically unstable world, where many seek escape from themselves in crowds and nightlife, this work moves in the opposite direction: towards nature, and through nature, towards a deeper form of self.

Nature is not background here; it is protagonist, therapist, witness, ally. It is the space where judgement falls silent and it becomes possible to loosen one's defences, to stop performing, to breathe again.

This book is a celebration of love, life, freedom, equality and unpretentious beauty. It is an ode to a specific moment in the year: the end of summer, when the heat softens, tourists disappear and places return to those who truly inhabit them. It is also an act of gratitude towards the landscapes that made this inner transformation possible, and towards a planet that can no longer tolerate our maximalism.

The Possible Dream is exactly that: a possible dream.

Not an abstract utopia but something tangible – a body at ease in its own skin; a time no longer fractured by notifications; a landscape not consumed but respected; a life that does not need too much to feel full.

MATTEO MAMMOLI

ACKNOWLEDGEMENTS

I wish to convey my profound appreciation and gratitude to all of you listed below. Hugo, it´s been delightful to work with you once again and I thank you for your patience with me on the layout! Curt, thank you for making this possible once more.

Matteo, your words have deeply resonated with me and they reflect my vision beautifully. To the following people who believed in me to portray them in their authentic selves, I am tremendously grateful that you all contributed to this chapter of my life.

Malina, Bella, Ioanna, Marguerite, Gemma, Ayse, Iana, Clément, Léa, Vlada, Mariia, Amos, Fanny, Paula and to everyone else, grand merci.

The photographs featured in this book were taken between 2020 and 2025.

To those who have bravely survived, or are currently enduring domestic violence, be it emotional abuse, physical or sexual abuse, I hear you, I see you, and most importantly I believe you.

A member of Verlagsgruppe Random House GmbH
Neumarkter Straße 28 • 81673 Munich
produktsicherheit@penguinrandomhouse.de

First Edition

Library of Congress Control Number is available; British Library Cataloguing-in-Publication Data: a catalogue record for this book is available from the British Library

Editorial direction: Curt Holtz
Design and layout: Hugo d´Alte, Helsinki
Retouching: Paul Drozdowski
Production management: Luisa Klose
Separations: Reproline Mediateam, Munich
Printing and binding: Livonia Print SIA, Riga
Paper: Magno Matt

Verlagsgruppe Random House FSC® N001967

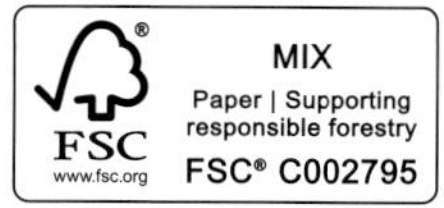

Printed in Latvia

ISBN 978-3-7913-9406-0

www.prestel.com

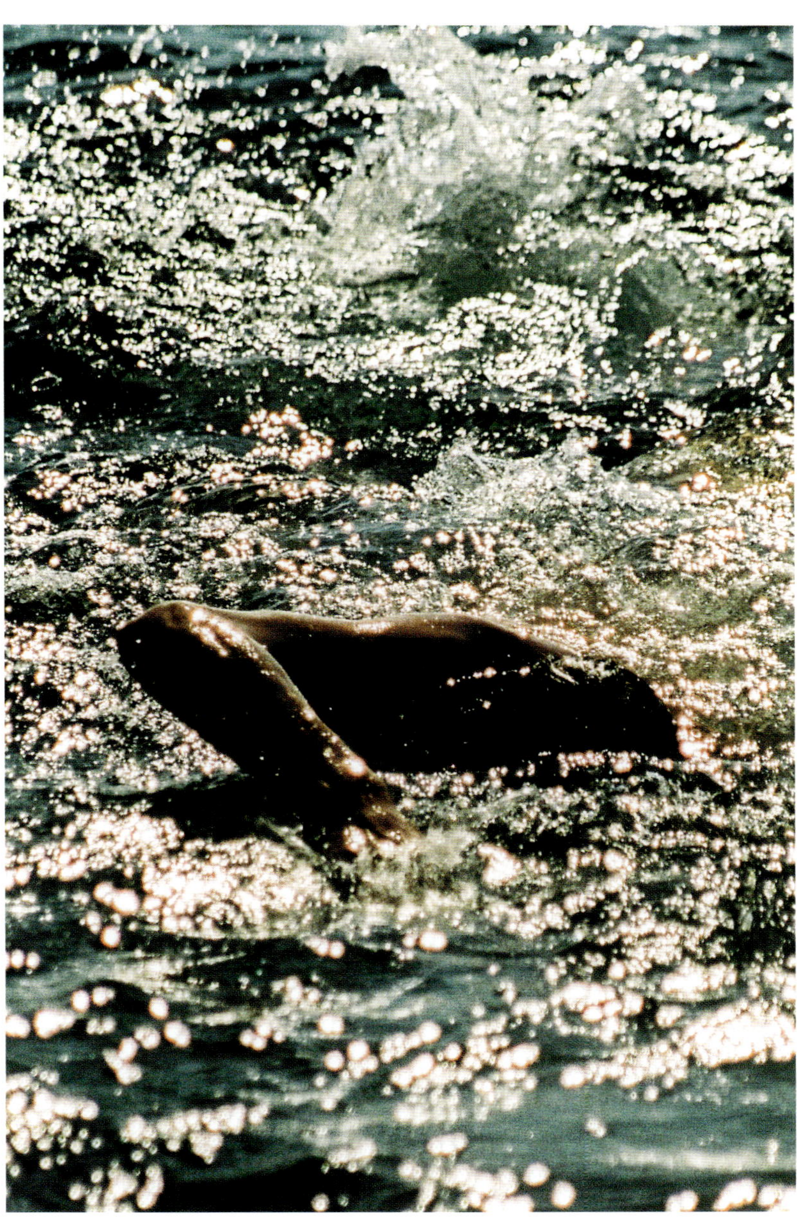

"Someone I loved once gave me a box
full of darkness. It took me years to understand
that this too was a gift."

Mary Oliver